LIBRARY OF HEBREW BIBLE/
OLD TESTAMENT STUDIES

565

Formerly Journal for the Study of the Old Testament Supplement Series

Editors
Claudia V. Camp, Texas Christian University
Andrew Mein, Westcott House, Cambridge

Founding Editors
David J. A. Clines, Philip R. Davies and David M. Gunn

Editorial Board
Alan Cooper, John Goldingay, Robert P. Gordon,
Norman K. Gottwald, James Harding, John Jarick, Carol Meyers,
Patrick D. Miller, Francesca Stavrakopoulou,
Daniel L. Smith-Christopher

BREAKING MONOTHEISM

Yehud and the Material Formation of Monotheistic Identity

Jeremiah W. Cataldo

BLOOMSBURY
NEW YORK · LONDON · NEW DELHI · SYDNEY

Bloomsbury T&T Clark
An imprint of Bloomsbury Publishing Inc

1385 Broadway	50 Bedford Square
New York	London
NY 10018	WC1B 3DP
USA	UK

www.bloomsbury.com

Bloomsbury is a registered trade mark of Bloomsbury Publishing Plc

First published 2012
Paperback edition first published 2014

© Jeremiah W. Cataldo, 2012

All rights reserved. No part of this publication may be reproduced or transmitted in any form or by any means, electronic or mechanical, including photocopying, recording, or any information storage or retrieval system, without prior permission in writing from the publishers.

No responsibility for loss caused to any individual or organization acting on or refraining from action as a result of the material in this publication can be accepted by Bloomsbury or the author.

Library of Congress Cataloging-in-Publication Data
A catalog record for this book is available from the Library of Congress

ISBN: HB: 978-0-567-11093-0
PB: 978-0-567-40217-2

Typeset by Forthcoming Publications Ltd (www.forthpub.com)

For Elisha, in whose smile I have no questions.

And

*For Gene Carpenter (1943–2012), friend and mentor.
May you find that place you seek.*

Contents

Acknowledgments	xi
Abbreviations	xiii
INTRODUCTION	1

Chapter 1
WHAT IS MEANT BY MONOTHEISM? 5
  1. Defining Monotheism 10
    a. Defining "Monotheistic Body" and "Monotheistic Identity"
      (and Further Defining Monotheism) 13
  2. Identifying Monotheism 19
  3. The Problem of an Axial-age Shift 21
  4. A Word on "Member" as a Subcategory of Monotheistic
    Identity 30
  5. Why Employing the Theories of Michel Foucault
    and Gilles Deleuze and Felix Guattari Is Helpful 35

Chapter 2
HOW MONOTHEISM CREATES A NEW NORMATIVE ORDER
IN SUPPORT OF ITS OWN AUTHORITY 39
  1. Interrupting Authority: The Material Construction
    of Monotheistic Identity 40
    a. Authority Is a Natural Production of the Social Body
      and Religious Authority Must Be Imposed 51
    b. Inscribing Authority: Defining Meaning and Order 53
    c. Resistance as Necessary in the Production
      of Monotheistic Identity 55
    d. Addressing the Function of Authority in Yehud 62
    e. Coding (Religious) Authority within Social-Political
      Identity 66
    f. Zerubbabel and the "Restoration" of Political Authority? 67
    g. Restoration, Reconstruction, and Exclusion as Discourses
      on Identity Formation within the Monotheistic Body 73
  2. The Legitimation of Authority Requires an Apparatus
    of Punishment 78

Chapter 3
SOCIALIZATION AND CONFLICT AS FORCES PRODUCTIVE
OF IDENTITY … 82
1. Resistance and Separation as Processes in the Formation of Class Identity within Monotheism … 84
   a. Economy as a Productive Force in Rewriting Class Identity as Religious Identity … 89
   b. Rewriting Production as a Divine Activity … 101
2. The Nature of Desire Production as Mode of Production for the Monotheistic Body … 108

Chapter 4
DIVINE LAW AS A DOMINANT DISCOURSE
OF THE MONOTHEISTIC SELF … 113
1. Understanding the Function and Force of Law as Discourse: Some Preliminary Remarks on the General Concept … 114
2. So Then, What Is at Stake if a Religious Law Governs a Social-Political Body? A Theocracy? … 123
   a. A Few More Words Regarding Understanding Law as Constructive and Relevant for Monotheistic Identity … 129
3. The Exclusionary Nature of Monotheistic Law … 133
   a. Further Understanding Law as a Framework for Restoration … 138
   b. Further Clarification of Monotheistic Law as an External Law … 141
   c. Constructive Law and the Monotheistic Ideal … 144

Chapter 5
CLARIFYING LAND AS THE ARENA FOR RESTORATION … 149
1. Defining Land as the Space for Restoration … 152
   a. Inscribing the Land in a Public Display of Divine Authority … 156
2. Understanding Production and Perception of the Land in the Process of Restoration … 159
   a. Monotheism's Ideological Definition of "Land" as an Argument in Support of Authority Over the Land in the Material Sense … 171
   b. The Necessity of (Re)Figured History and (Re)Defined Geography for Restoration … 173
3. Brief Remarks on Debt and the Distribution of Land … 180
   a. First Strategy … 181
   b. Second Strategy … 184

Chapter 6
THE NECESSITY OF AN "OTHER" FOR MONOTHEISTIC IDENTITY   186
1. Understanding the Role of Differentiation within
   the Monotheistic Identity   189
2. Strategies of (Social) Identity Formation
   as Relevant for Monotheistic Identity   194
   a. Resistance (Discourse) as Productive of Identity   198
3. Discourses of Resistance on Land and Authority   202
   a. Walls, Social Identities, and Authority:
      Components of Monotheism's Discourse of Resistance   209

Chapter 7
THE MONOTHEISTIC BODY WITHIN VIEW:
UNDERSTANDING THE PARAMETERS OF THE MODEL   218
1. Authority, Law, and an Apparatus of Control   221
2. Deviance as a Threat to Monotheistic Identity   227
3. Discourses of Resistance   232

Bibliography   237
Index of References   252
Index of Authors   256

Acknowledgments

> The woods are lovely, dark, and deep, but I have promises to keep. And miles to go before I sleep, and miles to go before I sleep.
> —Robert Frost

While writing this book I found myself thinking frequently about this section of Robert Frost's poem "Stopping by the Woods on a Snowy Evening." Over time, for me, this section took on a life of its own and divorced itself from the larger poem. In doing so, its meaning changed. Not only were the woods a seductive mistress that one must leave reluctantly, the woods took on a terrifying quality. There is always so much to see, so many connections to make, and so many different themes to trace out. That is largely how I felt about the inherent complexity of this work. Accounting for every aspect of that complexity, however, would prove disastrous.

For that reason I am extremely thankful to those who have pointed me in the right direction. Showing themselves to be editors of a higher caliber, Andrew Mein and Claudia Camp persistently directed me back when my tendency was to get caught up in the details along the way. More than once, Andrew's comments demonstrated admirable insight. Chuck Pazdernik happily took on the challenge of reading early drafts of this work. He consistently and rightfully pushed me to test the limits of my own theories rather than allow me to recline in the shade of what was comfortable. Likewise, Peter Anderson willingly shared with me, sometimes unknowingly, the highs and lows of this journey through conversation, recreation, and by assisting me through the belligerence of various chapters.

My colleagues in the History Department and the Honors College at Grand Valley happily gave me the space needed to take on this project. As my previous home, the History Department gave me the opportunity to teach a course on the subject of this study while I was writing it. The students of that course eagerly took on the challenge of blazing new trails and repeatedly reminded me to maintain a concrete anchor to my theoretical musings. Such an opportunity is of inestimable value. My new home, the Honors College, has excitedly embraced both me and the different paths I take with my research. They too have unfailingly encouraged me to bring my research into the classroom, giving me the opportunity to develop the courses through which to do so.

Lastly, my family has patiently endured the highs and lows of writing and my frequent "absences" taken to my study. In light of that, I will always be thankful for my son's repeated interruptions to remind me of the books that were in my study or that my office light was "on."

This "journey through the woods" would not have been possible without all of these individuals. And in saying that I am reminded that no journey is truly embarked upon alone.

ABBREVIATIONS

ABD	*Anchor Bible Dictionary*. Edited by D. N. Freedman. 6 vols. New York, 1992
AJP	*The American Journal of Philology*
ARS	*Annual Reviews of Sociology*
BA	*Biblical Archaeologist*
CBQ	*Catholic Biblical Quarterly*
EJS	*European Journal of Sociology*
ET	English translation
HB	Hebrew Bible
INJ	*Israel Numismatic Journal*
JAAR	*Journal of the American Academy of Religion*
JBL	*Journal of Biblical Literature*
JHS	*Journal of Hebrew Scriptures*
JNES	*Journal of Near Eastern Studies*
JR	*The Journal of Religion*
JSNT	*Journal of the Study of the New Testament*
JSOT	*Journal of the Study of the Old Testament*
JSOTSup	Journal for the Study of the Old Testament: Supplement Series
LHBOTS	Library of Hebrew Bible/Old Testament Studies
PEQ	*Palestine Exploration Quarterly*
RB	*Revue Biblique*
SJA	*Southwestern Journal of Anthropology*
SJOT	*Scandinavian Journal of the Old Testament*
TWOT	*Theological Wordbook of the Old Testament*. Edited by R. L. Harris and G. L. Archer Jr. 2 vols. Chicago, 1980
VT	*Vetus Testamentum*
WBC	Word Biblical Commentary

INTRODUCTION

It is appropriate at the beginning to offer some clarification of my intent for this work, as well as to express some important limitations. On both a personal and an academic level, I have become increasingly interested in understanding the influence that strict monotheistic religions[1] have upon social-political institutions in the societies in which they are observed. This interest has stemmed in part from both a curiosity and a concern regarding monotheism's seemingly ever-present anxiety over the nature of political powers. In this, modern monotheisms are nearly identical to their more ancient counterparts. Acceptance of the very idea of a universal and absolute God, and so also a corresponding absolute power, demands that political powers be understood as subservient to a greater force symbolized in and by the monotheistic community. This demand in itself reflects a fundamental contest that resides at the heart of every monotheistic religion: a contest for land and authority, where land, first material and later in the ideological sense, represents the basis of power and authority, including control over material resources. In addition, the idea of a monotheistic God is, at the core of monotheism's symbolic system, no more than the "objectivated truth"[2] of the community's self-perception and its desire for absolute (the imperial model is not too far from this) authority. This constituted in part the preliminary hypothesis with which I approached this work.

While not a complete picture, Persian-period Yehud offers us an excellent example of the birth of one form of monotheism, and from which a model for understanding the common structural development of monotheism may be constructed. There we see a strict and rigid articulation of a monotheistic identity uttered in consequence of an insecure hold over the province by the *golah* community. To be sure, this monotheistic

---

1. My use of the term "monotheism," which will be defined in the first chapter, refers to the different forms of strict monotheism, unless otherwise noted.
2. "Objectivated," as P. Berger (*The Sacred Canopy: Elements of a Sociological Theory of Religion* [2d ed., New York: Anchor, 1990 [1st ed., 1967], 87) defines it.

form was a more "compact" form of monotheism than its later counterparts (e.g. the more modern forms of Judaism, Islam, and Christianity). By "compact" we mean that its nature and identity were less encumbered with layers of ideologies and doctrines and that it was still reliant on the material circumstances that surrounded it to support its contest for authority. More "complex" forms of monotheism are those that follow a monotheistic transition from a reliance upon material circumstances into one based within the ideological world.[3] The complex of layers of beliefs, doctrines, ideologies, and ritualized "truths" are based upon the "new" presupposition that divine authority does not require material confirmation, that the religious community may be kept indefinitely at the fringes of power, but that the Divine will eventually overturn the order of the material world and dismiss the previously established institutions and structures of power and authority. The perceived need of this final act, which is referred to as "restoration," is common to all forms of monotheism—restoration is one of three pillars[4] we will discuss at length that constitute the common structural framework of monotheism.

In using the *golah* community as a case study for analyzing the material origins of monotheism, I am not arguing that all later forms of monotheism are direct forms of Yahwism. To prioritize one form of monotheism as the source for all others is, I believe, to be guilty of the same overly reductive theorizing of which Axial-Age theorists are guilty.[5] Monotheism is, I believe, a product of distinct occurrences of a confluence of events that, while unique, has been found in similar (but not identical) forms in multiple social and historical environments. Nevertheless there is, I also believe, enough evidence to conclude that *golah*-Yahwistic monotheism did influence later forms of monotheism, either directly, such as in the case of Rabbinic Judaism, or indirectly, such as in the case of Christianity and Islam.[6] Yet to argue that Islam, for example, exists only because the *golah* community produced its form of monotheism is to overlook grossly the unique material, social, and political circumstances that created an environment for Islamic monotheism. Moreover, I would argue *not* that monotheism is primarily an *intellectual* achievement of higher-order thinking (in contrast to Axial-Age and social-evolutionary theorists) but that it is the institutionalized product of a (religious) community's attempt to realize its desire of

---

3. We will discuss this transition at length throughout this work.
4. Together they are, revelation, law, and restoration.
5. The problems of Axial-Age theory will be discussed in Chapter 1.
6. As an imperial power, the Roman Empire did much to facilitate this influence.

authority over the broader social-political body in which it exists. What might appear as evolutionary is the accumulating process of society—that is, the process of incorporating and expanding upon existing structures and characteristics. In contrast to most evolutionary theories, however, there is no form of perfection toward which social institutions are innately transforming themselves. As we will demonstrate in this work, the *monotheistic* perception of God, with which we are most familiar (and not, in contrast, any pre-institutionalized views), was *initially* defined in reaction to the multiplicity of competing authorities by a solitary community desiring authority for itself.

That we have an incomplete picture of the social environment in Yehud poses unavoidable limitations upon our study. Yet we are able to work partly around those limitations by working with structural elements common to all monotheisms. Because of that, it is possible to identify in later monotheisms common structural elements that can be identified subsequently in the *golah* community. More importantly, the monotheism of the *golah* community presents not only the first concrete example of monotheism (as can be solidly identified, in contrast to Zoroastrianism),[7] it also preserves the material aspects of the community's struggle for authority, of which its monotheism was a product. That is not to say that monotheism was the end goal, but that it was a product of the community's "desire production."[8] The strict form of *golah* monotheism was produced by the community's struggle against and its retreat to religion to justify that struggle with the broader social-political body in which it existed. Of course, the reasons for this will be discussed throughout the length of this work.

Because this work is occupied primarily with the nature of a social-religious institution, much of its dialogue employs the vocabulary of theory. The historical and material particularities of its subject are in no way ignored but rather explained through the lens of the theory that is being developed within the work itself. Explaining something via something that is itself in the process of development is always difficult and can at times find itself to be dealing with presumption rather than conclusion; however, to avoid the obvious pitfalls, I have made a concerted effort to revisit important historical and material particularities from

---

7. We will also discuss in the following chapter why I am not at the moment considering earlier, pre-institutionalized forms of monotheism (which some describe as "primitive").

8. "Desire production" is a phrase that I am borrowing from G. Deleuze and F. Guattaria, and a concept that we will discuss at greater length in the following chapters.

different angles in order to verify the conclusions drawn. I also recognize the necessity of further studies in which the theory developed here is systematically applied to individual analyses of the more modern forms of monotheism. I initially envisioned doing that to a limited basis here but came to realize that anything short of an isolated focus would not do the theory or the monotheistic religion justice. It would run the risk of being overly reductive in its constant return for validation to the theory and the case study that are the primary focus of this work.

Finally, I feel it is important for some who may read this to point out that I do not have an "agenda." My intent is neither to discredit nor affirm monotheism or any of its different forms[9] but only to *understand* the material characteristics and origin of its development.

---

9. As some might interpret to be the case in my explanation of ideological "truths" as being historical interpretations of a contingent material reality.

Chapter 1

WHAT IS MEANT BY MONOTHEISM?

> Humankind would never have progressed to monotheism in the natural course of events, in the sense of a gradual evolution. Monotheism demands emigration, delimitation, conversion, revolution, a radical turning towards the new resulting from an equally radical break, abnegation, and denial of the old.[1]

Monotheism demands, in other words, a fateful contest.

Past analyses focusing on the development of monotheism have traditionally appealed to a common set of ideas: that monotheism followed or developed out of polytheism, that monotheism was somehow connected to the social-political rise of a monarchy or empire, that monotheism was an *intellectual activity* supporting ideologies tending toward exclusion and universalism, and that monotheism represents a culmination of higher-order ethical thought. Yet in all of this, there is absent a sufficient explanation as to why monotheism became a social-religious reality, with specific reference to the material conditions—as the environment that all cultural institutions must acknowledge through support of or resistance to—that supported its development. While I agree to an extent with the general previous set of ideas, they, and the arguments that employ them, offer only descriptive attributes or qualities of monotheism. They tell us *about* monotheism and how to identify it. Moreover, arguments that have depended entirely upon this set of ideas have tended to focus on one type of "paradigmatic" monotheism, assuming that the historical and religious particularities of its culture were broadly translatable.[2] There is a commonality, to be sure, but it lies not in historical

---

1. Jan Assmann, *The Price of Monotheism* (Stanford, Calif.: Stanford University Press, 2010), 118.
2. And this is true also for works by scholars whose area of expertise lay outside ancient Israel; for example, note the works of Jan Assmann, *Moses the Egyptian: The Memory of Egypt in Western Monotheism* (Cambridge, Mass.: Harvard University Press, 1997), and *The Price of Monotheism*.

or other particularities but in the human desire for authority. To this point, there has yet to be offered a suitable model through which the origins of different monotheistic religions could be explained: *that at its origin monotheism was a consequence of a material contest over land and authority.* While each form or expression of monotheism has since followed its own developmental path, it has not strayed far from this structural origin. Its tendencies toward exclusion, toward a codified regulation of social-religious behavior, toward its ideological ownership of universal and absolute truths, toward its privatization of God, and toward its apocalyptic hopes of a new or restored world order in which the righteous community is ushered into a position of authority, can all be traced back to that very starting point.

In this view, monotheism was not a necessary logical, evolutionary "next step" out of polytheism—a point about which more will be said below—but was a consequence of chance material circumstances. Such circumstances created the possibility not only *for* monotheism, but also in response to those changing circumstances, provided it with the space and means with which to preserve itself.

With this developing understanding of monotheism we need not dismiss the idea that political institutions, such as those of monarchy and empire, were influential in the development of monotheistic thought (such as of the divine as a universal and absolute ruler and power). Social-political ideas of law, power, and land were important to the development of monotheism. Yet monotheism did not originate internal to any position of power. It developed from the periphery of material power—a power that it *desired*. Monotheism has been preserved through the rise of fall of social-political powers because its original structure developed external to social-political power, from the "bottom up," so to speak. The appeal made by monotheism to a universal God, to a universal law, to a universal collective body was in various circumstances, after it had developed into its more complex forms, attractive to kings and emperors looking beyond political centralization (for which polytheism was generally better suited) and toward a perpetual legitimation of their own power.[3] Nevertheless, the eschatological or apocalyptic "endgame" of monotheism cannot cease to remind us of its original, nascent desire: that a universal God would restore land, law, and "national" identity to the righteous community and establish its authority over those individuals

---

3. As Assmann writes, "Divine sovereignty…needs the king and the institutions of state in order to assert itself on earth…" (*The Price of Monotheism*, 68).

who were not members of the community.⁴ In its more mature or complex forms—those forms that follow monotheism's abandonment of an original reliance upon the material world for restoration—monotheism has been expressed in a variety of ways, such as "ethical" monotheism, "philosophical" monotheism, "prophetic" monotheism, and "spiritual" monotheism. Monotheism's focus on ethical power rather than material power in these forms supports its transition from a dependence upon material conditions to ideologically constructed ones for the basis of its power and authority.

The exclusivity of monotheism is not solely the product of the quantitative nature of the divine but is also initially a contingent product of the material conditions surrounding the monotheistic community. Monotheism is dependent upon the material conditions constitutive of its origin. Statements, therefore, such as the following by Mark Smith, that make monotheistic exclusivity contingent upon the abstract but quantitative nature of the divine both appeal primarily to a more complex form and symbol system of monotheism and reverse the processual relationship between monotheism and exclusion. But monotheism is not exclusive because of the existence of a single God. A single God is thought to exist because monotheism is exclusive—a point that can be more clearly seen in the material conditions out of which monotheism (or *a* monotheism) developed:

> Monotheistic exclusivity is not simply a matter of cultic observance, as in the First Commandment's prohibition against "no other gods before me" in Exodus 20:3 and Deuteronomy 5:7. It extends further to an understanding of deities in the cosmos (no other gods, period).⁵

And while there is truth to that, Mark Smith's statement, which reflects a sentiment shared by the majority of scholarship, does not seek out the structural nature of monotheistic exclusion dependent upon historical and material priorities and circumstances. Instead, it depends weakly on a debatable, evolutionary view of religion—a view that holds monotheism to be a progressive stage beyond polytheism. Yet what if despite

---

4. Or, as R. Karen puts it, "What we normally think of as monotheism—the institutional monotheism of organized religions—arose for many purposes, some of them political, related to group cohesion, the establishment of law, the maintenance of authority, and nation building" ("Two Faces of Monotheism," *Contemporary Psychoanalysis* 39, no. 4 [2003]: 643).

5. Mark S. Smith, *The Origins of Biblical Monotheism: Israel's Polytheistic Background and the Ugaritic Texts* (New York: Oxford University Press, 2001), 151.

scholarly tendencies to view it as an "intellectual breakthrough," monotheism was not the necessary or expected conclusion to polytheism—a view that attributes polytheism to more "elementary" forms of religion and intellect? And what if we conclude, as Robert Bellah seems to do, that *both* religious forms are susceptible in their own rights to an independent development from compact to complex symbol systems?[6] In other words, that the teleologies of both polytheism and monotheism, while not necessarily exclusive, may reflect relatively independent developments. If so, then we must ask: What were the original forces at work on the identity of monotheism if it were not the consequence of polytheism?

We would, perhaps, begin from this premise—a premise that understands relations of alliance and conflict to be at the heart of all human engagements: at its heart, monotheism embodies a contest over land and authority—a (political and economic) contest that is determined by historically contingent conditions. To test this hypothesis we will begin with the development of monotheism in Persian-period Yehud. Yehud offers an important case study because the monotheism developing there was still consciously reacting to the material conditions that surrounded and influenced it. Using that original and raw material, and constructing from it a theoretical model, one of our goals for this volume will be to identify the structural qualities common to all forms of monotheism. Yet, it should also be noted that it is neither necessary nor sufficient to claim that polytheism is an incipient stage of monotheism. It is also not necessary to exclude the possibility that polytheisms sharing similar structural qualities to monotheism need be excluded from the proposal that conflict arriving out of material conditions is an impetus for religion; the focus here, however, is upon monotheism specifically. And with a concern for limiting the scope of our discussion, what was said of polytheism should also be said of henotheism, which can be defined as "the adherence to one god out of several, especially by a family, tribe, or other group."[7] In this discussion, henotheism is distinguished primarily from strict monotheism due to its acceptance of the possible existence of other deities. While it too may share certain structural qualities with monotheism, such as possible exclusivist tendencies, like polytheism its primary *raison d'être* is not found in conflict.

---

6. Robert Bellah, "Religious Evolution," in *Reader in Comparative Religion: An Anthropological Approach* (ed. William A. Lessa and Evon Z. Vogt; New York: Harper & Row, 1972), 36–50.

7. *New Oxford American Dictionary.*

1. What Is Meant by Monotheism?

Toward that end, our working hypothesis, as more clearly stated, is this: the *origin* of monotheism is found in a material contest for land and authority between a religious community and a larger social body; the impetus for the development from compact to complex symbol systems in monotheism is driven by an unresolved conflictual power relationship over land and authority, which is produced by different historically particular and contingent sets of material conditions.[8] Within the parameters of this contest, which are determined by the cultural ethic of the religious community—note that this contest is perceived only by the community to be a contest—monotheism at its birth existed on the periphery of social-political power. It existed, and exists, in dialectical relationship with the social body—a relationship in which it perceives itself as a subjugated body. Yet the very nature of this contest assumes that in the wake of a divine restoration overturning prevailing social-political powers the monotheistic community will be ushered into a position of authority. Monotheistic identity, therefore, is preserved through discourses of resistance that engage the larger social body, the "other." Divine law codifies these discourses, situates them within the context of divine revelation, and affirms itself as a *constructive* ideal toward which the created world must strive. The transition from a material rationale of control or authority to one constituted by ideals such as belief, dogma, and "truth" occurs for monotheism when restoration within the material world fails to be immanent.[9] This transition is itself a part of the process of monotheism's "maturation" into its more complex forms (read monotheistic identities [a term defined below]). All of this undergirds a crucial point: a "monotheistic" people is a prerequisite for a monotheistic God. Or to put it differently, the *idea* of an absolute, solitary God depends upon the outward expression of a community self-identifiable through its attitude of exclusion. In other words, a *monotheistic* God is the ideational product of a self-awaredly exclusionary community.

This discussion will consistently bear in mind two distinct but related "streams": (1) the material conditions contributing to the "objective structure of monotheism," for which Yehud will be our primary focus; (2) the material and historical conditions contributing to the distinct but interdependent monotheisms of Judaism, Islam, and Christianity. Since the focus of this work is on developing a model it will attend to how the

---

8. Charles Pazdernik helped me clarify this point in a private conversation.

9. For example, in the case of Yehud this occurred within or alongside the transition from prophecy to apocalyptic. See J. Berquist's discussion of the transition from prophecy to apocalyptic in *Judaism in Persia's Shadow: A Social and Historical Approach* (Minneapolis: Fortress, 1995), 221–40.

former sets up the possibility for the latter. While this work itself will make overtures toward this, subsequent studies must delve more specifically into a sustained focus on each the individual monotheisms.

1. *Defining Monotheism*

Before defining monotheism itself, it is helpful to identify where the boundaries of monotheism may be drawn. In this regard, Hinduism is a good example of a religion that is significantly older than monotheism, shares a number of similar characteristics with monotheism, and has been characterized both as monotheistic and polytheistic. Yet while there has been some discussion, for reasons not without merit, regarding Hinduism as a religious tradition perhaps more closely aligned with monotheism than polytheism—in that all deities can be considered manifestations of a singular godhead—it is not a strict, absolute monotheism in the same vein as Islam, Judaism, and Christianity.[10] In other words, Hinduism's personalizing of and its amiability toward multiple and varying divine manifestations are somewhat prohibitive of any all-encompassing absolutist ideal or ideology.[11] Thus, by strict monotheism we mean a monotheism, as will be defined below, that actively pursues an absolute, divine claim to authority which entails the privatization of three main pillars: revelation, law, and restoration. It rejects as impossible all truths save for the one—which it deems absolute in nature—that resides at the core of its own identity. In contrast, Hinduism tends to emphasize *puja* (worship) as expression of devotion (*bhakti*) to a *personal* rather than universal deity.[12] While the idea of a personal deity does not simultaneously reject the idea of a universal, absolute deity, it also does not dogmatically emphasize a singularly absolute identity;

---

10. Moreover, it is questionable that one can even speak of Hinduism as a single religious tradition. R. King ("Orientalism and the Modern Myth of 'Hinduism'," *Numen: International Review for the History of Religions* 46, no. 2 [1999]: 146) suggests that reference to Hinduism as a single religion is the product of Western Christian interpretation.

11. Texts such as the Puranas, while addressing the rise of *bhakti* (devotion) to a personal God (*Bhagavan*) or Goddess (*Bhagavati*), do not exclusively focus on a single deity but present a pantheon of deities that corresponds to different Brahmanic perceptions of the world (cf. Gavin D. Flood, *An Introduction to Hinduism* [New York: Cambridge University Press, 1999], 103, 110–13). But one should also compare the view found in the Upanishads that there is a supreme, distinct God (*Bhagavan*) or Goddess (*Bhagavati*) who creates, sustains, and eventually destroys the world (cf. ibid., 114).

12. Ibid., 103.

some have pointed out that exclusive devotion to a particular deity, even if a personal deity within a "pantheon," reveals monotheistic tendencies.[13] But those that make such an argument tend to view monotheism as the *next* stage in an evolutionary development.[14] Thus Hinduism represents institutionalized religion before it is sterilized of multiple truths. This evolutionary theory of religion, which focuses on the ideal of institutionalized religion, tends to overlook specific historical circumstances in which a particular form of religion is practiced. Yet religious development is inseparable from the material circumstances that define it. While there may be similar structural and ideological responses across history, they are similar in that they are responses to similar material circumstances and the power structures against which those circumstances are measured. Hinduism's inherent theological pursuit of understanding the relationship between a single, all-pervasive divine essence and the many different divine expressions remains prohibitive of an absolutized, exclusivist dogma on divine essence that has characterized strict monotheism.[15] As Gavin Flood writes,

> Apart from its concern with language and its relation to being, Hindu theologies have been interested in the relation of 'the one' to 'the many.' That is, Hindu revelation and yogic experience refer to an absolute reality which is unitary and without second, yet experience of the world tells us that existence is manifold and diverse. What is the relation between this unique one and the diversified many? Some Hindu theologies maintain that the relation is one of identity, the absolute is ultimately identical with the many and difference is merely illusory; some say that the relation is of difference and that the one and the many are quite ontologically distinct; while others maintain that both identity and difference are true of the relation between the one and the many. Hindu theologies arrive at different positions with regard to this fundamental question.[16]

Even with its belief in a singular, non-personal, all-pervading divine essence, Hinduism's refusal to be intolerant of other deities sets it apart from Islam, Judaism, and Christianity.[17] This distinction was in part the

---

13. Cf. Robert Karl Gnuse, *No Other Gods: Emergent Monotheism in Israel* (JSOTSup 241; Sheffield: Sheffield Academic, 1997), 217.
14. Gnuse, for example, praises Israelite monotheism as a paradigmatic example of this evolutionary step (cf. ibid., 177–228, but also passim).
15. It should also be noted that Jews and Muslims might make a comparable claim about Christian Trinitarianism.
16. Flood, *An Introduction to Hinduism*, 229–30.
17. Cf. Nicol Macnicol, *Indian Theism: From the Vedic to the Muhammadan Period* (London: H. Milford, Oxford University Press, 1915), 10–19, 88, 102, 192–93.

result of the historically and materially contingent conditions of its origin in the Indus River Valley region—the need or demand for social-political unity and stability—conditions that imposed cooperation, at least initially, as defined by a dominant group feeling in Vedic culture, over conflict.

With that said, defining monotheism alone as "the belief in one God" is insufficient—such a definition does not exclude religions such as Hinduism. Moreover, it explains neither *why* a single god has been isolated to the expense of all others nor what monotheism is as a practicable religion.[18] It virtually ignores the sociological development of monotheism as a religious system constructed by human agents in relation to each other. Or, as Martin Jaffee notes, "What troubles me…is the suspicion that to focus on the divine unity and transcendence as the principal taxonomic markers of monotheism over other systems of religion—and the primary principle of its superiority as a religious worldview—*is at the same time to ignore much that characterizes monotheism as a system of religion.*"[19] Monotheism is not a belief in the existence of a single God. Conviction that there is absolutely only one God is, instead, a monotheistic belief.

Perhaps more importantly, any definition of monotheism must include monotheism's inherent struggle for land and authority—at its heart a *materialist* struggle. Thus, while there is nothing wrong in saying that monotheism values the *belief* in one God, one must clarify that monotheistic belief, including its ideas of universalism and absolutism, is a reaction to historically specific material conditions or realities. Monotheism, in short, is a consequence of a material contest conducted at the margins of power. Its dedication to a singular authority and its own future vindication—from the authority of the external social-political world—is the result of its desire to correct this original peripheral status.

It is through monotheism's rejection of its materialist origins—and subsequently the broader social world through exclusion, since the material sphere remains within the jurisdiction of the social world and

---

18. As M. Jaffee ("One God, One Revelation, One People: On the Symbolic Structure of Elective Monotheism," *JAAR* 69, no. 4 [2001]: 755) complains, "[H]overing behind virtually all discussions as an assumed, circumambient discursive atmosphere, is the confidence that monotheism's own theomorphic formulations are a sufficient foundation for sketching its phenomenological outlines as a historical pattern of religion. Virtually every author I consulted seemed satisfied to identify as the primary taxonomic marker of monotheism an insistence on the numerical oneness and qualitative uniqueness of the divine Being whose activity accounts for the creation of the world and in relation to whom human beings discover and fulfill the purpose of their own creation."

19. Ibid., 755–56, emphasis mine.

not the religious body—and its embrace of ideological explanations for identity, structure, and power that we see monotheism's maturation into its more complex forms.[20] The lack of any foreseeable realization of monotheistic desire—namely for land and authority—within the material sphere provides the impetus for monotheism's maturation as it looks elsewhere for fulfillment. Subsequently, such desires must be preserved in the ideological world, through beliefs, dogmas, traditions, identities, and rituals.[21]

In other words, it was, ultimately, and we will discuss this more fully, the failed realization of monotheism's desired restoration in the historical, material world that provided its successful self-preservation. Monotheism was not, as might be the conclusion of an Axial-Age theory, solely the result of imperialization. "It is," we must bear in mind, "too easy to make imperialization (or oppression) the originating state that people…resist."[22] While imperialization may have shaped the circumstances that would lead to the development of monotheism, monotheism was not born out of oppression, as a situation in which the community would be openly and aggressively abused by someone in power. Moreover, the decentralization that occurred under imperial conquests, which created the possibility of contests for authority, was one, albeit one important, influence among a number whose confluence permitted, *but did not provide the central reason for*, the development of a monotheistic worldview.

a. *Defining "Monotheistic Body" and "Monotheistic Identity" (and Further Defining Monotheism)*
I employ the terms "monotheistic body" and "monotheistic identity" as labels drawing a distinction between (1) the structure that is common to all monotheistic religions and (2) the different expressions of identity that are unique to each monotheistic religion, but which also portray the collective framework by which the members of the religious community are defined. With the term "religious community" I refer broadly in this

---

20. Again, as noted in a previous footnote, one can see an early example of this development in the transition from prophecy to apocalypticism in Persian-period Yehud.

21. P. Bourdieu (cf. "Genesis and Structure of the Religious Field," *Comparative Social Research* 13 [1991]: 14) describes the assumption of an ideological "function" a rational outcome of religion's attempt to consecrate its explanations of its relationship to the natural and social world.

22. Jon L. Berquist, "Constructions of Identity in Postcolonial Yehud," in *Judah and the Judeans in the Persian Period* (ed. Oded Lipschits and Manfred Oeming; Winona Lake: Eisenbrauns, 2006), 62.

work to those who are members of a particular monotheistic tradition in order to ease the discussion of the structure common among the different monotheisms and to avoid become mired in the particularities built upon that structure. This work focuses on understanding that structure as something distinguishable from historical particularities. Monotheistic identity, to describe it differently, is the collective projection of an identity framed by the common structural qualities of the monotheistic body. As it depends less upon material conditions and more upon ideologically constructed beliefs, a monotheistic identity is a collectively externalized product that is internally and externally identifiable. The common structure or set of qualities upon which different monotheistic identities are based is the monotheistic body. The monotheistic body, which is fundamentally the structuring qualities of monotheism,[23] is sustained by three pillars: revelation, law, and restoration. The fundamental basis for conflict between any of the different monotheistic religions, or monotheistic identities, themselves arises out of their unique attempts to privatize these pillars. That is to say, each identity contests the claim of the others to ownership of divine revelation in the social, material world; to divine law as the universal source of regulated order; and, to the future complete restoration of divine authority within the natural world. Put simply, "monotheistic body" refers to the objective structures held together by the three pillars mentioned previously, and "monotheistic identity" refers to the historically contingent identity built upon the structure that is the monotheistic body. By "objective structures" we mean that there are basic elements that can be found in identifiably similar forms in any number of historical times or cultures.

Revelation means divine revelation, the moment, or process, in which the Divine "entered" the social and material world to begin the process of restructuring social-political systems in support of divine authority. The manner in which this occurs differs among the different monotheistic identities. Revelation is a process, an atemporal instance rather, that begins a process.[24] That is, revelation does not secure authority for the religious community but inaugurates the process toward restoration in which divine authority would be absolutely (re)established and in which the religious community would be granted the benefits of divine authority.

---

23. In other words, the monotheistic body is not monotheism but is the basis or structure upon which a monotheistic religion is constructed and sustained.

24. As M. Eliade (*The Myth of the Eternal Return: Cosmos and History* (trans. Willard R. Trask; Princeton: Princeton University Press, 2005; repr. New York: Bollingen Foundation, 1954], 111–12) notes, revelation is both an instance and a process during which archetypes are revealed.

"The LORD says to my lord," for biblical example of this, "'Sit at my right hand until I make your enemies your footstool.' The LORD sends out from Zion your mighty scepter. Rule in the midst of your foes" (Ps 110:1–2). The end result of revelation is restoration, a created or restored reality in which all authorities that compete against divine authority have been defeated. Initially, monotheistic restoration was thought by early monotheistic communities to be materially immanent; however, the seemingly failed historical validation required revised expectations. Revelation took on a more eschatological tone before its previous historical and material expectations and became "unassailable" by empirical invalidation.[25]

The second pillar of monotheism is law. "Law," as George Mendenhall explained, "rests upon commonly accepted opinion that certain acts are wrong and must be punished or otherwise compensated for; and, if someone has been injured, he has a right to appeal to the coercive power of the community to obtain redress."[26] Mendenhall's description of natural[27] law proves true also for divine law, with the exception that the "coercive power of the community" is a power gifted to the community by the divine rather than being perceived as something "natural." In contrast to natural law, divine law is prescriptive, or constructive; it regulates the behavior and identity of a religious community toward a desired restoration. More importantly, divine law is always believed by the religious community to be superior to any social body and is therefore never believed to be a product of it. Legislated power and power structures exist consequently apart from the larger social body, but, because the religious community believes divine law to symbolize divine claim over the natural world, act authoritatively upon it; and in this sense, it bridges ideological and material worlds by focusing on actions undertaken within the natural world. The law, in other words, is the manner through which divine authority can be perceived and known.

While natural laws tend to be codified around the preservation of justice, and function often in a descriptive sense, divine laws tend to focus on a prescriptive justice. But in the latter case, justice, as each monotheistic identity perceives it, refers to the ultimate subordination of

---

25. See also Berger, *Sacred Canopy*, 73.
26. George Mendenhall, "Ancient Oriental and Biblical Law," in *The Biblical Archaeologist Reader*, vol. 3 (ed. Edward F. Campbell and David N. Freedman; Garden City: Anchor, 1970), 3.
27. "Natural" is being used as a contrast to supernatural, or divine. Thus, in this context, natural refers to that which human agents and institutions produce through their interactions with each other.

natural social-political authority to divine authority. In its earliest forms, justice was not primarily an issue of "moral principle"—that is, when morality is considered an ideal toward which one must strive—but an issue of socially determined "right" and "fair" behavior, or "blame" versus "shame," as it related to systems of material exchange and of class relations. In other words, it referred to systems of reward and punishment rooted in the material conditions of existence, as well as the proper treatment of those over whom authority could be exercised.[28]

Moreover revelation, law, and restoration cannot escape their collective origin as products of the material contest for authority that underlies the very nature of the monotheistic body. On a conceptual level, there is a comfort of certainty within an identity found through acquiring a power greater than those of the natural world, comfort in knowing that that power can sustain or alter the order of the world at any given moment for the benefit of the obedient, and relief in the knowledge that when the natural order is finally overturned the survival of the "faithful community" will be insured. On a material level, these pillars as their primary purposes, at the very heart of their *raison d'être*, interrupt, reinterpret, or overturn the productive order of that world. They alter the way human beings associate with, control, or are controlled by each other—in other words, they alter what constitutes the fundamental core of authority (and power) in all its forms, and they do this by transforming culturally defined reciprocal relations between humans and between human beings and their material circumstances into an a-cultural, quasi-reciprocal, creditor–debtor relationship between the divine—which, as we will see, can also be sufficiently defined as the monotheistic body—and humanity. As created beings, and therefore dependent upon their creator, the debt owed by human beings to a divine Creator is infinite; and because that debt is infinite, the authority of the divine creditor is absolute.[29] Ezra's proclamation "We are slaves" (Ezra 9:9), which was inspired by the material conditions surrounding the *golah* community as a result of the community's guilt before the divine (cf. v. 7), carries with it a haunting echo of this reconfiguration of relations.

---

28. A focus on the material impacts of a transgression and its punishment is generally obvious in ancient Near Eastern laws. Before the influence of Hellenism, such laws did not typically attempt to regulate purely ideological abstracts in morality.

29. On the idea of infinite debt, see Gilles Deleuze and Félix Guattari, *Anti-Oedipus: Capitalism and Schizophrenia* (Minneapolis: University of Minnesota Press, 2005), 196–97. See also R. Smith ("The Economy of Guilt," *Political Theory* 3, no. 2 [1975]: 200–201), who equates "debt" with "guilt."

If these pillars form the foundation upon which monotheistic self-awareness is expressed, this self-expression, according to Robert Gnuse, emphasizes the human tendency toward what we already described as "privatization." He writes, "Identity is connected to owning land, which reinforces human desire to possess, defend, and conquer. Monotheism thereby becomes political when land is bequeathed to a people by God and its possession is insured by obedience to that God, so that the people defend the land passionately to prove they are obedient."[30] Obedience to the divine or a divine law, which is also a type of political behavior, reflects at its heart not a desire for any moral goodness but, on the part of the obedient, a desire for divine control—an altered political structure—and that the obedient, and not the disobedient, be the beneficiaries of that control.[31] As it identifies a characteristic of the monotheistic body, Gnuse's concept of land ownership pinpoints a component that is just as relevant for the more compact forms of monotheism in the distant past as it is the more complex forms of the more recent past and present. But where monotheistic communities of the distant past focused on land as value in the material sense, more recent focus, which has zeroed in on "matured" forms of monotheism, has been on the value of land in a more abstract sense—the land in question is the "new" or "restored world," one that remains utopian until divine power overturns the extant orders of the natural world. The more modern trend of "globalization" of monotheism—which is the result of its development from historical, material expectations into universal, ideological expectations—has shifted monotheism's gaze from restoration as possibly occurring in any defined historical or material point in time toward an absolute, universal restoration.

Religious morals, values, and ethics, the control over which characterizes authority within a monotheistic community, which are ideologically dominating concerns in monotheistic religions, can be traced back to monotheism's original, material concerns. These are, after all, cultural ideas expressed on the subjects of preservation of self and community, regulated behavior—and are thus related to divine law—and the manner through which the religious group may be distinguished from "everyone else." Divine revelation, according to M. Jaffee, supports these concerns

---

30. R. Gnuse, "Breakthrough or Tyranny: Monotheism's Contested Implications," *Horizons* 34, no. 1 (2007): 81.

31. As C. Ake ("A Definition of Political Stability," *Comparative Politics* 7, no. 2 [1975]: 271) describes, obedience to a particular law upholds the authority of those who make decisions about what the law should be and how it should be enforced.

because its purpose—although I would clarify that this be understood as *one* of its self-expressed goals and not its sole purpose—is to bring "all of humanity into proper moral relationship with the Creator."[32] The benefits of this relationship are the realization of the previously stated concerns as well as being allied in relationship with the de facto authority over the natural, *created* world. Yet what remains unstated in Jaffee's proposal is that a whole-scale worldwide, historical conversion of *all* humanity into a "proper moral relationship" is a statistical impossibility. Moreover, monotheism requires the simultaneous existence of insiders and outsiders to confirm the boundaries of its own identity. Each monotheistic identity is best known fundamentally by who and what it rejects; the three pillars of monotheism continually reaffirm the importance of a clearly articulated boundary between member and non-member.

As expressed by the different monotheistic identities, the nature of monotheism is subject to change among different historically contingent material conditions.[33] Yet the structural qualities of each monotheistic identity, which are elements of the monotheistic body, remain constant.

This work will focus on the original development of monotheism expressed within the *golah* community in Persian-period Yehud.[34] It will articulate monotheistic qualities both particular and general as it works toward identifying the structural components of the monotheistic body. To meet its goal, this analysis focuses on several important areas: power relations in the province of Yehud, land as private property, land's economic impact, political structure and the "rule of law," *golah*-Yahwistic religious identity and its tendency toward "cultural" exclusion, and social group formation in the midst of conflict. The *golah* community's presence within and engagement of these areas produces some of the fundamental structures common to monotheistic identities throughout history. By treating this community as a model case study, this analysis will introduce those structures that are "genetic characteristics" of the monotheistic body. In this discussion, then, we accept that the structural components or qualities of the monotheistic body are genetic in that they are shared by and govern the development of each monotheistic identity.

---

32. Jaffee, "One God, One Revelation, One People," 760.

33. For this reason, L. W. Hurtado ("First-Century Jewish Monotheism," *JSNT* 21, no. 71 [1999]: 5) is correct when he emphasizes the importance of proceeding inductively when using categories such as monotheism.

34. I am using *golah* as a social category as defined in Jeremiah Cataldo, "The Crippled *Ummah*: Toward Redefining *Golah* in Ezra–Nehemiah," *The Bible and Critical Theory* 4, no. 1 (2008): 6.1–6.17.

2. *Identifying Monotheism*

Yet we must emphasize that we are not referring to any proposed "final" form of monotheism, nor initially to monotheism in what we might refer to as its modern state. We are referring to the *structural origin* of a strict, or exclusive, monotheism—a monotheism that, like its later forms, rejects absolutely the existence of all other gods. Issues of so-called "primitive monotheism," therefore, will not be considered.[35] Such religious expressions are described by some as being monotheistic because they betray tendencies interpreted from a modern, monotheistic point of view as being on the trajectory of monotheism. Adherents of "primitive monotheism" as a social-religious category, which were prevalent in the early twentieth century, have generally assumed monotheism to be the logical development out of polytheism. Archaic predispositions or proclivities toward the idea of an all powerful deity—an "All-Father"— were interpreted as the first murmurings of a singular, universal deity.[36] Such tendencies, it was assumed, could be found among early societies because they reflected a collective, unconscious need to return to some original belief in a singularity of supra-human, natural and otherwise, forces. Rudolph Otto's *mysterium tremendum*, for example, refers to this belief through the vocabulary of an instinctual, response mechanism—a "numinous consciousness."[37] This response, according to him, is, and was, a type of residue of a divine imprint upon humanity that instinctually recognizes the absolute nature of divine authority.[38]

Analyses of monotheism subsequent to Otto's discussions of monotheism have tended to focus at the wrong level of social-political complexity in their evaluations of monotheism. These have zeroed in on the political power of monarchy and empire as the central catalyst behind the development of monotheism. Moreover, these have continued the a priori assumption that monotheism was a logical, evolutionary development out of polytheism rather than an event dependent upon unique historical and material circumstances. Robert Gnuse, for instance, who even though

---

35. Cf. Paul Radin, *Monotheism Among Primitive Peoples* (London: G. Allen & Unwin, 1924); E. O. James, "Primitive Monotheism," *Sociological Review* 27 (1935): 328.
36. Cf. the larger discussion in James, "Primitive Monotheism," 328.
37. Rudolph Otto, *The Idea of the Holy: An Inquiry into the Non-Rational Factor in the Idea of the Divine and Its Relation to the Rational* (Oxford: Oxford University Press, 1958), 25, but see his larger discussion in pp. 12–40.
38. Cf. Rudolph Otto, "The 'Idea of the Holy': Mysterium Tremendum," *Parabola* 23 (1998): 75.

he described a "paradigm shift" in biblical scholarship away from any perception of a monolithic Jewish monotheism,[39] employed Karl Jaspers' model for an axial age in his argument of an evolutionary development of monotheism.[40] For him, monotheism was a result of general burgeoning of creative intellectual activity.[41] Along similar lines, Juha Pakkala posits that the monotheism of the Deuteronomistic Historian—thus, the precursor to Judaism and Christianity—was "nationalistic"; that is, this "preliminary monotheism" was not a self-aware monotheism as much as it was an attempt to restore a political-religious nationalism.[42] A. M. Hocart too argued that "the germ of monotheism lies in the doctrine of divine kingship."[43] V. Nikiprowetzky has proposed that ethical monotheism is the result of a "universalist religion enclosed within the categories of a transcendental nationalism, or Zionism."[44] Chiara Peri argues that monotheism was a culmination of culture's rational thought in which old words and traditions were "de-semanticized" and infused with newer meanings. Thus, while a link with Israel's polytheistic past was maintained, interpretations of that past were corrected.[45] Jan Assmann distinguished between "primary" and "secondary" religions and argued that Israelite monotheism was a secondary religion that developed out of polytheism as its primary, or original, form or source of religion: "All secondary religions, which are at the same time book, world, and…monotheistic religions, look down on the primary religions

---

39. As clearly represented in the work of William Foxwell Albright, *From the Stone Age to Christianity: Monotheism and the Historical Process* (2d ed.; Garden City: Doubleday, 1957). As C. Peri observes, Gnuse associates the works of T. L. Thompson (*The Historicity of the Patriarchal Narratives: The Quest for the Historical Abraham* [Harrisburg: Trinity Press International, 2002]) and J. Van Seters, *Abraham in History and Tradition* [New Haven: Yale University Press, 1975]) with the beginning of that shift. His observation is echoed in Philip R. Davies, "What Separates a Minimalist from a Maximalist? Not Much," *Biblical Archaeology Review* 26 (2000): 24–27, 72–73.

40. Cf. Gnuse, *No Other Gods*, 226.

41. Cf. Ibid., 129–76.

42. Juha Pakkala, "The Monotheism of the Deuteronomistic History," *SJOT* 21, no. 2 (2007): 159–78. He writes, for example, "The authors are convinced that there is no other deity but Yahweh, but all the consequences of this view have not yet been drawn" (ibid., 159).

43. A. M. Hocart, "The Origin of Monotheism," *Folklore* 33, no. 3 (1922): 290.

44. V. Nikiprowetzky, "Ethical Monotheism," *Daedalus Daedalus* 104, no. 2 (1975): 85.

45. Chiara Peri, "The Construction of Biblical Monotheism: An Unfinished Task," *SJOT* 19, no. 1 (2005): 41.

as pagan."[46] Overall, there has been an inconsistency in the manner in which scholars have identified and described monotheism—an inconsistency due in part to a limited understanding of the structure upon which a monotheistic identity is built.

3. *The Problem of an Axial-age Shift*

To varying degrees, each of the scholars discussed above has tended to view Israelite monotheism in particular as a, and for some *the*, "breakthrough" in intellectual, religious thought corresponding to a broader (worldwide, for some) intellectual shift—a progressive intellectual shift not unknown to Modernist theory.[47] The Axial Age, as proposed by Jaspers and refined by Eisenstadt, offers a possible rationale for that shift. Yet while it may satisfy some, it explains sufficiently neither the material circumstances that gave way to monotheism nor the shift within monotheism from the immanent material realm to the ideological, or spiritual, realm as the context for its restoration. In short, it does not explain monotheism's transition from the concrete to the abstract, which was brought on by monotheism's failure to substantiate fully absolute, divine authority within the historical, material world. Despite a possible Axial-age rationale, the argument should be made more clearly.

Karl Jaspers wrote, "The axis of history is to be found in the period around 500 B.C., in the spiritual process that occurred between 800 and 200 B.C." And further, "Man, as we know him today, came into being."[48] It was during this time, according to Jaspers, that a great intellectual shift occurred; it was a historical range that was chosen in part, as Robert Bellah observes, because it was then that figures such as Confucius, Buddha, the Hebrew prophets, and the Greek philosophers lived, and who still "are alive to us, are contemporary with us, in a way that no earlier figures are."[49] As empires dotted the landscape, a change that decentralized local powers and set small states into competition, an

---

46. Assmann, *The Price of Monotheism*, 1.
47. On the nature of Modernism, see the overview, including variations of modernist thought, in Anat Matar, *Modernism and the Language of Philosophy* (London: Routledge, 2006), 1–9.
48. Karl Jaspers, *The Origin and Goal of History* (London: Routledge & Kegan Paul, 1953), 1. Note, in comparison, that A. Momigliano (*Alien Wisdom: The Limits of Hellenization* [Cambridge: Cambridge University Press, 1975], 8–9) redefines the axial period to 600–300 B.C.E.
49. Robert N. Bellah, "What Is Axial About the Axial Age?," *EJS* 46, no. 1 (2005): 73.

environment was produced consequently in which intellectuals were free to pursue activities outside of any controlled bureaucracy, such as in a priesthood.[50] Thus, it is important to note that Jaspers' so-called axial shifts did not occur in imperial centers but in the smaller states.[51]

S. N. Eisenstadt describes the Axial Age (which he dates from 500 B.C.E. to the first century C.E.[52]) as a "revolutionary process" that "took place in several major civilizations including Ancient Israel, Ancient Greece, Early Christianity, Zoroastrian Iran, early Imperial China, and the Hindu and Buddhist civilizations."[53] During the first millennium B.C.E., he argues, the intellectual elite of these societies became actively aware of a need to construct a world that was in line with a collective transcendental vision.[54] Similarly, Benjamin Schwartz refers to the Axial Age as a period of transcendental breakthroughs reflective of changes occurring within a common plane in human intellectual life.[55] These "breakthroughs" were in fact revolutions whose aftershocks were felt in the social, political, and religious spheres. Or, as Eisenstadt writes, "The revolution, or series of revolutions, which are related to Karl Jaspers' 'Axial Age,' have to do with the emergence, conceptualization, and institutionalization of a basic tension between the transcendental and mundane orders."[56]

Of the seven "civilizations" that Eisenstadt mentions, five seem to be restricted to a particular religious framework or identity:[57] ancient Israel

---

50. As noted by ibid., 74
51. Again, as noted by ibid.
52. Shmuel N. Eisenstadt, "The Expansion of Religions: Some Comparative Observations on Different Modes," *Comparative Social Research* 13 (1991): 46.
53. S. N. Eisenstadt, "Introduction," in *The Origins and Diversity of Axial Age Civilizations* (Albany: State University of New York Press, 1986), 1. He writes further, "Although beyond the Axial Age proper, it also took place in Islam" (ibid.). Note also that Bellah omits Zoroastrian Iran from his discussion because of the general uncertainty surrounding Zoroaster's life, whether he might have lived during the middle of the second millennium BCE or the middle of the first ("What is Axial About the Axial Age?", 75).
54. Eisenstadt, "Introduction," 1.
55. Benjamin I. Schwartz, "The Age of Transcendence," in *Wisdom, Revelation, and Doubt: Perspectives on the First Millennium B.C.* (ed. Benjamin I. Schwartz), *Daedalus* (1975): 3–4.
56. Eisenstadt, "Introduction," 1.
57. In ancient Greece, Xenophon's "monotheistic tendencies," according to Gnuse, never fully embraced monotheism (*No Other Gods*, 225). Note also Pettazzoni and Meslin who argue that while the pre-Socratic thinkers merged all gods in the Hellenistic world into a single divine principle, their views remained "monotheistic institutional possibilities" that were never thoroughly employed.

1. *What Is Meant by Monotheism?* 23

(by which he presumably means Judah, given his dates for his Axial Age proper, and which he appears to assume was predominantly Yahwistic[58]), Early Christianity, Zoroastrian Iran, and the Hindu and Buddhist civilizations. Yet what he determines to be a civilization is somewhat problematic; religion, in particular, cannot comprise a civilization. In his very use of the term, it would appear that Eisenstadt has divorced from its material conditions, which define the identity of any civilization, a "civilization's" ideological expressions of identity (which makes it easier for him to show a transcendentalization of the divine). In short, by focusing almost exclusively on an ideological basis for identity he has converted "civilization" into an abstract idea that can be defined without specific concern for the cultural, material, and historical circumstances that delineate a civilization. It also suggests a somewhat Orientalist[59] undertone to speak rather monolithically of "the Hindu and Buddhist civilizations." With that, he has described people groups at the very least ranging from Southwest Asia to East Asia! The label "Early Christianity" is not much better. At its birth, Christianity was a Jewish movement, and one response among several to a desired national restoration constantly prohibited by the presence of foreign imperial powers. As such, at the time of its origin it remains consistent with his description of ancient Israel and does not demand unique attention. Its "uniqueness" was found later in the first millennium C.E., and substantially well after the first century C.E., as it developed an identity that rewrote any residual Jewish traditions and was based on a culture that was brought in by "Gentile" converts, who were predominantly Roman. Thus, Christianity was not an isolatable civilization—much less a civilization. It would be better described, in the manner that Eisenstadt does of Islam, as a related development that occurs outside the axial age proper.[60]

Bellah is correct in saying that Eisenstadt's Zoroastrian Iran cannot be considered accurately in the discussion.[61] The time in which Zoroaster lived is simply not certain, nor is it very clear that Zoroastrianism was culturally dominant. Moreover, there is no real evidence of a *Zoroastrian* Iran since the Persian kingdom resulted from an amalgamation of

---

58. By "Yahwistic" we refer specifically to the monotheistic variant described in the biblical texts. Yet one cannot speak of a *monotheistic* Judah. And one can only speak of Jewish monotheism after the politically defined kingdom had lost its material definition.
59. For more on this concept see Edward W. Said, *Orientalism* (New York: Vintage, 1994; repr. 1979).
60. See again Eisenstadt, "Introduction," 1.
61. Again see Bellah, "What Is Axial About the Axial Age?," 75.

different tribes, who likely held on to their tribal deities for as long as possible.[62] If Zoroastrianism should be excluded due to uncertain dates, perhaps Islam and Christianity, both of which developed more significantly after the first century C.E. (Islam was entirely after), should also be excluded. This would leave Eisenstadt's "major civilizations" at ancient Israel, ancient Greece, and early Imperial China—only one of which it can be said to have developed a strict monotheistic religion, and even the inclusion of China in that list is not without its problems.[63] Given the evidence under discussion, an "axial period" does not appear to be a sufficient causal explanation for the development of monotheism.

But according to Eisenstadt, Israel's tribal organization, its continual encounters with other settled and nomadic peoples, and its location at the crossroads of "great empires of antiquity" created a circumstance that was "the continuous fluidity and openness of political boundaries: the constant flow and mobility of people; difficulties in the maintenance of a stable, compact political entity and even of a distinct identity."[64] In addition, he describes Israelite identity as being marked by a tension between ethnic identity and a "religious-cultural" identity. The former was based on a strong historical consciousness, a strong "primordial kinship identity" based on the traditions of the Patriarchs, and a political identity. The latter, as he puts it, was an "identity couched in potentially universalistic terms."[65] It was Israel's internal struggle to maintain a collective distinctiveness from other peoples and cultures, thus its tendency toward segregation, that constructed within Israelite identity a monotheistic possibility.[66] Moreover, through the people's desire to separate in universalistic terms themselves from other peoples "by claiming to transcend their particularistic religious symbols," Israel's monotheism took

---

62. For an overview of the Persian pantheon, especially the resurgence of deities during the reign of Artaxerxes II, see S. A. Niogosian, "The Religions in Achaemenid Persia," *Studies in Religion* 4, no. 4 (1974): 378.

63. As Bellah describes ("What Is Axial About the Axial Age?", 77, see also p. 75), Eisenstadt's distinction between transcendental and mundane has been questioned in the case of China because of its "inveterate 'this-worldliness.'" See also Mark Elvin, "Was There a Transcendental Break-Through in China?," in Eisenstadt, ed., *The Origins and Diversity of Axial Age Civilizations*, 325–59. Even Eisenstadt himself has tempered his earlier assertion (Jóhann Páll Árnason, S. N. Eisenstadt, and Björn Wittrock, eds., *Axial Civilizations and World History* [Jerusalem Studies in Religion and Culture 4; Leiden: Brill, 2005], 533).

64. S. N. Eisenstadt, "The Axial Age Breakthrough in Ancient Israel," in Eisenstadt, ed., *The Origins and Diversity of Axial Age Civilizations*, 128.

65. Ibid., 131.

66. Ibid., 131–32.

on a tone of universalism.⁶⁷ With the eventual destruction of the nation and the peoples seemingly perpetual existence under foreign powers—described alternatively as "waves of conquest and settlement"—the tension between an ethnic identity and a religious-cultural identity increased and resulted further in the transcendentalization and universalization of the divine.⁶⁸ In the face of a tumultuous political environment, Eisenstadt contends, the Jewish people "developed and continued claims of the universal validity of their religion and tradition."⁶⁹

There is some agreement to be had with Eisenstadt's statement: "[W]hat was characteristic of the Jewish situation during this period—and later on—was the combination of a precarious political and economic situation with attempts at intensive participation in the political and cultural life of the period."⁷⁰ But what he describes as the "Jewish situation" during the Axial Age proper and shortly following is in fact based on the described experiences of a community of Judean immigrants who traveled from Babylonia to Yehud—that is, the *golah* community in Persian-period Yehud. His description does not accurately reflect the circumstances of an entire civilization.

Aware, possibly, of the dangers that Eisenstadt's rather broad statements pose, Robert Bellah warns:

> In discussing the axial age it is all too easy to read in our own presuppositions or to take one of the four cases (usually Israel or Greece) as paradigmatic for all the others.⁷¹

The problem of assuming one case to be paradigmatic for others with respect to Axial Age theory is that it avoids the historical and material particularities of individual social-political contexts. The danger lies not in employing one case as a model but in accepting it as a credible explanation for all possible occurrences. That said, however, Bellah still believes there is a framework through which to interpret the intellectual shift to which Jaspers and Eisenstadt have pointed:

> Is there a theoretical framework in which to place the axial age that will help us avoid these pitfalls as much as possible? I believe there is: the framework of the evolution of human culture and cognition.⁷²

---

67. Ibid., 132.
68. Ibid., 132–34.
69. Ibid., 132.
70. Ibid.
71. Bellah, "What Is Axial About the Axial Age?", 77.
72. Ibid.

Bellah sees the Axial Age as a stage in the evolutionary development of human intellect and social-cultural patterns of engagement. He equates the Axial Age with Merlin Donald's fourth stage of human development.[73] This stage is marked by a theoretic attitude—reflection for the sake of reflection—an intellectual posture to which Yehuda Elkana refers as "second-order thinking."[74] Bellah argues that it is precisely this second-order thinking, "the idea that there are alternatives that have to be argued for," that is characteristic of the Axial Age.[75] But the cultural transformations of the societies that define the Axial Age are not uniform. Moreover, while Greece, Israel, China, and India in the first millennium B.C.E. approach, as Bellah describes, the capacity of "theoretic culture for second-order thinking," such thinking is limited to an intellectual elite and never a popular enterprise.[76] And those individuals who were responsible for leading such innovations were seldom successful in the short term.[77] As even Jaspers declares, "The Axial Period too ended in failure."[78] But as Bellah states, "The insights, however, at least the ones we know of, survived."[79] In short, while the individual endeavors of the Axial Age were a failure, the repercussions of those intellectual endeavors were felt and embodied by others.

However, the rather Durkheimian concept of what appears to be a global collective unconscious upon which the axial period seems to

73. M. Donald describes these stages in *Origins of the Modern Mind: Three Stages in the Evolution of Culture and Cognition* (Cambridge, Mass.: Harvard University Press, 1991), passim.

74. Ibid., 341; Yehuda Elkana, "The Emergence of Second-Order Thinking in Classical Greece," in Eisenstadt, ed., *The Origins and Diversity of Axial Age Civilizations*, 40–64. Bellah describes Elkana's theory, "For Elkana, first-order theory can be quite complex, as for example mathematics and the beginning of algebra in Babylonia, or…calendrical astronomy…but it involves straight-forward rational exposition, not reflection about the basis of the exposition. Second-order thinking is 'thinking about thinking,' that is, it attempts to understand how the rational exposition is possible and can be defended. One of the earliest examples is geometric proof, associated with Pythagoras in early Greece. Geometric proof not only asserts geometric truths, but the grounds for thinking them true, that is, proofs that in principle could be disproved, or replaced by better proofs" ("What Is Axial About the Axial Age?," 80).

75. Ibid.

76. Ibid., 88.

77. Ibid., 89.

78. Jaspers, *The Origin and Goal of History*, 20. Or even, "The axial age was shattered. History continued" (Japsers, "The Axial Age of Human History," *Commentary [New York]* 6 [1948]: 435).

79. Bellah, "What Is Axial About the Axial Age?", 89.

1. What Is Meant by Monotheism?

depend is problematic.[80] A singular period in which world civilizations somewhat uniformly developed a consistent appreciation and practice of higher-order thinking cannot avoid sounding overly reductionist or simplistic. Even Eisenstadt has more recently proposed "multiple axialities"[81] because he himself has recognized that a singular axiality assumes what I would call a "psychic homogeneity"[82] across the world's civilizations. And with multiple axialities, one is no longer beholden to a single historical period or causal explanation as a rationale for any cosmic intellectual shift. Instead, "axiality" should be considered a model denoting structural qualities with which to analyze similar developments in different cultures. In that way, one may still appropriately account for the material conditions unique to each historical-cultural context. All this would suggest that there exists no true Axial Age, that the cultural responses used previously to define that age were not characteristic of a worldwide historical phenomenon. They were instead the variegated responses to different historical circumstances produced by trends both unique and similar among different cultural-historical contexts. Eisenstadt has recently admitted that the theory requires "a differentiated approach to pre-axial or non-axial civilizations."[83] And further, "It is important to analyze these civilizations, their reproduction and dynamics in their own terms and not only as precursors of axial civilizations or as 'failed' axialities."[84] Perhaps more important are his following concessions that fundamentally reject the original premise of axial-age theory, which had required that there was a collective movement throughout the world in response to eerily similar circumstances. These are the third and fourth points out of seven in a program for reconsidering the Axial Age that Eisenstadt proposes:

> Third is the necessity to distinguish systematically, to a far greater extent than we have, among the different components of axial civilizations: basic cultural orientations, cosmological visions, and institutional formations, with special emphasis on the development within them of multiple constellations of power, collective identities and economic formations. Fourth, and closely connected with the preceding consideration, is the

---

80. It is interesting that Eisenstadt will later accuse Jaspers of an apparent reliance upon this concept (Árnason, Eisenstadt, and Wittrock, eds., *Axial Civilizations and World History*, 532–33).

81. S. N. Eisenstadt, "Axial Civilizations and the Axial Age Reconsidered," in Árnason, Eisenstadt, and Wittrock, eds., *Axial Civilizations and World History*, 561.

82. Might some call this the divine?

83. Ibid., 531.

84. Árnason, Eisenstadt, and Wittrock, eds., *Axial Civilizations and World History*, 531–32.

recognition of the importance of the autonomous dynamics of political spheres, the constitution of collective identities as well as of economic formations; of the different modes in which they were interwoven with different axial cosmological visions, giving rise to different institutional patterns without assuming the existence of a natural correlation between any specific cosmological vision and any political regime, patterns of collective identity or economic formation."[85]

In the same more recent work, Eisenstadt proposed that axial civilizations are characterized by a "core of affinity," which entails

a certain openness in the constitution of these dimensions of social order and of the relations between them. This openness is manifest in the decoupling of the different components or dimensions of social order—the structural and the symbolic—from the frameworks within which they presumably were embedded in earlier, pre-axial periods of their respective societies, or which can be identified in non-axial societies with which they share some basic structural characteristics.[86]

This "decoupling," which Eisenstadt presumably still maintains was the consequence of decentralized powers, forced a structural differentiation "best manifest in the crystallization of specific organizationally distinct organizations, collectivities and even roles such as for instance distinct occupational ones; as against their being firmly embedded in different family, kinship or local settings; of 'free' non-embedded resources and of the concomitant development of new integrative problems and mechanisms."[87] Distinctive elite functions crystalized as a consequence; such functions were not only economic and political in orientation but were given to "the constitution of trust, regulation of power and provision of meaning."[88] Within a decentralized context that collapsed previous organizational structures, the disembodied function of the elite became the basis upon which a newer differentiated power could be based. "Second-order" thinking and reflexivity in their concomitant organization of "different worlds of knowledge" concretized "new 'civilizational' institutional formations" in place of traditional social formations, or power structures, that were previously responsible for maintaining social order.[89] All said, an axial-age explanation, which has itself become increasingly dubious, does not sufficiently account for the origin of monotheism. Its focus on "thinking about thinking," to put it baldly,

85. Ibid., 532.
86. Ibid., 533.
87. Ibid., 534.
88. Ibid.
89. Ibid., 537–42.

does not explain monotheism's focus on a "restoration" of authority in or by overturning the conditions of the material world.

Monotheism instead, as we will show, was the consequence of material circumstances produced in an environment in which the monotheistic community was on the periphery of authority. It was not the sole property of a seemingly global paradigm shift in intellectual thought, but the consequence of an historical contest for authority. Monotheism became an exercise of a "second-order thinking" *after* its desired restoration was not made materially manifest. One can accept that second-order thinking, and so a transition from concrete to abstract, was a vehicle (but not the only one!) through which monotheism was preserved in the face of its own failure to garner material power and achieve its desired "restoration," but it was not the medium of its birth.

Neither, as we will clarify in this work, was monotheism a *necessary* evolutionary stage in human cognition and interaction. The relative paucity of true monotheistic religions—that is, in terms of individual types and not modern geographic spread—among the world's civilizations suggests instead that monotheism was an arbitrary consequence of material conditions that may themselves have been produced in different stages of human-social development, and not a singular or common stage. Its continuing prevalence is due largely to the structural qualities upon which each expression of monotheism was built. These qualities are common not because early monotheistic communities were somehow linked into the same collective unconscious,[90] but because the same desire or contest for authority that is inherent within all human societies resides at the heart of monotheism. Authority, then, as we are using it, means more than the ability to control. It includes also the capacity to define, organize, and situate material objects, forces, and ideas in a definitive manner within a culture. The basis for authority is often found in material circumstances but develops as well into an inclusion of ideas and the forces that motivate them. Thus, for example, we can speak of a "symbolic power"[91] because the idea of power and a corresponding authority were first recognized with control over land and resources.

90. Again, I am using "collective unconscious" as Durkheim defined it (*The Elementary Forms of the Religious Life* [trans. Karen E. Fields; New York: Free Press, 1995], passim). For contrast note K. Mannheim (*Ideology and Utopia: An Introduction to the Sociology of Knowledge* [trans. Louis Wirth and Edward Shils; New York: Harcourt Brace Jovanovich, 1936], 6, emphasis mine), "It is one of the fundamental insights of the sociology of knowledge that the process by which collective-unconscious motives become conscious cannot operate in every epoch, *but only in a quite specific situation.*"

91. As the term is defined in Bourdieu, "Genesis and Structure," 25.

Axial-age theories fail to account adequately for the structural development of monotheism. In addition, these theories, among others, fall short in their general lack of attention to the constructive role that active preservation of the boundary between member and non-member plays.

4. *A Word on "Member" as a Subcategory of Monotheistic Identity*

As a subcategory of monotheistic identity, "member"—and by that we mean the identifiable member of a monotheistic community who is distinguishable as one who has been encoded with the community culture—and its distinction from "non-member" reflect the more general, base division (which takes place first in the monotheistic body) between natural and divine authorities. Thus, the fundamental separation in monotheism between member and non-member is the result not of any original sin (Christianity) or any covenant breaking (Judaism). It is foremost an ideological division that is itself the consequence, a reaction, rather, of an unsupportive historical context. In other words, at its core the separation between insider and outsider exists because the religious community sees itself in contest with (prevailing) natural authorities. And it is a contest in which, from a material perspective, natural authorities have the upper hand. This contest is clearly expressed in Ezra–Nehemiah's focus on the dogged separation of communities (including the expressed distaste for "foreigners"[92]), an expressed presumed entitlement to the land (including the Jerusalem temple), the described imposition of an external, religious law, and even the selective attention given to some of the imperially appointed political officials (notably governors). For example, it is stated in Nehemiah,

> So the descendants went in and possessed the land, and you subdued before them the inhabitants of the land, the Canaanites, and gave them into their hands, with their kings and the peoples of the land, to do with them as they pleased... Here we are, slaves to this day—slaves in the land that you gave to our ancestors to enjoy its fruit and its good gifts. (Neh 9:24, 36)

Historically, Israel and Judah were not "religious" nations in the sense that they were theocracies or nations whose primary mode of production

---

92. Cf. M. Liverani's discussion of the ethnic labels used and his conclusion they are false labels in *Israel's History and the History of Israel* (trans. Chiara Peri and Philip R. Davies; London: Equinox, 2005), 274–77. Liverani concludes that labels designating historical ethnicities were used to delegitimate their claims to the land of Yehud.

was identifiably religious. The idea portrayed in the biblical texts that Israel was a religiously patterned nation was one created by authors writing after the Babylonian exiles of 597 and 587 B.C.E. It is a mistake to take for granted that what the *golah* community desired most was religious fidelity. Rather than being a goal in itself, fidelity offered a possible mechanism of (desired) control. Or to phrase it somewhat differently, the codifying of religious law outlining group identity and behavior (thus culture) exemplified not an isolated concern to be religiously faithful for the sake of religious ethic alone but ultimately to provide a rationale for economic division. After all, the immigrating community held no valid economic anchors within the province. That is one reason why we see occur the practice of intermarriage—immigrants marrying into the social-economic hierarchy—a practice that Ezra–Nehemiah vehemently detests. Land, the biblical texts assume, was the unique property of Yahweh who could give it to whomever Yahweh pleased; it was not, in this spirit, the property of any "people of the land." And so Ezra–Nehemiah reduces within its narrative world all peoples not members of the community to a single category of "foreign." As foreigners, the people of the land would, presumably, have no legitimate claim to the land or its surpluses.

Such a utopian ideal, however—and it was utopian because it reflected a reality hoped for but not materially manifest—could not be maintained realistically. For instance, at the material level, the community could not afford financially to exclude all peoples.[93] More importantly, the *golah* community was not in any social or political position—in other words, they held not enough material power—to exclude people from engaging in the everyday activities of the province, or even only the city of Jerusalem. This utopian ideal, then, was the measure against that which was considered the prevailing normative; and restoration could occur only when the normative world was more closely aligned with the biblical perception of how that world *should* be.[94]

---

93. As Liverani (ibid., 358–59) notes, the Phoenicians were integrated because of their financial strength (cf. Neh 13:15–16). C. Carter (*The Emergence of Yehud in the Persian Period: A Social and Demographic Study* (JSOTSup 294; Sheffield: Sheffield Academic, 1999], 288–89) relatedly posits that the economic instability of Yehud created problems not only in meeting the burden of reconstructing the Jerusalem temple but also, in light of famine, general material surplus production.

94. D. Karp ("The Utopia and Reality of Sovereignty: Social Reality, Normative IR and 'Organized Hypocrisy'," *Review of International Studies* 34 [2008]: 316) describes this general tendency in utopian thought, and how it becomes political, as follows, "The 'utopian' mode of thought starts by fleshing out a normative position,

Had the *golah* community ideal held dominant political authority, we would likely have seen in its testifying texts an increased, critical focus on the economic and political activities, successes or failures, of its rulers, such as can be found throughout the book of Kings. What we see, on the contrary, is an appeal to religion as the primary, controlling sphere of authority.[95] Even so, the form of Yahwism to which the appeal was made was a new variant—one that was more rigidly defined around the *golah* community as the chosen remnant (cf. Ezra 9:1–8). This form of Yahwism, in other words, was one without strong institutional anchors within the dominant culture in Yehud.

As an immigrating community, the *golah* community insured loyalty to the group by defining itself as the sole divine remnant—a loyalty that was vital to the community's attempt to establish the land rights of its members.[96] Daniel Smith refers to this communal response as "defensive structuring":

> The preservation of an identity under threat calls for 'defensive structure.' If, as we have suggested, 'ethnic identity' is preserved by conscious choice in circumstances of intercultural contact, then an analysis of the social mechanisms of the Judean exiles in Babylon ought to reveal creatively structured identities in order to be 'the people of God' in a foreign land.[97]

and uses this position to arrive at prescriptions or conclusions about the descriptive world. When one translates this mode of thought into political action, one uses one's agency to (re)design political institutions, or to foster political events, such that the world is brought more closely into line with a normative idea about the way the world ought to be."

95. The general theme of the letter from Artaxerxes in Ezra 7:12–28 is on the construction and centralization of the Jerusalem temple and on the establishing of Ezra's Mosaic Law as normative in Yehud.

96. G. Ahlström (*The History of Ancient Palestine* [Minneapolis: Fortress, 1993], 846) offers a similar observation. M. J. Leith ("Israel Among the Nations: The Persian Period," in *The Oxford History of the Biblical World* (ed. Michael D. Coogan; Oxford: Oxford University Press, 1998], 397) writes that Ezek 11 tackles the issue of land claim by stating that Yahweh had deserted Judah and followed the exiled Judeans into Babylon. This was, according to Leith, a counterclaim to that made by the nonexiled Judeans that the land was theirs.

97. Daniel L. Smith, *The Religion of the Landless: A Sociology of the Babylonian Exile* (Bloomington: Meyer-Stone, 1989), 63. But compare J. Kessler ("Persia's Loyal Yahwists: Power, Identity, and Ethnicity in Achaemenid Yehud," in Lipschits and Oeming, eds., *Judah and the Judeans in the Persian Period*, 104) who is more confident regarding the social position of the Judean immigrants: "The Golah Returnees dominated the major institutions of Yehud. A combination of circumstantial factors and Persian imperial decisions placed the members of this group in an especially advantageous position and gave them virtual hegemony over the

Yet it is "defensive" not in that the community was on the verge of extinction—in point of fact, it is more likely the people of the land were accepting of the immigrants.[98] It was defensive in that the community perceived that its desired social-economic position was contingent upon its self-identification as an exclusive community[99]—a desire that was symbolized by the city of Jerusalem and the community's occupation of it.

The city of Jerusalem occupies the focus of the Persian-period biblical texts; their authors see in that city the seat of divine power and, subsequently, the center from which the radius of restoration proceeds.[100] The construction of the city's walls was interpreted—especially by Ezra–Nehemiah and Zechariah—as a manifest confirmation of the separation of that which represents the sacred from a profane "other."[101] Expressed

---

province." Outside of the various claims of the biblical texts, that the land was empty and that the returning community was bestowed, whether directly or circumstantially, with imperial authority, there is no strong supporting evidence for Kessler's proposal.

98. Different scholars have pointed to the likely "ethnic" diversity in Yehud (cf. Israel Eph'al, "Syria-Palestine Under Achaemenid Rule," in *Cambridge Ancient History*. Vol. 4, *Persia, Greece and the Western Mediterranean, C. 525 to 479 B.C.*, (ed. John Boardman et al.; Cambridge: Cambridge University Press, 1988), 147; Kenneth G. Hoglund, "The Achaemenid Context," in *Second Temple Studies, 1. Persian Period* (ed. Philip R. Davies; Sheffield: Sheffield Academic, 1991), 54–72; Ahlström, *The History of Ancient Palestine*, 822–23; Leith, "Israel Among the Nations," 381. See also both Leith and Gropp (Mary J. W. Leith, *Wadi Daliyeh: The Wadi Daliyeh Seal Impressions* [Discoveries in the Judaean Desert 24; [Oxford: Clarendon, 1997], 5–6, 11; Douglas M. Gropp, *The Samaria Papyri from Wadi Daliyeh: Wadi Daliyeh II and Qumran Cave 4: The Samaria Papyri from Wadi Daliyeh/Miscellanea*, Part 2 [Discoveries in the Judaean Desert 28; Oxford: Clarendon, 2001], 6) who discuss the demographic makeup of Samaria. And see A. Lemaire's discussion ("Populations et Territoires de Palestine à l'Époque perse," *Transeuphratene* 3 [1990]: 31–74) of larger Palestine.

99. This statement finds agreement in Morton Smith, *Palestinian Parties and Politics that Shaped the Old Testament* (2d corr. ed.; London: SCM, 1987), 75, 81.

100. Kessler states that the *golah* community's interest in Jerusalem was primarily an attempted cultural and religious identification with the heritage of the geographic site and less an economic or demographic venture ("Persia's Loyal Yahwists," 103). But to emphasize religious identity over economic factors as justification for control over Jerusalem given its history as a capital city seems to assume that the economic expense of the temple was not enough to warrant the concern of the people who were already in the land.

101. According to Durkheim, this binary categorical division is common to all humanity: "Whether simple or complex, all known religious beliefs display a common feature: They presuppose a classification of the real or ideal things that men

differently, those texts describe the *golah* community as embodying and repeating a self–non-self archetypal pattern—a pattern, one portrayed within the biblical texts as normative, most clearly expressed through the Exodus tradition in which the Divine selected a representative people from amidst others—by defining the community over and against the *am ha'aretz* and building walls to radically impose confirmation of this division.[102]

For us, however, understanding the *golah* collective identity (in contradistinction to that of the so-called *am ha'aretz*) is not the end result. What we seek to understand is how the community's identity was formed in reaction to social, political, and economic forces impacting not only the community but also the larger cultural context. While the cultural identity of the community enjoyed much structural formation in diaspora, as it is presented in the biblical texts, it betrays also an identity fashioned at the confluence of reactionary and assimilative forces that were natural to the context of Yehud. After a period of about seventy years, the "home" culture for the *golah* community was in its Babylonian community, and its subsequent development, through which it took on a

---

conceive of into two classes—two opposite genera—that are widely designated by two distinct terms, which the words *profane* and *sacred* translate fairly well. The division of the world into two domains, one containing all that is sacred and the other all that is profane—such is the distinctive trait of religious thought. Beliefs, myths, dogmas, and legends are either representations or systems of representations that express the nature of sacred things, the virtues and power attributed to them, their history, and their relationships with one another as well as with profane things" (*Elementary Forms*, 34).

102. K. Hoglund (*Achaemenid Imperial Administration in Syria-Palestine and the Missions of Ezra and Nehemiah* [SBLDS 125; Atlanta: Scholars Press, 1992], 208) states that the emphasis on Jerusalem's walls in Nehemiah was meant to focus attention on the formation of a holy community through the process of separating the community from surrounding peoples. Note also that the self–non-self archetype reflects an inherent binary opposition. As J. Alexander (*The Meanings of Social Life: A Cultural Sociology* [Oxford: Oxford University Press, 2003], 32) writes, "This contrived binary, which simplifies empirical complexity to two antagonistic forms and reduces every shade of grey between, has been an essential feature of all human societies but especially important in those Eisenstadt (1982) has called the Axial Age civilizations. This rigid opposition between the sacred and profane, which in Western philosophy has typically been constructed as a conflict between normativity and instrumentality, not only defines what people care about but establishes vital safeguards around the shared normative 'good.' At the same time it places powerful, often aggressive barriers against anything that is constructed as threatening the good, forces defined not merely as things to be avoided but as sources of horror and pollution that must be contained at all costs."

unique identity, was secured in Yehud.[103] With that said, it is by understanding where main points of resistance and acceptance occur that we may begin to understand the community's connection to the larger culture. For it is at those points where society and (sub-)culture "rub raw" that main (structural) issues are revealed. Moreover, such points reveal places wherein the social and political bodies find themselves either in conflict over the proper distribution of power or where a previously accepted distribution of power is or has been interrupted.

Monotheistic religion is not immune to this. Its struggle for power moves beyond a single social body and embraces the whole of the material and social realms. And yet it is precisely this "greediness" that produces the fundamental need, an exclusionary one, to define between the self and the non-self as those who "share in the throne of God" and those who "suffer hell." Monotheism's inherent tendency toward universalism and absolutism are readily employed by those seeking to establish any dominant claim to power.

5. Why Employing the Theories of Michel Foucault and Gilles Deleuze and Felix Guattari Is Helpful

Throughout this work I make reference to the works of Michel Foucault and Gilles Deleuze and Felix Guattari.[104] These scholars have focused in different ways on the construction and maintenance of the psychophysical body, or individual, and its relation to the social body, the latter which was itself composed by the former in great number. These scholars also accepted that the individual reflected, consciously and unconsciously, the body of knowledge contained within the social body. Individuals could be "created" and "re-created" based on the social body's shifting nature.[105] Foucault, in particular, was concerned with understanding power in terms of networks and relations between individuals and within

---

103. This observation is based on an understanding that immigrating cultures take on different developmental paths than those of their home cultures left behind. See, for example, the case studies of Lithuanian refugees conducted by Liucija Baskauskas, "The Lithuanian Refugee Experience and Grief," *International Migration Review* 15 (1981): 276–91; Raymond G. Krisciunas, "The Emigrant Experience: The Decision of Lithuanian Refugees to Emigrate, 1945–1950," *Lithuanian Quarterly Journal of Arts and Sciences* 29 (1983).

104. Specifically, I am drawing upon Foucault's *Discipline and Punish*, his *Archaeology of Knowledge*, and Deleuze and Guattari's *Anti-Oedipus*.

105. See also the summary of Foucault in David Armstrong, "Bodies of Knowledge / Knowledge of Bodies," in *Reassessing Foucault: Power, Medicine, and the Body* (ed. Colin Jones and Roy Porter; London: Routledge, 1994), 17–27.

society. In fact, individuals are always conditioned by society—the relationships they employ have already been in a sense predetermined for them. To understand the historical nature and development of these relationships, Foucault focused on understanding discontinuities, practices, and genealogies of knowledge.[106] He focused on specific moments to address general questions.[107] Or, as Felix Driver observes, "Foucault's histories do not present us with linear narratives. They are concerned less with the flow of individual intentions, actions and consequences than with discourses, practices and effects."[108] Individuals are important because of the discourse(s) they preserve throughout history and within the social body. More importantly, individual contribution to a larger discourse is the basis for identity. When we speak of the individual, we speak not of an isolated being but of a(n individual) reflection of the social body. Likewise, when we speak of individual texts or documents, we refer not to inert documents but to individual, cultural productions that reflect unities, disruptions, totalities, and relations characteristic of, ultimately, a social body.[109]

Deleuze and Guattari, particularly in *Anti-Oedipus*, likewise turned to the psycho-physical body as representative of the discursive formations, patterns, or "flows" (and their interruptions) of the social body. And like Foucault who focused on "madhouses and prisons," believing those institutions revealed the loose seams of social order—thus, the final separation between order and chaos—Deleuze and Guattari viewed the (schizophrenic) individual as symptomatic of the disjointed flows or productions of the social body. "For Deleuze and Guattari, to conceive of the social machine as a binary organization is to ignore the fact that something always escapes."[110] The social body is a producing body, a machine whose purpose is surplus production. It follows the pattern of the natural world as the primary producer. But Deleuze and Guattari do not content themselves with a staunch materialist explanation. For them, surplus production is in truth desire production; and this opens the body as machine to materialist *and* ideological possibilities, to representation

---

106. See also Felix Driver, "Bodies in Space: Foucault's Account of Disciplinary Power," in Jones and Porter, eds., *Reassessing Foucault*, 114.
107. Ibid.
108. Ibid., 115. M. Foucault himself writes, "History is not linear but a series of discursive formations" (*The Archaeology of Knowledge and the Discourse on Language* (trans. A. M. Sheridan Smith; New York: Pantheon, 1972], 188).
109. Cf. ibid., 7.
110. Mohamed Zayani, "Gilles Deleuze, Félix Guattari and the Total System," *Philosophy & Social Criticism* 26, no. 1 (2000): 97–98.

as an activity in itself no longer anchored by any material object.[111] Production is always dependent upon human relations, which themselves can be—and always are—interrupted, rejoined, or otherwise altered. As they write, "As a matter of fact, what is marked or inscribed on the socius—directly—is the producers (or nonproducers) according to the standing of their family or their standing inside the family."[112] Desire production, as they use the phrase, is not simply a process of material surplus production. It has been "deterritorialized" from being the sole possession of material forces.[113] Yet neither is it an act of ideological production devoid of material associations. It is the process by which the identity of the social body is formed and whose productive flows support the apparatus of power.[114] By revealing these flows and their interruptions, one lays bare the very cornerstone of the body's identity.

Foucault's and Deleuze and Guattari's understandings of the relationship between the psycho-physical and social bodies underlay my own understanding of the monotheistic body as a construct of material and ideological relations. Monotheistic religions are the evolving products of the engagement between the discursive formation that is common to all monotheisms and the social body. This discursive formation is largely the identifying process of the monotheistic body. Where these theorists prove most helpful is in dismantling social behaviors and identities to reveal the structural relationships, or even their absences, that support those behaviors and identities. This will prove extremely helpful when unpacking the discourse of monotheism in order to lay bare its structure and its origin. But in saying this, we recognize that any pursuit of a deeper meaning beyond discourse and the pursuit of a structure behind it may leave our theorists, especially Foucault, behind. Their theories are helpful precisely in their abilities to dismantle the social (and religious) body, to reveal networks of relations. They reveal the points of resistance between ideological and material explanations and causes. In other

---

111. They define "representation" as follows: "Representation no longer relates to a distinct object, but to productive activity itself. The socius as full body has become directly economic as capital-money; it does not tolerate any other preconditions. What is inscribed or marked is no longer the producers or nonproducers, but the forces and means of production as abstract quantities that become effectively concrete in their becoming related or their conjunction: labor capacity or capital, constant capital or variable capital, capital of filiation or capital of alliance" (Deleuze and Guattari, *Anti-Oedipus*, 263).
  112. Ibid., 262–63.
  113. Cf. ibid., 233.
  114. Cf. ibid., 139–40.

words, I employ the theories of Foucault and Deleuze and Guattari to strip away ideological layers of discourse to reveal monotheism's material underpinnings.

Based on this discussion, our working hypothesis, to review, is this: monotheism is a consequence of an original conflict—one that produces a concern for the division between member and non-member—within the material sphere. Analyses of monotheism must be equipped not only to identify monotheism's origin in the material sphere but also to explain its development from compact to complex forms, which entails a shift from a dependence upon the material to the ideological. This shift was brought on by monotheism's concern for its own acquisition of authority over the social body.

Chapter 2

How Monotheism Creates a New Normative Order in Support of Its Own Authority

> [Religions] must have a clear conception of what they feel to be incompatible with their truths if these truths are to exert the life-shaping authority, normativity, and binding force that they claim for themselves.[1]

As we previously noted, "authority" includes but is not limited to the capacity to define, organize, and situate within a social-political hierarchy a culture's material objects, its productive forces, the possible range and field for engagements of its individuals, and its dominant modes of ideation.[2] Moreover, it supports and preserves the power to organize reciprocal relations within a group or society. In part, because of these things, it is one of the principal purposes for which the three pillars (revelation, law, and restoration) sustain the monotheistic body. Their collective functional motivation is the attainment of an absolutely coercive power by which the monotheistic body can be imposed as an objective reality upon both accepting and reluctant individuals or institutional cultures within a corresponding social body.[3]

---

1. Assmann, *The Price of Monotheism*, 14. Assmann refers specifically to "secondary religions," which as we have noted previously includes monotheism, according to his classification.

2. This is true of authority generally and is not limited to its different types—a point also acknowledged by Weber in his discussion of the ideal types of authority (cf. *Economy and Society: An Outline of Interpretive Sociology* [trans. Ephraim Fischoff et al.; New York: Bedminster, 1968], 215–16, 241–54, 1111–57). See also Rodney Hall's proposal ("Moral Authority as a Power Resource," *International Organization* 51 [1997]: 591–622) that moral authority attending social identities derived from religious norms and principles can be a source of power. He shows that moral authority was employed in Medieval Europe as a power resource to define the rules of a hierocratic social order (ibid., 592).

3. I am borrowing here from Berger's discussion of coercive power and its ability to sustain the objective reality of a society (cf. *Sacred Canopy*, 11). Monotheism's use of coercive power is motivated by a self-perceived need to impose upon society its altered view of reality as objective reality.

Legitimated authority requires either that it be physically present within the social body or that it be represented by a symbol offering a continual reminder as to why the social body has legitimated that authority in the first place. Thus, revelation within the material world—that is, a disruption by divine authority—is crucial in terms of legitimation (and its subsequent representation by the law) for the monotheistic body. To be clear, revelation is interruption. It is the divine's, or monotheistic body's, intrusion into the social body's normative order for the purpose of refiguring the social body's established institution(s) of authority. It is, figuratively speaking, the Mosaic Law supplanting the priority of the king's law in Yehud (cf. Ezra 7:25–26). Consequently, the perceived legitimacy of divine revelation ultimately requires monotheism's absolute acquisition of authority within the material world, whether in the present moment or a future present moment. In the case of Yehud, the legitimacy of divine revelation and election of the *golah* community demanded the socially dominating imposition of *golah*-religious law as a representative form of authority and also the community's social-economic control over the city of Jerusalem and its temple. Without a viable or accessible military power, authority in Yehud required in the least an ascendancy over the utility of economic resources and their production, as well as their functional "mediums of exchange."[4] It would have been upon the basis of this ascendancy that was constructed the symbolic systems of monotheism as authoritative, the regulatory power of its law, the foundational distinction of its membership and its congruent claim to the land, and the expected restoration of divine authority—the effective utility of all these, in the context of Yehud, depended upon economic control. In short, in the context of Persian-period Yehud, without the force of a military, the *golah* community needed to control the economy in order to establish its (monotheistic) authority.

1. *Interrupting Authority:*
The Material Construction of Monotheistic Identity

The authority or power toward which monotheism, or more specifically the monotheistic body, directs its energy does not belong to it originally. It must be interrupted and redirected from those forces of power and

---

4. I am borrowing in part from Hall's initial definition of authority that he provides in his work discussing the construction and employment of moral authority as power (see "Moral Authority as a Power Resource," 591). In Yehud, however, while there was authority based on economic control, one cannot speak of the *golah* community as having moral authority over the population, a point we will continue to revisit throughout this work.

authority that have been institutionalized within the social body. But to understand the productive consequence of monotheism's attempted revision of the nature of authority, we must begin first by understanding the nature of the affected structures themselves. These, which are ontologically products of dialectical and material circumstances, are pillaged by the monotheistic body; their systems of production, whether that be of desire or material, are interrupted and redirected in support of monotheism's transcendent authority—an authority that assumes jurisdiction over the natural, or mundane, order of material production.[5] The Deuteronomist, for example, takes for granted the transcendent authority of Yahweh: "If you will only heed his every commandment that I am commanding you today—loving the LORD your God, and serving him with all your heart and with all your soul—then he will give the rain for your land in its season, the early rain and the later rain, and you will gather in your grain, your wine, and your oil; and he will give grass in your fields for your livestock, and you will eat your fill" (Deut 11:13–15). The author assumes that this transcendent authority controls the very economic function of the material world. In fact, divine control over the surplus production of the material world confirms for the author divine authority over the social body. This same assumption is also a characteristic quality of the monotheistic body, and as such is shared by every monotheistic identity.

Each monotheistic identity is constructed in part through an interruption of already institutionalized productive forces that constitute a basis for authority, a delegitimization of already existing social-political authorities, and a privatizing and institutionalizing of those forces by and within the divine realm. And further, from Deuteronomy, which puts it in terms of an identity based partly on conquest and land acquisition,

> You shall put these words of mine in your heart and soul, and you shall bind them as a sign on your hand, and fix them as an emblem on your forehead. Teach them to your children, talking about them when you are at home and when you are away, when you lie down and when you rise. Write them on the doorposts of your house and on your gates, so that your days and the days of your children may be multiplied in the land that the LORD swore to your ancestors to give them, as long as the heavens are above the earth. If you will diligently observe this entire commandment that I am commanding you, loving the LORD your God, walking in all his ways, and holding fast to him, then the LORD will drive out all these nations before you, and you will dispossess nations larger and mightier than yourselves." (Deut 11:18–23)

---

5. On the production of desire or "desiring production," see, for example, Deleuze, and Guattari, *Anti-Oedipus*, 116.

This passage also highlights the importance of ritual to the construction of a hierarchy of authority. According to Foucault, "The more one possesses power or privilege, the more one is marked as an individual, by rituals, written accounts or visual reproductions."[6] And it is precisely this ascending individuation—including especially rituals, written accounts, and visual reproductions, which delineate, define, and enforce a separation between religious identity and the larger social body—that the monotheistic identity vigorously engages. This identity fervently struggles to separate itself from, place itself in a position of authority over, the social body. One can see this clearly, for example, in the Islamic belief that the responsibility all political authorities share is to behave consistently toward divine law.[7] And in Christianity, which embraces a general posture expressed by the phrase, "Give unto Caesar what is Caesar's" (Matt 22:21), secular authorities are likewise judged, even while passive tolerance—waiting for the divine to bestow full authority upon the religious body—is earnestly admonished. Because the desire of the monotheistic body is universal and absolute authority, it cannot share authority. And so a distinctive monotheistic identity's "ascension into individualization" requires separation from the social body and a newly articulated self-identity. Or we might borrow from Deleuze and Guattari in saying, it "interrupts the productive flows" of the social body, to assert its own as authoritative.[8] Anything that competes with divine authority is subsequently rejected by monotheism as a "false god." This "production of desire" is monotheism's pursuit of a final and absolute authority over the material and social world. It is by its very nature production *toward* the fulfillment of desire not yet attained.

On the other hand, political authority, as a product of the social body, is a natural development.[9] The social body, in other words, produces

---

6. Michel Foucault, *Discipline and Punish: The Birth of the Prison* (trans. Alan Sheridan; New York: Vintage, 1995), 192.

7. Cf. John L. Esposito and Natana J. De Long-Bas, "Classical Islam," in *God's Rule: The Politics of World Religions* (ed. Jacob Neusner; Washington, D.C.: Georgetown University Press, 2003), 138.

8. "Productive flows" and the "production of desire" are concepts Deleuze and Guattari develop throughout their *Anti-Oedipus*.

9. Similarly, Ibn Khaldun describes royal (and by that he means political) authority as the natural outgrowth of "group feeling," or that common cultural identity that binds together members of a group. "It should be known that royal authority is the natural goal of group feeling. It results from group feeling, not by choice but through (inherent) necessity and the order of existence, as we have stated before" (*The Muqaddimah: An Introduction to History*, vol. 1 [trans. Franz Rosenthal; New York: Pantheon, 1958], 414).

naturally the legitimated authority by which it is governed. In comparison, the monotheistic body is fashioned out of a competition with a naturally produced social-political authority. Thus, when political and religious authorities are separate—their unification is always for the monotheistic body the goal, never the starting point—divine authority represents an interruption to already institutionalized distributed relations of power. In fact, we may say that all monotheistic identities begin as an interruption to a prevailing normative order.

Thus, interruption as a *productive* act is possible because authority within a social body is comprised of control over the body's forces of production and representation; interruption alters the flow of those original forces.[10] To be clear, production—whether of material surplus or of, in the word of Deleuze and Guattari,[11] desire, which is simultaneously material and ideological—is constructive; it is the process by which the survivability of the social body is insured, within which is also preserved the body's distribution of power.[12] In turn, representation, as Deleuze and Guattari explain it, defines the limits of this production for the social body. "[I]f it is termed representative, this is because it is equivalent to the noncodable, noncoded, or decoded flows."[13] Or to put it somewhat differently, a dialectic relationship—notably of resistance and opposition—with defined limits of production creates the fundamental definition of identity; moreover, it is the very basis upon which the original forces of differentiation and exclusion are based. As Deleuze and Guattari argue, the natural world is the *original* producer.[14] But the social body imposes its limits upon production, interrupting the original flows of the natural world, creating new, altered flows that produce the parameters of

---

10. Cf. Deleuze, and Guattari, *Anti-Oedipus*, 6–8. Foucault's perception of authority in meaning and language parallels his understanding of the social production of authority. Thus, he writes, "For a series of signs to exist, there must—in accordance with the system of causality—be an 'author' or a transmitting authority. But this 'author' is not identical with the subject of the statement; and the relation of production that he has with the formulation is not superposable to the relation that unites the enunciating subject and what he states" (*Archaeology of Knowledge*, 92).

11. Deleuze and Guattari, *Anti-Oedipus*, 139–40.

12. Karl Marx, "The German Ideology," in *The Marx–Engels Reader* [ed. Robert C. Tucker; New York: Norton, 1978], 172–73; Bourdieu, "Genesis and Structure," 31; Deleuze, and Guattari, *Anti-Oedipus*, 254–55. In addition, P. Kollock ("Social Dilemmas: The Anatomy of Cooperation," *ARS* 24 [1998]: 191) alludes to the constructive nature of production in his discussion of cooperation.

13. Deleuze and Guattari, *Anti-Oedipus*, 164.

14. Ibid., 140–41.

its identity.[15] It subsequently distributes individuals toward roles and responsibilities within those defined parameters, the defined space to which Bourdieu refers as *habitus*.[16] The limits of that defined space mark the socially perceived distinction between order and chaos. The nature of authority, the identity of it, is defined in resistance to those limits; it is never a demolition or a rejection of them. It is important to note that in the same way that the social world necessitates the original forces of production (and the natural world) against which to define itself, the monotheistic body requires the social body against which it defines itself through resistance and interruption in a process mimicking ascending individuation. Monotheistic interruption is productive through its emphasis (sometimes latent) on opposition. Opposition, in its fundamental construction of categories, is for monotheism the archetypal act by which authority is defined and also preserved.[17]

When we speak therefore of *golah* and *am ha'aretz* as social categories,[18] we do so with the understanding that as social categories they are consequences of the productive forces operative within Yehud.[19] Neither term bears any direct relevance outside that defined productive space.

---

15. Deleuze and Guattari write somewhat obliquely, "The productive synthesis, the production of production, is inherently connective in nature: 'and...' 'and then...' This is because there is always a flow-producing machine, and another machine connected to it that interrupts or draws off part of its flow (the breast—the mouth)" (ibid., 5).

16. "The habitus is at once a system of models for the perception and appreciation of practices. And in both cases, its operations express the social position in which it was constructed. As a result, the habitus produces practices and representations which are available for classification, which are objectively differentiated; but they are immediately perceived as such only in the case of agents who possess the code, the classificatory models necessary to understand their social meaning. Thus, the habitus implies a 'sense of one's place' but also a 'sense of the other's place'" (Pierre Bourdieu, *In Other Words: Essays Toward a Reflexive Sociology* [trans. Matthew Adamson; Stanford: Stanford University Press, 1990], 131). But note also that Weber used the term similarly in *The Sociology of Religion* [trans. Ephraim Fischoff; Boston: Beacon, 1993], 158–59.

17. For further reference on the idea of opposition in this sense, see Deleuze, and Guattari, *Anti-Oedipus*, 11–13.

18. Again note that I am using these terms as social categories as defined in Cataldo, "The Crippled *Ummah*."

19. Defining "*golah* community" as a social identity that denotes a minority group within the larger social body of Yehud alleviates the proposed problem that has tended to impede an understanding of the social composition in Yehud, a problem as described by J. Blenkinsopp (in *Isaiah 56–66: A New Translation With Introduction and Commentary* [New York: Doubleday, 2003], 49).

Nor is there any certainty regarding their statuses as categories of objective measure within the society and more specifically its productive space; they are, rather, the ideational products of a minority community (the *golah* community) whose identity was constructed on the periphery of authority.[20] This expressed uncertainty exists because the institutionalization of authority within Yehud—against which the community will come to define itself—occurred *before* the arrival of the *golah* community.[21] Any alteration of the social-political structures upon which authority was based, which would be necessary to legitimate the *golah* community as a group in a position of social-economic authority, would entail an interruption of the society's already extant "productive flows."[22]

And it is in that sense that divine revelation is an interruption of the normative social-political order.[23] Subsequently, the intent of divine law is to normalize divinely regulated patterns of behavior in place of what was previously naturally produced as normative. Thus, it is within the very nature of monotheism to interrupt that order, simultaneously rejecting all natural authorities in favor of the divine. That is, monotheistic revelation and law are founded on a rejection of the socially established order and its systems of distributed power when these are not consistent with the divine plan for restoration. For example, within the Islamic tradition, the Hadith preserve the belief that all human authority should be consistent with divine authority and if not, it should be rejected:

---

20. Both G. Ahlström and R. P. Carroll posit, though with different convictions as to what measure, that the community was on the periphery of economic authority. To be sure, the categories, even if only subjectively perceived measures of social distinction, are the consequences of real, objective forces of production. See R. P. Carroll, "Textual Strategies and Ideology in the Second Temple Period," in Davies, ed., *Second Temple Studies, 1*, 113–15; Ahlström, *The History of Ancient Palestine*, 846.

21. D. Smith ("The Politics of Ezra: Sociological Indicators of Postexilic Judaean Society," in Davies, ed., *Second Temple Studies, 1*, 95–96), for example, rejects the need to posit a foreign aristocracy in order for an "upper class" to exist in Yehud. In other words, the social body in Yehud, which was already predispositioned for class differentiation and institutionalized authority, would likely have replaced an absent aristocracy.

22. This is true of all modes of production and does not necessitate a highly stratified society. Carter, for example, argues that the economy of Yehud was predominantly village based (*Emergence of Yehud*, 249).

23. Deleuze and Guattari describe the interruption of the productive flows of society, upon which a society's institutions of authority are based, as the coupling of fragmentary objects—the consequence is the creation of a new system of production upon which the institutions of authority are based (*Anti-Oedipus*, 5).

> He said: The Messenger of Allah (may peace be upon him) called us and we took the oath of allegiance to him. Among the injunctions he made binding upon us was: Listening and obedience (to the Amir) in our pleasure and displeasure, in our adversity and prosperity, even when somebody is given preference over us, and without disputing the delegation of powers to a man duly invested with them (Obedience shall be accorded to him in all circumstances) *except when you have clear signs of his disbelief in (or disobedience to) God-signs that could be used as a conscientious justification (for non-compliance with his orders)*." (Muslim: Book 20: Hadith 4541, emphasis mine)

In addition, an oft-quoted manifesto within Christianity, "we are in this world, not of it," clearly reflects this rejection of earthly authority by separating religious identity from the authorities and cultures that form identity in "the world." This focus on separation is found in the Gospel of John: "I have given them your word, and the world has hated them because they do not belong to the world, just as I do not belong to the world. I am not asking you to take them out of the world, but I ask you to protect them from the evil one. They do not belong to the world, just as I do not belong to the world" (John 17:14–16).[24] The Quran states similarly, which strongly suggests a common element shared between the different forms of monotheism, "Anyone who, after accepting faith in Allah, utters unbelief—except under compulsion, his heart remaining firm in Faith—but such as open their breast to unbelief—on them is Wrath from Allah, and theirs will be a dreadful Penalty. *This because they love the life of this world better than the Hereafter*: and Allah will not guide those who reject Faith" (16:106–107, emphasis mine).

Quite tellingly, the same emphasis on interruption is shown in an earlier form of monotheism with the *golah* community in Yehud. Under successive empires, the province required political institutions capable of governing the territory, an especially important need given its multi-ethnic context or situation.[25] Such institutions and systems of distributed power may be safely assumed in the framework of any social-political analysis. Texts such as Ezra–Nehemiah, Chronicles, and Zechariah,

---

24. One might also note further: "If you belonged to the world, the world would love you as its own. Because you do not belong to the world, but I have chosen you out of the world—therefore the world hates you. Remember the word that I said to you, 'Servants are not greater than their master.' If they persecuted me, they will persecute you; if they kept my word, they will keep yours also" (John 15:19–20).

25. As noted also by Eph'al ("Syria-Palestine Under Achaemenid Rule," 147), who speaks of the broader Syria-Palestinian context, which includes Yehud. Such a framework is beneficial in that it reminds investigators Yehud did not exist autonomously or in a vacuum.

however, provide us with a very different picture. According to these, the land was "empty" of any established, operative social and political structures—an "empty" land waiting for the arrival of the divinely elected remnant.[26] But accepting that this presumption is true dismisses out of hand any possible discussion of a socially allocated power.[27] And it is clear that one cannot talk about society or government without taking these into account.

It is not difficult to see that the biblical account provides us with an irreconcilable proposal. Its seeming dependence upon the divine as a productive force suggests an incomplete understanding of Yehud's social-political reality. If we accept the biblical testimony that the land was empty then we have no reason not to accept Ezra–Nehemiah's inference that the *golah* community reconstituted society and all its institutions—a rather impressive feat!—as though a colony in an untamed, chaotic land.[28] If, on the other hand, we do not accept this then we should not feel obliged to dismiss the biblical texts all together; instead, we must look for points of divergence. Since we know that a province existed in some fashion before the arrival of the immigrant community in question (Gedeliah, for instance, was appointed governor over some semblance of a province [cf. 2 Kgs 25:22]), we can begin with certain presuppositions,

---

26. Cf. the discussions of R. P. Carroll, "Exile! What Exile? Deportation and the Discourse of Diaspora," in *Leading Captivity Captive: "The Exile" as History and Ideology* (ed. Lester L. Grabbe; Sheffield: Sheffield Academic, 1998), 62–79; Philip R. Davies, "Exile! What Exile? Whose Exile?," in Grabbe, ed., *Leading Captivity Captive*, 128–38; Hans M. Barstad, "After the 'Myth of the Empty Land': Major Challenges in the Study of Neo-Babylonian Judah," in *Judah and the Judeans in the Neo-Babylonian Period* (ed. Oded Lipschits and Joseph Blenkinsopp; Winona Lake: Eisenbrauns, 2003), 3–20. But compare B. Oded ("Where Is the 'Myth of the Empty Land' to be Found? History Versus Myth," in Lipschits and Blenkinsopp, eds., *Judah and the Judeans in the Neo-Babylonian Period*, 55–74), who argues that the land was not empty and that the returnees were inclusive of Judeans who remained in the land. His basic assumption is that Judaism is a "religion of historical memory, not a religion of inventing myths" (ibid., 71)

27. Such power is true of any society or collective body. For example, Marx states this is both produced by the *cooperation of different individuals* and is determined by a society's distribution of labor ("The German Ideology," 161). Or perhaps it is better stated by Bourdieu that *relationships of interdependence and reciprocity* are the backbone of any urban-based division of labor (Bourdieu, "Genesis and Structure," 5.).

28. As, for example, P. Bedford has incorrectly proposed ("Diaspora: Homeland Relations in Ezra–Nehemiah," *VT* 52 [2001], 153). Berquist once proposed something similar (*Judaism in Persia's Shadow*, 140), but has since reevaluated his previous position ("Constructions of Identity," 61).

namely that the community interacted with the people already in the land, that those peoples were governed by something resembling a political institution upon which power was distributed, and that the *golah* community could not have established a new political institution immediately upon its arrival. In other words, the already extant presence of organized people and communities—a society!—in the land rejects the hypothesis that the community created a previously non-existent polity.

Even in light of this conclusion we must be able to account for the testimony of the biblical texts. Ezekiel's symbolic address of the land,[29] for example, while not obviously obsessed with any division between *golah* and *am ha'aretz*, dismisses all previously established social-political structures as profane and, since the divine is *the* source of order, chaotic. Or, as Julie Galambush interprets Ezekiel's intent, "[t]o posit a land that is 'devastated,' 'empty,' or both is to posit both need and warrant for the return of the ruling classes *and the displacement of those whose control is defined as chaos.*"[30] Because the author of Ezekiel dismisses the validity of any current social-political authority the author is able to argue for the need of a new ruling class, or aristocracy. As we are discovering, however, the immigrating Judeans' initial engagement with the then extant social-political situation was one marked by reaction and interruption, not control. A fundamental act productive of identity, their reaction was to the then extant distribution and division of society and labor, some choosing to embrace the situation while others chose to reject it.[31] The latter, if we appeal to Morton Smith's observation, were known as the *golah* community (or *bene haggolah*) in Ezra–Nehemiah and the former as the *am ha'aretz*.[32]

As we will discuss in greater detail, texts such as Ezra–Nehemiah, Haggai, and Zechariah present portraits of an idealized society[33]—the

---

29. As J. Galambush notes ("This Land Is My Land: On Nature as Property in the Book of Ezekiel," in *"Every City Shall Be Forsaken": Urbanism and Prophecy in Ancient Israel and the Near East* [Sheffield: Sheffield Academic, 2001], 81–82), in Ezekiel the land symbolically represents the inhabitants who undergo destruction because of Israel's sin.

30. Ibid., 92, emphasis mine.

31. Smith, for reference, discusses a division between what he terms a "Yahweh alone" party and a more syncretistic party that sought to assimilate Yahwism and the majority culture (*Palestinian Parties*, 75–81). According to him, Ezekiel, along with Deutero-Isaiah, the Deuteronomic and Priestly traditions, as well as the Holiness Code were written or shaped by the former.

32. Ibid., 81.

33. As also noted by T. Dozeman in "Geography and History in Herodotus and in Ezra–Nehemiah," *JBL* 122, no. 3 (2003): 457.

points of resistance they describe are points at which the "objective" structures of this envisioned society are threatened by the "external" forces of the material world. They concern themselves not with understanding the relations of production and reproduction or the distribution of economic goods.[34] Nor do they seem clearly aware of any relations of interdependence and reciprocity.[35] The expected successful imposition of an external, divine law assumes the absolute power of a transcendental authority whose law is the blueprint for restoration (cf. Ezra 7:11–28). And it is assumed so at the expense of a law that is itself a product of the social body's productive forces. In fact, these texts are suspiciously silent on issues concerning the economy, perhaps one reason why we get rather impressive statements such as, "And whatever else is required for the house of your God, which you are responsible for providing, you may provide out of the king's treasury" (Ezra 7:20). Of whatever the community had need—a state of being whose qualities the community itself seems at liberty to define—it was free to take from the king's treasury; the Persian imperial government was, for all intents and purposes, the tool of Yahweh (cf. Ezra 1:1–2; Isa 45:1–3). Material production, in consequence, was projected as the responsibility of the land and of the people's god, and the community enjoyed the benefit of it by remaining faithful. Or, to put it in different terms, according to the community's religious-historical tradition, which was itself a projection of the community's own situation, it was God as absolute authority who performed society-building—that is, productive—labor. As Ezra describes this imperial role, "So the descendants went in and possessed the land, *and you subdued before them the inhabitants of the land, the Canaanites, and gave them into their hands, with their kings and the peoples of the land, to do with them as they pleased*" (Ezra 9:24, emphasis mine). Again,

---

34. Note also Bourdieu ("Genesis and Structure," 31) whose observation informs my own understanding. "The strictly religious authority and the temporal force that various religious claimants can enlist in their struggle for religious legitimacy is never independent of the weight that laypersons mobilize in the structure of the relations of force between classes. It follows that the structure of objective relations between claimants occupying different positions in the relations of production, reproduction, and distribution of religious goods tends to reproduce the structure of relations of force between groups or classes, but *under the transfigured and disguised form* of a field of relations of force between claimants struggling for the conservation or subversion of the symbolic order."

35. M. Harris, for example, defines reciprocity as, "a form of economic exchange that is primarily adapted to conditions in which the stimulation of intensive extra productive effort would have an adverse effect upon group survival" (*Cows, Pigs, Wars, and Witches: The Riddles of Culture* [New York: Vintage, 1974], 126).

surplus, and here one may assume spoils of conquest,[36] was produced for the pleasure of the elected community. It is through this, for lack of a better description, "aristocratic ideology"—that is, surplus is produced *for* us—that we must navigate while reading the Persian-period biblical texts.[37] Yet it is not clear that the *golah* community was in itself an aristocratic class, which it would have needed to have been if its vision of society were to have been true. In fact, as James VanderKam among others has pointed out, it appears that members of the community intermarried into aristocratic standing after they had immigrated into the province (cf. Neh 13:28)—a situation that implies the existence of an already established aristocracy.[38]

In addition, despite the eery absence of mentioned political officials in the Persian-period biblical literature, and its careful admission of only *golah*-community affiliated leaders, there is evidence suggesting the presence of officials not affiliated with the *golah* community, such as the list of governors reconstructed from papyri, coins, and pottery

---

36. Surplus may be acquired in multiple ways, as shown through an analysis of the historical development of societies, from growing and storing surplus, to trade, to conquest and the taking of another's surplus through force (the latter of which the Roman Empire was very proficient).

37. One may say that this aristocratic ideology is common among religions. As M. Weber writes, "Originally there must have been a union of political and religious authority everywhere, but with the development of theology and an educated priesthood functional specialization became inevitable. Great power remained in the hands of the priests, partly because of their wealth from temple lands and income, partly because the masses looked to them for salvation from punishment for sacrilege, and partly because they were originally the only men of learning. From this followed two important results: (1) in general, since priests enjoyed a monopoly of legal knowledge, and since the priesthoods were held by members of the aristocratic families, these families enjoyed a position of unassailable dominance as long as the law remained uncodified; (2) all education, especially in the bureaucratic monarchies, where training was necessary for employment in the administration, was almost entirely in the hands of priests. Throughout the Near East the priesthood strove to gain control of education; we see this tendency clearly in the Egyptian New Empire, where the priests displaced secular officials and secular education" (*The Agrarian Sociology of Ancient Civilizations* [trans. R. I. Frank; Foundations of History Library; London: NLB, 1976], 78–79).

38. As one may also read from passages such as Ezra 10:18 (see also James C. VanderKam, *From Joshua to Caiaphas: High Priests After the Exile* [Minneapolis: Fortress, 2004], 53–54). Moreover, this practice leads L. Fried to conclude that the prohibition of intermarriage in Nehemiah was an attempt to limit the influence and power of the landed aristocracy (see *The Priest and the Great King: Temple–Palace Relations in the Persian Empire* [Biblical and Judaic Studies; Winona Lake: Eisenbrauns, 2004], 211). See also Ahlström, *The History of Ancient Palestine*, 861.

fragments—a list that is increasingly becoming widely accepted.[39] Perhaps more importantly, it would have been uncharacteristic of the Persian imperial government to grant autonomy (in the way a theocracy would require) to individual territories under its control.[40] In short, the social-political vision portrayed in the Persian-period biblical literature, if we were to accept it as an accurate historical portrayal, must be clearly shown as having been institutionalized on both local and imperial levels.

All said, our first strategy should be to read the Persian-period biblical texts as historical reflections of attempts to interrupt pre-existing structures of authority. The effectiveness of this strategy and its translatability to other forms of monotheism will be pursued throughout the remainder of this work.

a. *Authority Is a Natural Production of the Social Body and Religious Authority Must Be Imposed*

> Because religion is comprehensive, it is fundamentally about power; it therefore cannot avoid politics.[41]

Ideally, divine law codifies a religious authority that has been inscribed upon the social body—an authority and its corresponding law that are both presumed authoritative by virtue of the corresponding divine revelation.[42] This expectation can be seen in the Ezra's letter from Artaxerxes (see again Ezra 7:11–28), in which the "law of your god" imposes its framework upon the law of the king, as the initial object and its conjunctive clause seem to indicate: *dt' dy-'lhk wdt' dy mlk'*. The promised punishment for disobedience is bodily inscription *par excellence*, and

---

39. On the other hand, there is some rather meager evidence from which one might read some amount of priestly authority. Based on a silver coin bearing the inscription "Yohanan, the priest," D. Barag ("A Silver Coin of Yohanan the High Priest and the Coinage of Judea in the Fourth Century B.C.," *INJ* 9 [1986]: 4–21) concludes that the high priest held a certain amount of "secular" power. While there was a certain Yohanan mentioned in Neh 12:22, *Ant.* 11.297–301, Elephantine letter Cowley 30, Barag is correct to conclude that it cannot be the same Yohanan that served during the fifth century (ibid., abstract)

40. See the larger discussion in Jeremiah W. Cataldo, *A Theocratic Yehud? Issues of Government in Yehud* (LHBOTS 498; London: T&T Clark International, 2009), 33–66.

41. William Scott Green, "Religion and Politics—a Volatile Mix," in Neusner, ed., *God's Rule*, 2.

42. A relatively recent example of this is Ruhollah Khomeini's linking of property rights in Iran (ca. 1979) to the existence of a clerical state (cf. Ervand Abrahamian, *Khomeinism: Essays on the Islamic Republic* [Berkeley: University of California Press, 1993], 44).

one whose purpose takes for granted that the individual comes to represent the collective (in the sense of individuation through the exercise of power).[43] Divine law is a representation of divine revelation, itself an interruption of the productive flows of the social body, which as inscribed upon the social body institutionalizes a divine authority that reorders those productive flows.

When a governing authority is not imposed by an external power, it is the natural outgrowth of material and ideological productions.[44] It is the "natural" result of the forces of material production, providing an implicit and generative function of order, that is fashioned and refashioned by the ideological forces of action and interaction (antagonism and cooperation) among and between the agents of the social world. It is generally predisposed toward relations of class, gaining material and symbolic strength initially through class antagonisms—or, to employ the discussion above, opposition and its subsequent construction and confirmation of boundaries of authority. Class, when considered the basic structure upon which authority is distributed toward individuals or groups, is not, among other things, an arbitrary self-perception but a division that is a result of these social, economic, and political forces.[45]

With the social vision of Ezra–Nehemiah in view, we must note that divine law or its corresponding religious institution and authority is not uniquely or wholly generative of class or class relations. It takes for granted the already established distributions of power and production within the social body—distributions that produce class relations.[46] It enjoys not an autonomous existence but one defined by the same social

---

43. On the act and purpose of inscribing punishment upon the body, see Foucault, *Discipline and Punish*, 3–31, esp. 25–26.

44. Note also Marx, "The German Ideology," 161.

45. On class antagonism and class as a structure upon which authority is distributed, see Bourdieu, "Genesis and Structure," 3. See also G. Deleuze and F. Guattari (*A Thousand Plateaus: Capitalism and Schizophrenia* [Minneapolis: University of Minnesota Press, 1987], 216) who, while taking aim at Marxism, emphasize that antagonism as a source of definition is true only at macro level; otherwise, at the micro level, thus dealing with groups and individuals, definition occurs primarily through "mass movements," which entails cooperation as much as antagonism. Ibn Khaldun's understanding of group feeling finds agreement with this emphasis.

46. Note also Bourdieu, who writes, "That is to say that monotheism, totally ignored by societies whose economies relied on crops, fishing, and/or hunting, is encountered only in the dominant classes of societies already based on a developed agriculture and a division into classes (some West African societies, the Polynesians, the Dakota and Winnebago Indians) in which the advances of the division of labor are accompanied by a correlative division of religious work" ("Genesis and Structure," 8).

body its members often reject; that is, the religious institution belongs to the same habitus in which the political institution is produced. Patterns of power relations supporting an institutionalized authority within the social body are duplicated in the monotheistic body. But where in a social body forces of production are initially focused on material surplus, production in the monotheistic body focuses on monopolization of spiritual or symbolic "capital" in the absence of any control over material surplus. Ezra's speech in Nehemiah (9:1–37) supports this conclusion with its simultaneous focus on maintaining a categorical distinction in group identity (member/non-member) and on the group's position on the periphery of social-economic authority ("we are slaves" [cf. v. 36]).[47] And from a more modern perspective, Bourdieu describes the general religious pattern (to which the *golah* community seems to be fitting) of a monopolization of spiritual capital as a mechanism for establishing the internal hierarchical stratification of the monotheistic body, thus, the (re)inscription of authority into the ideological sphere—a possibility due the monotheistic body's marginality:

> Inasmuch as it is the result of the monopolization of the administration of the goods of salvation by a body of religious *specialists*, socially recognized as the exclusive holders of the specific competence necessary for the production or reproduction of a *deliberately organized corpus* of secret (and therefore rare) knowledge, the constitution of a religious field goes hand in hand with the objective dispossession of those who are excluded from it and who thereby find themselves constituted as the *laity* (or the *profane*, in the double meaning of the word) dispossessed of *religious capital* (as accumulated symbolic labor) and recognizing the legitimacy of that dispossession from the mere fact that they misrecognize it as such.[48]

b. *Inscribing Authority: Defining Meaning and Order*
With the inscription of any authority, a corresponding system of meaning and order that supports or legitimates that authority is necessary. On a theoretical level, then, Michel Foucault is partly correct that social-political order is produced and maintained only when punishment is

---

47. That the so-called confession separates the narratively present community from the iniquities of its ancestors, while making it the object of reference when referring to its social-economic travails supports this proposal that the community viewed itself to be the heir of social-economic authority in the province—as shown by the narrative progression from expressed plight, to unilateral pledge of loyalty to Yahweh, to the temple, and to the divine law (see also Tamara Cohn Eskenazi, "Nehemiah 9–10: Structure and Significance," *JHS* 3 [2001], §§2.8-9).

48. Bourdieu, "Genesis and Structure," 9.

written upon the body.⁴⁹ This "marking out" confirms and legitimates class relations and the structured relations of authority, as well as the meanings associated with both. There must always be a "source" or "Actor" who is or who represents authority, a body upon which power relations are inscribed, and an audience who observes, remembers, and legitimates:

> But the body is also directly involved in a political field; power relations have an immediate hold upon it; they invest it, mark it, train it, torture it, force it to carry out tasks, to perform ceremonies, to emit signs. This political investment of the body is bound up, in accordance with complex reciprocal relations, with its economic use; it is largely as a force of production that the body is invested with relations of power and domination; but, on the other hand, its constitution as labour power is possible only if it is caught up in a system of subjection...⁵⁰

If we treat "body" as a metaphor for the social-political body, similar can be said of the monotheistic body because its producing source is the social body—a filiation, nonetheless, that the monotheistic body resists. Consequently, the authority of the divine and the religious "aristocracy," or those who control the symbolic capital within the related religious sphere, is written upon the non-member for the benefit of the aristocracy and the larger membership of a particular monotheistic identity. Through dissociation the religious member excludes the non-member upon whom the price for non-membership (hell, rejection by God, eternal torture without respite) is inscribed. It is too late for the sinner who must endure eternal condemnation; his pain in fact is meaningless for him but meaningful for the audience, or religious membership. His unrealized but unavoidable⁵¹ damnation constitutes partially the desire production of the monotheistic body. For it is in that absolutizing act—writing the member's salvation upon the damned body of the non-member—that the authority of the monotheistic body is rendered. As Deleuze and Guattari explain regarding this general human tendency, "Cruelty"—and this includes damnation in monotheism—"has nothing to do with some ill-defined or natural violence that might be commissioned to explain the history of mankind; cruelty is the movement of culture that is realized

---

49. As noted throughout his work *Discipline and Punish*.
50. Ibid., 25–26.
51. I am not implying a strictly Calvinist explanation here. Outside of a monotheistic meaning world or system, the non-member (or "sinner") does not recognize his own damnation and can never avoid it without first becoming a member and being appropriately encoded with the relevant meaning system.

in bodies and inscribed on them, belaboring them... [E]ven death, punishment, and torture are desired, and are *instances of production...*"[52] Rejection, punishment, and marking upon—even if only ideological—are all events that monotheism employs both to demonstrate and legitimate its authority in contest with the social body.

This brings us to the following issue. Do the religious ideologies expressed in the Persian-period biblical texts reflect the social body or are they constructed in reaction to the social body? If the ideologies themselves are natural outgrowths of the social-religious body inhabiting Yehud, we might expect the expressed ideologies to reflect a dominant religion of the province. And at first blush they may seem to do so. Yahwism, according to Ezra–Nehemiah (Ezra 4:1–2), was practiced in the province and in Samaria before the arrival of the immigrant (*golah*) community. Yet Ezra–Nehemiah also expresses a rejection of the people already in the land—who seem to be represented by Sanballat the Horonite, Tobiah the Ammonite, and Geshem the Arab, and who themselves are assuredly social-political authorities—by declaring they were without historic claim or right in Jerusalem (cf. Neh 2:20).[53] Such exclusion of the larger social body, and those related to it, as we will discuss further, was not a natural production of the social body but the ideological production or creation, driven by resistance to the social body itself, of the *golah* community.

c. *Resistance as Necessary in the Production of Monotheistic Identity*
Resistance, that is, to the social body and its institutionalized law that represents the structures and systems of authority within the social body. The pretext to resistance is established by divine law, which itself is a consequence of divine revelation as an interruption to the social body's normative order. The force of divine law, its regulating effectiveness, requires resistance to the institutionalized authority of a more natural law. The basis of power and authority that the *golah*-Yahwistic law was intended to preserve, and which did not yet exist, required that the law

---

52. Deleuze, and Guattari, *Anti-Oedipus*, 145, emphasis mine.
53. Note also that Hoglund (as argued throughout *Achaemenid Imperial Administration*, 217–26) suggests that the opposition between Nehemiah and Sanballat specifically indicates a change in the political relationship between Samerina and Yehud. If one accepts this to be true then one must also conclude that the biblical author usurped a political event, stripped it of its strictly political meaning, and re-infused the event with a meaning that was directly relevant for the religious community. Thus, a political contest of authority becomes framed as a contest supporting the monotheistic body's, in the form of the *golah* community's, claim to authority.

first be established as the absolute paradigm of regulated order. Only by interrupting the productive forces of the social body and inscribing upon that body a monotheistic identity from which the social body as non-member had been rejected could this basis in fact be established. Re-inscribing the distribution of power and authority, in other words, entails an immanently *acting* process of exclusion providing the base upon which a revised social-political hierarchy could be built. The principle of communication between the social body and the monotheistic body is contestation, which, because no monotheistic identity can exist without it, necessitates the act of exclusion in the process of identity formation. Thus, the monotheistic body appropriates the productive forces of authority, displacing and reorganizing them in its own fashion.[54]

To understand, then, resistance as production in the previously described manner, with our focus on Yehud, we seek within the biblical texts discourses of "reverse socialization." Socialization within this context occurs in reverse because the monotheistic body, through its absolutizing of divine law, claims the authority of social control, which is more natively the institutionalized production of the social body.[55] The discourses contained within the Persian-period biblical literature are constructed upon points of resistance or opposition that occur between the monotheistic community and the larger social body. For example, Zechariah's oracles, which stem from a context of frustrated restoration, and which react to that situation, reflect a consequent reinterpretation of divine revelation as being intended for a more narrowly defined community. While the Exodus tradition of divine revelation provides the foundational support for the oracles, the recipients of divine selection have been identified more narrowly than those that the Exodus tradition itself identified specifically:[56]

---

54. Deleuze and Guattari describe this type of appropriation metaphorically as characteristic of the struggle between the (holy) family, as the basic social unit, and the State (*Anti-Oedipus*, 124).

55. For the purpose of clarifying the terms, Berger defines "socialization" as the pursuit to ensure a continuing consensus concerning the most important features of the social world. "Social control" is defined as the imposed parameters of society to keep group and individual resistances under tolerable limits. Cf. *Sacred Canopy*, 30.

56. R. J. Coggins (*Haggai, Zechariah, Malachi* [Sheffield: JSOT, 1987], 7) suggests that Haggai and Zech 1–8 correspond to the period during which Persian rule was first being established in Syria-Palestine. Assuming this to be correct, oracles may be read in part as responses to perceived (or perhaps a hoped-for) lapse in power within Yehud—a lapse that may cultivate aspirations for social control and authority.

Up, up! Flee from the land of the north, says the LORD; for I have spread you abroad like the four winds of heaven, says the LORD. Up! Escape to Zion, you that live with daughter Babylon. For thus said the LORD of hosts regarding the nations that plundered you. Truly, *one who touches you touches the apple of my eye.* (1:6–8, emphasis mine)

The prophet's proclamation emphasizes several important issues for a projected social hierarchy. First, the recipients of divine favor are those who have been exiled to Babylon; these are the people of Yahweh.[57] Thus, the initial mechanism for social division—upon which the *golah*-Yahwistic understanding of the distribution of power is also based[58]—is fashioned out of a perceived divine selection. The construction of this "mechanism" speaks to an underlying expression of collective identity that overwrites any previous identity. That is, the Babylonian Judean identity contains within it the belief that it was the exiled Judeans alone upon whom Yahweh had expressed favor and in whom was bestowed social, political, and religious authority. It would be through this community that Yahweh would enact restoration (cf. Zech 2:10–11).[59]

There is both a future and a past connection being developed here. Yahweh will "return" to Zion, a name used to refer to historical Jerusalem before the events of the Babylonian exiles. Thus, within the biblical texts the return of Yahweh implies a restoration of the nation of Judah. For example, "The LORD will inherit Judah as his portion in the holy

---

57. This is in line with S. Cook's suggestion (*Prophecy and Apocalypticism: The Postexilic Social Setting* [Minneapolis: Fortress, 1995], 123) that Zech 1–8 is the product of the Zadokite priesthood.

58. But note that the term *golah* is not used as a category in Zechariah as it is in Ezra–Nehemiah. In fact, as J. Weinberg (*The Citizen-Temple Community* [trans. Daniel L. Smith-Christopher; JSOTSup 151; Sheffield: JSOT, 1992], 69) notes, Zechariah uses *am ha'aretz*, the "other" category of Ezra–Nehemiah, to refer to the returning community. Nevertheless, the different use of the labels does not negate a similar structural view of social division. Zechariah, like Ezra–Nehemiah—and this will be shown throughout this work—*does* maintain a member–non-member distinction, especially in regard to institutionalized authority. Thus, Bedford's claim ("Diaspora," 150) that there is no conflict between the "remnant" and the "people of the land," while technically correct because it focuses on *labels*, fails fully to appreciate the underlying discourse of resistance in Zechariah.

59. J. M. Balcer (*Sparda By the Bitter Sea: Imperial Interaction in Western Anatolia* [Brown Judaic Studies 52; Chico, Calif.: Scholars Press, 1984], 138) likewise sees this undertone in Zechariah; however, he proposes that Yehud took part in a rebellion against Darius. J. A. Soggin (*Introduction to the History of Israel and Judah* [trans. John Bowden; London: SCM, 1993], 282) offers a similar proposal. However, there is no substantial archaeological evidence in excavated Persian-period sites supporting any rebellion (cf. Carter, *Emergence of Yehud*, 320).

land, and will again choose Jerusalem" (Zech 2:12). Jerusalem's restoration, together with Yahweh's return, idealizes a restoration of political authority vested with divine favor (cf. 1 Kgs 11:13, 32, 36). In making this claim, the passage combines religious and political authorities into one.[60] Yet even in their telling of this "history" the biblical texts cannot avoid acknowledging, especially in the voice of the Deuteronomist and the prophets, that neither the law of the land nor the law of the king was a *religious* law reflecting an institutionalized divine authority. Examples of this, such as the following, in which the king or nation acts outside the framework of religious law (and are therefore accordingly criticized), are replete throughout the Deuteronomistic History:

> "I will not cause the feet of Israel to wander any more out of the land that I gave to their ancestors, if only they will be careful to do according to all that I have commanded them, and according to all the law that my servant Moses commanded them." But they did not listen; Manasseh misled them to do more evil than the nations had done that the LORD destroyed before the people of Israel. The LORD said by his servants the prophets, "Because King Manasseh of Judah has committed these abominations, has done things more wicked than all that the Amorites did, who were before him, and has caused Judah also to sin with his idols; therefore thus says the LORD, the God of Israel, I am bringing upon Jerusalem and Judah such evil that the ears of everyone who hears of it will tingle." (2 Kgs 21:8–12)

Behind the criticism of the Deuteronomist lays the hope of return. Yet the biblical description of return, as a prerequisite step in restoration, demands that we ask whether the portrayal of the "realities" of the province were similar to life before the exiles, or if the described realities of a social-political world governed by religious law were in fact utopian.[61] If we for the moment accept the latter possibility as true, then what do the biblical texts relevant to the Persian Period say, if anything, about the distribution of power and authority? According to Zechariah (2:4 [2:8 HB]) Jerusalem shall be "open" (*przwt tsb yrwslm*). This seems to imply that the previous boundaries, marked by its walls, will be insufficient to enclose the population of the city. Instead, it will expand beyond its previous limits and will necessitate a divine wall of protection. We should not read this as the result of an absorption of the peoples of the

---

60. In fact, as Cook (*Prophecy and Apocalypticism*, 128) observes, divine intervention in Zechariah has universal implications, which is very much in line with the ontology of restoration in the monotheistic body.

61. And it is with this sentiment that we might also recognize, as Said notes generally, "that we can better understand the persistence and the durability of saturating hegemonic systems like culture when we realize that their internal constraints upon writers and thinkers were *productive*, not unilaterally inhibiting" (*Orientalism*, 14).

land but as a promise that is very much in line with the traditional barren-to-pregnant motif found throughout the Pentateuch. The remnant itself will multiply—a parallel perhaps found in the rapid growth of the Hebrews in Egypt (cf. Exod 1:7). In other words, the description is a metaphorical argument that the small "remnant" community will no longer be a minority but the majority (cf. again Zech 2:11–13). The separation of the chosen community from the "other" remains in force with Yahweh promising to be a "wall of fire" around the city and the "glory within it" (2:5). Such a prophecy certainly implies that the community will rely less upon any earthly authority—the natural outgrowth of any social-political body—and more upon a divine authority whose walls will blaze divine glory.[62]

Zechariah's oracles advocate a transformation from political authority into divine authority.[63] Or more specifically, the prophet advocates for the existence of an absolute, divine authority not restricted to the machinations of the social body.[64] Thus, the position of individual leaders is

---

62. Both Weinberg and Coggins, among others, conclude that the Jerusalem high priest became the sole leader of the Jerusalem community (Coggins, *Haggai, Zechariah, Malachi*, 13; Weinberg, *Citizen-Temple Community*, 124–25). See also, P. Dion, "The Civic-and-Temple Community of Persian Period Judaea: Neglected Insights from Eastern Europe," *JNES* 50 (1991): 284; Jonathan E. Dyck, *The Theocratic Ideology of the Chronicler* [Biblical Interpretation Series 33; Leiden: Brill, 1998), 3–4.

63. As C. Meyers and E. Meyers (*Haggai, Zechariah 1–8* [AB 25B; Garden City: Doubleday, 1987], 335–36) write, "Zechariah's visions all, in greater or lesser measure, confirm the fact that establishing the priesthood as the civil and religious authority of the state is acceptable. The visions may succeed in accomplishing this legitimization, ironically shifting the pattern of legitimization in the ancient world in which the temple was the symbol of the approval of the gods for a dynastic power." See also R. Wilson, who states confidently that Zechariah operated within priestly circles (*Prophecy and Society in Ancient Israel* [Philadelphia: Fortress, 1980], 289); although, according to Cook, Zechariah's emphasis on a future Davidide ruler resisted the hegemony of the priests (*Prophecy and Apocalypticism*, 144; VanderKam [*From Joshua to Caiaphas*, 42] makes a similar observation).

64. Which, in part, is what led J. Bright (*A History of Israel* [2d ed.; Philadelphia: Westminster, 1972], 373), for example, to conclude that the Persians removed Zerubbabel from office, allowing Joshua to take full authority. Yet one need not conclude similarly. As Fried (*Priest and the Great King*, 205) remarks regarding the second crown in Zechariah's vision (6:9–14), "The second crown made by Zechariah is put away in the temple as a remembrance. It is not to be held in safekeeping for a future Davidic king, as suggested by most commentators; rather, it is put in the temple as a reminder that the true king is YHWH." In other words, while both see a dismissal of Zerubbabel, Bright expects historical accuracy from the text

"legitimated" by their having been hand-selected by the deity, which is rather baldly proposed by the statement, "Is not this man a brand plucked from the fire" (Zech 3:2). And that followed by a statement that gives the contestation of authority a decidedly juridical or ceremonial coloring, "Thus says the LORD of hosts: If you will walk in my ways and keep my requirements, then you shall rule my house and have charge of my courts, and I will give you the right of access among those who are standing here" (3:7). But this authority cannot exist without its having been inscribed upon the body of the non-member, which the figure of the satan seems to represent in this case (cf. Zech 3:2). While the term *stn* is often translated in this verse as "Satan," a proper noun, it is more accurately a common noun with an included definite article. In other words, the term may better be translated as "the adversary" or "the one who withstands."[65] Joshua, "pulled from the fire," stands before the community's adversary in a rhetorical display of power. Upon the body of the non-member, the so-called adversary—perhaps the non-member as representation of an object against which resistance to a competing form of authority is directed—is despotically inscribed the separation between member and non-member. And in this separation lay a new power relation, absolutized within the monotheistic body. That Joshua is given "clean clothes" undoubtedly implies that the adversary has nothing to contest either regarding Joshua's authority or the superiority of religious authority symbolized in the office of the high priest. Even the presence of the adversary, who seems to act within a courtly hierarchy and system of precedence, infers that he too is subject to divine authority that is mediated through Joshua.[66]

If this oracle is directed toward a revised nature of authority, what is the economic and class impact of this vision? It is often the case that high priests were members of the aristocracy.[67] Joshua's investiture signals he was to be a member of the aristocratic ruling class; however, this makes the most sense only with the rejection of the landed aristocracy and the people of the land who do not support the claim of the

of Zechariah. Fried, on the other hand, accepts Zechariah's prophecy as a vision for a future society.

65. The Septuagint translates the term as *diabolon*, "devil."

66. Liverani, for further reference, observes, "[The monarchic option] was defeated by another utopia, the priestly vision, projected into the future and pursued with great determination. In theory this envisaged God's direct sovereignty: Yahweh malak, 'God reigns,' as the Psalms say, once royal but now adapted to this new ideology..." (*Israel's History*, 324).

67. Cf. VanderKam's discussion (*From Joshua to Caiaphas*, 53–54) of high priests and aristocratic class within the framework of intermarriage.

2. How Monotheism Creates a New Normative Order

so-called remnant to divine election—an idea that biblical texts making similar claims before Zechariah's prophecy seem to have recognized (cf. 2 Kgs 25:12 [but compare 25:22]; Jer 39:10; 52:16 [but compare 40:6]).

We can be confident that enough people remained in the land to require an appointed political authority after the second Babylonian exile. Nebuzaradan, captain of the Babylonian guard, for example, appointed Gedaliah son of Ahikam son of Shaphan as governor over "the people who remained in the land of Judah" (2 Kgs 25:22). An empty land would require no governor. And with a social body containing political and economic differentiation, we can expect the legitimated existence of some form of aristocratic class.[68] Zechariah proclaims Joshua to be the divinely chosen authority (cf. 3:9; 6:11); that authority was expressed in rhetorical opposition to an already established institutionalized authority, with a political-economic differentiation that would comprise the division of social-economic classes.[69] Joshua does not fit within any preexisting political framework; the monotheistic identity, which has become necessary for Joshua's position, entails as an identity a reaction to any authority outside the control of the monotheistic body—thus, either of the imperial body or the social body of Yehud.[70] The prophet describes a new system of power relations, which is implied in his vision of two crowns (6:9–15). Within this new system, the body upon whom divine law would be inscribed was not that of the law breakers themselves but upon those who were unable to obey the law.[71] To the member of the monotheistic body, the non-member is the always-present symbol, the "criminal" caught in a cycle of negligent disobedience. His presence outside the body and his rejection from it must be repeated as often as

---

68. A general sociological pattern is as also noted, for example, by Timothy K. Earle, "Chiefdoms in Archaeological and Ethnohistorical Perspective," *Annual Review of Anthropology* 16 (1987): 290.

69. With respect to this opposition to an already institutionalized authority, Ahlström (*The History of Ancient Palestine*, 820) argues that the investiture of Joshua in Zech 3 indicates that Zerubbabel, as the political authority, was "no longer in command."

70. The interpretation of Meyers and Meyers (*Haggai, Zechariah 1–8*, lv) of Zechariah's vision of the flying scroll as symbolic of Jerusalem's self-rule emphasizes Zechariah's focus on a self-autonomous polity.

71. As Foucault (*Discipline and Punish*, 128–29) writes, "And, ultimately, what one is trying to restore in this technique of correction is not so much the juridical subject, who is caught up in the fundamental interests of the social pact, but the obedient subject, the individual subjected to habits, rules, orders, an authority that is exercised continually around him and upon him, and which he must allow to function automatically in him."

possible—whether through text, ritual, or other ideological expression of identity. "[T]he punishments," Foucault reminds us, "must be a school rather than a festival; an ever-open book rather than a ceremony. The duration that makes the punishment effective for the guilty is also useful for the spectators."[72] The spectators are the *golah* community, the guilty the *am ha'aretz*, and this "school" occurs in the constant remembrance of the exile.[73] If for Zechariah the ancestors are identified with the *am ha'aretz*, then the benefits of the divine–human relationship, as the prophet understands them, are directed toward the remnant, or the *golah* community:

> For thus says the LORD of hosts: Just as I purposed to bring disaster upon you, when your ancestors provoked me to wrath, and I did not relent, says the LORD of hosts, so again I have purposed in these days to do good to Jerusalem and to the house of Judah; do not be afraid. (8:14–15)

Resistance, therefore, is productive of identity when its coordinated patterns are consistent with the divine law that is itself a blueprint for restoration. Restoration requires a successful contest against the more natural forms of authority.

d. *Addressing the Function of Authority in Yehud*

While the general practice of Near Eastern empires was to adopt local administrative systems, most local populations did not notice any significant changes in regime. Imperial governments tended to recognize that order was best maintained when the most accessible form of political organization was a local, cultural production. This required further that the temporally situated political organization of the province, whatever

---

72. Ibid., 111.

73. R. Gibbs' description (*Why Ethics?* [Princeton: Princeton University Press, 2000], 375) of the semiotics of remembering is apropos here: "The role of remnant is central to Jewish existence since the time of the prophets. It performs the responsibility of remembering and hoping in a way that can model the social form of remembrance. The remnant makes the one who remembers herself into a sign of loss, [a] sign of suffering of the others who cannot be fully remembered, and a sign for others to interpret… The remnant waits and promises to remain. Or perhaps it is promised to remain—it is assigned a post it cannot renounce: it must remain until the redemption. As a history of a remnant, history is the witness of suffering in anticipation, a witness to exposure that cannot be renounced." While Gibbs refers to a more modern Jewish concept of "remnant," the term not only sufficiently describes Zechariah's understanding of the identity of the remnant in light of the loss occurring with the Babylonian exile, but it also addresses the responsibility of the remnant (the monotheistic community): "it must remain until redemption," or one may say "restoration."

its "face," not be divorced from the economic and cultural systems of the social body, which itself had endured years of production and transformation. For this reason, constructivist assertions, such as found in Ezra–Nehemiah and Zechariah, that the law of the land was religious law and that the authority over the province was religious authority, cannot be accepted without hesitation. These texts offer nothing in the way of explaining how a social body and its existing political organization wholly restructured itself within the foreign framework of religious authority.[74] To his credit, Joel Weinberg attempted to provide an economic rationale and justification for religious authority in Yehud. However, his theories have several times been shown incorrect.[75] The general tendency in studies of Yehud has been, however, to view authority as something unencumbered by social or economic anchors, something easily modifiable and transferable. It is as though many scholars accept the premise, as articulated by Weber, that "[t]he church advances its demands toward political power [merely] *on the basis of its claims to office charisma.*"[76] And is that not precisely what Zechariah's prophecies regarding Joshua imply, that he was chosen based on his divinely selected and charismatic stature? That anterior to his selection, a newly institutionalized divine power was already victorious over the power or authority that existed previously? Perhaps, but we also see the presence of an imperial juridical system inferred in 2 Kings:

> Gedaliah swore to them and their men saying, "Do not be afraid because of the Chaldean officials; live in the land, serve the king of Babylon, and it shall be well with you." But in the seventh month, Ishmael son of Nethaniah son of Elishama, of the royal family, came with ten men; they struck down Gedaliah so that he died, along with the Judeans and Chaldeans who were with him at Mizpah. Then the people, high and low and the captains of the forces set out and went to Egypt; for they were afraid of the Chaldeans. (2 Kgs 25:24–26)

Those responsible for murdering Gedeliah and his entourage did not suffer directly under the retributive system of the Babylonian king.

---

74. In saying this I am acknowledging that I do not accept that the land was "empty" following the Babylonian exiles. For more discussion on the so-called empty land, see Davies, "Exile! What Exile?"; Carroll, "Exile! What Exile?," 64–65; Barstad, "After the 'Myth'"; Oded, "Where Is the 'Myth'?"; Bob Becking, "'We All Returned as One!' Critical Notes on the Myth of the Mass Return," in Lipschits and Oeming, eds., *Judah and the Judeans in the Persian Period*, 7.

75. Cf. Carter, *Emergence of Yehud*, 294–307; Jeremiah Cataldo, "Persian Policy and the Yehud Community During Nehemiah," *JSOT* 28 (2003): 240–52.

76. Weber, *Economy and Society*, 1164, emphasis mine.

Instead, they fled (2 Kgs 25:25–26). But in taking action, they recognized they were challenging the Babylonian king's superiority and that ultimately they would lose that challenge based on the balance of material power. Their "strike" was against the political body, and it was the Babylonian empire, with Gedeliah its physical representative, as body that made this act meaningful.[77] In other words, the political authority of the Babylonians was not some distant idea, but it was manifest, structured, paramount within provincial territories. Thus, an attack on Gedeliah's body was an attack on the political body of the empire. The guilty fled because such an attack must be punished for the sake of imperial authority; the law, as it were, must be inscribed upon the body of the criminal.[78]

Furthermore, no political vacuum existed under the Persian Empire; thus, a political authority was present to greet the Judeans immigrating from Babylon. One can be confident that the administrative and political structures in place under Babylonian authority continued relatively unchanged under subsequent Persian authority.[79] Or to put it differently, there existed a political system within Yehud before and during the time of the Persian empire—one in which the imperial government appointed

---

77. Foucault writes, "The right to punish…is an aspect of the sovereign's right to make war on his enemies: to punish belongs to 'that absolute power of life and death which Roman law calls *merum imperium*, a right by virtue of which the prince sees that his law is respected by ordering the punishment of crime' ([quote from] Muyat de Vouglans, xxxiv)" (*Discipline and Punish*, 48).

78. See also Foucault's discussion of bodily inscription in ibid., 3–31.

79. For reference, M. Dandamaev and V. Lukonin write, "Under the Achaemenids, Babylonian law reached its pinnacle. It was the model for the legal norms of the countries of the Near East and began to spread West. Babylonian private law, as well as the formulae of documents, was not substantially changed under the Persians, although many public institutions were subjected to Iranian influence and many Iranian terms were encountered in legal documents of the fifth century. Furthermore, at the end of Darius I's reign, reforms in the economic structure and state administration also entailed some changes in the field of private law. Nevertheless, the Achaemenid administration utilized the local law during contact with the Babylonians, and the Persians, who had begun to take an active part in the business life of the country, were guided by the Babylonian law" (Muhammad A. Dandamaev and Vladimir G. Lukonin, *The Culture and Social Institutions of Ancient Iran* [trans. Philip L. Kohl; Cambridge: Cambridge University Press, 1989], 121). For further reference, see also Barstad, "After the 'Myth'," 4; Lester L. Grabbe, "The 'Persian Documents' in the Book of Ezra: Are They Authentic?," in Lipschits and Oeming, eds., *Judah and the Judeans in the Persian Period*, 534–35.

provincial and local authorities.[80] There is no evidence (nor is there any reason) to suggest that the existing political system decayed during Babylonian rule or after the arrival of Persian rule.[81] On the contrary, there is a history of imperial political involvement in Yehud and Samaria (the latter being relevant to our discussion due to cultural and presumably economic exchanges[82]).

The biblical authors seem to treat authority in many ways as the charismatic ideal embodied in divine favor (as one may interpret from Zech 4:8–14). And it is the utopian dream of direct rule by Yahweh that haunts authors such as the Deuteronomistic Historian when he tells the story of the people's desire for a king (1 Sam 8:5). As an expression of religious authority, this dream or vision is based on a manna-in-the-wilderness type of concept—that the divine will provide economic well-being. Can we not read this in the declaration from Haggai: "Is there any seed left in the barn? Do the vine, the fig tree, the pomegranate, and the olive tree still yield nothing? From this day on I will bless you" (2:19)?

80. Cf. Matthew W. Stolper, *Entrepreneurs and Empire: The Murašû Archive, the Murašû Firm, and Persian Rule in Babylonia* (Publications De L'Institut Historique et Archéologique Néerlandais de Stamboul; Leiden: Nederlands Historisch-Archaeologisch Instituut te Istanbul, 1985), 38–39; Joachim Schaper, "The Jerusalem Temple as an Instrument of the Achaemenid Fiscal Administration," *VT* 45 (1995): 528–39, and "The Temple Treasury Committee in the Times of Nehemiah and Ezra," *VT* 47 (1997): 200–206; Fried, *Priest and the Great King*, 32. One could even go as far back as the Assyrian empire to show a relatively consistent pattern (see Adam Zertal, "The Province of Samaria [Assyrian *Samerina*] in the Late Iron Age [Iron Age Iii]," in Lipschits and Blenkinsopp, eds., *Judah and the Judeans in the Neo-Babylonian Period*, 381).

81. Such might also be said with the problematic argument Yehud was a part of Samaria until the Persian empire took control of the territory (on this see Albrecht Alt, "Die Rolle Samarias bei der Entstehung des Judentums," in *Festschrift Otto Procksch zum sechzigsten Geburtstag* [Leipzig: Deichert & Hinrichs, 1934, 5–28 [repr. *Kleine Schriften zur Geschichte des Volkes Israel I* (Munich: Beck, 1953), 316–37], and "Die Landnahme der Israeliten in Palästina," in *Kleine Schriften zur Geschichte des Volkes Israel* [Munich: Beck, 1953], 89–125 [ET "The Settlement of the Israelites in Palestine," in *Essays on Old Testament History and Religion* (Oxford: Blackwell, 1966), 135–69]; Sean McEvenue, "The Political Structure in Judah From Cyrus to Nehemiah," *CBQ* 43 [1981]: 353–64; Weinberg, *Citizen-Temple Community*, 113; Bedford, "Diaspora," 45; Liverani, *Israel's History*, 332; contrast with Eph'al, "Syria-Palestine Under Achaemenid Rule," 160; Blenkinsopp, *Isaiah 56–66*, 46).

82. This is based on, among other things, the practice of intermarriage between aristocratic families of Samaria and Yehud (cf. Frank Moore Cross, Jr., "A Reconstruction of the Judean Restoration," *JBL* 94 [1975]: 6; VanderKam, *From Joshua to Caiaphas*, 53–54).

And relatedly, the biblical tradition of the exodus, which played an instrumental role in the identity formation of the *golah* community (if the tradition was not entirely written by it or its contemporaries), under Moses states, "See! The LORD has given you the sabbath, therefore on the sixth day he gives you food for two days; each of you stay where you are; do no leave your place on the seventh day. So the people rested on the seventh day. The house of Israel called it manna..." (Exod 16:29–31). What is the moral of this if not that the national god of Israel provides food, as both a metaphor and a reality of economic well-being, for the people? Certainly this is not the narrative of a people in the wilderness nor of one living comfortably in the city. It is not honest about the harsh realities of nomadic life in the wilderness. And it does not offer any reflection of class distinction or surplus distribution the urbanite has come to know. Instead, it reflects a situation similar to that in which the *golah* community found itself: existence as a community with no immediate perceivable control over land or its surplus production.[83] Within Yehud, authority was preserved within a social-political system that preexisted the arrival of the *golah* community.

e. *Coding (Religious) Authority within Social-Political Identity*
Ezra (cf. 10:1–12) responds in part to the preexisting (i.e. before the arrival of the *golah* community) authority within Yehud by implying that there can exist only one class, and it is a status not accessible to non-members. As is true of the monotheistic identity, with its reactionary tendency, the religious community embraces this simple, binary opposition, a common human and social pattern that is also explained by Deleuze and Guattari:

> It will be said that there is nonetheless a class that rules and a class that is ruled, both defined by surplus value... But this is only partially true... [T]he theoretical opposition is not between two classes, for it is the very notion of class, insofar as it designates the "negative" of codes, that implies there is only one class... The opposition is between the class and those who are outside the class.[84]

Heuristically, this quote helps illuminate possible rationale explaining why Jerusalem high priests participated in the practice of intermarriage, marriages that joined families in political alliance; and it offers a basis—that is, the pursuit of power through the body of *the* class—for under-

---

83. Cf. Smith, "Politics of Ezra," 95–96; Hoglund, *Achaemenid Imperial Administration*, 221; Fried, *Priest and the Great King*, 211.
84. Deleuze and Guattari, *Anti-Oedipus*, 255.

standing why members of the immigrating community incorporated themselves into landed aristocratic families (cf. Neh 13:28).[85] Such actions do not mirror the biblical testimony that the *golah* community was indeed the ruling authority, or the class in power. Instead, they testify to an already existing social body defined by an array of functioning systems and distributed relations. They testify, in other words, to an already existing—i.e., before the arrival of the *golah* community— habitus. It was a similar understanding that served as the basis for Morton Smith's analysis of, what he terms, the "'Yahweh-alone' party."[86] And while one need not agree with all of his conclusions, his work has correctly shown that a number of biblical texts (such as Ezekiel, Second Isaiah, the Deuteronomistic and Priestly traditions, and the Holiness Code in addition to Ezra–Nehemiah) were written or shaped by a community that viewed exclusion and separation as *the fundamental basis of collective identity*.[87] These texts not only present a program for coding religious authority, they offer a historical revisionism intent on recoding political authority, making it the product of divine favor rather than an imperial or even a natural "outgrowth" of the provincial social-political body.

f. *Zerubbabel and the "Restoration" of Political Authority?*

As we have been discussing, the figures of Zerubbabel and Joshua described in the texts of Haggai and Zechariah represent the re-ordering of political and religious authority. Both texts infer the submission of Zerubbabel's political authority to divine authority represented in the Jerusalem temple and in the figure of Joshua as the high priest. For example,

> In the second year of King Darius, in the sixth month, on the first day of the month, the word of the LORD came by the prophet Haggai to Zerubbabel son of Shealtiel, governor of Judah, and to Joshua son of Jehozadak, the high priest: Thus says the LORD of hosts: These people say the time has not yet come to rebuild the LORD's house. (Hag 1:1–2)

---

85. See also VanderKam, *From Joshua to Caiaphas*, 53–54.
86. Cf. Smith, *Palestinian Parties*, 75–77, 81–82.
87. Smith writes, "The quantity of the material testifies to the importance of this period in the history of the party. It seems to have been the time of formation. The national disaster is plausibly supposed to have made the survivors collect and edit those few written texts which had survived, and write their own accounts of the material of texts which had been lost and of material which had hitherto been preserved orally by institutional groups like the priesthoods of the various holy places" (ibid., 76–77).

Haggai's specific address of Zerubbabel and Joshua suggests that Yahweh, through the voice of the prophet, acknowledged the relative authority of the two leaders—something, however, with which Zechariah may not agree (cf. Zech 6:9–15).[88] And while this acknowledgment might suggest a separation of powers, political and religious respectively, Haggai seems to reject the possibility of any such separation. Zerubbabel is mentioned only once in isolation from Joshua and the Jerusalem temple.[89] His first responsibility, in other words, was to aid Joshua in rebuilding the Jerusalem temple. When he is mentioned alone (Hag 2:20–23) it refers not to any description of the present moment but to a future, albeit uncertain, possibility provided by Yahweh:[90]

> Speak to Zerubbabel, governor of Judah, saying, I am about to shake the heavens and the earth, and to overthrow the throne of kingdoms; I am about to destroy the strength of the kingdoms of the nations, and overthrow the chariots and their riders; and the horses and their riders shall fall, every one by the sword of a comrade. On that day, says the LORD of hosts, I will take you, O Zerubbabel my servant, son of Shealtiel, says the LORD, and make you like a signet ring; for I have chosen you, says the LORD of hosts. (Hag 2:21–23)

"It is preferable," offers John Kessler, "to interpret Zerubbabel's destiny in 2:20–23 in a way that parallels the temple's in 2:1–9."[91] There is merit in that preference; however, Kessler merely "connects dots," so to speak, without fully addressing the productive forces behind them. This is

---

88. See also the discussion above. According to R. P. Carroll ("Ancient Israelite Prophecy and Dissonance Theory," *Numen: International Review for the History of Religions* 24 [1977]: 146), both Haggai and Zechariah express "elements of dissonance" regarding Zerubbabel's position; that is, their expectations of him do not match up with his seeming failure to fulfill them.

89. O. Margalith's statement that Zerubbabel is part of an oligarchy ("The Political Background of Zerubbabel's Mission and the Samaritan Schism," *VT* 41 [1991]: 317–18) is, I believe, one that accepts as true the biblical texts' "veiling" of actual political authority and relations of power with religious utopianism. It accepts that the aristocratic ruling class was comprised of members from the *golah* community. The same may be said of G. Garbini's proposal that a hierocracy was in place following Zerubbabel to 152 B.C.E. (*Myth and History in the Bible* [trans. Chiara Peri; JSOTSup 362; Sheffield: Sheffield Academic, 2003], 106), a conclusion that seems to follow the proposal offered by Cross ("Reconstruction," 16) and possibly also that of Bright (*A History of Israel*, 373).

90. But even as a future reference the oracle lacks any specifics regarding the nature of Zerubbabel's position (see also John Kessler, *The Book of Haggai: Prophecy and Society in Early Persian Yehud* [Atlanta: Society of Biblical Literature, 2007], 236–37).

91. Ibid., 238.

2. How Monotheism Creates a New Normative Order 69

likely due his focus on prophecy as an overt social exercise in reaction to rather than, for comparison, as a generative force of identity production.[92] We should state it rather that religious authority, and we see this in the framing of Zerubbabel's destiny, makes overtures toward subsuming political authority, taking on its role of preventing civil disorder—a role Foucault would describe as being a continuation of the military model of prevention.[93] Monotheism carries out this role by creating a dichotomized reality of member and non-member. And indeed, Foucault's "continuation" fits well with Haggai's employment of "LORD of hosts."[94] But to what purpose? Zerubbabel would be *khwtm* ("as a seal, signet," Hag 2:23) of the deity, a promise that is offered *only after Zerubbabel's responsibility to Joshua and the Jerusalem temple had been clearly explained*.[95] In other words, Zerubbabel's position of authority is contingent upon his acceptance of the absolute authority of the divine.[96] According to Haggai, political authority would remain restrained within the jurisdiction of religious, or divine, authority.[97] But religious authority is in this situation—which is utopian because it is a vision of restoration as a *new* reality—a "need" produced by a desire, which would be consistent with human and social motivation. Or, as Deleuze and Guattari clarify, "Desire is not bolstered by needs, but rather the contrary; needs are derived from desire: they are counterproducts within the real that

---

92. Ibid., 266–69.
93. Foucault, *Discipline and Punish*, 168.
94. The term, "LORD of hosts," usually demanded a military connotation (cf. Max Weber, *Ancient Judaism* [trans. Hans H. Gerth and Don Martindale; New York: Free Press, 1952], 82–84; Norman K. Gottwald, *The Tribes of Yahweh: A Sociology of the Religion of Liberated Israel 1250–1050 B.C.E.* [Maryknoll: Orbis, 1979], 281–82).
95. D. Edelman (*The Origins of the "Second" Temple: Persian Imperial Policy and the Rebuilding of Jerusalem* [London: Equinox, 2005], 133–34) suggests that had restoration continued on Haggai's given trajectory, and Judah become again an independent kingdom, Zerubbabel's role would have been framed by his responsibility to the Jerusalem temple, and defined as "temple restorer."
96. Haggai and Zechariah only speak of Zerubbabel as he fits their visions of restoration. Cf. Carroll, "Ancient Israelite Prophecy," 146; Smith, *Palestinian Parties*, 82; Cook, *Prophecy and Apocalypticism*, 132; VanderKam, *From Joshua to Caiaphas*, 12–14. See also the more restrictive proposal offered by Weinberg (*Citizen-Temple Community*, 114–15), who posits that Zerubbabel was not a governor but an unofficial leader of the community of returnees.
97. Cf. Julian Morgenstern, "Jerusalem—485 BC," *Hebrew Union College Annual* 27 (1956): 160; Soggin, *Introduction to the History of Israel and Judah*, 282; Berquist, *Judaism in Persia's Shadow*, 134; Oded, "Where Is the 'Myth'?," 62. In addition, Coggins (*Haggai, Zechariah, Malachi*, 12–13) notes that Haggai emphasizes divine authority to the expense of political authority.

desire produces."[98] Understood this way, Haggai's "need" for an established religious authority reflects a collective or communal desire for political autonomy, and this need represents the lack thereof. This desire is typically expressed by Persian-period biblical texts in the vocabulary of "restoration." From Zechariah, for example, "Thus says the LORD: I *will return* to Zion, and *will dwell* in the midst of Jerusalem; Jerusalem shall be called the faithful city, and the mountain of the LORD of hosts shall be called the holy mountain" (Zech 8:3, emphasis mine).

While recognizing Zerubbabel's political position, the oracle seems to highlight obliquely the governor's relative powerlessness.[99] In that regard, Morton Smith's proposal that Zerubbabel was the leader of the Yahweh-alone party (or *bene haggolah*) and that this party was recognized as the legitimate political authority and took control of rebuilding the Jerusalem temple is interesting but fails. It centers authority, both political and religious, on the *unbuilt* Jerusalem temple.[100] Or as John Kessler writes, "The oracle to Zerubbabel contains an implied dramatic conflict, relating to the disparity between the reality of Yehud's subjection to Persian rule, and the grandiose promises found in Israelite traditions regarding its place in the world of nations, the role of the Davidic dynasty, and the universal recognition of Israel's deity."[101]

---

98. Deleuze and Guattari, *Anti-Oedipus*, 27.

99. The idea that Zerubbabel represents a possible restoration of the Judean dynasty (cf. Blenkinsopp, *Isaiah 56–66*, 44) is not necessarily contradictory. Zerubbabel may simply be an ideal figure, a symbol representing a connection, a fluidity rather, with the past. This does not mean he necessarily is given power but that he fundamentally represents divine power. Viewing Zerubbabel as a symbolic figure here allows some parallel between Haggai and Zechariah to be maintained, especially in light of Zech 3 and 6:9–14, which seem to indicate that Joshua, not Zerubbabel, was "in charge" (as noted by Ahlström, *The History of Ancient Palestine*, 820). Edelman (*The Origins of the 'Second' Temple*, 122–23) suggests that the lack of any direct assertion that Yahweh will place Zerubbabel on the throne in place of the Persians in Haggai (ch. 2) is meant to reinforce the deity's direct rule. Kessler (*Book of Haggai*, 259–61) concludes a notable lack of specifics may suggest Zerubbabel does not represent an actual restored monarchy. Alternatively, Cook (*Prophecy and Apocalypticism*, 132) states that Haggai (2:20–23) grants Zerubbabel messianic status.

100. Smith, *Palestinian Parties*, 107–9.

101. Kessler, *Book of Haggai*, 220. Compare with "What exactly does Haggai [Hag 2:21–23] destine for Zerubbabel the son of Shealtiel? Apparently his prophecy is an antithesis to the prophecy of Jeremiah [Jer 22:24]" (Sara Japhet, "Sheshbazzar and Zerubbabel Against the Background of the Historical and Religious Tendencies of Ezra–Nehemiah: Part 1," in *From the Rivers of Babylon to the Highlands of Judah* [Winona Lake: Eisenbrauns, 2006], 63). It is a point Kessler also makes:

2. How Monotheism Creates a New Normative Order

Perhaps this disequilibrium results in Haggai's petition of the "LORD of hosts" (*yhwh tsb'wt*). In some cases, this god performs whatever political action is necessary, and at others, a champion fights in his name (e.g. 1 Sam 17:45). Zerubbabel, according to Haggai, is not the latter.[102] Even still, the general expectation was that the LORD of hosts himself would restore the "remnant" of Judah. As, for example, Haggai writes, "For thus says the LORD of hosts: Once again, in a little while, I will shake the heavens and the earth and the sea and the dry land; and I will shake all the nations, so that the treasure of all nations shall come, and I will fill this house with splendor, says the LORD of hosts. The silver is mine, and the gold is mine, says the LORD of hosts" (2:6–8). There is a parallel from Judean tradition in 2 Kings, where Isaiah son of Amoz tells Hezekiah, "The surviving remnant of the house of Judah shall again take root downward, and bear fruit upward; for from Jerusalem a remnant shall go out, and from Mount Zion a band of survivors. The zeal of the LORD of hosts will do this" (19:30–31). This god's role is also exemplified in the Psalms, for example, "The LORD of hosts is with us; the God of Jacob is our refuge. Come, behold the works of the LORD; see what desolations he has brought on the earth. He makes wars cease to the end of the earth; he breaks the bow, and shatters the spear; he burns the shields with fire" (46:7–9). How does he make wars cease? By defeating in battle all (his) enemies, while leaving some behind for the benefit of the faithful community. "If the LORD of hosts had not left us a few survivors, we would have been like Sodom, and become like Gomorrah" (Isa 1:9). And further, "Therefore says the Sovereign, the LORD of hosts, the Mighty One of Israel: Ah, I will pour out my wrath on my enemies, and avenge myself on my foes" (Isa 1:24)! Haggai's expectation appears well-established within the religious-cultural traditions of Judah.

By describing the LORD of hosts as taking on the role of restorer, Haggai implies that the current state of the Jerusalem temple (unbuilt) and the state of the community (responsible to imperial authority) would be remedied through divine restoration. Consequently, the political office of governor would become a sign, a divine "seal" confirming that the divine actions of restoration had been successful.[103] In this role, there is

---

"[T]he extended metaphor of Yahweh's setting Zerubbabel upon his finger like a signet ring serves several purposes and makes several points. The image provides a further comment on Jer 22:24 and juxtaposes Zerubbabel's faithfulness to Jehoiachin's lack thereof" (*Book of Haggai*, 234).

102. Cf. Cook, *Prophecy and Apocalypticism*, 132.

103. While Haggai seems, as Coggin has defended (*Haggai, Zechariah, Malachi*, 13–14), to acknowledge Zerubbabel as governor, the issue is not the person in the

no clear indication that this political position would continue in perpetuity or that it would gain any independent status.[104] According to Haggai (cf. again 2:21–23), as an office independent of the cult it did not represent the "true" social-political body; accordingly, the office and Zerubbabel were "coopted" by Yahweh.[105] Or as John Kessler argues, "I would see the avoidance of [explicitly royal] language as a *deliberate reticence* to portray the future as an exact replica of the past."[106] Haggai, in other words, does not clearly envision a monarchy; instead, a theocracy might be nearer his vision of "restored" society. But that desire, when desire is considered to be a *lack* of need, is underscored by its very lack of fulfillment: the Jerusalem temple remains unfinished.

Thus, we should be hesitant to interpret Haggai's oracle, as C. Meyers and E. Meyers have done, as a direct indication of the growing power and centrality of the Jerusalem high priesthood.[107] The texts are not the outward expressions of desire of the provincial social-political body reflecting, consequently, entrenched relations of power. Theirs is a petition to put power *into* the hands of the priesthood; it is this that explains the presence of the figure Joshua in Haggai and Zechariah (Hag 1:12, 14; 2:2, 4; Zech 3 et passim; 6:11). Both describe an act or reality in which political authority is subsumed within religious authority on an ideological level—that is, that governors ought to be subordinate to priests in a "restored" society directed by Yahweh. But this "ideology" does not reflect the desire production of the larger provincial social-political body. In other words, it is utopian, a reaction to social-political realities not in alignment with the vision of the *golah*, or "Yahweh-alone," community.

---

position but the text's interpretation of how power in relation to the position is distributed.

104. It is generally argued that the reference to "the Branch" in Zechariah (cf. 3:8; 6:12) does not refer to Zerubbabel (cf. Cook, *Prophecy and Apocalypticism*, 134–35; VanderKam, *From Joshua to Caiaphas*, 31; but note also Ahlström, *The History of Ancient Palestine*, 820).

105. While I would not agree with his conclusion that Yehud become a "hierocratic enclave," G. Garbini's observation (*History and Ideology in Ancient Israel* [trans. John Bowden; New York: Crossroad, 1988], 71) that economic activity seems to be surprisingly absent among those things considered important by the biblical texts is worth noting and a point that finds agreement with this author. The absence of any direct reference to economic issues in the biblical discussions of political authority casts into suspicion the biblical conclusions regarding political authority as the exercise of the religious community.

106. Kessler, *Book of Haggai*, 237.

107. Meyers, and Meyers, *Haggai, Zechariah 1–8*, xxxix.

g. *Restoration, Reconstruction, and Exclusion as Discourses on Identity Formation within the Monotheistic Body*

> [E]xclusions can arise only as a function of inhibiters and repressers that eventually determine the support and firmly define a specific, personal subject. No chain is homogenous; all of them resemble, rather, a succession of characters from different alphabets in which an ideogram, a pictogram, a tiny image of an elephant passing by, or a rising sun may suddenly make an appearance… Each chain captures fragments of other chains from which it "extracts" a surplus value, just as the orchid code "attracts" the figure of a wasp…[108]

As we have seen, this biblical portrayal of religious authority, from the *golah* or Yahweh-alone perspective, focuses on excluding any uncontrolled—that is, that which is not confined within the monotheistic body—existence or function of a natural, political authority. Yet in the same way that some modern religious ideologues hate, but cannot exist without, a democratically liberal and critically thinking government, religion and religious authority cannot exist without the material productions of the social body. Recasting behaviors of the political body into those more characteristic of what is possible within the restraints of divine law imperializes the productive forces of the social-political body. It is in this sense that Sheshbazzar, who should be considered a governor,[109] appears within Ezra–Nehemiah only as he relates to religious ceremony and artifact. Ezra (1:8) mentions him as the "prince of Judah" to whom the vessels of the Jerusalem temple were counted out.[110] The rather overt claim there seems unmistakable: political authority, as symbolized by the role *nsy'*, should be an authority subordinate to religious authority, which is symbolized by the Jerusalem temple and the high priest as the temple's representative. Of the four times Sheshbazzar is mentioned, three refer to his receiving the temple vessels (1:8, 11; 5:14). Ezra 5:14 states additionally that King Cyrus made Sheshbazzar governor, but the text admits this only within the narrative framework of

---

108. Deleuze and Guattari, *Anti-Oedipus*, 39.
109. Cf. Meyers and Meyers, *Haggai, Zechariah 1–8*, xxxiv; Fried, *Priest and the Great King*, 184–86; VanderKam, *From Joshua to Caiaphas*, 101; Edelman, *The Origins of the "Second" Temple*, 155. Contra Weinberg, *Citizen-Temple Community*, 114–15; Soggin, *Introduction to the History of Israel and Judah*, 280–81.
110. Why does Ezra use both titles ("prince of Judah" and "governor") to described Sheshbazzar? While the title "governor" was an imperial appointment, "prince of Judah" seems to emphasize the author's expectation of restoration. Thus, the title seems to be used in an ideal sense.

his having received the temple vessels.[111] Ezra mentions further that Sheshbazzar laid the foundations of the Jerusalem temple.[112] And while Sheshbazzar's role in building the temple may be in question, textual intent seems fairly clear: Sheshbazzar, a governor, is not mentioned without reference to the Jerusalem temple, whether of its construction or of his handling of the temple vessels. His office is narratively stripped of all characteristics of a natural, political authority and recast as a function of the divine purpose in restoration.

Ezra 2:2 lists Zerubbabel as one of the leaders of the "returnees." While this presentation may seem somewhat innocuous, there is within it an inherent bodily claim to territoriality: the political office that Zerubbabel holds is important because through it he would lead the *golah* community, a collective defined according to religious ideology, into the land. There he would establish an authority that would subject political authority to divine will. This framing of Zerubbabel is ideal, as the phrase "the number of the Israelite people" (Ezra 2:2; Ezra defines "Israel" as the *golah* community) suggests. For the author, "Israel" and the assumed future restoration of the kingdom (of Judah, really) refers to and will originate with the *golah* community.

This religious frame continues in Ezra 3:2 where Joshua and Zerubbabel, with their respective entourages, joyously set out to build the altar of the "God of Israel" (again note Ezra's definition of the term "Israel") so that the community may offer burnt offerings upon it "as prescribed in the law of Moses the man of God." After sacrificing day and night, they (presumably the *golah* community has actively joined Joshua and Zerubbabel in the proceedings) observe the festival of booths.[113] And in the second year after their arrival "at the house of God at Jerusalem"

---

111. Weinberg (ibid.; also cited above) suggests that Sheshbazzar was not governor of the province but of the *golah* community. It is rather difficult, however, to conclude that the imperial government was directly involved with appointing community leaders.

112. This, of course, is a much debated point in scholarship. My intention here is not to decide whether Sheshbazzar could have been responsible for laying any temple foundations but how the text is portraying the subservience of political authority. For a few references on the debate, see Weinberg, *Citizen-Temple Community*, 114–15; Fried, *Priest and the Great King*, 170, 177; VanderKam, *From Joshua to Caiaphas*, 9; Japhet, *From the Rivers of Babylon*, 204–14.

113. The festival serves as a reminder that the people were once slaves in Egypt (Deut 16:12–13). That the *golah* community alone observed the festival, a required observance according to Mosaic Law, further confirms the connection between the community and the religious tradition of the Exodus, which was also about, among other things, immigrating into the land of Canaan to possess it.

2. How Monotheism Creates a New Normative Order 75

Joshua and Zerubbabel *hllw* (Ezra 3:8), which the NRSV translates as "made a beginning" but whose etymology is uncertain. In its causative sense the action implies the inauguration or "beginning" of change prompted by a program of reconstruction. Within this movement, they appoint the Levites to have oversight of the work on the Jerusalem temple. Again the temple figures centrally in the actions that unfold. And even when Ezra acknowledges the existence of other people in the area (but only after labeling them "adversaries"; these are the *am ha'aretz*, whose members include M. Smith's "syncretistic" party) who approach Zerubbabel and the heads of families asking to aid in building the Jerusalem temple, it is Zerubbabel and Joshua with the heads of families who refuse the aid (Ezra 4:1–3). In their answer, they confirm perceived boundaries of religious membership, "our God...the God of Israel" (v. 3). Ezra also credits them (Joshua and Zerubbabel) with "setting out to rebuild the house of God in Jerusalem" (Ezra 5:2).[114] Nehemiah's references to Zerubbabel are limited to associating him as one of the leaders of the *golah* community (making little, as does Ezra, of his political office as one that exists outside religious function) and to using both him and Nehemiah as chronological markers during which "all Israel" (read *golah* community) gave daily portions to those employed in the Jerusalem temple (cf. Neh 12:47).

Haggai's references to Zerubbabel position him ideologically alongside Joshua, and they center on the figures' combined role in rebuilding the Jerusalem temple (cf. Hag 1:1, 12, 14). Haggai refers to Zerubbabel as governor usually when it also designates Joshua the high priest (cf. Hag 1:14; 2:2). Only once does it refer to Zerubbabel as governor without referring to Joshua (Hag 2:21), and there it emphasizes Zerubbabel's instrumentality contrasted directly with divine agency. Likewise in Zechariah, Zerubbabel's instrumentality is emphasized. There Zerubbabel is

---

114. S. Japhet addresses the literary confusion in Ezra regarding Sheshbazzar and Zerubbabel by suggesting a break in the collective memory of the community. "We have seen that Sheshbazzar's figure and actions did not leave an imprint on the people's memory, and that already in the days of Darius his figure has become remote and unfamiliar. Nevertheless, the people did remember a connection between him and the transfer of the temple's vessels from Babylon to Jerusalem. In contrast, Zerubbabel's figure becomes more prominent and comes to occupy the entire historical stage. These facts constitute a stimulus to the historiographical process, resulting in the magnification of the scope of Zerubbabel's activities—both in terms of the time in which they occurred and in terms of their contents—and in the perception of Zerubbabel as responsible for the deeds performed by others" (ibid., 212). While that may certainly have been the case, it seems to absolve of responsibility the biblical authors pursuing any particular agenda.

described as the one who by the spirit of Yahweh makes mountains into plains (Zech 4:7) and whose hands both laid the foundation of the Jerusalem temple and will complete it (4:9). But even in this active role, his position is still confined within the "desiring-production," as Deleuze and Guattari phrase it, of the *golah*, or Yahweh-alone, community—a desire for the Jerusalem temple as symbol of divine authority, surplus production, and the community's monotheistic identity. This pattern of confinement, of imprisoning political authority within the long, dark hallways of divine authority, is similar to that found in the Deuteronomistic History wherein kings were judged on how well their actions and rules supported the legitimation of divine authority: "Manasseh was twelve years old when he began to reign; he reigned fifty-five years in Jerusalem… *He did what was evil in the sight of the LORD*" (2 Kgs 21:1–2, emphasis mine). And Zerubbabel's actions are successful only because the spirit of Yahweh restricts production to that which benefits the community. While Zechariah seems to look favorably on Zerubbabel as an active figure, it nevertheless subjects him to a religious framework and makes little of his political office. In fact, it makes no mention of Zerubbabel being governor and devotes only one chapter to him before moving on to another "Branch"[115] in ch. 6. There Zechariah is instructed to place a crown upon the head of Joshua (v. 11) and proclaim "behold a man whose name is branch" (*hnh-'ys tsmh smw*, v. 12). Does this proclamation refer to Joshua or some other unnamed individual?[116] If it is

---

115. Note also Cook, who writes, "A significant difference between Zechariah and Haggai is that Haggai does grant a definite messianic status to a contemporary, namely Zerubbabel (Hag. 2:20–23). In contrast, though Zechariah at one time may have looked to Zerubbabel with messianic hopes (see Zech. 4:6–10a, an early addition to the vision), for this prophet he was only a messianic candidate; and the Zechariah tradition soon pointed its hopes to a future Davidide, referred to as the *tsmh* ('sprout, branch'). The term *tsmh* in earlier prophecy (Jer. 23:5; 33:15; compare Isa. 4:2; [11:1]) emphasized a coming ideal Davidide who would execute justice on the earth. Zechariah's use of the term is probably based on Ezekiel's reference to these prophecies (Ezek. 17:22–24)" (*Prophecy and Apocalypticism*, 132).

116. Ahlström (*The History of Ancient Palestine*, 820) states that the term "branch," a royal epithet, is used in Zech 6:12 of Joshua. Cook (*Prophecy and Apocalypticism*, 134–35), however, argues that Joshua does not fill the messianic expectation and Zechariah looks to a future Davidide branch. VanderKam (*From Joshua to Caiaphas*, 31) also argues that the term does not refer to Joshua: "Uffenheimer, who has examined other biblical uses of the word *tsmh*, contends that it never refers to an individual existing at the present time of the writer but always to an ideal figure of the future. In light of this scriptural usage and the fact that Zerubbabel and Joshua were contemporaries and apparently in office at the time when this

meant for Joshua, then we may read the vision of the two crowns (as noted in the Hebrew, Zech 6:9–15) in the following manner: one crown symbolizes Joshua's new political power in addition to his religious authority, possibly suggesting the creation of a theocratic polity.[117] Such a polity, of course, would be utopian, especially so given the nature of the Zechariah text, as we have been discussing it. If it refers to an as-of-yet-unnamed Davidide ruler, then Joshua serves *ad litem*, so to speak. In either case, in the absence of a Davidide ruler, both in terms of the actual office and the "right" person, political authority is collapsed into religious authority and made subject to it. This prophetic myopia confines the social body to the monotheistic body. In other words, it makes society a product of religious forces, being either their object or their consequence. Nevertheless, whatever one decides on the identity of the branch, the city of Jerusalem continues to serve as a symbol of divine authority:

> Peoples shall yet come, the inhabitants of cities; the inhabitants of one city shall go to another, saying, "Come let us go entreat the favor of the LORD, and to seek the LORD of hosts; I myself am going." Many peoples and strong nations shall come to seek the LORD of hosts in Jerusalem, and to entreat the favor of the LORD. (Zech 8:20–22)

Ultimately, however, Zerubbabel's crown, which was never his but which seems to represent political office, is repressed and the authority of the office subverted. While the two crowns might have created an interpretive problem, the author puts Zerubbabel's immaculate crown in the care of Heldai, Tobijah, Jedaiah, and Josiah son of Zephaniah for "remembrance," a memorial in the temple of the community's god. Whatever happens regarding the political office, whether Joshua or an unnamed individual carries out a messianic role, it is a messianic role, bringing restoration through an overturning, that is needed. Only a messiah can overturn the prevailing social-political order in an act of "restoration," thereby redirecting the eyes of the world upon the national deity of the "remnant." We can say then that the intent is the glorification

---

passage was written, it seems preferable to see in Zechariah's Branch a ruler who *will* come from David's line (see also Zech 6:12)."

117. One should not make the immediate connection between a priest in authority and theocracy (cf. as argued extensively in Cataldo, *A Theocratic Yehud*). What one would read in this instance is the *suggestion* (a utopian one to be sure) of a theocracy, which in addition to the religious authority being the political authority without separation in the office nor in its relation to the social-political body requires an establishment, systems of production and distribution, etc., capable of sustaining a theocracy (again, see ibid.).

of the community through the glorification of its god. Moreover, that the crown intended for remembrance is cast to emphasize the crown on Joshua's head.

In light of what has been discussed, it seems clear that the biblical texts focus on (re)construction rather than description. They do not tell the story of the political body, of its marking out and being marked out through the material productions of its members. They say nothing about the material basis of class division and of the distribution of authority based on those divisions. They speak obliquely of class but of class being comprised by the *golah* community. But can we speak of an aristocracy when we must first speak of immigrant? This biblically narrated program, or process, of restoration ignores the material and economic realities of the province. It focuses instead on the reconstruction of the Jerusalem temple in the hands of the remnant. The temple becomes the connection between the people and their god, between the land and a (possible) future nation. Relatedly, the "signet ring," as Zerubbabel was described, becomes an extension of the temple as the symbol of divine authority. But reconstruction is not restoration in the proper sense. The authority of this polity is, unlike the Israel and Judah of the past, centered in the Jerusalem temple. This program speaks of a world that has never existed nor can it ever exist without divine intervention. It is, to be sure, utopian in the fullest sense.

2. The Legitimation of Authority Requires an Apparatus of Punishment

> The art of punishing, then, must rest on the whole technology of representation. The undertaking can succeed only if it forms part of a natural mechanics.[118]

If, for theoretical argument, it were true the *golah* community was the ruling class of the province[119] and that after Nehemiah the high priest took over political authority, then we must demand an answer to the following question: What apparatus of punishment that supported the authority of the *golah* community was established in the province?[120]

---

118. Foucault, *Discipline and Punish*, 104.
119. It does us no good to speak only of a meager city. The Persian empire never established a pattern of granting autonomy to cities within a province.
120. Weber's comments on the use of force for control are helpful here: "[The state] has been successful in seeking to monopolize the legitimate use of physical force as a means of domination within a territory. To this end the state has combined the material means of organization in the hands of its leaders, and *it has expro-*

Ezra tells us that the law of Moses was synonymous with the law of the king, and on account of this was the law of the province (Ezra 7:26). But here we must protest. This law was not a "natural" product of the social body in Yehud. Moreover, the so-called imperial decree from Artaxerxes (see Ezra 7:11–26) demands that if one were to accept its authenticity (without its having been amended) one must accept that the imperial government was doing something unique in Yehud. And that is precisely what the monotheistic identity of the *golah* community demands of us— a recognition that imperial political authority was a divine handmaiden for the establishment of divine authority, one through which the social body of the *am ha'aretz* could be inscribed upon.

Exclusion is certainly one method of enforcing regulated behavior within the political body, but its method is meant more to address the audience of members than the one excluded.[121] The separation between the *golah* community and the *am ha'aretz* could be read as a legitimation of the (new, monotheistic) political body only if one accepts that the majority of the social body in Yehud was, metaphorically speaking, criminal. And that is precisely what the biblical texts we have discussed seem to claim (in a manner very similar to the way Canaanites were described in the tradition of land conquest under Moses and Joshua).

But that is a utopian or highly idealistic claim. Within an understanding of the monotheistic ideology of exclusion, "criminalizing" the non-member (i.e. social body) offers no obvious, material benefit to the new social–political–religious body after it has been excluded. The *am ha'aretz* become simply a characters in the *golah* community's drama, a tired foil against which the community casts its own pristine image. It finds a modern parallel in the overcrowded prisons of the modern world, circumstances that no longer serve a purpose of rehabilitation but that have been reduced to the separation of one social group from another. These have become a sort of anti-world both romanticized and feared by those who have never experienced such forced exclusion first hand. They are an enclosed "outside." When an individual transgresses the law of the political body, he or she is removed from one society and forced outside

---

priated all autonomous functionaries of estates who formerly controlled these means in their own right" (Max Weber, "Politics as a Vocation," in *From Max Weber: Essays in Sociology* [ed. Hans H. Gerth and C. Wright Mills; New York: Oxford University Press, 1958], 82–83 [emphasis mine]).

121. Assmann's comments on the "oneness" of God in the monotheistic sense are apropos here: "God's oneness is not an invention of monotheism, but the central theme of polytheistic religions as well… God's oneness is not the salient criterion here but the negation of 'other' gods" (*The Price of Monotheism*, 29).

into an enclosed (marked out in geographic space by use of walls, barbed wire, sniper towers, etc.), excluded society. The image of the prison and the space it carves out are symbolic, not for the inmates, or enclosed "outsiders," but for the outside "insiders"—or: member, citizen, non-criminal. The latter are the audience of this "apparatus" of punishment.[122] It is to them a prison's solemn inference is addressed, "*lasciate ogne speranza, voi ch'intrate.*"[123]

This parallel with Yehud works if one clearly recognizes that it is the *golah* community, the social–political–religious body, that has walled itself within demarcated space—it has, in other words, inverted the paradigm for the purpose of excluding the member or citizen from the "criminal." This space is symbolized by Jerusalem's walls as both metaphor and physical representation of community separation from the people of the land.[124] Religious understanding of sacred and profane has forced the community's hand here. Throughout the ancient Near East that which was sacred was kept in isolation from profane, a practice resulting in spaces dedicated as inner sanctuaries or a "holy of holies" wherein only a high priest could annually venture.[125] "To safeguard sacred from profane" was the highest order of every religious official and obedient worshiper.[126] And it is in this way that the *golah* community, as a collective body, reflexively viewed itself as the material representation of (but not actually) the sacred (cf. Ezra 9:2; Neh 11:1). Consequently, the *am ha'aretz* was labeled by the *golah* community as profane, "criminal," and (ideologically, since the absence of material power on the part of the *golah* community) removed from productive engagement with the member.

It is important to realize what has happened. The biblical texts have metaphorically collected all the people in the province who are not members of the *golah* community and placed them, to continue the analogy,

---

122. For more on the role of punishment and punishment's audience, see Foucault, *Discipline and Punish*, 73–131.

123. Italian text from Robert Pinsky, *The Inferno of Dante* (New York: Farrar, Straus & Giroux), 18.

124. See Jeremiah Cataldo, "Whispered Utopia: Dreams, Agendas, and Theocratic Aspirations in Persian-Period Yehud," *SJOT* 24, no. 1 (2010): 53–70.

125. Note, for example, the recounting of tradition given by the author of Hebrews (9:3–7).

126. M. Douglas' work (*Purity and Danger: An Analysis of Concept of Pollution and Taboo* [Routledge Classics; London: Routledge, 2006]) has done much to clarify how deeply entrenched within cultural practices concerns for the separation between sacred and profane, or clean and dirty, were within ancient Near Eastern, as well as other, cultures.

in prison. And the law by which all people have been judged is that whose purpose is to facilitate the process of restoration, from which only the religiously obedient community would benefit. In this situation, religious ideology constitutes the fundamental nature of the so-called apparatus of punishment. More importantly, the real social-political power relations that define a society's apparatus of punishment have been inverted. It is as though the ruler has locked him/herself in jail and shouted through the bars at external society, "You are the criminals! In here I am sacred, the chosen of God!" But without a material basis upon which one's authority can be legitimated—and this is a point that we have both begun addressing and will continue to do so—legitimation requires, in theory, an unnatural, or supernatural, act. We must, in short, see the radical materialization of a utopian ideal; in a word, restoration.

In summary, monotheism creates a new normative for authority by interrupting, or resisting, the preexisting normative and by creating boundaries between member and non-member, forming or producing identity through acts of exclusion. It must preserve that authority by inscribing it upon the body of the non-member, whose identity as an outsider is based entirely on his own exclusion.

Chapter 3

SOCIALIZATION AND CONFLICT AS FORCES PRODUCTIVE OF IDENTITY

Our discussion to this point seems to be confirming that conflict is necessary for both the creation and the preservation of a monotheistic identity. This conflict, which is driven by a pursuit for authority, is at its most fundamental level a material conflict. Consequently, rationales, justifications, arguments, or other ideological explanations, upon which later religious beliefs may be based, are initially productions defined by identifiable material and historical contingencies. Ideological forces and symbol systems within monotheism, which over time take on lives of their own apart from material conditions, were originally for monotheism products of a material conflict for authority and its concomitant socialization of social actors. Socialization, to be clear, is a community-building act. By extension, the concept "weakly socialized," which may best describe the original development of a monotheistic community or identity, can identify the development of a community within a larger community through simultaneous processes of dependence and resistance. Understanding the nature of socialization and the different degrees to which it may occur will help us better understand conflict as productive for a monotheistic identity.

Or to be more specific, social-political actors who have been "socialized" within the parameters of a monotheistic identity are "weakly socialized actors."[1] "[W]eakly socialized actors...do not take the standard of legitimacy either for granted or as a moral imperative that directly motivates their goals and behaviors. They confront the standard of legitimacy as an *external institutional resource and constraint*. As such, it affects both the mode of interaction between political actors and their relative power over outcomes."[2] The monotheistic body is "weakly

---

1. I am drawing from the theory discussed in Frank Schimmelfennig, "The Community Trap: Liberal Norms, Rhetorical Action, and the Eastern Enlargement of the European Union," *International Organization* 55, no. 1 (2001): 62–63.
2. Ibid., 63.

socialized," and its actors likewise, because it belongs to the social body, whose norms it shares, but it defines itself in contradistinction to the collective identity of the social body; thus, conflict creates the environment for weakly socialized actors. As though in a schizophrenic relationship, the monotheistic body simultaneously rejects the social body and depends upon it for its own existence. In addition, it views any authority legitimated by the social body, but not simultaneously so by the monotheistic body, as a threat. If political legitimacy is based on the characteristics of collective identity and distinguishes between rightful and improper ways of acquiring, transferring, and exercising political power, we must accept that "rightful" and "improper" are defined according to the desire, and its concomitant production, of the social body. Thus, political legitimacy is a naturally produced act that is simultaneously relative to a particular body and, as an objectified fact, that acts back upon the body. And while the monotheistic body will acknowledge this act of legitimacy as necessary for the social body, it rejects it as its own.

Within the framework of its monotheistic identity, the *golah* community was self-perceivably a consecrated body—note the collective body itself, but not a body of sacred individuals—inasmuch as it was associated with or held possession of the land, which ultimately symbolized obedience—an idea best expressed in the religious injunction: "You shall be holy, for I the LORD your God am holy" (Exod 19:2).[3] Displacement from and a return to the land, from which Yahweh had also departed and returned (cf. Ezek 10), determined the first act in a pattern of legitimacy. It was a *community building* act, separating the member from the nonmember. And it can be found at the heart of the conflict in Yehud and sustained by differing notions of identity. "On that day they read from the book of Moses...it was found written that no Ammonite or Moabite should ever enter the assembly of God... When the people heard the law, they separated from Israel all those of foreign descent" (Neh 13:1–3). Socialization creates the parameters for legitimation. And further, as Schimmelfennig writes, "By linking distributional conflict [which for our purposes occurs between the monotheistic body and the social body]

---

3. This injunction reveals a view in contrast to that portrayed in Ezekiel in which only the divine could be perceived as holy. (This view in Ezekiel was brought to my attention by Andrew Mein.) As M. Douglas (*Purity and Danger: An Analysis of Concepts of Pollution and Taboo* [London: Routledge & Kegan Paul, 1966], 49) notes, the injunction is to *be* holy. And relatedly, Hoglund (*Achaemenid Imperial Administration*, 208) observes that Nehemiah's focus is on the formation of a holy community. Apart from Ezekiel, a priest, there exists, it would seem, a belief that the community can and should strive to be a holy community.

with the collective identity and the constitutive values and norms of the community, rhetorical action changes the structure of bargaining power in favor of those actors that possess and pursue preferences in line with, though not necessarily inspired by, the standard of legitimacy."[4] So we should view the standard of legitimacy *as described* in the *golah*-oriented biblical texts (e.g. Ezra–Nehemiah, Haggai, Zechariah, Ezekiel)—particularly those produced by the Yahweh-alone party, as Morton Smith first identified it—as a product of the *golah*-community's desire production. Its dogged self-perception as a distinct and a monotheistic community reflects its desire for legitimated authority—a desire written within the cultural code of a monotheistic identity. Its resistance to natural social-political authority repeats the archetype of the monotheistic body's resistance to its origin in the social body. And its "distributional conflict" is found in its resistance to the norms and values of the social body it tries to forget, to write over, with those constructed from the monotheistic community's own desire production. This conflict, whose secondary intent is to redefine the class structure, is an act of resistance, rewriting, and redefinition of identity.

To understand the relationship between the primary (acquiring authority) and secondary (articulating collective identity) intents of this conflict and its consequent effect on the socialization of its actors, we look in this chapter for how the monotheistic identity resists the authority of the social body, rewrites the forces of desire production, and redefines the identity of, in the case of Yehud, the people already in the land resulting in a community socialized within the cultural framework of a monotheistic identity but weakly socialized within a corresponding framework of the social body. This chapter will also employ "discourse of class" as a heuristic device that understands the process of socialization or identity production in its analysis of the *golah* community in order to emphasize the nature of the community's relationship to the forces of production over which the *golah*-Yahwistic monotheistic identity assumes claim.

1. *Resistance and Separation as Processes in the Formation of Class Identity within Monotheism*

> It will be said there is nonetheless a class that rules and a class that is ruled, both defined by surplus value, the distinction between the flow of financing and the flow of income in wages.[5]

---

4. Schimmelfennig, "The Community Trap," 63.
5. Deleuze and Guattari, *Anti-Oedipus*, 254.

3. Socialization and Conflict

If we borrow the theoretical understanding of Deleuze and Guattari, in terms of materialist production and of an objective structure or form, there is only one class. "[I]t is the very notion of class, insofar as it designates the 'negative' of codes, that implies there is only one class."[6] And further, "The opposition is between the class and those who are outside the class."[7] It is difficult, therefore, to speak, as Mario Liverani does, of a "political class" and an "educated class" without glossing over the negative resistances that define "class" in a social-political body.[8] Class, to be clear, is not simply about one's location in a given social-economic hierarchy but about the *processes*, or "flows" as Deleuze and Guattari term it, that define one's position in that hierarchy of power.[9] Nor, as Deleuze and Guattari explain, is it about value as much as it is about the *production* of value and identity, the latter which is conditioned in part by the institutionalization of the former and the socialization of its actors in support of that institution.[10] Therefore it is appropriate to speak not only of position but of the processes of production (and consumption[11]) that hasten the institutionalization of identity and authority.[12] In addition, the accompanying forces of resistance and separation are those that identify and define the "class" in power; they are part of a social body's "discourses of class."[13] These discourses depict the formation of a social-economic hierarchy and the relevant distribution of agents[14] within that hierarchy. When we refer to "class" in Yehud, therefore, we speak less about any categorical position and more about the social-economic *production* of identity as an aspect of socialization—but an identity, in the case of the *golah* community, that was on the periphery of

---

6. Ibid., 255.
7. Ibid.
8. Liverani, *Israel's History*, 256.
9. Cf. Diane Reay, "Rethinking Social Class: Qualitative Perspectives on Class and Gender," *Sociology (Oxford)* 32, no. 2 (1998): 260.
10. Deleuze and Guattari, *Anti-Oedipus*, 254–56.
11. As Reay ("Rethinking Social Class," 262) writes, "Class relations are increasingly construction through patterns of consumption and their associated technologies of desire. Consumption no less than production is a classed and classifying process."
12. There are certainly two sides to the debate on whether class is an identifiable position or whether it is something more fluid. For an overview of this debate and the scholars that lines themselves on either side of it, see ibid.
13. Reay (ibid., 261–63) discusses in helpful detail what constitutes discourses of class and classlessness, the latter depending upon the existence of the former.
14. On the definition and function of social agents, see Bourdieu, *In Other Words*, 9–10.

power.[15] Consequently, monotheistic resistance to an already institutionalized order and its focus on rewriting the socialization process emphasizes the monotheistic belief in the superiority of divine law over the production of value within the social body.

If we consider the separation of the urban and rural spheres within the biblical texts as symptomatic of a contest over a centralized, legitimated authority, then, for instance, the material bases for Ezra–Nehemiah's focus on the separation between member and non-member can be made clearer. Jerusalem's walls, as both metaphor and reality, portray the contest, or resistance, between the monotheistic (*golah*) community and the larger social body. This contest is inculcated within their construction, because though a seemingly arbitrary act their delineation of space presents a divine claim over property. And to be sure, private property is a variable that must be considered in any discussion of class and identity. It is, for reference, upon the basis of private property as authority over the forces of production, that Deleuze and Guattari, drawing in part from Marx, situate their understanding of class distinction. "Private property as private property, as wealth, *is compelled to preserve its own existence and thereby the existence of its opposite…*"[16]

It is in that, the simultaneous affirmation and revision of social-political identity that we find the identity of the *am ha'aretz* as articulated by the *golah* community. The community, as does the monotheistic identity generally, attempts to "deterritorialize" the social body by "de-identifying" it—that is, by removing from it the domain of production and the force of authority by creating a new order in which the social body comprises at most weakly socialized actors in relation to the prevailing monotheistic identity.

Along these lines, the text of Jeremiah contributes to an overall sense of the production of class identity by emphasizing "internal" and "external" forces of production when he states, "But Nebuzaradan the captain of the guard left some of the poorest people of the land to be vinedressers and tillers of the soil" (52:16). Those left in the land were commissioned, the text charges, to care for the land. But doing so was not for their own benefit, as their identity had already been limited to the "poorest people of the land."[17] Moreover, their rejection from attaining

---

15. Again, note that I am using heuristically *golah* as a class or identity reference as defined in Cataldo, "The Crippled *Ummah*."

16. Marx, "Alienation and Social Classes," 133, emphasis mine.

17. The statement in Jeremiah goes along with the prophet's gesture of burying a land deed, as Carroll ("Textual Strategies," 113–16) has already convincingly demonstrated.

"private property" left them at the mercy of the "rightful" landowners, for whom they were left to serve.[18] Hope in the belief that Yahweh would maintain the distributed relations that form the backbone of private property prompted Jeremiah to buy land from his cousin, "Thus says the LORD of hosts, the God of Israel: Take these deeds, both this sealed deed of purchase and this open deed, and put them in an earthenware jar, in order that they may last for a long time. For thus says the LORD of hosts, the God of Israel: Houses and fields and vineyards shall again be bought in this land" (32:14–15; see also the broader context in vv. 6–25).

Like the text of Jeremiah, the text of Ezekiel (33:23–25, 29) advocates preemptive action on the issue of land ownership: "The word of the LORD came to me: Mortal, the inhabitants of these waste places in the land of Israel keep saying, 'Abraham was only one man, yet he got possession of the land; but we are many; the land is surely given us to possess.' Therefore say to them, Thus says the Lord GOD: You eat flesh with the blood, and lift up your eyes to your idols, and shed blood; shall you then possess the land?... [T]hey shall know that I am the LORD, when I have made the land a desolation and a waste because of all their abominations that they have committed." Those who had not endured geospatial displacement, who had instead remained in the land, had been rejected by divine authority and must be treated appropriately.[19] Yahweh, according to Ezekiel, had chosen in the Babylonian Judeans a remnant, whose own identity was linked to the privatization of the land.[20] Those who had not been displaced were considered profane, or having an identity no longer linked to the land or to divine favor—thus, they were without legitimate claim to the land.[21]

---

18. The "poorest" of the land, who are lumped into the *am ha'aretz*, must, for the *golah* worldview to be considered legitimate, accept their own "de-facing" to emphasize the face of the "remnant" community. And note how the concept of remnant is played by the authors against the body of the *am ha'aretz*. The community is considered that which is preservable and identifiable, but that is an identity that can only be maintained before the faceless body of the *am ha'aretz*. Or, in the vocabulary of Marx (cf. "Alienation and Social Classes," 133), the *am ha'aretz* are alienated and identified only as other because, according to certain biblical texts, their contribution to the productive forces confirms the identity of the *golah* community as the divinely chosen remnant.

19. As Galambush (*This Land Is My Land*, 75) has pointed out, the restoration of the community in Ezekiel entails the elimination of "wild animals" from within and around the community and land.

20. Cf. ibid., 90–91.

21. Note also, "As I live, says the Lord GOD, surely with a mighty hand and an outstretched arm, and with wrath poured out, I will be king over you. I will bring you out from the peoples and gather you out of the countries where you are

This "de-facing" of the other to inscribe the identity of the self is similar to the manner in which class division is "a process of identity"—one that is defined from the perspective of a ruling class.[22] As an expression of the monotheistic identity, the Persian-period biblical texts sought to establish and legitimate divine authority over the social body. And so our question must again be: Against whom or what were their

> scattered, with a mighty hand and an outstretched arm, and with wrath poured out; and I will bring you into the wilderness of the peoples, and there I will enter into judgment with you face to face. As I entered into judgment with you ancestors in the wilderness of the land of Egypt, so I will enter into judgment with you, says the Lord GOD" (Ezek 20:33–36). In terms of shifting patterns of identity, D. N. Freedman argues that in Ezekiel Israel is no longer a witness for Yahweh but evidence of the deity: "It was during the years after the exile that Yahwism again became a religion based on a story, not bound to any human institution other than the community of those who heard that story and were gladdened in their bones" ("Son of Man, Can These Bones Live?," *Interpretation* 29 [1975]: 181). The role of narrative in the formation of cultural identity is certainly a valid point (see Elinor Ochs and Lisa Capps, "Narrating the Self," *Annual Reviews in Anthropology* 25 [1996]: 19–43), but the primacy to which Freedman seems to give narrative is somewhat problematic. Narrative was both an expressed and expressing ideology but it alone cannot bear the weight of maintaining a religion. For a comparative example one might look at the *ummah* in Medina during Muhammad's lifetime (for further discussion see [Cataldo, "The Crippled *Ummah*"). Primarily this was a social collective defined by a common creed or faith, the essence of which is shared (similar) to "moral of the story" for the Babylonian exiles. Yet it depended upon human institutions, despite its religious appeals, namely, those produced by the economic and political spheres. Story, narrative, creed, or ideology alone cannot maintain the rigorous demands of preserving a social collective. Because it is a form of cultural memory (an argument Philip R. Davies makes at length of the biblical texts, but see *Memories of Ancient Israel: An Introduction to Biblical History—Ancient and Modern* [Louisville: Westminster John Knox, 2008], 146), and memory is definition by looking at the past (cf. Kenneth H. Tucker, *Classical Sociological Theory: A Contemporary Approach* [Malden: Blackwell, 2002], 27), who writes that narratives "formulate the idea of a distinctive national past"), it must have an anchor of response in the material, human institutions of society. In other words, narratives function as responses to physical, social and economic situations (cf., in his analysis of the Marxist method, Roland Boer, *Jameson and Jeroboam* [Atlanta: Scholars Press, 1996], 1). Or, to use D. Schiffrin's ("Narrative as Self-Portrait: Sociolinguistic Constructions of Identity," *Language in Society* 25, no. 2 [1996]: 170) description, "The way we tell our stories also reveals a self that exists within a cultural matrix of meanings, beliefs, and normative practices."

> 22. Cf. Marx's description ("Alienation and Social Classes," 133–35) of the proletariat as a "destructive" class due to its legitimating of its position imposed upon it by the bourgeois (or ruling class, shown by its control of private property and material production).

authors reacting? Theirs are texts written in resistance to an already institutionalized authority. That is, the *golah* community immigrated into a province whose social body was already divided according to a distribution of economic relations. And it is likely that the *golah* community could have fully integrated into the preexisting social order—in fact, Ezra–Nehemiah suggests that some did (cf. Ezra 10:10, 18, 44), which implies also that the *golah* ideology as expressed in the biblical texts was not shared by even all members of the immigrant community.[23] The existing reality that produced the strongly felt need to separate in resistance, to exclude, was the presence of people in the land, as representation of an already existing institutionalized authority.[24]

a. *Economy as a Productive Force in Rewriting Class Identity as Religious Identity*

> When the people heard the law, they separated from Israel all those of foreign descent. Now before this, the priest Eliashib, who was appointed over the chambers of the house of our God, and who was related to Tobiah, prepared for Tobiah a large room where they had previously put the grain offering, the frankincense, the vessels, and the tithes of grain, wine, and oil, which were given by commandment to the Levites, singers, and gatekeepers, and the contributions for the priests. While this was taking place I was not in Jerusalem... (Neh 13:3–6)

---

23. Liverani's observation (*Israel's History*, 270) of the community's use of Yahwistic religious traditions is noteworthy here: "The 'oaths' or 'promises' of Yahweh to Abraham and then Moses correspond, at the mythical level, to the legal function of the edicts of the Persian emperors: they provide legitimation for the return and bestow entitlement of property to the land. But at the practical level, the actual return of exiles and their takeover of Palestine required another model. The patriarchal traditions could be used by the returnees as a prefiguration of their presence in the country; but the remainees could equally appeal to them as a model of coexistence between complementary groups. These stories offered the returnees a 'weak' yet realistic model of return: in small groups, without direct conflict, by agreement with the residents and surrounding peoples, sharing the land and its resources. The traditions of the conquest offer a 'strong' model, preferred by the supporters of violent confrontation and of the exclusion of 'extraneous' people. These were logically (or at least narratively) connected to the 'exit from Egypt' that marked the liberation of the people from slavery in a foreign land."

24. There is certainly a confirmation of this general human tendency in socialization and its concomitant production of identity found in Miroslav Volf's observation (*Exclusion and Embrace: A Theological Exploration of Identity, Otherness, and Reconciliation* [Nashville: Abingdon, 1996], 78): "We exclude because we want to be at the center and be there alone, single-handedly controlling 'the land.'"

Despite vociferous protest of intermarriage in Ezra–Nehemiah, the practice does not seem to have been uncommon.[25] Members of the immigrating *golah* community appear well enough to have married "foreign" women (cf. Ezra 10:18–44), though "foreign" is a problematic term here. Its use by the author inverts the traditional model of internal-versus-external space as a component in defining identity. If there was any social-political "native" to the internal space of Yehud it was the so-called *am ha'aretz*. The *golah* community, on the other hand, moved inwardly from "outside" this space. Nevertheless, the text inverts the spatial positioning of the groups (categories it itself has defined) making the *golah* community internal, thus "native," to the land by virtue of divine election and a desire to force out all others (cf. Ezra 10:2–5).

That Ezra–Nehemiah defines this social division based on a particular religious perspective should make us somewhat suspicious. It says next to nothing about the state of the economy within the province, leaving us to grasp at offered threads that when pulled seemingly lead back to religion. Its presentation of society is that society is but a facet of religion, as though a tent to be raised when the community has found a suitable space. Its author treats society not as a social world full of acting and interacting agents who produce culture, surplus, even religion, but a religious world, a framed portrait even, in contrast to a space of infinite possibility, wherein agents are strategically distributed and categorized by the divine. Class within this ideological frame is not defined according to systems of relation and distribution of power and material production (surplus) but according to whom the authors *perceive* to have been divinely selected.

Textual silence regarding provincial economy should not go unnoticed, especially as it is one reason why some scholars have hastily proposed a "temple economy" for Yehud.[26] Grain seems to have been an economic mainstay for the province.[27] And it is possible, as Joachim Schaper proposes, for its economic distribution to have been centered in a

---

25. As noted by Cross, "Reconstruction," 6; Smith, *Palestinian Parties*, 65; Ahlström, *The History of Ancient Palestine*, 861; Fried, *Priest and the Great King*, 211; VanderKam, *From Joshua to Caiaphas*, 53–54.

26. Notably Weinberg in *Citizen-Temple Community*.

27. Carter, *Emergence of Yehud*, 255–56; Edelman, *The Origins of the 'Second' Temple*, 321; Oded Lipschits, *The Fall and Rise of Jerusalem: The History of Judah Under Babylonian Rule* (Winona Lake, Ind.: Eisenbrauns, 2005), 212–61; Oded Lipschits, "Achaemenid Imperial Policy, Settlement Processes in Palestine, and the Status of Jerusalem in the Middle of the Fifth Century B.C.E.," in Lipschits and Oeming, eds., *Judah and the Judeans in the Persian Period*, 24.

temple.[28] But that a date for the Jerusalem temple's completion remains elusive threatens any longed for certainty in our understanding of the province's economic system. Moreover, we should note that when temples were used as distribution centers under the Babylonian and Persian empires, the imperial governments typically stationed an imperial representative, who answered to the king and not the religious authority, within the temple.[29] As Schaper writes, "Concerning those taxes which the temples collected for and passed on to the Persian king and his administration, it must be stressed that the sanctuaries—among them the Jerusalem temple—merely acted as outlets of the imperial 'Inland Revenue.'"[30] One might see in this statement an analogy of a bank with the imperial capital city representing the "corporate office" while temples represented "branch" or "satellite" locations. With respect to provincial economy, in other words, temples did not act autonomously. They were answerable to and with in-flow and out-flow activities monitored by the imperial government through its imperial representative.[31] None of this, however, is mentioned by Ezra–Nehemiah.

In fact, economic issues are relegated as being secondary to religious obedience.[32] "In those days," writes Nehemiah (13:15–16), "I saw in Judah people treading wine presses on the sabbath, and bringing in heaps of grain and loading them on donkeys; and also wine, grapes, figs, and

---

28. Schaper, "Temple Treasury Committee," 200–206. Note also that Edelman (in *The Origins of the 'Second' Temple*) has recently argued at length that the temple was built during the reign of Artaxerxes I.

29. Cf. Stolper, *Entrepreneurs and Empire*, 43–44; Schaper, "Jerusalem Temple," 529; Fried, *Priest and the Great King*, 9–11.

30. Schaper, "Jerusalem Temple," 539.

31. L. Fried makes a similar argument in "The ʿam hāʾāreṣ in Ezra 4:4," in Lipschits and Oeming, eds., *Judah and the Judeans in the Persian Period*, 137–41.

32. Where, for instance, is any text mentioning daily economic transactions in the province (or even in Yehud) similar to those found in Babylonian al-Yahudu? Cf. F. Joannès and André Lemaire, "Trois Tablettes cunéiformes à l'Onomastique Ouest-Sémitique," *Transeuphratene* 17 (1999): 17–33; Laurie Pearce, "New Evidence for Jews in Babylonia," in Lipschits and Oeming, eds., *Judah and the Judeans in the Persian Period*, 399–411. The evidence of Judeans engaging in everyday economic activities suggests they had fully integrated into Babylonian economic society (see also Cataldo, *A Theocratic Yehud*, 72–73). Does the lack of a similar corpus of evidence or discussion of similar activities in the biblical texts suggest the *golah* community as a whole had not fully assimilated? On a related note, and in some agreement with Becking ("Critical Notes," 11–12), more and more evidence of permanent Judean settlements is turning up suggesting that the number of Judeans who returned to Judah was actually small. This would further confirm the hypothesis that the *golah* community as a minority among the inhabitants of Yehud.

all kinds of burdens, which they brought into Jerusalem on the sabbath day; and I warned them against selling food. Tyrians also, who lived in the city, brought in fish and all kinds of merchandise and sold them on the sabbath to the people of Judah, and in Jerusalem." While referencing the materiality of the city's economy, the text seems instead more concerned with the buying and selling of food to and by Judeans, those who are religiously proscribed to "Remember the sabbath day, and keep it holy" (Exod 20:8).

How does this offer anything informative about a definition of class? Scholars who argue that imperial representatives had no real power in Yehud, and that power was in the hands of the *golah* community leaders, must do so by either accepting that religious ideology provided the fundamental basis for economic division and distribution of power or by disregarding economy altogether and compartmentalizing economy into religious categories. In addition, they must accept that it was from the religious culture of the *golah* community that came the forces of socialization for the people already in the land. In short, they must make religious ideology the productive source of class identity and its underlying distribution of authority.

Nehemiah contains another economic mention. During a time of famine there was a "great outcry" of "the people and of their wives against their Jewish kin" (5:1). It is a classic glimpse of the role of surplus production in its attention to a basic social need. To survive, surplus enough to pay taxes and feed one's family must be produced within the context of Nehemiah. There must have been a dramatic eagerness on the part of some to assert themselves (and their statuses) as members of an aristocratic class. In the process, it was the people who supported "class" through their labor, from whom "class" was validated, who produced the material product from which power and authority were bled. "Social classes may be said to exist whenever one social group is able to appropriate a part of the surplus labor product of other groups. In such a situation of exploitation, wealth and power accrue disproportionately to those who are able to claim and dispose of what others produce."[33] The distribution of economic-based power relations always contains oppression.[34] The basic social unit, as Aristotle (*Pol.* 1.1252a) once described the family, was no longer bound by sentiment or any group feeling. Kinship and loyalty, those things that once bound tribes together, had

---

33. Norman K. Gottwald, "Social Class as an Analytic and Hermeneutical Category in Biblical Studies," *JBL* 112, no. 1 (1993): 4.

34. When oppression is defined as a mechanism of control over access to power (cf. Foucault, *Discipline and Punish*, 170–77).

been replaced by the cold, functional gears of, in the words of Deleuze and Guattari, a surplus producing machine. The text of Nehemiah obliquely admits to a larger economic field than it is either fully conscious of or one to which it would admit. Furthermore, a sustained analysis of the social-political environment in Yehud reveals that the *golah* community did not have all economic means at its disposal to assert its position as a landed aristocracy. The community, in the face of economic breakdown, threatens internal dissolution: "We are having to pledge our fields, our vineyards, and our houses in order to get grain during the famine... We are having to borrow money on our fields and vineyards to pay the king's tax" (Neh 5:3–4). What else can be concluded here than the very tale repeated throughout the history of urban societies and the greedy consumption of private property? Wealthy large-land owners buy the lands of smaller landowners who cannot afford to pay all required taxes—note these are not temple taxes!—and still put food on the table.[35]

Nehemiah's appeal (Neh 5:4–5) to kinship in economic hardship is interesting. Economic distribution of and the buying up of land does not reflect a kinship-based society whose economy is based on communal

---

35. The same social-economic breakdown has occurred in nearly every urban-based society. In Egypt, for corresponding example, "the creditor could inflict every kind of indignity and torture upon the body of the debtor; for example, cut from it as much as seemed commensurate with the size of the debt... I consider it as an advance, as evidence of a freer, more generous, *more Roman* conception of law when the Twelve Tables of Rome decreed it a matter of indifference how much or how little the creditor cut off..."(Friedrich Wilhelm Nietzsche, *On the Genealogy of Morals; Ecce Homo* [trans. Walter Arnold Kaufmann and R. J. Hollingdale; New York: Vintage, 1989], 64) Rome's fall, according to some ancient historians, was due in large part to the rapid urbanization brought on by displaced free citizens who were forced to sell their lands and were rejected from paying jobs because of the society's large dependence upon slavery. Latifundialization changed radically surplus production but the Roman social body was left without a free working class base to support the newer economy. As Pliny railed, "*Verumque confitentibus latifundia perdidere italiam, iam vero et provincias*" (*Historia Naturalis* [T. Mayhoff] 18.11). And Seneca warned, "How far will you extend the bounds of your possessions? A large tract of land, sufficient heretofore for a whole nation, is scarce wide enough for a single lord" (*Epistles* 89). In Yehud we may see a similar idea, though to a lesser degree: "And there were those who said, 'We are having to borrow money on our fields and vineyards to pay the king's tax. Now our flesh is the same as that of our kindred; our children are the same as their children; and yet we are forcing our sons and daughters to be slaves, and some of our daughters have been ravished; we are powerless, and our fields and vineyards now belong to others'" (Neh 5:4–5).

ownership. Cities or towns[36] are not polities organized by kinship principles but by a group feeling[37] that determines the quality of the social-political body and the distribution of power. The economic forces of the city are bound together by laws regulating and maintaining production, the distribution of power, and social-economic relations. So the appeal from a group that was undoubtedly urban by definition of its collective identity leaves little room but to interpret the outcry as both an appeal to utopia and a feeling of disenfranchisement.[38] If we take the text of Nehemiah at face value, the appeal worked. Nehemiah chastises the nobles and officials and calls a "great assembly" against them (Neh 5:7). There seems little doubt the purpose of this assembly was to manipulate a desired response. During the assembly Nehemiah accuses these of "getting into bed" with the enemies of the *golah* community and of being religiously disobedient: "The thing that you are doing is not good. Should you not walk in the fear of our God, to prevent the taunts of the nations of our enemies?" (v. 9). To set an example, Nehemiah states he and his "brothers" (5:10; most likely subordinate officials) have been providing loans without interest to those who were in need. But even this must be a reflection of the narrator's ideal (or self-aggrandizing on the part of Nehemiah) because it has the governor of the province working within the religious framework of *golah* Yahwism, the religion of a

---

36. M. P. O'Connor ("The Biblical Notion of the City," in *Constructions of Space II: The Biblical City and Other Imagined Spaces* [ed. Jon L. Berquist and Claudia V. Camp; LHBOTS 490; New York: T&T Clark International, 2008], 18–39) makes an interesting argument that biblical scholars often confuse the terms "city" and "town" when translating various terms from Hebrew that refer, for lack of a better phrase, to urban developments. He writes, for example, "The scholarly treatment of the biblical city is confused, I have argued, for a variety of reasons; this confusion is most manifest in the plethora of works intended for the general reader. The confusion is not, however, limited to those works. Two competing accounts of the biblical city, the literary-theological and the archaeological, have made difficult a reading of the biblical evidence informed by historical and philological approaches… One way out of the impasse sketched here involved acknowledging that the usage of English 'city' in the Bible is not an ordinary part of English usage. Biblical English 'city' is a calque, a term that transfers into another language the range of meanings and associations found in the source language" (ibid., 34).

37. "Group feeling" as Ibn Khaldun defines it (cf. *Muqaddimah*, 1:414, 428).

38. It seems to appeal to the religious agrarian tradition of the exodus in which the Hebrews were "family," with each tribe positioned metaphorically around Yahweh: "The Israelites shall camp each in their respective regiments, under ensigns by their ancestral houses; they shall camp facing the tent of meeting on every side" (Num 2:2).

provincial minority.³⁹ And in this seemingly utopian vision what other result can there be than this, "We will restore everything and demand nothing more from them. We will do as you say" (Neh 5:12)?

From an economic standpoint, Nehemiah should have had no issue with the buying and selling of land. Within the Persian imperial system land was a fundamental unit of economic value. Pierre Briant, for related example, writes,

> Aux yeux des auteurs grecs, en effet, le système tributaire est fondé sur une gigantesque appropriation des terres et des hommes, via les productions que les paysans réalisent par leur travail. C'est là une vision développée avec une pariculière faveur par Xénophon, qui insiste à de nombreuses reprises sur les droits illimités du vainqueur sur les gens et les choses. *Il est clair que, du point de vue de l'idéologie impériale achéménide elle-même, es terres conquises relèvent de l'autorité royale, sans exception aucune: c'est une telle réalité dont rend compte le term* būmi.⁴⁰

Within the imperial system, land was a basic economic component of any value and exchange systems.⁴¹ And all land became the de facto property of the imperial government upon conquest. While local territories maintained their local economies, these economies must be consistent with the imperial economic system. In other words, it seems somewhat questionable that an imperial representative whose loyalty was to the imperial government would risk the ire of nobles and officials and any "king's eyes and ears" among them.⁴² The macroeconomic benefit of debt relief is not in question here, especially in our pursuit of a structural model, but the broadly indiscriminate, or unconditional, return of private property is.⁴³ It is one thing to have relief in one's debt. It is quite another

---

39. Fried (*Priest and the Great King*, 210) observes similarly that the actions described in Neh 5 reflect an attempt to position a strong free peasantry against a landed aristocracy.

40. Pierre Briant, *Histoire de l'Empire perse: de Cyrus à Alexandre* (Paris: Fayard, 1998), 427, emphasis mine.

41. In fact, S. Hornblower goes so far as to say the Persian empire was feudal: "Feudalism is a system of loyalty in return for benefits, usually land. In that general sense Achaemenid Persia was feudal" (*The Greek World 479–323 BC* [New York: Routledge, 1991], 67, and see also 157–60). One might consider also Dandamaev and Lukonin, *Culture and Social Institutions*, 147–50, 194.

42. For more on the "king's eye," see Jack Martin Balcer, "The Athenian Episkopos and the Achaemenid 'King's Eye'," *AJP* 98 (1977): 252–63; Dandamaev and Lukonin, *Culture and Social Institutions*, 111; Hornblower, *Greek World*, 67–68; Fried, *Priest and the Great King*, 106.

43. Debt forgiveness can have a positive socioeconomic impact (as noted, for example, by Ariane De Bremond, "The Politics of Peace and Resettlement Through

to get everything back without having to repay one's debt. Thus, the picture presented implies the extension of funds by the upper classes and the consequent rising status of the smaller landowners. The latter live off the surpluses of the former and still retain their own economic holdings. Such a push for equalization does not reflect a context wherein the *golah* community was the aristocratic class—economic equality, whether in spiritual or material terms, between member and non-member is not consistent with the monotheistic identity.

Moreover, the wide-scale absolving of debts accompanied by the return of all (claimed) previously private properties may create more problems than it would solve.[44] It would interrupt, among other things, the distribution of power relations and surplus production. Herein we see economic equality as a possible threat to economic stability.[45] The utopian vision of a theocratic classless society—that is, there would exist no class division within the membership—becomes not the defender of any current existence but its revolutionary. It cries for change, but it knows only the end product and not how to get there. To see the process in motion, it appeals to Yahweh to bring about, to make good, the necessary change.[46] This dependence upon the divine suggests an appeal

---

El Salvador's Land Transfer Programme: Caught Between the State and the Market," *Third World Quarterly* 28, no. 8 [2007]: 1537–56). But compare this to W. Easterly's discussion ("Debt Relief," *Foreign policy* 127 [2001]: 20–26) of the problems of unconditional debt relief, though he focuses on a modern context, which is helpful in clarifying some of the structural and procedural problems of debt relief.

44. Again, see Easterly's discussion (ibid.) emphasizing structural issues of debt relief.

45. But note also that, as M. A. Dandamayev notes, there are a number of documents from the Murashu Archive (second half of the fifth century in the Nippur region) that attest to debt exploitation in which the Murashus and their agents confiscated all movable property of their debtors. "It must be said, however, that such actions were illegal, and, in a number of cases, the Murashus had to restore the harm caused by them" ("Achaemenid Imperial Policies and Provincial Governments," *Iranica Antiqua* 34 [1999]: 276). While it may be tempting to draw a parallel between that event and what is described in Ezra–Nehemiah, the protests recorded in the latter do not express any awareness of a legal transgression—one also cannot equate the return of movable property with a hypothetical return of children. Moreover, what is described in the Murashu Archive is not a whole-scale absolving of debts, which Ezra–Nehemiah wants to see, but the correction of exploitation above and beyond the normal credit–debt system.

46. Can we get around comparing this *golah* ideology with Esposito and De Long-Bas's analysis of Islam, "[B]eing a Muslim has been not just a matter of belonging to a community of fellow believers, but also to live in an Islamic community or state governed by Islamic law (in theory if not always in practice). *In this*

to a power greater than the "obstacle" the community cannot remove; it appeals to an authority that is in direct contest with the naturally produced political authority. This vision is partly responsible for the lack of materials testifying to the daily, local activities of economic exchange in the province.[47] It focuses on what Yahweh will do, not on what the people will do. Dependence upon the divine as aristocratic protector of and provider for the community is characteristic across monotheistic identities. This dependence ultimately frames the religious community's perception of the monotheistic body or God.[48]

Common to economies under the Neo-Assyrian, Neo-Babylonian, and Persian empires was a dependence upon the private household for tax income, out of which it maintained its official staff and army.[49] The substance of the response in Nehemiah (noted above), if we look at it without obligation to any religious framework, might reflect a concern for the sustainability of this model. The greater the amount of free, working small-landowners the greater the amount of taxable income. And the less that a local economy is centralized in the hands of an aristocratic elite, the better able the imperial official is to govern the social-political body and defend against bids for power made by a landed elite.[50] Local recognition of this idea, however, only comes after the economic situation has lent itself to significant class division, creating a

---

utopian vision of the Islamic state, political authority is understood to be the instrument for carrying out the divine message. Sovereignty, therefore, is the embodiment of the Word of God in the Shariah (Islamic law), rather than a power that belongs to the ruler or the clergy" ("Classical Islam," 138, emphasis mine).

47. This lack is not unique to studies of Persian-period Yehud. M. Van de Mieroop (*The Ancient Mesopotamian City* [Oxford: Oxford University Press, 1997], 13–19) notes this is also common among the available evidence from Mesopotamian cities.

48. This is true of even more recent forms of monotheism. For example, dependence is defined in both positive and negatives senses in post-Shoah Judaism. To note, "(Divine) withdrawal or contraction, at the time of creation, produces the evil side or evil face of G-d in the world. G-d emerges as a presence who is unjust and an abuser in relation to human beings whom G-d has created and who are dependent upon G-d. Just as victims of abuse must learn to stand up to the abuser and ultimately to forgive the abuser in order to reintegrate themselves and place their own lives back in order, so Jews must learn to forgive the abusive G-d, not because G-d deserves it in any way, but because such forgiveness of the abuser is the necessary precondition for the recovery of the victim of abuse" (Marvin A. Sweeney, *Reading the Hebrew Bible After the Shoah: Engaging Holocaust Theology* [Minneapolis: Fortress, 2008], 16).

49. Cf. Dandamayev, "Achaemenid Imperial Policies," 269.

50. Examples of this can be found throughout history from, for example, the Roman empire to various dynasties in East Asia (e.g. Han, Ming).

framework in which large landowners have largely begun acquiring the holdings of small landowners, either creating a new class of landless poor or increasing the social body's social-economic dependence upon slavery. While the passage in Nehemiah can be read to reflect this real economic concern, its being situated by the author within an almost wholly religious framework is problematic. It is difficult to conclude that a landed aristocracy gave up a large basis of its power because it felt obligated to obey the religious law of an immigrating community.

Moreover, we need not argue for a monolithic royal economy preceding the Persian empire to conclude that local economies needed to integrate into an imperial economic system.[51] And even if we conclude that the socioeconomic structures under the Persian empire were diverse, as M. Dandamayev does (though he tends to see in this a rationale for an autonomy held by provinces),[52] we still must find in Yehud counterparts from the nations Israel and Judah. These "counterparts," or even stages in an evolutionary, social-political process, point not to a theocracy nor any economic system trapped within the framework of religion.[53] We cannot conclude as Dandamayev does that the high priests of the Jerusalem temple "gradually became the governors of the province."[54] Even he notes, "[E]ach province remained [a] socio-economic unity with its own social institutions, internal structure, *old local laws, customs, traditions, systems of weights and measures, and monetary systems*,"[55] none of which, regarding Yehud, traditionally included priestly political authority.[56] While we need not argue for the existence of a hegemonic

---

51. Dandamayev, for instance, writes, "But already during the period preceding the Persian conquest of Mesopotamia, the royal economy in Assyria and Babylonia had not occupied a large share of the economy of these [Mesopotamia, Elam, Syria] countries. In the first millennium an enormous royal economy would have been an anomalous phenomenon" (ibid.).
52. Ibid., 270.
53. For a larger discussion on this subject, see Cataldo, *A Theocratic Yehud*.
54. Dandamayev, "Achaemenid Imperial Policies," 273.
55. Ibid., 272 (emphasis mine).
56. The ingredients for a temple-centered province are not present in the social composition of the province, and proposing one requires the rejection of already extant functioning systems. The existence of a coin containing the name of a high priest, while notable, is not enough to prove high priests governed the province. And in saying this I am not dismissing the generally accepted, and plausible, conclusion that there is significance in having one's name inscribed upon a monetary unit. Yet as Dan P. Barag ("Some Notes on a Silver Coin of Johanan the High Priest," *BA* 48 [1985]: 166–68) observes of the silver coin inscribed "Yohanan, the priest," the coin contains "pagan" imagery. Thus, while the coin demands the heed of those paying

imperial economic system, sustained analysis shows that the imperial government created an administrative system whose first priority was loyalty to the imperial government.[57] While freedoms would have been permitted for local territories, they could only be conducted within the framework of this priority.

To sum up, the Persian-period biblical texts present an ideologically transmuted world. Positive descriptions are in many instances negatively perceived realities. For example, Ezra–Nehemiah describes a social context in which all foreigners are driven out (of families and communal engagements). To take this text in a positive fashion would be to accept simultaneously a society whose body was comprised of the *golah* community alone. It is also to assume that the community had the material means to sustain itself as a unique society, that it was able to dictate and control economic forces which would define its collective identity. The text of Nehemiah admits that foreigners continued to live and engage in economic transactions (thus, the material production of the society): "Tyrians also, who lived in the city, brought in fish and all kinds of merchandise and sold them on the sabbath to the people of Judah, and in Jerusalem" (Neh 13:16). There, in this whispered observation, is a partial economic description: in Jerusalem some form of market economy seems to have existed. Yet the author writes not from the perspective of one in control over the economy, who not only enjoyed the fruits of surplus produced by others, but as one having the ability to control material production. Instead, he writes from the position of one who sits just outside authority, appealing to the divine for legitimation of the social-economic claims being made. As a brief example, we note: "Then I remonstrated with the nobles of Judah and said to them, 'What is this evil thing that you are doing, profaning the sabbath day? Did not your ancestors act in this way, and did not our God bring all this disaster on us

---

attention to economic exchange and suggests the priest held some amount of secular economic power, it is not a coin that would be consistent with imagery permitted within religious law of *golah* Yahwism. In addition, it should be noted this coin was found among others inscribed *yhzqyh hphh*, which can be dated to around the same period (see Uriel Rappaport, "The First Judean Coinage," *Journal of Jewish Studies* 32 [1981]: 6–7). N. Avigad (*Bullae and Seals from a Post-Exilic Judean Archive* (Qedem 4; Jerusalem: Hebrew University, 1976], 35) dates the small, silver *yhzqyh* coins to about 330 B.C.E. His association of the name with a 66-year-old priest mentioned in Josephus (*C. Ap.* 1.187–89) is dubious. Rappaport ("Judean Coinage," 16) and VanderKam (*From Joshua to Caiaphas*, 118), by contrast, have shown that the Persian imperial government did not generally give the offices of governor and high priest to the same person.

57. See the larger argument in Cataldo, *A Theocratic Yehud*, 33–66.

and on this city? Yet you bring more wrath on Israel by profaning the sabbath'" (Neh 13:17–18). Here we must read the inferred separation. If the nobles of Judah were thought to be members of the *golah* community then their engagement with the social-economic systems of the province outside the parameters of any *golah*-Yahwistic law shows that not all members of the community were of equal mind. On the contrary, these seem, as the text infers, to have recognized their position as an immigrant community and integrated themselves into the already functioning social-economic system.[58] The passage, especially within the larger frame of Neh 13, appeals to an ideal reality that attests to a social context thriving but restricted within a religious framework. In this reality, aristocratic nobles accept that they are powerless before the divine and those who represent the divine. This speaks to the large-scale divorce the text of Ezra describes (Ezra 10:1–14). While such an event seems to reflect more a utopian ideal than an actuality, it exemplifies the framework within which the author is working. It also obliquely acknowledges that members of the community intermarried with aristocratic families in the province to advance their own standing.

Rejection of intermarriage seems also to reflect an ideological confrontation on several fronts. This may certainly reflect, as Douglas argues, a strong xenophobia, but it seems also to have a strong material basis,[59] specifically as an issue of land ownership.[60] Land as we have already noted represents the source of surplus production, it was fundamentally the material basis for the distributed relations of power and economic exchange. As an immigrating community, any claim to the land made by the *golah* was subject to rejection by those already in the land, the latter having already established socially and economically legitimated claims of ownership over it. This again explains the appeal to religion by the community, to the divine to create utopia, or a new normative order. By subjecting all aspects of society to religion, by revising the forces of production, so the very idealistic theory goes, social-economic authority would be in the hands of the *golah* community. And the monotheistic body would secure its authority over the social

---

58. Based on the work of Josephus, Smith (*Palestinian Parties*, 65) states many Yahwist priests were involved in intermarriage and that this reflects what was a common state of affairs. See also Phyllis Trible, *Texts of Terror: Literary-Feminist Readings of Biblical Narratives* (Philadelphia: Fortress, 1984), 6; Ahlström, *The History of Ancient Palestine*, 861; VanderKam, *From Joshua to Caiaphas*, 53–54.

59. See Mary Douglas, "Responding to Ezra: The Priests and the Foreign Wives," *Biblical Interpretation* 10 (2002): 1–23.

60. See also Tamara Cohn Eskenazi, *Ezra–Nehemiah* (exp. ed. with Apocrypha; Women's Bible Commentary; Louisville: Westminster John Knox, 1998), 24.

body. It is toward that event, which is an aspect of restoration, that a monotheistic identity rewrites notions of class identity—socializing its members accordingly—in support of its own members by appealing to the divine as the stable economic force behind production.

b. *Rewriting Production as a Divine Activity*
The concept of "remnant" is a cornerstone of the *golah* community's claim over production within the context of Yehud. Its foundation rests on a systematization of society into two overly simplified, religiously defined categories. "'What do you see, Jeremiah?' I said, 'Figs'... Thus says the LORD, the God of Israel: Like these good figs, so I will regard as good the exiles from Judah, whom I have sent away from this place to the land of the Chaldeans" (Jer 29:3, 5). And the "bad figs"? "I will make them a horror, an evil thing, to all the kingdoms of the earth—a disgrace, a byword, a taunt, and a curse in all the places where I shall drive them. And I will send sword, famine, and pestilence upon them, until they are utterly destroyed from the land that I gave to them and their ancestors" (Jer 24:9–10).[61] This dichotomy Ezra–Nehemiah shares.

The passage from Jeremiah, and we find similar in Ezra–Nehemiah and Isaiah, emphasizes a divine restructuring of the social order. Any sense of class or other identity must, according to these authors, begin there. As Ezra's prayer (9:5–15) suggests, the remnant community waits passively for the surplus-producing actions of the divine—actions that are contingent upon obedience to the divine law. Third Isaiah also emphasizes divine control over surplus production when he puts expectantly in the mouth of Yahweh, "I will extend prosperity to her like a river, and the wealth of the nations like an overflowing stream; and you shall nurse and be carried on her arm, and dandled on her knees" (66:12). It is a utopian view of a covenantal relationship that assumes divine control over surplus production, which is itself a productive force acting upon class identity. Isaiah's insistence on prosperity in addition to the preservation of life, for example, emphasizes divine control over material production and divine intent for the remnant to be the direct beneficiary.[62]

---

61. B. Porten ("Settlement of the Jews at Elephantine and the Arameans at Syene," in Lipschits and Blenkinsopp, eds., *Judah and the Judeans in the Neo-Babylonian Period*, 457) agrees that Jeremiah's allegory of the good and bad figs refers to the Judean exiles and those Judeans who remained in the land, respectively.

62. This is consistent with the scholarly view, as expressed by J. McKenzie (*Second Isaiah* [AB 20; New York: Doubleday, 1968], 209), that the community which benefits from divine action is the "pious poor." Existing on the negative side of a class division, the community waits for a restoration of social-economic order in which the community's negative position becomes a positive one: "The prophet

This "remnant" ideology is based on a redefinition of social-economic order and a corresponding reorientation of political space, in which the city of Jerusalem and its temple are the axis.[63] This statement finds agreement with Liverani, who writes, "The returnees, during their exile, had built up a 'strong' ideology, based on the new covenant, on Yahweh's exclusiveness, on the 'remnant that shall return'" (*shear-jashub* is the name given by Isaiah to his son: Isa 7:3; see 10:21).[64] From this described ideology are found foundations upon which the divine may construct a (utopian) society. Such "foundations" create a social organization in which one is only considered a legitimate member by being one of the Babylonian diaspora—a rather restrictive and exclusive claim, to be sure.[65] The consuming focus of Ezra–Nehemiah, for example, on the city of Jerusalem shows that the return of the remnant cannot be considered complete until the city is itself restored: "Any of those among you who are of his people—may their God be with them!—are now permitted to go up to Jerusalem in Judah, and rebuild the house of the LORD, the God of Israel—he is the God who is in Jerusalem" (Ezra 1:3).

But, and we must ask this with some concern—especially when dealing with surplus or desire production—what *type* or *function* of city,

---

is sure that the saving act will come suddenly; it is like conception and birth in a single day. The saving act means the sudden appearance of a large number of true Israelites; this again suggests that the prophet and his followers formed a minority" (ibid.). In addition, in Isaiah's words regarding prosperity can we not hear an echo of Thomas More: "[I]n Utopia…*no one doubts, provided only that the public granaries are well filled, that the individual will lack nothing for his private use*" (*Utopia* [Yale ed. of the Complete Works of St. Thomas More 4; New Haven: Yale University Press, 1965], 239, emphasis mine)?

63. J. Wellhausen (*Prolegomena to the History of Israel* [Scholars Press Reprints and Translations Series; Atlanta: Scholars Press, 1994], 421) makes a similar observation: "So closely was the cultus of Jerusalem interwoven with the consciousness of the Jewish people, and so strongly had the priesthood established their order, that after the collapse of the kingdom the elements still survived here for the new formation of a 'congregation' answering to the circumstances and needs of the time. Around the ruined sanctuary the community once more lifted up its head (1 Kings viii.; Hagg. i. seq.; Zech. 1. seq.). The usages and ordinances were, though everywhere changed in detail, yet not created afresh. Whatever creating there was lay in this, that these usages were bound together in a system and made the instruments of restoring an organisation of 'the remnant.'"

64. Liverani, *Israel's History*, 256.

65. Bedford makes this similar observation (see "Diaspora," 153), though he will conclude differently that the land was empty and that those who remained in Babylon held, within imperial limits, authority over the "repatriates" in Yehud (cf. ibid., 156).

since this reveals something of the forces acting upon the collective social-political identity? When the biblical texts refer to the city of Jerusalem, how was it perceived? How do its characteristics reflect the city's mode of production?

To help answer those and similar questions, Michael Patrick O'Connor suggests there were three main types of cities within the ancient Near East, one of which likely accurately describes Jerusalem: bureaucratic, industrial, and ceremonial.[66] According to him the bureaucratic city is an administrative center for a region, the industrial type is a surplus capital (storing and producing), and the ceremonial city is a center for regulating "symbols that undergird and constitute a society."[67] If, as the relevant biblical texts suggest, the *golah* community represents the "center" of an urban space (also of power and authority), we must understand the nature of the space. Rather, we must understand the experiential and ideological function of material production as it defines that urban space. Yet, the general silence of biblical texts such as Ezra–Nehemiah, Haggai, and Zechariah on administrative (apart from forced divorce) and economic issues suggests that the authors did not have a bureaucratic or administrative model of city in mind. Imperial interest in Jerusalem as a center in Yehud would certainly have been a combination of these two models and not, in comparison, the ceremonial variant. On the other hand, the biblical authors seem to view Jerusalem with ceremonial intent. Yet the sluggardly pace in which the city and its temple seem to have been rebuilt in material space does not support any conclusion positing Jerusalem as a ceremonial center effectively regulating symbolic systems.[68]

A ceremonial vision for Jerusalem correlates with the monotheistic agenda of the *golah* community. The biblical allusion of the remnant to the "Hebrews of the wilderness" tradition illustrates, as Liverani puts it, "The extraordinary insistence on national self-identification though observance of a divinely-given law…and answers the precise needs of a nation lacking the normal geopolitical coordinates."[69] For the former, this insistence is on the desire for a *restored* nation, the blueprint for which the divine law provides, as it does also for the idealized Mosaic tradition. Divine law, with its focus on an exclusionary distinction

---

66. O'Connor, "The Biblical Notion of the City," 31–32.
67. Ibid., 32.
68. For an alternative opinion, Edelman (throughout her work in *The Origins of the 'Second' Temple*) presents a counterargument for a shorter time span in which the Jerusalem temple was rebuilt (thus, sixth century B.C.E. in the fourth year of Darius rather than some time during the fifth century B.C.E., as is generally accepted).
69. Liverani, *Israel's History*, 344.

between member and nonmember, facilitates in this situation the self-identification of the remnant as the citizenry of a future restored but presently utopian nation. But the charisma of Moses was for the *golah* community mechanically supplanted by the structured order of law (cf. Ezra 3:2). In other words, for the *golah* community there was no pre-urban formation of identity, and its allusion to the Mosaic tradition is in truth a fusion of an idealized pre-urban situation with its own desire for a restored nation. After all, a legal code inscribed upon a political body demands the existence of an *urban* polity that both legitimates codified law and supports the systems of relation through which power is distributed. And as Garbini suggests, the self-identification of the remnant with Israel employed a radical division between the members of the remnant and everyone else:

> In Achaemenidean Jerusalem a small group of those who had returned from the Babylonian exile considered themselves the only legitimate "remnant," not only of the kingdom of Judah which had disappeared but of the whole people of Israel. Jerusalem represented all the tribes because it considered itself, in polemic against the Israelites of Shechem, to be the sole people of God: a sacred people who had the mission of serving God in his temple and in his dwelling, Jerusalem.[70]

That the idea of remnant is first presented in Israel's so-called Ancestral Narratives (Gen 12–50) should not go unnoticed, even more so if we accept that either the Narratives were written during the Persian Period or that they were at least given then a final redaction.[71] In either scenario, the religious tradition reflects a nuanced perspective that lends itself easily to the situation in which the Babylonian diaspora found itself. The diaspora's collective religious *Weltenschauung* was framed by a belief that Yahweh preserves what Yahweh desires and that Yahweh manipulates political powers (should there be any surprise that these are almost always foreign?) to get what Yahweh wants—an idea that is consistent throughout the Hebrew Bible. For example, "God sent me before you to preserve for you a remnant on earth, and to keep alive for you many survivors. So it was not you who sent me here, but God; he has made me a father to Pharaoh, and lord of all his house and ruler over all the land of Egypt" (Gen 45:7–8). The reason? The Hebrews, as the story goes,

---

70. Garbini, *History and Ideology*, 126.
71. John Van Seters, *Prologue to History: The Yahwist as Historian in Genesis* (Louisville: Westminster John Knox, 1992), 250, 294.

would conquer Canaan (with the help of Yahweh) and establish a nation. Compare for instance 1 Chr 4:43, "they destroyed the remnant of the Amalekites that had escaped, and they lived there to this day," a statement meant to indicate continued obedience to divine will in routing out the "foreign" from the "Promised Land." And even in this we have a parallel to the *golah* community. Ezra–Nehemiah, for example, plays fast and loose with the term "foreign." Invariably, when the term is used to describe peoples in the land of Canaan it refers to those who are inhabitants of the land, who can be considered *native* to it. On the other hand, the self-proclaimed natives constitute an immigrating community (i.e. the *golah* community).[72] It creates an ideological counter-movement. The primary, understandable purpose behind this dramatic polarization was to make manifest in collective memory the rigid categorization of who was acceptable (who was "in") and who was not (who was "out"). This isolationist push betrays a programmatic agenda intent on revising the social-economic hierarchy.[73] Religious exclusivity and divine election map out for the self-proclaimed remnant a new brand of social organization. And it is from this (reorganized) social(-religious) body that the realization of a religious nation was thought to spring, a utopia in the midst of a struggle for survival (cf. 2 Kgs 19:30–31). Sacred fertility is found in the surviving remnant from which the city of Jerusalem and Mount Zion would again be animated with social-religious community. The remnant perceives of itself as the seed, the center from which "restoration" will radiate throughout Judah and Israel (or the territories previously known by those designations). "Then I myself will gather the remnant of my flock out of all the lands where I have driven them, and I

---

72. I am not dismissing the possibility of "Israel" and "Judah" being internal developments—peasant revolt, peaceful infiltration, or other. Cf. George Mendenhall, *The Tenth Generation* (Baltimore: The Johns Hopkins University Press, 1973); Gottwald, *Tribes of Yahweh*. Liverani, among others, follows A. Alt's proposal that Yehud was annexed to Samaria until the arrival of Nehemiah (*Israel's History*, 332). My comment is restricted to the biblical presentation of land acquisition.

73. N. Gottwald ("Two Models for the Origins of Ancient Israel: Social Revolution Or Frontier Development," in *The Quest for the Kingdom of God: Studies in Honor of George E. Mendenhall* [ed. H. B. Huffmon, F. A. Spina, and Alberto Ravinell Whitney Green; Winona Lake: Eisenbrauns, 1983, 7) describes a similar event, which is highlighted by his peasant rebellion model for the "conquest" of Canaan. "The historical reality underlying the two polarized equations of 'Canaanite = bad' vs. 'Israelite = good' was not in the first instance an ethnic or religious polarization but a social structural polarization around the divisions between those who upheld the reigning hierarchic social order and those who struggled to bring a more egalitarian free peasant society into existence."

will bring them back to their fold, and they shall be fruitful and multiply" (Jer 23:3). And how will this be accomplished? "I will raise up shepherds over them who will shepherd them, and they shall not fear any longer, or be dismayed, nor shall any be missing, says the LORD" (v. 4). We find something quite similar in Zechariah: "But now I will not deal with the remnant of this people as in the former days, says the LORD of hosts. For there shall be a sowing of peace; the vine shall yield its fruit, the ground shall give its produce, and the skies shall give their dew; and I will cause the remnant of this people to possess all these things" (8:11–12). Once a revised social organization had been established, Yahweh would control surplus production for the benefit of the remnant.

And what of the proposed role of the remnant? Isaiah's suffering servant, which may refer to the remnant, is offered as a "light to the nations" through which divine authority is mediated (cf. Isa 42:6).[74] This role originates from an ideological center, namely the Jerusalem temple, which requires the existence of a city (Jerusalem). A distribution of labor, and a system for storing surplus, must be in place before the existence of the temple;[75] and these things must be deemed "sacred," or capable of being accepted as such, by driving out all of those things proclaimed profane. In the same way that the city is the "mediator between various permanent and seasonal settlements in its surroundings,"[76] the remnant and the religious city mediates between the member and non-member: the binary opposition as defined within the monotheistic identity.

What must be stressed here is the city's role in preserving exclusion. Jerusalem, as we have been discussing it, emphasizes this separation.[77]

---

74. Cf. the discussion in McKenzie, *Second Isaiah*, 133–36.

75. We might read as a counter opinion the statement in 2 Sam 7:6, "I have not lived in a house since the day I brought up the people of Israel from Egypt to this day, but I have been moving about in a tent and a tabernacle." While the larger narrative describes the building of and the maintaining of a kingdom, this statement shows a reaction to the temple because it is an urban product.

76. Van de Mieroop, *The Ancient Mesopotamian City*, 11.

77. Even if Lipschits is correct that the social-economic elite of the province lived in (or moved to) Jerusalem after it was rebuilt (see "Achaemenid Imperial Policy," 31–32; note also that he states that Jerusalem did not become a "real urban center" until the Hellenistic period [ibid., 40]), we should not conclude (as some have done [such as Weinberg, *Citizen-Temple Community*]) that this elevated the status of the *golah*-Yahwistic priesthood. While the biblical texts may imply that the transfer of the provincial capital was due to the restoration of the Jerusalem temple, that is unlikely. It is more accurate to say that the restoration of the Jerusalem temple was possible because of a change of the political capital. For example, D. Webster (*The Fall of the Ancient Maya: Solving the Mystery of the Maya Collapse* [London:

The city's walls, while also built for defense, emphasized the separation of that which belonged to the divine, the space for divine creation and preservation as forces of production, from the profane. To put it differently, Jerusalem—and we recognize here that the primary focus of all Persian-period biblical texts focusing on restoration is on the city of Jerusalem—was to be recognizable in not only geographic and material space, but in ideological space as well.[78] But with the monotheistic dependence upon this pattern, (desire) production must fit within the regulating framework of divine law.

The *golah* community's identification of itself as the remnant in contrast to the people already in the land is fundamentally an argument

Thames & Hudson, 2002], 78) argues it is incorrect to decide on a society's urban status based on ceremonial facades such as temples, which have produced now-abandoned models such as the "priest–peasant" model, which saw essentially a two-class society with the priests as the aristocratic class and essentially everyone else as surplus producers (thus "peasant") for the priesthood. Unfortunately, the so-called priest–peasant model, or something similar, is still used in studies of Yehud, shown by those works assuming the existence of a theocracy; cf. Roland de Vaux, *Ancient Israel: Its Life and Institutions* (trans. John McHugh; New York: McGraw-Hill, 1961), 98–99, 141; Otto Plöger, *Theocracy and Eschatology* (trans. S. Rudman; Oxford: Blackwell, 1968); Paul Hanson, *The Dawn of Apocalyptic: The Historical and Sociological Roots of Jewish Apocalyptic Eschatology* (Philadelphia: Fortress, 1979), 211–20; Weinberg, *Citizen-Temple Community*, 112–26; Wellhausen, *Prolegomena*, 411–22; Dyck, *Theocratic Ideology*, 1–4, to name but a few, basing an overly simplistic social-economic division on agenda-driven religious texts. The establishment of a military garrison north of the city of Jerusalem (cf. Hoglund, *Achaemenid Imperial Administration*, 224) indicates not an imperial glorification of a priestly aristocratic class but the establishment of a social-economic, even political, center from which the imperial government through its appointees (governors and other) administered the province. One thing we certainly need not do is conclude along with W. Dever that "urban" is the result of centralization ("Archaeology and the 'Age of Solomon': A Case-Study in Archaeology and Historiography," in *The Age of Solomon: Scholarship at the Turn of the Millennium* [ed. Lowell K. Handy; Leiden: Brill, 1997], 244). "Urban" is the result of a complex network of systems of relation and production that may be centralizing (as may be shown in "urbanization") but not always automatically so.

78. But in saying this we need not necessarily conclude with Hoglund, who writes, "The presence of urban fortifications allowed a city to consider itself independent of the empire, capable of determining its own destiny. Such independent thinking was naturally fraught with the potential for rebellion" (*Achaemenid Imperial Administration*, 210). Urban ideological space does not automatically lend itself to independent thinking and whispers of rebellion. Cities fortified by the empire would presumably have been marked by a conscious imperial ideology regarding fortification.

for the community's control over the forces of production. Likewise, its association of Jerusalem as a sacred space identifies the city as the space in which restoration would occur (or perhaps better stated "begin"). These actions reflect the monotheistic community's apparent attempt to control the forces of production by rewriting the social-political structure—a revision that supports divine authority by imposing a boundary between member and non-member, according to which only the member would be considered a contributing agent in the new system, or mode, of production.

2. *The Nature of Desire Production as Mode of Production for the Monotheistic Body*

Different modes of production, as Marx has pointed out historically, determine different epochs that frame the conditions of a social-political identity.[79] "Each of these epochs," writes Gottwald, "was characterized not only by a mode of production in the sense of techniques, materials, and human labor power (forces of production), but simultaneously by a mode of production in the sense of forms of activity in distinctive social and political relations with other producers (relations of production)."[80] From a society's mode of production are derived its relations of power, production, and authority, along with the formation of class as the core in which these forces intersect. "The production of ideas, of conceptions, of consciousness, is at first directly interwoven with the material activity and the material intercourse of men, the language of real life. Conceiving, thinking, the mental intercourse of men, appear at this stage as the direct efflux of their material behavior. The same applies to mental production as expressed in the language of politics, laws, morality, religion, metaphysics, and so on, of a people."[81] And further, "The nature of individuals thus depends on the material conditions determining their production."[82]

---

79. Marx writes ("The German Ideology," 42), "Men can be distinguished from animals by consciousness, by religion or anything else you like. They themselves begin to distinguish themselves from animals as soon as they begin to *produce* their means of subsistence, a step which is conditioned by their actual physical organization. By producing their means of subsistence men are indirectly producing their actual material life. The way in which men produce their means of subsistence depends first of all on the nature of the actual means of subsistence they find in existence and have to reproduce."
80. Gottwald, *Tribes of Yahweh*, 632.
81. Marx, "The German Ideology," 47.
82. Ibid., 42.

This supports what we have been saying regarding monotheistic identity in that monotheistic identity, a religious identity, is also a social-political identity that is subject to conditions or processes of identity formation determined by the productive relationship between social agents and the material world.

In the strictest sense, Marx's theory on mode of production posits that human agents' relation to material production determines their role within the social body as well as their forms of consciousness. And Deleuze and Guattari, who draw partly from Neo-Marxist theory, argue that mode of production is in its purest form really desire production permitting the simultaneous influence of material and ideological forces. In this way, they account for the social body's strong material bases while allowing patterns of ideation to be explanatory of different forms of social relations and production:

> Let us remember once again one of Marx's caveats: we cannot tell from the mere taste of wheat who grew it; the product gives us no hint as to the system and the relations of production. The product appears to be all the more specific, incredibly specific and readily describable, the more closely the theoretician relates it to *ideal forms of causation, comprehension, or expression*, rather than to *the real process of production on which it depends.*[83]

Material production provides the underlying support for desire production because it meets the basic need of survival—and survival is the basic need of all social collectives, both physically and in terms of identity. "Desire is not bolstered by needs, but rather the contrary; needs are derived from desire... Lack is a countereffect of desire; it is deposited, distributed, vacuolized within a real that is natural and social."[84] There is, in other words, desire and the absence of desire at the heart of all production. "Desire does not lack anything; it does not lack its object. It is, rather, the *subject* that is missing in desire, or desire that lacks a fixed subject..."[85] Marx's "mode of production" is for Deleuze and Guattari the production of surplus as the production of desire. Surplus is, in other words, a product as well as an object of desire: "Desire always remains in close touch with the conditions of objective existence; it embraces them and follows them, shifts when they shift, and does not outlive them."[86]

---

83. Deleuze and Guattari, *Anti-Oedipus*, 24.
84. Ibid., 27.
85. Ibid., 26.
86. Ibid., 27.

With that in mind, the monotheistic body inherits from the social body its patterns of production and the concomitant patterns of religions among social agents. But it takes for granted, because of its relationship to the social body, the material means of subsistence production. There is, therefore, an initial disconnect between the monotheistic body and the social body that serves as the catalyst for the conflict over authority. For the monotheistic body, which is inherently predisposed to fulfill functions of association and dissociation,[87] the object of desire is the right of authority over the social body and an alleviation of the previous disconnect. Jewish monotheistic identity, as expressed by Donniel Hartman, for example, demonstrates this by imposing restrictions on marriage, or legalized membership within its body—thus, a prohibition against intermarriage: "Being classified as an insider is accompanied by various consequences, rights and benefits, all of which may be called into question when one's basic status is being redefined… *As distinct from the non-Jew who is legally not capable of generating a binding marriage*, being part of the 'Community of Israel' is attested by the right to marry within the community, a right that cannot be revoked given the immutable nature of one's membership."[88] While the monotheistic body presumes material production to be a given fact, mode of production is made subservient to the production of symbolic power: "The power of imposing a vision of divisions, that is, the power of making visible and explicit social divisions that are implicit, is the political power par excellence: it is the power to make groups, to manipulate the objective structure of society."[89] That, after all, is the idealized form and intent of monotheism: a space demarcated within space, a dichotomy between member and non-member, the monotheistic body carving out space from the social body, desire defined by its absence, lack. For it is in controlling this distribution of symbolic power that the monotheistic identity asserts its authority, its ultimate desire, over both the social body and the social body's forces of material production. Yet therein is also the

---

87. I am drawing here from Bourdieu, who says of religion in general, "Because religion, like all symbolic systems, is predisposed to fulfill a function of association and dissociation or, better, of distinction, a system of practices and beliefs is made to appear as *magic* or *sorcery*, an inferior religion, whenever it occupies a dominated position in the structure of relations of symbolic power, that is, in the system of relations between the systems of practices and beliefs belonging to a determined social formation" ("Genesis and Structure," 12).

88. Donniel Hartman, *Boundaries of Judaism* (London: Continuum, 2007), 23, emphasis mine.

89. Bourdieu, *In Other Words*, 138.

materialist origin from which the monotheistic body cannot shake itself free; its ideological truths remain forever chained to the material realities that frame the space of production within the social body—free to move about but never to exist freely autonomous. Monotheistic identities compensate for this through their explanations of authority as being ultimately determined and shaped by divine revelation. And if we might look briefly ahead in historical development, for each, Islam, Judaism, and Christianity, the material world and its forces of production are, following that revelation, always in a state of increasing subservience to divine authority, which will be revealed absolutely at the dawn of a "new age." This age is a divine revision of the forces and distributed relationships of the material world. In a word, restoration. In a restored order, all authority is the product and exercise of the divine alone. Every member's responsibility is to testify to this coming reality through obedience to divine authority.

That this responsibility is inherent within the nature of the monotheistic body, and so shared by the different monotheistic identities, can be demonstrated. The following three different examples from three different traditions speak to this expected responsibility. In addition, the similarity of their messages offers strong support for our developing argument that restoration is a pillar shared among the different monotheistic religions. Hans Küng speaks out of a progressive Catholic Christian perspective (which led in part to his rejection of papal infallibility, and the Vatican's subsequent removal of his authority to teach Catholic theology). Rabbi Moshe ben Maimon (Maimonides), who during his lifetime endured strong criticism and outright rejection within Jewish circles regarding both his rulings and his writings, was posthumously acknowledged to be one of the greatest rabbinic thinkers. In contrast to both Küng and Maimonides, however, the hadith of Imam Bukhari are widely accepted as one of the most reliable and authoritative collections of hadith. Despite their different perspectives and their different positions relative within the monotheism to which they belong (i.e. having moved from the center to the margins, having moved from the margins to the center, or having remained at the center), their messages are consistent, which is a testament not only to the fundamental qualities, in terms of structure, that are shared by the different monotheistic identities but even to the ranges that a particular monotheistic identity accommodates.

Hans Küng:
> [The fellowship of believers] is a living invitation to the world to unite itself with the Church and join in testifying to the great things the Lord has done, not only for the Church but for the whole world. The whole of

mankind is called upon to share in giving praise and thanks, to hear the word of grace and to celebrate the meal of love once again, in order to bear witness to Christ in the everyday life by being men who not only love each other, but all men... The whole of mankind is called upon to share in giving praise and thanks. [T]he Church has a future; it has the future. This is the eighth day which passes description and cannot be foreseen, the day on which God will complete his work of creation, the Church will reach the goal of its pilgrimage and the world will recognize its Lord.[90]

Maimonides:

The Eleventh Foundation is that God, blessed be He, gives reward to one who obeys the commandments of the Torah and punishes one who violates its prohibitions. The greatest reward is the World to Come, and the greatest punishment is kareis (spiritual excision, "cutting off"). We have already said enough on this topic [earlier in the Commentary]. The verse which teaches this foundation is [when Moshe says to God], "And now, if you will forgive their sin; and if not, please remove me [from your book which you have written]" to which God responds, "...Whoever has sinned against me, him will I blot from my book" (Shemos [Exodus] 32:32—33). This indicates that He knows the servant and the sinner, to give reward to this one and punishment to the other.[91]

Imam Bukhari:

Narrated Anas: The Prophet said, "(The people will be thrown into Hell (Fire) and it will keep on saying, 'Is there any more?' till the Lord of the worlds puts His Foot over it, whereupon its different sides will come close to each other, and it will say, 'Qad! Qad! (enough! enough!) By Your 'Izzat (Honor and Power) and YOUR KARAM (Generosity)!' Paradise will remain spacious enough to accommodate more people until Allah will create some more people and let them dwell in the superfluous space of Paradise." (Hadith Bukhari 9 93:481)

---

90. Hans Küng, *The Church* (trans. Ray Ockenden and Rosaleen Ockenden; New York: Sheed & Ward, 1967), 487–88.
91. Rabbi Moshe ben Maimon, *Mishneh Sanhedrin* 10 (trans. Eliezer C. Abrahamson).

Chapter 4

DIVINE LAW AS A DOMINANT DISCOURSE OF THE MONOTHEISTIC SELF

The divine law of the *golah* community (which we can find referred to by Ezra) was a prescriptive rather than descriptive law. Its purpose, as is common to monotheistic laws, was to regulate actions toward the realization of restoration. As a prescriptive law, its fundamental purpose was to facilitate restoration. The extent to which divine law was effectively productive of the monotheistic identity as a social-political identity can only be determined after the nature of divine law, as well as law generally, is defined:

> Few questions concerning human society have been asked with such persistence and answered by serious thinkers in so many diverse, strange, and even paradoxical ways as the question "What is law?"[1]

> And what are these laws of nature that have displaced God in the minds of millions? Law has two meanings. One is an external rule enforced by authority, such as the common rule against robbery and assault. The word is also used to denote the uniform way things act in the universe, but this second use of the word is erroneous. What we see in nature is simply the paths of God's power and wisdom take through creation. Properly these are phenomena, not laws, but we call them laws by analogy with the arbitrary laws of society.[2]

Divine law exists not because it is the ideal form, toward which, subsequently, natural law would aspire. *Divine* law, rather, expresses an alternative; it demands a pattern of behavior that supports an authority alternative to that which already has been naturally institutionalized.[3] In

---

1. H. L. A. Hart, *The Concept of Law* (2d ed.; Oxford: Clarendon, 1994), 1.
2. Aiden W. Tozer, *The Knowledge of the Holy: The Attributes of God: Their Meaning in the Christian Life* (New York: HarperSanFrancisco, 1961), 66.
3. That the nature of law is to support authority is generally accepted. As Ake ("A Definition of Political Stability," 271) writes of laws and political behavior generally, "Obedience to the law constitutes political behavior just as much as

other words, divine law is an interruption to the productive flows that form natural law and its corresponding authority; it is an alternative whose ontological core is characterized by reaction and whose ultimate aim is to facilitate a new reality. And because, as Robert Wilson previously observed, notions of judicial authority are already strongly linked with a society's social structure,[4] and because divine law is not a natural product of such preexisting forces, the authority upon which divine law depends is known or manifest through revelation, which is an interruptive act that at times implicitly and at others overtly challenges the established structures of a society. Divine law both systematizes and categorizes that revelation.

1. *Understanding the Function and Force of Law as Discourse: Some Preliminary Remarks on the General Concept*

In a general sense, law is a functional, regulative pattern of engagement that defines acceptable and sometimes productive relations between social agents.[5] It is "repressive" in that it articulates the limits of the

---

contesting elections does. For, whether intended or not, the effect of obedience to the law is to uphold the authority of those who make decisions about what the law should be, and how it is to be enforced. To uphold this authority is to aid in maintaining aspects of the distribution of power to make decisions for society."

4. Robert R. Wilson, "The Mechanisms of Judicial Authority in Early Israel," in Huffmon, Spina, and Green, eds., *The Quest for the Kingdom of God*, 60.

5. Within the society itself we recognize further that there is no human act that is intrinsically non-political (as noted by Ake, "A Definition of Political Stability," 271). We should note further that according to Hart (*The Concept of Law*, 13–17), there is no suitable, accepted definition of "law." While it belongs to the general family of "rules of behavior" and while it is recognizable, it is not entirely definable. We can only therefore speak of the concepts that comprise it. Note specifically, "It is this requirement [i.e. that there be a genus under which a word, concept, or definition may be applied] that in the case of law renders this form of definition useless, for here there is no familiar well-understood general category of which law is a member. The most obvious candidate for use in this way in a definition of law is the general family of rules of behaviour; yet the concept of a rule as we have seen is as perplexing as that of law itself, so that definitions of law that start by identifying laws as a species of rule usually advance our understanding of law no further" (ibid., 15). Given even political science's struggle to define an important concept such as "law" we will begin with an understanding that law is either prescriptive or descriptive of social-political relations, that it is culturally produced, and that it corresponds to the hierarchical distribution of power in a society. We follow Hart's distinction between morality and law (that law is not always a moral judgment): "The most fundamental difference relating to connections between law and morality between

socius, defining the "territoriality" of the social body. But it fills this role only because law is itself a production of the social body. Deleuze and Guattari describe the repressive function of law in the following manner:

> This repression determines what part of the influx [of intensity] will pass through and what will not in the system in extension, what will remain blocked or stocked in the extended filiations, and on the contrary, what will move and flow following the relations of alliance, in such a way that the systematic coding of the flows will be carried out.[6]

While the purpose of their laws is similar, there is a crucial difference between ancient and modern societies as to what constituted the fundamental nature or form of law. On the average, modern polities tend toward a text-oriented law.[7] In contrast, law in ancient polities generally differs from a codified set of laws in that social-political law may be unwritten, and may be constituted solely by the word of the king. Whereas in societies of written law the "letter" of the law regulates standards, expectations, and acceptable patterns of behavior. Law codes of the ancient world, such as the laws of Hammurabi, Eshnunna, Ur-Namma, and even the Mosaic Law, or the Deuteronomic Law by extension, not only aggrandize the individual through whom a deity bestowed the law but also represent idealized patterns of behavior.[8] Or as

---

legal theory developed in this book and Dworkin's theory concerns the identification of the law. According to my theory, the existence and content of the law can be identified by reference to the social sources of the law (e.g. legislation, judicial decisions, social customs) without reference to morality except where the law thus identified has itself incorporated moral criteria for the identification of the law. In Dworkin's interpretive theory, on the other hand, every proposition of law stating what the law or some subject is, necessarily involves a moral judgment, since according to his holistic interpretive theory propositions of law are true only if with other premises they follow from that set of principles which both best fit all the settled law identified by reference to the social sources of the law and provide the best moral justification for it" (ibid., 269). Hart's distinction here stems from his understanding that there can be legal rights and duties which have no moral justification or force (ibid., 268).

    6. Deleuze and Guattari, *Anti-Oedipus*, 164.

    7. Or, as Barak Obama describes, albeit somewhat superficially, "[L]aws are just words on a page—words that are sometimes malleable, opaque, dependent on context and trust as they are in a story or poem or promise to someone, words whose meanings are subject to corrosion…" (*The Audacity of Hope: Thoughts on Reclaiming the American Dream* [New York: Vintage, 2008], 92).

    8. With respect to the so-called Mosaic Law, this observation is not meant to disregard its development into a descriptive inspiration for "educated and pious Jewish lifestyle" (Philip R. Davies, "'Law' in Early Judaism," in *Judaism in Late Antiquity*. Vol. 3, *Where We Stand: Issues and Debates in Ancient Judaism* [ed.

Michael LeFebvre puts it, "The law *as practiced* in those societies often differed from, even contradicted, the laws *as stated* in the collections."[9] In the ancient Near East, laws did not replace kings, as one might suppose from a modern vantage point. Even in Israel under Josiah's reform, the Deuteronomic Law did not become the codified regulation of the social-political body. As LeFebvre again writes, "It ought not to be supposed that Deuteronomic scribes invented the idea of written legislation as a replacement for kings. The 'intermediate' stage represented by the Deuteronomic law looks like an enhanced juridical treatise (even kings are taught by it), but law writings are not yet perceived as *being* 'the law.'"[10] We are, in other words, still caught in the vicious cycle of the king as despot—the regulating "flows" projected from the king are returned in the form of surplus and allegiance, that is, desire production, from which kingly power, rather than power of the law, is legitimated. But this legitimation, according to Deleuze and Guattari, creates an oppressive relationship between an authority and those over whom that authority is exercised—a model that the monotheistic body attempts to replicate. By "overcoding," then, is meant the process of acculturation into a new normative order. To meet that end, law must either support the existing order or contain a blueprint for a new order; the latter option must be capable of engaging the previous social-political order in a "vengeful" contest in order to establish its own authority. Or, as Deleuze and Guattari write,

> Overcoding is the essence of the law, and the origin of the new sufferings of the body. Punishment has ceased to be a festive occasion, from which the eye extracts a surplus value in the magic triangle of alliance and filiations. *Punishment becomes vengeance*, the vengeance of the voice, the hand, and the eye now joined together on the despot—the vengeance of the new alliance, whose public character does not spoil the secret: "I will bring down upon you the avenging sword of the vengeance of alliance." For once again, before it becomes a feigned guarantee against despotism, the law is the invention of the despot himself: *it is the juridical form assumed by the infinite debt.*[11]

Jacob Neusner and A. J. Avery-Peck; Leiden: Brill, 1999], 18). Rather, it is an observation that the law was not originally descriptive for a social-political body but became at a later point simultaneously descriptive and prescriptive for a religious community. See also M. Lefebvre's discussion in *Collections, Codes, and Torah: The Re-Characterization of Israel's Written Law* (LHBOTS 451; New York: T&T Clark International, 2006), 1–30.

    9. Ibid., 1.
    10. Ibid., 87, emphasis in original.
    11. Deleuze and Guattari, *Anti-Oedipus*, 212–13, emphasis in original.

The functional nature of law usually directs itself toward one of two aims, which political scientists tend to describe as either prescriptive or descriptive, following constructivist and realist modes of thought, respectively.[12] In either case, or even in a blending resulting in perhaps a prescriptive realism or a descriptive constructivism (possibly resulting in a philosophy of power as decentralized from the individual, of which Foucault has been a prominent voice), functional law must be upheld not simply by a constant display of power but also by the everyday actions and decisions of the social-political body—a body that must legitimate the law by operating within the parameters it itself defines. One cannot agree with Gunther Teubner's argument that law "as a communicative process...produces human actors as semantic artifacts."[13] Law alone cannot produce. Without human agency, without socially constructed relations of power, it is but a passive artifact itself. The desire of law is in truth the desire of the social-political body. The productive flows that law mimics are those produced out of or by human agency. In other words, law is the codified regulation, a cultural artifact, of the desire production of the social body. Its goal is not power. It is not creation. Its goal is the preservation and stability of the productive processes, including power, that define and identify the social body.

Among its other roles, law preserves the classification systems of a society until times of usually radical political change.[14] It preserves through either, or both, coercion—the force of which is not inherent within the law but is found in a power utilizing the law—or regulation. Coerced behavior results when power is exercised by an authority through the legal system to control the parameters of possible behaviors.[15] Regulated behaviors are those behaviors permitted to individuals by the governing system so as not to be found guilty of transgressing the law, or the "rules of the game" according to Pierre Bourdieu.[16] These may be described as informing the individual of what not to do: "In any

---

12. But note also that some, such as J. S. Barkin ("Realist Constructivism," *International Studies Review* 5, no. 3 [2003]: 325–42) and G. Teubner ("How the Law Thinks: Toward a Constructivist Epistemology of Law," *Law & Society Review* 23, no. 5 [1989]: 727–58), would see constructivist epistemology and realist theory as compatible and not forced into binary opposition.

13. Ibid., 730.

14. Again note Wilson, "The Mechanisms of Judicial Authority in Early Israel," 60.

15. Mendenhall ("Ancient Oriental and Biblical Law," 3–4) points out that the social-political body (but what he terms "community") has the coercive power to enforce obedience to the law.

16. Cf. Bourdieu, *In Other Words*, 9–10.

large group general rules, standards, and principles must be the main instrument of social control, and not particular directions given to each individual separately."[17] These classification systems, serving regulatory roles, mold principles that define the structured identity that both unifies a social body and separates it from others. The same is true also for groups within a social body. "Hence the law must predominantly, but by no means exclusively, refer to classes of person, and to classes of acts, things, and circumstances; and its successful operation over vast areas of social life depends on a widely diffused capacity to recognize particular acts, things, and circumstances as instances of the general classifications which the law makes."[18] Bourdieu expands upon this general understanding, "Through classification systems...inscribed in law, through bureaucratic procedures, educational structures and social rituals...the state molds mental structures and imposes common principles of vision and division..."[19] Political structures define and solidify role expectations within the lines of political behavior (in both its positive [promoting political stability] and its negative [promoting political instability] senses). As Claude Ake puts it, "Thus, the network of political role expectations, or the political structure, constitutes a system of channels or obstacles that control the flow of political exchanges (that is, the transactions and communications) between political actors, preventing political exchanges from fluctuating beyond certain limits and giving them a general regularity without making them perfectly predictable. Political structures may thus be called the 'pattern of the flow of political exchanges.'"[20]

As a mechanism for social control, and so also a medium through which power is legitimately exercised, law maintains perceived social and political stability by insuring the distribution of power within the social-political body and supporting its related authority.[21] But this necessitates a preexisting structure within which a law is legitimated and in which legislation may be performed in a manner consistent with the established structure. Or, as Hart writes, of an authority that depends

17. Hart, *The Concept of Law*, 124.
18. Ibid.
19. Pierre Bourdieu, *Practical Reason: On the Theory of Action* (Stanford: Stanford University Press, 1998), 45–46.
20. Ake, "A Definition of Political Stability," 273.
21. Note Hart, "The doctrine [of sovereignty] asserts that in every human society, where there is law, there is ultimately to be found latent beneath the variety of political forms, in a democracy as much as in an absolute monarchy, this simple relationship between subjects rendering habitual obedience and a sovereign who renders habitual obedience to no one" (*The Concept of Law*, 50).

upon structure rather than charisma, and so may be preserved beyond the life of any one ruler, "[E]ven before a new legislator has begun to legislate, it may be clear that there is a firmly established rule giving him, as one of a class or line of persons, the right to do this in his turn."[22] This is possible in part because law reflects the way in which individuals engage (find themselves) in reciprocal relations with the "state," or the distributed power over a social-political body. We can argue then that laws are not functional replacements for authority, nor are they preconceived to write a new distribution of power, as a constructivist might argue. They are intended to safeguard, to regulate, and to control the power and authority already established.[23]

---

22. Ibid., 58. And note further, "Just because the scope of a rule accepted at a given time by a group may look forward in general terms to successors in the office of legislator in this way, its acceptance affords us grounds both for the statement of law that the successor has a right to legislate, even before he starts to do so, and for the statement of fact that he is likely to receive the same obedience as his predecessor does. *Of course, acceptance of a rule by a society at one moment does not guarantee its continued existence. There may be a revolution: the society may cease to accept the rule*" (ibid., 58–59, emphasis mine).

23. Hart describes two main types of rules that function in this way. He describes "primary rules of obligation" as what governs a society "where the only means of social control is that general attitude of the group towards its own standard rules of obligation." He writes further, "If a society is to live by such primary rules alone, there are certain conditions which, granted a few of the most obvious truisms about human nature and the world we live in, must be satisfied. The first of these conditions is that the rules must contain in some form restrictions on the free use of violence, theft, and deception to which human beings are tempted but which they must, in general, repress, if they are to coexist in close proximity to each other... Secondly, though such a society may exhibit the tension already described, between those who accept the rules and those who reject the rules except where fear of social pressure induces them to conform, it is plain that the latter cannot be more than a minority, if so loosely organized a society of persons, approximately equal in physical strength, is to endure: for otherwise those who reject the rules would have too little social pressure to fear. This too is confirmed by what we know of primitive communities where, though there are dissidents and malefactors, the majority live by the rules seen from the internal point of view" (ibid., 91–92). There are, according to Hart, three primary "defects" of primary rules (see ibid., 92–94). The first is uncertainty, which results because the rules do not form a system but exist as a set of separate standards "without any identifying mark, except of course that they are the rules which a particular group of human beings accepts" (ibid., 92). The second is the static character of the rules, for which change only comes through a slow process of growth. And the third is the inefficiency of the social pressure by which the rules are maintained. For these "defects" he argues there exist secondary rules, which he describes as "remedies": "[T]hey may all be said to be on a different level from the primary rules, for they are all about such rules; in the sense that while primarily rules

Because of the monotheistic body's pursuit of authority, similar can be said of law within the framework of a monotheistic identity. Monotheistic religious laws fulfill this purpose by regulating all productive flows toward the monotheistic body. The desire of the monotheistic body, its absolute authority, is unique in contrast to social-political law in that this authority is taken for granted a priori, as though an exogenous mechanism of social-religious control.[24] This idea is made clear in Deuteronomy: "*If* you obey the commandments of the LORD your God that I am commanding you today, by loving the LORD your God, walking in his ways, and observing his commandments, decrees, and ordinances, *then* you shall live and become numerous, and the LORD your God will bless you in the land *that you are entering to possess*" (Deut 30:16, emphasis mine).

If there are some similarities between the social body and the monotheistic body regarding the function of law and authority, can the same be said of the system or institution in which law and authority are preserved? Ake writes, "The legal system or the institution for binding arbitration of the group or society has the same effect as custom. It limits the variability of behavior in given situations by authoritatively defining what we ought to do (obligations), what we may do (rights), and what we can do (powers)."[25] How we present ourselves and how we engage others within society is determined by a legitimate system of rule and restraint, which preserves the hierarchy of authority and its supporting distribution of power. But that is not to say that this determined engagement is fully conscious. Some obligations function on an unconscious, but nevertheless culturally encoded, level. And here we see the semantically sticky situation of distinguishing between laws and morals.[26] Human actors or

---

are concerned with the actions that individual must or must not do, these secondary rules are all concerned with the primary rules themselves. They specify the ways in which the primary rules may be conclusively ascertained, introduced, eliminated, varied, and the fact of their violation conclusively determined" (ibid., 94).

24. P. Tillich (*Systematic Theology* [3 vols.; Chicago: University of Chicago Press, 1951], 1:85) describes something similar as "theonomy." "Theonomy does not mean the acceptance of a divine law imposed on reason by a highest authority; it means autonomous reason united with its own depth. In a theonomous situation reason actualizes itself in obedience to its structural laws and in the power of its own inexhaustible ground. Since God (*theos*) is the law (*nomos*) for both the structure and the ground of reason, they are united in him, and their unity is manifest in a theonomous situation."

25. Ake, "A Definition of Political Stability," 274.

26. Note Hart's statement that "Moral rules impose obligations and withdraw certain areas of conduct from the free option of the individual to do as he likes. Just

agents are not encoded with fundamental notions of right and wrong from birth; they are behaviors learned on both conscious and unconscious levels,[27] though in contrast, religious laws assume that these notions are either inherent within individuals (Islam and Christianity) or within the community (Judaism, by virtue of divine election; also Islam). For example, the Christian might say that divine grace and sovereignty is "a sovereign grace that grasps the human subject and evokes from it the creaturely responsibility for which it has a capacity but which, on account of false pride and sloth, it fails to make good. In other words, it is a gospel that frees us from self-preoccupation in order for us to become responsive to the Torah of conscious, deliberate, and joyful participation in the divine governance of creation."[28] In contrast, laws of a society are based on socially constructed evaluations of "right" and "wrong." They reflect that which has been accepted and legitimated by society as acceptable modes of behavior and action. Thus, "Legal control is... primarily, though not exclusively, control by directions which are... general."[29]

The preservation of the evaluative distinction between "right" and "wrong" requires some form of codified behavioral patterns, which may also be identified as "political behaviors." Ake writes,

as a legal system obviously contains elements closely connected with the simple cases of order backed by threats, so equally obviously it contains elements closely connected with certain aspects of morality. In both cases alike there is a difficulty in identifying precisely the relationship and a temptation to see in the obviously close connection an identity. Not only do law and morals share a vocabulary so that there are both legal and moral obligations, duties, and rights; but all municipal legal systems reproduce the substance of certain fundamental moral requirements" (*The Concept of Law*, 7).

27. Bourdieu (*In Other Words*, 9–10) describes it as an engagement within and of the habitus: "Action is not the mere carrying out of a rule, or obedience to a rule. Social agents, in archaic societies as well as in ours, are not automata regulated like clocks, in accordance with laws which they do not understand. In the most complex games, matrimonial exchange for instance, or ritual practices, they put into action the incorporated principles of a generative habitus: this system of dispositions can be imagined by analogy with Chomsky's generative grammar—with this difference: I am talking about dispositions acquired through experience, thus variable from place to place and time to time. This 'feel for the game,' as we call it, is what enables an infinite number of 'moves' to be made, adapted to the infinite number of possible situations which no rule, however complex, can foresee."

28. Douglas John Hall, *Imaging God: Dominion as Stewardship* (Grand Rapids: Eerdmans; New York: Friendship, 1986), 51.

29. Hart, *The Concept of Law*, 21.

> Political behavior takes place in organized society, that is, in a situation in which men are in a state of interaction, as opposed to having random contact. For people in random contact, behavior is infinitely variable and, hence, unpredictable. People in interaction behave in the context of shared expectations about what can legitimately be done in any given situation. For these people in interaction, the variability of behavior patterns is limited so that behavior can be predicted to some extent. The congeries of standardized expectations that are the basis of the predictability of behavior are called "roles."[30]

Given Ake's proposal, is it possible then for a social body whose own political ideology is antithetical to that of a larger society to maintain an autonomous existence within that society? Or to rephrase it, can we speak of a "social community" that consciously rejects *on a structural level* the very society upon which it depends, in the manner that the *golah* community is described by Ezra–Nehemiah to have done in relation to the *am ha'aretz*? Rejection is by definition political behavior that it is acted out against the dominant political and legal system. Whether it is coexistent or resistant to the dominant political structure the variability and possibility of its choice of action is still determined by the dominant political machinery. One cannot, for example, have a purely democratic community living within and by the systems of a monarchic society—a social community cannot exist outside the social-political parameters determined by the dominant and dominating systems of the society *upon which it depends* for its very own existence. It is, however, possible, on a theoretical level, to have a democratically *minded* community within a monarchic society, but it would still be a community within a monarchic society that happens to hold to a democratic ideology. The existence of such communities are what have historically made revolutions possible. The Iranian Revolution of 1978–80, for example, was the result of communities harboring ideological agendas different from the dictatorial or imperialist regime of the Shah. Thus, enthusiasm for the revolution was carried out under the banners of anti-imperialism, republicanism, communism (of the Marxist variant) and Shi'i Islam, banners that reflected

---

30. Ake, "A Definition of Political Stability," 272. Note further: "It is more accurate to define the political in terms of an effect—namely, the alteration or maintenance of patterns of the distribution of the power to make decisions for the society. In that way, we arrive at a definition of the 'political' which compels us to assume that all human behavior is potentially political… The definition of the political is not a problem of making declarations about intrinsic differences between particular acts, but rather one of specifying a particular effect. If it is clear what this effect is, then the political is defined, whatever the variety of particular acts that may be associated with this effect" (ibid.).

the ideologies of different communities within the systems that defined "Iran" and "Iranian."[31] The Iranian revolution ultimately resulted in a theocratic political structure after religious authorities became political authorities, and who were thereby able to cause changes in the political structure so as to support a theocracy.[32] Yet one cannot say of Iran that there was an autonomous republic or an autonomous communist social-political body within the imperial-based society; each are political definitions that speak directly to the dominant distribution of power.[33]

2. So Then, What Is at Stake if a Religious Law Governs a Social-Political Body? A Theocracy?

The purpose of law is to offer a codified regulation of political behavior that supports the identity of the social-political body and is enforced by a legitimated authority. When the general function and force of law are properly understood, including the ways they impact social-political identity, we must reject the very basis of statements such as, "Members

31. As noted by Ervand Abrahamian, "The Making of the Modern Iranian State," in *Comparative Politics At the Crossroads* (ed. Mark Kesselman et al.; Lexington: D. C. Heath, 1995), 693–95, 716–19. One might also note further the observation of G. Burns ("Ideology, Culture, and Ambiguity: The Revolutionary Process in Iran," *Theory and Society* 25 [1996]: 358, see also 363–64) that rebellions against the Shah did not involve widespread calls for a theocracy, even though it became the ultimate outcome of the revolution.

32. That a theocracy is foremost a political structure is confirmed in Khomeini's acknowledgment that the complexities of the state precluded the creation of a self-evident (utopian) theocracy. As Abrahamian (*Khomeinism*, 54) writes, "The class forces unleashed by the revolution prompted Khomeini not only to redraw his picture of society but also to pay greater attention to the role of the state—an entity that had hardly figured in his early works. The contemporary state, he had liked to argue, should be no more complex than the early caliphate, in which Imam Ali had been able to administer a vast region from the corner of a simple mosque. God's will could be carried out without a vast army of tax collectors, bureaucrats, and military officers. The states's main functions were simple: to implement the sacred law, provide law and order, allow local judges to make swift and final decisions, keep a healthy balance between the social strata, spend no more than it collected in the khoms taxes, and, most significant of all, restrain people's evil instincts, especially their instinct to steal."

33. In the case of Iran, the political revolution failed to be a social revolution, as argued by Amjad, because the class structure of society (distributed relations of power) remained intact. Despite the different political ideologies of communities taking part in the revolution the political structure as determined by the society remained largely intact (cf. Mohammed Amjad, *Iran: From Royal Dictatorship to Theocracy* [New York: Greenwood, 1989], 131).

of theocratic communities within liberal democracies do not receive appropriate treatment under popular legal standards, and they need a new framework under which to be treated by law."[34] Such statements are not adequately aware of what is meant in such political terms as "political structure," "political behavior," or even "law." And we must be clear on this, "theocracy" *is*, without variance, a political term.[35] It does not, as some seem unwilling to relinquish, designate a religious institution with political aspirations or a religious community living under the authority of a non-theocratic political government. Theologically minded definitions cannot hold sway, a theocracy is not a theology, nor can any discussion of one reject the material realm, as monotheistic views of the world tend to do.[36] Understanding the parameters of a theocracy is important for identifying the nature of restored order according to monotheism. "Theocracy" best describes the end-goal of the restorative process. Each monotheistic identity considers of theocratic organization as the truest form of social organization, and an ideal form from which humans in their agency originally fled. Hall, writing from a Christian vantage point, describes this in terms of the preservation of membership in contrast to outsiders, or non-members—in short, social relationship as understood by monotheism. He states, for instance,

---

34. Lucas A. Swaine, "How Ought Liberal Democracies to Treat Theocratic Communities?," *Ethics* 111, no. 2 (2001): 302.

35. The importance of recognizing that theocracy is without fail a political term has been discussed at length in Cataldo, *A Theocratic Yehud*.

36. A point that P. Valliere, despite working within a theological framework, comes close to making (though he never fully dismisses theocracy as being primarily a theological ideal) while discussing Soloviev's term "free theocracy": "Soloviev makes an analogous argument for the incorporation of nature into the theocratic ideal. Nature and economy (the molding of nature by human beings) are the material means for realizing theocracy. The material realm must not be excluded from the ideal, for precisely because of its material (non-ideal) status it is 'the source of real force for the idea.' Without material embodiment theocracy hangs in the air" (*Modern Russian Theology: Bukharev, Soloviev, Bulgakov—Orthodox Theology in a New Key* [Grand Rapids: Eerdmans, 2000], 134). Contrast this, for instance, with the theologically laden use of the term theocracy in Allen Verhey, *Remembering Jesus: Christian Community, Scripture, and the Moral Life* (Grand Rapids: Eerdmans, 2002), 338. Even Ruhollah Khomeini's initial, idealized vision of Islamic government is insufficient in this regard: "The fundamental difference between Islamic government, on the one hand, and constitutional monarchies and republics, on the other, is this: whereas the representatives of the people or the monarch in such regimes engage in legislation, in Islam the legislative power and competence to establish laws belongs exclusively to God Almighty" (*Islam and Revolution: Writings and Declarations of Imam Khomeini* [trans. Hamid Algar; Berkeley: Mizan, 1981], 55).

4. Divine Law

> The human being is being-with-God, who is source and ground of all being; it is being-with-the-human-counterpart (*Mitmenschen*); and it is being-with-nature. Humanity in God's intention means existing in dynamic, harmonious relationships with these three counterparts of our being. To be *imago Dei* implies that, standing within the relationship with God, the human creature reflects God's vicariousness and gracious *Mitsein* in its life vis-à-vis these others... By contrast, sin in this same tradition is a condition of not only being-alone (attempting autonomy) but also being-against.[37]

Where a theocratic government distinguishes itself from other political governments is through its complete adoption and assimilation of a society's culturally dominant religious institution and structure.[38] This adaptation expresses itself through the religious law that becomes (in both the constructive and descriptive senses) the regulating framework that preserves the normative order. This is a point to which, for example, the first *faqih* of the Islamic Republic of Iran—which is the closest historical example of a pure theocracy, admits,

> Since Islamic government is a government of law, knowledge of the law is necessary for the ruler, as has been laid down in tradition. Indeed such knowledge is necessary not only for the ruler, but also for anyone holding a post or exercising some government function... Knowledge of the law and justice, then, constitute fundamental qualifications in the view of the Muslims. Other matters have no importance or relevance in this connection. *Knowledge of the nature of the angels, for example, or of the attributes of the Creator, Exalted and Almighty, is of no relevance to the question of leadership.*[39]

In other words, being absorbed in extra-curricular pursuits of angels or other things, or even being a theological expert, is not sufficient (or in the case of the former, helpful) alone to function as an authority in a theocracy. One must possess an expertise in law—which is intended to regulate the social–political–religious body, the mediation and enforcement, rather, must be capable of regulating the relations between members and broader social world (which in the case of Iran was the international community). This last is a temporary allowance in the process of restoration.

---

37. Hall, *Imaging God*, 127–28.
38. The religious structure must be culturally dominant if it is to be accepted and legitimated by the social body upon which the laws are inscribed. Theocracies, as all other political institutions, are socially produced. While the theocratic citizen may claim that the political model originated with the divine, and in a theocracy that belief becomes a defining ideology, it is above all a human institution.
39. Khomeini, *Islam and Revolution*, 59, emphasis mine.

With that said, our discussion, especially in its concern for Yehud, has been progressing toward this verdict: a purely theocratic state—this is the monotheistic body's ideal system of governance—cannot be *theocratic* and exist simultaneously under the laws and standards of a monarchic or other society. Neither is it possible to speak of a purely theocratic community or social-political body existing autonomously within a larger and otherwise-oriented society, such as a monarchy. To argue this possibility is to confuse subcultural identity as the characteristic of an autonomous political structure.[40] In contrast, the stability of cultural identity amidst its randomness and variability are made possible by the parameters of possible actions regulated by laws enforced by social-political institutions, which are constructed by the very body they are organizing.[41] In the midst of variance, in the face of possible dissolution into chaos, law, whether a "king's law" or a written law, enforces stability.[42] But within the material conditions of existence, a political government or institution is not created by its law. According to Deleuze and Guattari, "*[L]aw is the invention of the despot himself.*"[43] Yet that is true only if "despot" is the symbolic figure, personhood, or other ("God" in a

---

40. Cook (*Prophecy and Apocalypticism*, 163) observes similarly, "The objection that it was the priests, not civil leaders, who were in charge of Persian-period Yehud, having ascended to governmental hegemony, is now known to be overstated. Nehemiah 3:7 and 5:15 indicate that various civil governors ruled the restoration community long after the tenure of Zerubbabel. In Nehemiah 5:15, Nehemiah states: 'The former governors who were before me laid heavy burdens on the people, and took food and wine from them... Even their servants lorded it over the people.' The reference to a פחה ('governor') in Mal. 1:8 indicates that such a civil leader was still in power c. 520–400 B.C.E. The Yehud seals and coins published by Nahman Avigad support the biblical data, refuting the idea that Yehud was theocratically managed in the Persian period."

41. In light of this function of law, E. Nicholson's reminder (*The Pentateuch in the Twentieth Century: The Legacy of Julius Wellhausen* [Oxford: Clarendon, 1998], 3) that little or nothing of Yahwistic law seems to have been known in the pre-exilic period is poignant. It reminds us that the *golah* community's version of Yahwistic law was not based on any prior precedent in which religious law constituted the core of a Judean cultural identity.

42. And this is the role that religious law desires over the social-political body, the pursuit of which produces a contest with the social body and its law (Cf. Paul-Eugène Dion, "La Religion des Papyrus d'Éléphantine: un Reflet du Juda d'avant l'Exil," in *Kein Land für sich allein: Studien zum Kulturkontakt in Kanaan, Israel/Palästina und Ebirnâri für Manfred Weippert Zum 65. Geburtstag* [ed. Ulrich Hübner and Ernst Axel Knauf; Orbis Biblicus et Orientalis; Göttingen: Vandenhoeck & Ruprecht, 2002], 243–54).

43. Deleuze and Guattari, *Anti-Oedipus*, 213.

monotheistic identity) of a collective body. Law is created by the very same forces (and desires!) that created a social-political body's government. It is this very point, this very *reality*, that the monotheistic identity contests in the articulation of its own divine law. In protest it foists divine law as a prescriptive law, as a path toward *constructing* a divinely sanctioned reality as substitute for that defined by a social body's material conditions—as though a "true" form offered in place of a poor reflection.

Therefore, the basis for theocratic law in Yehud must be bound inextricably to the religious law of the dominant (and dominating) religious institution; in this case, any preexisting Yahwistic institutions must be considered illegitimate by the *golah* community (cf. Ezra 4:2–3). In a theocracy, law must also be bound to the political institution because it defines the legitimated exercise of material and political power—thus it simultaneously regulates religious, political, and social patterns of behavior. As a system of control, it insures that material power resides in the hands of the leaders of the dominant religion by insuring that the political behavior of its citizens does not undermine the legitimated distribution of power.[44] As a component in the system of governance it insures that the obedient citizen is both socially *and* religiously obedient; there no longer exists any distinction between the social body and the religious body. For this reason, any definition of a theocracy as simply "submission to divine rule" is woefully inadequate.[45] In the specific case

---

44. Ake ("A Definition of Political Stability," 271) defines "political behavior" as "any act by any member of a society that affects the distribution of the power to make decisions for that society. Political behavior is ubiquitous. Members of society behave politically insofar as, in obeying or disobeying the laws of the society, they support or undermine the power stratification system. Obedience to the law constitutes political behavior just as much as contesting elections does. For, whether intended or not, the effect of obedience to the law is to uphold the authority of those who make decisions about what the law should be, and how it is to be enforced. To uphold this authority is to aid in maintaining aspects of the distribution of power to make decisions for society. Similarly, all violations of the law constitute political behavior; every violation of law is ipso facto a defiance of constituted authority. It threatens the maintenance of the existing pattern of distribution of the power to make decisions for society. If the incidence of violations of law continues to increase, political authority eventually atrophies; that is axiomatic."

45. In contrast with B. Harvey ("Insanity, Theocracy, and the Public Realm: Public Theology, the Church, and the Politics of Liberal Democracy," *Modern Theology* 10 [1994]: 50–52), among others, who claims a theocracy is simply submission to divine rule and is the means through which an individual can interact with God from the "profane" realm.

of Yehud, Ezra's Mosaic Law, with its basic constitution being foreign to the provincial social body, could not become a statutory constitution through demanded *religious* obedience without it being a despotic law.[46]

To function as the descriptive, regulative law of a society, divine law must be capable of regulating the *social-political* behavior of human actors. And to meet this end, it must make the transition from prescriptive if not utopian idealism to descriptive realism. This is why the religious institution must be that of the culturally dominant religion, divine law must be produced culturally if it is to be the law governing a society and supporting a theocracy. Or to put it differently, the law that governs a theocracy is a law that has been culturally legitimated, by the dominant power which is social-political *and* religious. Whereas religious law "forms a principal medium of religious action, thought, and expression,"[47] usually directed toward a religiously articulated utopia, theocratic law governs and defines all possible actions, thoughts, expressions, and distributed relations of power for the social–political–religious body. Indeed, and this deserves the emphasis, in a theocracy the socius is no longer a social-political body, nor is it simply a religious body; it is a *social–political–religious* body.

For monotheism, a theocracy is the paradigm after which perceptions of a restored society are usually patterned. Because a theocracy, as are other forms of government, is based on the society's mode of production, as well as authority over it, it will not be found in a social-political context wherein an alternative form of government and society are found. For example, a theocracy, which would support the authority of the *golah* community, and be regulated by the community's religious law, did not exist in Yehud, whose social-political body supported an alternative form of government. But that is a point we must discuss further in the following sections. For the immediate discussion, what we can

---

46. In addition, Lisbeth Fried ("'You Shall Appoint Judges': Ezra's Mission and the Rescript of Artaxerxes," in *Persia and Torah: The Theory of Imperial Authorization of the Pentateuch* [ed. James W. Watts; Society of Biblical Literature Symposium Series; Atlanta: Society of Biblical Literature, 2001], 63–90, but compare to Hoglund [*Achaemenid Imperial Administration*, 230], who argues Ezra's law did become dominant legal expression) argues that Ezra's mission to appoint judges (cf. Ezra 7:11–26) would have been conducted with the assumption that religious law was the measure by which these judges would arbitrate matters in Yehud but that their decisions would have been in accordance with Persian imperial law.

47. As described by Jacob Neusner and Tamara Sonn, *Comparing Religions Through Law: Judaism and Islam* (London: Routledge, 1999), 5.

identify is that the desire for a theocracy, which is common to all monotheisms, is conditioned by monotheism's contest with prevailing social-political authorities. Consequently, monotheistic visions of theocracies, and the laws that support them, are constructivist in nature.

a. *A Few More Words Regarding Understanding Law as Constructive and Relevant for Monotheistic Identity*

> Politics are made up of two elements—utopia and reality—belonging to two planes which can never meet. There is no greater barrier to clear political thinking than failure to distinguish between ideals, which are utopia, and institutions, which are reality.[48]

"Constructivism," in the sociological and political senses, may be defined as the process of constructing a social-political reality according to a collective vision.[49] In its early form, constructivism was a philosophical concept advocated by Immanuel Kant arguing that reality was constructed in terms of one's own perceptions. To an extent, this view maintained that reality existed primarily not on a material plane but on a plane of ideals. N. Luhmann describes constructivism in its radical form as a stance positing "the world as it is and the world as it is observed cannot be distinguished."[50] Observation in this sense implies a perspective shaped by one's idea about what reality is, and that what is, in terms of being, is ultimately perfectible.

In light of that we must ask if the biblical authors perceived human nature as ultimately perfectible, allowing for, from an epistemological

---

48. Edward Hallett Carr, *The Twenty Years' Crisis, 1919–1939: An Introduction to the Study of International Relations* (New York: Palgrave, 2001), 87, cited in Karp, "The Utopia and Reality of Sovereignty," 313.

49. Barkin ("Realist Constructivism," 325) notes that scholars in the area of international relations define "constructivism" as either an ontology, epistemology, or methodology: "As such, it is usually defined as being distinct from either materialism or rationalism." He offers a definition of "constructivism" as it is generally used in studies of international politics: "Constructivists see the facts of international politics as not reflective of an objective, material reality but an intersubjective, or social, reality. In other words, what actors do in international relations, the interests they hold, and the structures within which they operate are defined by social norms and ideas rather than by objective or material conditions" (ibid., 326).

50. Citation from N. Luhmann and W. Rasch, *Theories of Distinction: Redescribing the Descriptions of Modernity* (Palo Alto: Stanford University Press, 2002), 11, cited in Nicolas Carrier, "Speech for the Defense of a Radically Constructivist Sociology of (Criminal) Law," *International Journal of Law, Crime and Justice* 36, no. 3 (2008): 169.

perspective, a complete constructive process, thus taking a view more modernly described as "radical constructivism":[51]

> What is radical constructivism? It is an unconventional approach to the problem of knowledge and knowing. It starts from the assumption that knowledge, no matter how it is defined, is in the heads of persons, and that the thinking subject has no alternative but to construct what he or she knows on the basis of his or her own experience. What we make of experience constitutes the only world we consciously live in. It can be sorted into many kinds, such as things, self, others, and so on. But all kinds of experience are essentially subjective, and though I may find reasons to believe that my experience may not be unlike yours, I have no way of knowing that it is the same. The experience and interpretation of language are no exception.[52]

Was the society in Yehud in all its "imperfections" the end-product of human interaction or a by-product of it? Ezra–Nehemiah may suggest both. Society in which the *golah* community existed (into which it immigrated, but from which it "separated" itself) could only be considered profane within *golah* ideology. The author(s) anticipate(s) a perfected, restored society cleansed of all profanity—such a society would arguably be the end-product of a divine plan.[53]

And is that not a function of law, that is, maintaining the political structure and preserving the distribution of power to the favor of those in power? We certainly see such ideas present in Ezra–Nehemiah.[54] But the

---

51. Presented as a rhetorical question, the answer would be "no," unless one assumed the biblical text accurately reflected a literal, absolute truth. But that is the proposition of monotheism, that its truths and its revelations are absolute and objective. An alternative perspective is described by Davies (*Memories of Ancient Israel*, 131), "The biblical sources, I have suggested, convey cultural memories, which have their own purposes in constructing identity and making sense of the present and the future. These memories can be relied on to reflect the view of the past that the authors wish to present."

52. Ernst von Glasersfeld, *Radical Constructivism: A Way of Knowing and Learning* (London: Falmer, 1995), 1.

53. Japhet ("Sheshbazzar and Zerubbabel, Part 1," 65–66) clarifies, "The Book of Ezra–Nehemiah describes the period of the Restoration from a historical distance and after a period of time during which those hopes and ferments flickered and were suppressed. The starting point of the book is not only a different perception of the course of events, but also a different political stand—the essence of which is an acceptance of political facts. This acceptance is not expressed as a political theory and a guide to political action, but takes form as a religious conviction and a way of understanding God's ways with His people."

54. Dozeman ("Geography and History in Herodotus and in Ezra–Nehemiah," 464) asserts that for the author of Ezra–Nehemiah, *eber-nahara(h)* represents a "new world order and environment in which law replaces monarchs." The "space" of

power motif that drives the text appears not to be one of preservation but of construction.[55] Faced with a perceived dystopic reality—a reality that required restoration—the authors propose an alternative that would be wholly regulated by divine law.[56] This alternative, which was really the result of restoration, was thought to fix or correct the encountered state of reality. Yet Nehemiah admits that divine law was not the status quo even for the community itself, "So they read from the book, from the law of God, with interpretation. They gave the sense, *so that the people understood the reading*" (Neh 8:8, emphasis mine). Because the very nature of the religious law was formulated on the rejection of the people already in the land (compare Exod 19:5–6), those who sought to impose it as normative must, to be successful, and in contrast to John Bright's proposal,[57] hold both the material and military (or "police") power to enforce obedience. Toward this end, which understands that the biblical portrayal of social-political relation to be motivated by visions of utopia, there is much revealed in Karp's analysis of utopian thought,

> The "utopian" mode of thought starts by fleshing out a normative position, and uses this position to arrive at prescriptions or conclusions about the descriptive world. When one translates this mode of thought into political action, one uses one's agency to (re)design political institutions, or to foster political events, such that the world is brought more closely into line with a normative idea about the way the world ought to be.[58]

eber-nahara(h), but Yehud more specifically, represents, therefore, the possibility in which a new political structure supported by religious law could be established.

55. Note also, "Rules can be taken as descriptive if and only if they are strictly followed, causing states to act in the real world in accordance with them. If rules merely prescribe 'appropriate' action, but actors feel free to do inappropriate things, then rules are normative. They belong in the realm of utopia, not the realm of reality" (Karp, "The Utopia and Reality of Sovereignty," 323). If *golah*-religious law was the political law of the province, where is the evidence that non-members (individuals outside the *golah* community) felt obliged to obey it?

56. T. Eskenazi's suggestion (*In an Age of Prose: A Literary Approach to Ezra–Nehemiah* [Atlanta: Scholars Press, 1988], 126) that an overarching concern for Ezra–Nehemiah was to protect the reader from confusing an "ideal community" with an "idyllic or idealized community" is interesting but helpful only for later readers of the text. It sees Ezra–Nehemiah as something of a humanitarian-oriented text with broad cultural-theological import concerned with the identity and stability of the community—thus, something akin to a survival mechanism (compare with Smith, "Politics of Ezra")—but not a text that reveals any social-political posturing, an activity in which members of the *golah* community were unquestionably involved.

57. Bright (*A History of Israel*, 391) proposed that Ezra imposed the law as normative.

58. Karp, "The Utopia and Reality of Sovereignty," 316.

The "normative" position, "ideal" rather, characterizing Ezra–Nehemiah is based upon acquired authority by the *golah* community—an authority that would be legitimated by a "restored" cultus. Yet we cannot say that a theocratic utopia, as is suggested or proposed by Ezra–Nehemiah and Zechariah, became an "institutional fact" for Yehud.[59] In truth, we are left without evidence toward which to point in order to show that the utopian descriptions articulated by the *golah* community (representatives of) were recognized and legitimated by external polities. A secret theocracy, a revolution in waiting, a construct of ideological aspiration, exists only in utopia, the only realm in which it can exist without destruction. The best hope a theocratic ideal might have in this situation is to affect change within already existing social-political structures. But it cannot hope to construct such structures. That is where texts such as Ezra–Nehemiah, Haggai, and Zechariah are caught. They are caught in a constructivist desire to realize utopia, to set aside constructivist vocabulary to take on descriptive vocabulary. Not to amend social-political reality but to construct it. Of the examples, the prophetic texts are perhaps more obvious in their ensnared position. As prophetic texts they seek change; they do not describe what has changed structurally. Ezra–Nehemiah, on the other hand, presents itself as historiography. Yet because the text proposes a social-political reality and structure different from what had existed prior to the arrival (or arrivals) of *golah* community members it is with the biblical texts that the more radical theory exists. Where Ezra–Nehemiah describes law, which is always for the text a religious law, it does so in a constructivist sense, to use it as the mechanism *through which to bring about a new reality*—Ezra, as we have discussed, must *teach* the law. As it is described in Ezra, the law does not function as either a "constitutive" or a "regulative" set of rules within the province.[60] That is, it neither already governs (or establishes

---

59. Karp defines "institutional fact" as the descriptive aspects of something, such as sovereignty, that can be treated as ontologically real. An institutional fact may be said to exist based on shared human beliefs and knowledge even if it cannot be said to exist "physically" (see ibid., 333–34).

60. Karp uses the illustration of chess to clarify these two concepts: "In the game of chess, there are rules that regulate the game, and rules that constitute it. The rule that one must move a piece if one touches it is a regulative rule. One can break this rule and still be playing the game of chess. By contrast, an example of a constitutive rule is that bishops can only move diagonally. If John Smith is using a chess board and chess pieces, but plays a game with those material objects in which his 'bishops' move vertically, there is a sense in which John is not playing the same game as the rest of us when we say that we are 'playing chess.' Another standard example is money. That a five-pound note is a piece of paper is a 'brute fact' [X]. That a five-

as the only possible choice[s]) the range of possible actions determined and legitimated by the social-political body, nor does it seem capable of regulating for the entire province interactions between individuals engaged in surplus, or desire, production. It functions on these levels for a religious community, a sub-culture defining itself in reaction to already established social and political norms. Yet the intent of the religious law, which must be read as part of the contest for authority, was to construct a new normative order for the social-political body. In order to do so, however, it must focus on exclusion so that it might be part of the process of rewriting social-political identity and the normative order.

3. *The Exclusionary Nature of Monotheistic Law*

There is a crucial point at which the religious law of the *golah* community fails at being political law. It was neither an imperial law (despite the aggrandizing claim of Ezra 7:25–26) nor was it a descriptive law, as that which already regulates a political body, in Yehud.[61] Notwithstanding the fanfare and ceremony of Ezra–Nehemiah, in which the divine law of *golah* Yahwism enjoyed center stage, the *golah* community was in relation to the people already in the land an immigrating community. Its religious law was to Yehud's already extant social-political body an *external* law. Moreover, textual laws were at this time not the bases for practiced law: "By Ezra's time, Torah was emphasized for the edification of leaders and commoners... Scholars are correct to note the development of Torah's *content* and *esteem* in these reforms; but it is assuming too much to posit in these periods an innovation in the *nature* of law writing."[62] In addition, while there were undoubtedly similarities between this religious law and the religious laws of the various forms of Yahwism practiced in the province, it distinguished itself so far as we know by virtue of its exclusion of everyone else. How, then, could it have hoped

---

pound note is money is an 'institutional fact' [Y], which depends entirely upon people in the context of British society [C] continuing to recognise it as such. Pieces of paper [X] become constituted as money [Y] within the context of a certain society [C], and this process confers value upon them beyond that of the 'brute facts' of the paper and ink" (ibid., 325–26).

61. Garbini (*Myth and History*, 110) suggests that the narrative of Ezra should be read not as historical confirmation of the dominance of religious law, but as a dividing line between the authority of the priests and the rabbis. If Garbini is correct, then Ezra's discussion of the law is less about suggesting political dominance and more about a contest for authority between priests and teachers of the law.

62. LeFebvre, *Collections, Codes, and Torah*, 143.

to regulate political behavior? It could not. And the best we can offer is to say that it was a "rival claim to govern without authority under the existing system."[63]

However, let us assume that the religious laws preserved in the Hebrew Bible are the same or similar to those maintained by the *golah* community, which is hardly a stretch according to Ezra–Nehemiah (Ezra 3:2; 7:6; Neh 8:1, 14; 10:29). Let us even further assume that the law referred to in Ezra–Nehemiah was a version of the Deuteronomic Law, to which the "book of the law of Moses" mentioned in Neh 8:1 refers. As Naomi Steinberg observes, there is in the Deuteronomic Law an obvious shift in focus toward state centralization.[64] Re-centralized power would undoubtedly be a concern for the *golah* community as it established its presence in Yehud. But if law supports the already established distribution of power, since *law does not create government*, the imposition of a new law—especially in view of any intrinsic tendency toward state centralization—would require a focused reorganization of distributed power. While the Deuteronomic literature, a possible source for Ezra's law,[65] offers a "new attitude" toward law, in contrast to earlier uses and understandings, it remains highly ideal and ritualistic while *anticipating* itself as prescriptive law.[66] And it is this thread of anticipation that weaves itself through Ezra–Nehemiah. Nehemiah's response to debt as an economic injustice in Neh 5:1–13, which LeFebvre entitles "Nehemiah's Lawsuit," offers to us an informative example:

> [A]t the end of the trial, the verdict implemented was "these words" which Nehemiah had spoken (vv. 12–13): the only prescriptive order emerging from the narrative *is the verdict stipulated by Nehemiah*. This scenario is startling if post-exilic Yehud was reorganized under Torah as a statutory constitution. As seen, there is plenty of Pentateuchal material Nehemiah could have drawn upon to justify his verdict. That he turned, however, to traditional forms of persuasion—and not to the law book—is telling.[67]

---

63. Hart, *The Concept of Law*, 118. Hart describes this type of "breakdown" as enemy occupation. While the described actions of the *golah* community may seem to fit the definition, and while it presents a superior and antagonistic attitude in its relation to the people already in the land, the phrase "enemy occupation" does not work well with this discussion of the social-political systems in Yehud.

64. Naomi Steinberg, "The Deuteronomic Law Code and the Politics of State Centralization," in *The Bible and the Politics of Exegesis* (ed. David Jobling et al.; Cleveland: Pilgrim, 1991), 166.

65. Cf. Raymond Westbrook, "Biblical Law," in *An Introduction to the History and Sources of Jewish Law* (ed. Neil S. Hecht et al.; Oxford: Clarendon, 1996), 3–4.

66. See LeFebvre's discussion in *Collections, Codes, and Torah*, 55–95.

67. Ibid., 128.

LeFebvre's conclusion may be overly ambitious; appeals to persuasion, and so also reason, can be offered within the framework of a prescriptive law. Nevertheless, Nehemiah's appeal to the divine as a source of punishment, thereby centralizing power on Yahweh,[68] rather than upon a textual law or the imperial king, *does* strongly suggest the absence, within the employed religious framework, of a prescribed legal structure through which punishment might be mediated. "The resulting appearance is very similar to that of Josiah's reforms. Citation of the law book is an important basis for restoring a defunct cultus. It is not used prescriptively for that reform, however. Nor is the book cited at all for social reform. There is actually no evidence in Ezra–Nehemiah of any effort to enforce Torah judicially."[69] Nehemiah's appeal, in other words, was not to an already social-politically legitimated power. Nor was his appeal one demanding a return to what was traditionally normative. He appeals to an idealized pattern of behavior wherein fidelity to Yahweh is socially constructive: "Should you not walk in the fear of our God, to prevent the taunts of the nations our enemies?" (5:9).

"[T]he defining characteristic of a legislative text," LeFebvre notes, "is when the text *is itself* 'the law'…"[70] Certainly an example of an appeal to a written text is found in ch. 13: "On that day they read from the book of Moses in the hearing of the people, and in it was written that no Ammonite or Moabite should ever enter the assembly of God" (v. 1). Despite the sense of "finding written" this was an idealistic, *constructive* appeal. Note that this appeals to the exclusionary nature of monotheistic identity, and so seeks to reinforce its own identity by isolating the religious community. Moreover, "[t]here is no real basis…for supposing Israel had come to the idea that law itself (any more than love or wisdom) could be embodied in words."[71]

This same process of producing collective identity is behind Ezra–Nehemiah's prohibition on intermarriage. It is framed by the theme of divine election found in, for example, Deuteronomy:

> When the LORD your God brings you into the land that you are about to enter and occupy, and he clears away many nations before you—the Hittites, the Girgashites, the Amorites, the Canaanites, the Perizzites, the Hivites, and the Jebusites, seven nations mightier and more numerous

---

68. As Foucault has widely demonstrated (but see especially his work in *Discipline and Punish*.), the ability to punish is power.
69. LeFebvre, *Collections, Codes, and Torah*, 68.
70. Ibid.
71. Ibid., 142.

than you[72]—and when the LORD your God gives them over to you and you defeat them, then you must utterly destroy them. Make no covenant with them and show them no mercy. Do not intermarry with them, giving your daughters to their sons or taking their daughters for your sons, for that would turn away your children from following me, to serve other gods. Then the anger of the LORD would be kindled against you, and he would destroy you quickly. (7:1-4)

Can we not hear echoes of this in Nehemiah? Nehemiah 9:7-8 reads:

> You are the LORD, the God who chose Abram and brought him out of Ur of the Chaldeans and gave him the name Abraham; and you found his heart faithful before you, and made with him a covenant to give his descendants the land of the Canaanite, the Hittite, the Amorite, the Perizzite, the Jebusite, and the Girgashite; and you have fulfilled your promise, for you are righteous

And we should also note,

> In those days also I saw Jews who had married women of Ashdod, Ammon, and Moab; and half of their children spoke the language of Ashdod, and they could not speak the language of Judah, but spoke the language of various peoples. And I contended with them and cursed them and beat some of them and pulled out their hair; and I made them take an oath in the name of God, saying, "You shall not give your daughters to their sons, or take their daughters for your sons or for yourselves. Did not King Solomon sin on account of such women?" (Neh 13:23-25)[73]

The reference to Solomon certainly refers to religious pursuits that did not include Yahweh:

> King Solomon loved many foreign women along with the daughter of Pharaoh: Moabite, Ammonite, Edomite, Sidonian, and Hittite women... and his wives turned away his heart. For when Solomon was old, his wives turned away his heart after other gods; and his heart was not true to the LORD his God, as was the heart of his father David. (1 Kgs 11:1, 3-4)

---

72. The comparison here assumes that all parties involved are in fact nations but are compared based on their "numbers." A slip of this type usually reflects a passage written after the fact, that is, the writer was writing out of the background of an Israelite (Judean) nation.

73. Traditionally, the city of Ashdod was inhabited by Philistines. But according to Isa 20:1, the Assyrian commander-in-chief sent by King Sargon conquered Ashdod. If the traditional Assyrian practice of deportation was employed, then there would likely have been a greater diversity of ethnicities represented. Jeremiah, in fact, describes Ashdod as a remnant (Jer 25:20; v. 21 also includes reference to Ammon and Moab), while Zechariah states, "a mongrel people shall settle in Ashdod" (Zech 9:6).

In what might be described as a standard monotheistic response, the author equates intermarriage with infidelity, a stepping outside defined parameters of a "permitted" behavior articulated by religious law. That the society engaged the practice, even so that its kings did, suggests it was an acceptable practice when considered outside a religious, monotheistic-oriented law framework.[74]

According to Ezra 3:2, Joshua and Zerubbabel built an altar to the god of "Israel" as prescribed in the law of Moses (cf. Deut 12:27; 27:5–6). If we accept the criteria stipulated by Nehemiah for membership in the "assembly," which according to Ezra–Nehemiah was also "Israel," we can be sure this statement in Ezra is not simply one of religious fidelity but of associative identity. That the presentation of religious law (in Ezra–Nehemiah) focuses more on identity definition—note the focus on religious and ethnic identities—than on regulating the political behavior of a social-political body should indicate for us the law's position before the "reality" it describes. It is a *constructivist* proposal, not a *descriptive* reality.[75] Furthermore, this should emphasize that the intent of the law was prescriptive, that it sought to construct a social-political reality by regulating it into existence—a proposal that is strongly supported by Ezra–Nehemiah's primary use of the law for the purposes of separation and identification.[76]

References to the law in Ezra–Nehemiah focus on exclusion for the purposes of preventing lawlessness and distinguishing a singular collective body—that is, a "remnant," the new "Israel" (cf. Neh 8:13–18; note esp., "And they *found it written in the law*…that the *people of Israel* should live in booths… *And all the assembly of those who had returned from the captivity made booths and lived in them*…" emphasis mine). By virtue of what constituted obedience to the law, we can surmise that lawlessness referred not to unregulated political behavior strictly, nor simply an acting out against laws governing behaviors within the social

---

74. Based on an analysis of the priesthood, VanderKam confirms (in *From Joshua to Caiaphas*, 53–54) that intermarriage was a fairly common occurrence within Yehud.

75. Though compare the works of R. Westbrook ("Biblical and Cuneiform Law Codes," *RB* 92, no. 2 [1985]: 253–58; *Studies in Biblical and Cuneiform Law* [Cahiers De Revue Biblique 26; Paris: Gabalda, 1988], 2–5; "Cuneiform Law Codes and the Origins of Legislation," *Zeitschrift für Assyriologie* 79 [1989]: 202), and B. Jackson (*Studies in the Semiotics of Biblical Law* [JSOTSup 314; Sheffield: Sheffield Academic, 2000], 141–42) who posit that a prescriptive use of Law/Torah emerges in Ezra–Nehemiah.

76. See also LeFebvre, *Collections, Codes, and Torah*, 139–40.

political body. The very concept of lawlessness as it related to religious law sought to identify and categorize identities and actions formed and undertaken *outside* the cultural framework defined by religious law (cf. Neh 9:28–30); in other words, the primary focus of the religious law was on *religious behavior* as a defining characteristic of collective identity (cf. Ezra 9:1–2).[77] For it is in this way that is stipulated who is and who is not a member of the community or assembly. Moreover, the narrative context of the law implies an association of the *golah* community, those who "returned from the captivity," with the Hebrews of Israelite (Judean) religious tradition to whom Yahweh promised the land of Canaan, at the expense of people already in the land. This focus on exclusion as constructive of identity, the like of which is characteristic of monotheistic identities generally, is, I propose, a consequence of a utopian agenda, which maintains that utopia would be realized by regulating behavior according to religious law. It does not describe a functioning political law animating the provincial political structure or the movement of the social-political body within that province. Or as LeFebvre puts it, "Ezra–Nehemiah does not display a concern for the enforcement of Torah's stipulations. What the records show is a concern to demonstrate that the post-exilic *cultus* was reformed in harmony with the Mosaic religion."[78]

a. *Further Understanding Law as a Framework for Restoration*
If *golah*-religious law was social-political law, it regulated political behavior. In consistency with laws generally, this may take one of two primary dispositions: on the one hand by regulating the individual through discipline, or on the other hand by regulating the social body. The former tends toward punishment after the fact; that is, the focus there tends to be more upon regulation through correction. "The chief function of the disciplinary power is to 'train'… Discipline 'makes' individuals; it is the specific technique of a power that regards individuals both as objects and as instruments of its exercise."[79] Of the latter, regulation focuses on risk management, that is, it looks toward future

---

77. LeFebvre's position (ibid., 115) is noteworthy here: "The Mosaic law book, itself, is treated as a situational application of law. Actual law is an unwritable divine ideal… When Ezra finds how Moses applied divine justice to circumstances similar to his own, Ezra makes a customized application of the same practice for his own day. His reference to the Mosaic law book is not as a source code of stipulations, but as an exemplar—a role model."
78. Ibid., 129.
79. Foucault, *Discipline and Punish*, 170.

events and actions while focusing on prevention and minimizing risk.[80] Foucault, for instance, describes this as the economy of the body:

> But we can surely accept the general proposition that, in our societies, the systems of punishment are to be situated in a certain "political economy" of the body: even if they do not make use of violent or bloody punishment, even when they use "lenient" methods involving confinement or correction, it is always the body that is at issue—the body and its forces, their utility and docility, their distribution and their submission.[81]

Dominant focus on Jerusalem's walls within Nehemiah reflects a concern for regulated space—and therefore regulation of the social-political body inhabiting that space. This concern is shown through Nehemiah's refusal, whether actual or narrative, to open wide the city gates on the Sabbath and thereby prevent foreign merchants entering sanctifiable space (Neh 13:91–21).[82] This action is consistent with Sally Merry's description of "spatialized regulation." As she puts it,

> Spatialized regulation is always also temporal as well. Regulations excluding offensive behavior usually specify time as well as space. Systems such as curfews designate both where and when persons can appear. Spatial regulations may interdict particular kinds of persons from an area only during certain times, such as business hours, or prohibit behavior…[83]

Nehemiah 13:21 tells us that this control was enforced with brutality: "But I warned them and said to them, 'Why do you spend the night in front of the wall? If you do so again, I will lay hands on you.'" Yet it is important that Nehemiah appeals not to the law as a source for regulated behavior—and if it truly were the law of the province, it would have been applicable here.[84] Punishment as described here depends not upon

---

80. As described by Sally Engle Merry, "Spatial Governmentality and the New Urban Social Order: Controlling Gender Violence Through Law," *American Anthropologist* NS 103, no. 1 (2001): 16.

81. Foucault, *Discipline and Punish*, 25.

82. Hoglund (*Achaemenid Imperial Administration*, 208) suggests that Nehemiah's actions were part of an attempt to focus attention on the formation of a holy community. His proposal, however, assumes that the imperially appointed governor was loyal foremost to the *golah* community.

83. Merry, "Spatial Governmentality," 17.

84. As discussed above, LeFebvre (*Collections, Codes, and Torah*, 125–28) makes a similar observation regarding Nehemiah's actions in Neh 5:1–13. For example, note specifically, "This scenario [i.e. Neh 5:7–13] is startling if post-exilic Yehud was reorganized under Torah as a statutory constitution. As seen, there is plenty of Pentateuchal material Nehemiah could have drawn upon to justify his verdict. That he turned, however, to traditional forms of persuasion—and not the law

law but upon Nehemiah's personal power, an exercise of power that seems to mimic what Foucault describes the "personal power of the sovereign."[85] In truth, the rationale behind Nehemiah's reaction seems somewhat unclear since the merchants were outside the city, the gates were closed, and they were not bringing "burdens" in on the sabbath day (v. 19). At the least, the presence of the merchants near the city of Jerusalem represents encroachment upon space the author has designated sacred, a designation confirmed by the author's interpretation of the city's walls and the function of its gates. What is important here seems to be a concern for control over operative forces and actions within defined space. As Merry describes further, "[Spatial forms of regulation] produce social order by creating zones whose denizens are shielded from witnessing socially undesirable behavior..."[86] Such forms reflect control, even if in this moment idealized, over space to regulate, in a preventative sense, lawlessness. We certainly see this in the action of closing the city gates on the sabbath day.[87]

This pattern of regulating behavior follows parameters of identity formation stipulated in Yahwistic religious law. "When the LORD your God brings you into the land you are about to *enter and occupy*, and he *clears away* many nations before you...and when the LORD your God gives them over to you and you defeat them, then *you must utterly destroy them*. Make no covenant with them and show no mercy" (Deut 7:1–2, emphasis mine). Extant citations of law suggest that the law had either been accepted by the community as, what LeFebvre terms, a "practical" text, or it was a blueprint for constructivist application. "The *presence* of citation therefore indicates practical use of the law text."[88] However, to appreciate it as descriptive of reality either requires that the religious law of an immigrating community created and sustained the framework of social-political behavior, which would necessitate legitimation by the whole of society, or it requires that the defined behavioral patterns were definitive of the religious community alone. To accept the former requires us to explain how and why a provincial governor focused

---

book—is telling. That this lack of judicial citation from the law book is paralleled by frequent cultic law book citations in Ezra–Nehemiah is even more telling" (ibid., 128).

85. Foucault, *Discipline and Punish*, 79–81.
86. Merry, "Spatial Governmentality," 17.
87. But in this case, spatial regulation is supported by what Merry has termed generally disciplinary regulation. Merry (ibid.) describes "disciplinary regulation" as regulation that "focuses on the regulation of persons through incarceration or treatment."
88. LeFebvre, *Collections, Codes, and Torah*, 96–97, emphasis in original.

on a solitary city seemingly at the expense of other cities in the province without losing his job. One possible way around this is found in Joseph Blenkinsopp's proposal that Nehemiah's "mission" was a response to the revolt of the local satrap Megabyzus. "If the Jews of the province had participated in the revolt, we would have an explanation for the fortification of Jerusalem and the countermeasures of the authorities in Samaria of which we hear in the misplaced section Ezra 4:7–23. In that case we could more easily understand in what frame of mind Nehemiah approached Artaxerxes with his request to rebuild the city its walls (Neh 2:3–5)."[89] However, apart from the lack of evidence for Jewish participation in the revolt,[90] this does not explain why or how any existing social-political law could have been replaced by the religious law of the *golah* community. On a theoretical level, Blenkinsopp's proposal offers an explanation for the textual focus on the walls of Jerusalem during Nehemiah's tenure as governor. But that explanation does not support the seeming suggestion of Ezra–Nehemiah that Nehemiah's actions were part of a process of divine restoration, which may be the result of authorial thievery—that is, interpreting events to be meaningful in ways they were not originally intended. The discrepancy, even on this theoretical level, emphasizes for us how the biblical authors framed events and ideas with an agenda that sought to realize utopia. According to Blenkinsopp's proposal, Nehemiah's actions would have been for the primary purpose of military and political control. Yet according to the author of Ezra–Nehemiah, Nehemiah's actions, as overtly understood, were driven primarily by a concern for demarcating and enforcing the religious division between spaces sacred and profane.

b. *Further Clarification of Monotheistic Law as an External Law*

> Artaxerxes, king of kings, to the priest Ezra, the scribe of the law of the God of heaven: Peace. And now I decree that any of the people of Israel or their priests or Levites in my kingdom who freely offers to go to Jerusalem may go with you. For you are sent by the king and his seven counselors to make inquiries about Judah and Jerusalem according to the law of your God, which is in your hand... (Ezra 7:12–14)

---

89. Joseph Blenkinsopp, "The Mission of Udjahorresnet and Those of Ezra and Nehemiah," *JBL* 106 (1987): 415.
90. See Meyers and Meyers, *Haggai, Zechariah 1–8*, xxxix; Leith, *Wadi Daliyeh Seal Impressions*, 9; Briant, *Histoire de l'Empire perse*, 704; Carter, *Emergence of Yehud*, 277–79, contra Balcer, *Sparda*, 138; John W. Betlyon, "The Provincial Government of Persian Period Judea and the Yehud Coins," *JBL* 105 (1986): 633–42; Blenkinsopp, "Mission of Udjahorresnet," 415, and *Isaiah 56–66*, 51.

Based on our discussion of law this far, one cannot accept the biblical proposal that Ezra introduced and enforced a relatively new religious law upon Yehud without glossing over the nature and function of law within the imperial context.[91] Moreover, it unrealistically assumes that society remained in a static state—unchanged by productive forces, which themselves must also become desires frozen in time—in the approximate seventy years from the fall of Judah to the trumpeted appearance of Ezra. Society in Yehud changed on a different trajectory than those of the Judean communities in Babylonia. For this reason we must, unless we wish to make an argument for an "empty land," accept that society continued in Yehud without the exiled Judeans, and that the forces of desire production, while interrupted, continued unabated, changing alongside developing social and historical circumstances. Furthermore, the laws by which people were governed did not share the same fundamental, material bases as the religious law of the *golah* community. There was no historical precedent in which the Mosaic Law was the statutory law for either Israel or Judah.[92]

Moreover, we cannot overlook the biblical portrayal of Ezra as a priest and scribe (cf. Ezra 7:21; Neh 8:9) intent on purifying the cultus.[93] By casting him as a priest and by making him the recipient of an imperial decree (cf. Ezra 7:21), Ezra–Nehemiah intimately connects the religious community and the imperial government, proposed religious and actual political authorities.[94] Linking the *golah* community to the mighty imperial king would seem to validate a *golah* claim to social-political authority. Moreover, by connecting the *golah*-religious law to the law of the imperial king, Ezra–Nehemiah equates with constructivist enthusiasm sovereign power with religious law. Yet the relative ease with which this seems to occur—"Then all the assembly answered with a loud voice, 'It is so; we must do as you have said'" (Ezra 10:12)—should remind us that this is utopian thinking of a high order. That even Ezra–Nehemiah suggests that the religious law was unknown in the province is reason enough for pause. "For Ezra had set his heart to study the law of the LORD, and to do it, and to *teach* the statutes and ordinances in Israel"

---

91. For further reference, note LeFebvre's discussion (*Collections, Codes, and Torah*, 96–145) of written law in Persian-period Yehud

92. On this, see LeFebvre's discussion in ibid., 31–95.

93. Cf. Ahlström, *The History of Ancient Palestine*, 877, 886–87.

94. Berquist's statement (*Judaism in Persia's Shadow*, 143) that Ezra encouraged allegiance to the Persian empire by equating the law of God to the law of the emperor would provide an alternative reading if we limit Ezra's audience to the *golah* community.

(Ezra 7:10, emphasis mine).[95] Given such a lack of knowledge, acceptance of a new law, as we have discussed already, would require coercive power from an external source. While this is certainly a role the imperial government could have taken there is more evidence of the imperial government utilizing the political structures already established rather than creating relative chaos by imposing and externally enforcing a newer law.[96] Moreover, the imperial government appointed officials who were loyal to it to important posts throughout its empire.[97] And it was the practice of the author of Ezra–Nehemiah to claim such appointees, where possible, as divinely appointed representatives.[98] Where they no longer supported the appropriate agenda, they are dismissed from the pages of history. Some, rather many, are not even mentioned.[99] Subsequently, any

95. LeFebvre (*Collections, Codes, and Torah*, 131–32) notes a similar emphasis in Neh 7:1–18). He concludes that the focus of the passage is on a encouraging public understanding of Mosaic Law.

96. Cf. Hoglund (*Achaemenid Imperial Administration*, 234–35), though he argues that Ezra's activity was to establish a new imperial legal apparatus within the legal structures already in place. Compare Fried's argument ("You Shall Appoint Judges," 63–90) that Ezra's commission was limited to appointing judges in the province (see also *Priest and the Great King*, 220). Dandamaev and Lukonin (*Culture and Social Institutions*, 121) also observe that the Persian imperial government tended to utilize the administrations and structures already in existence in local territories, although they take the argument further: "Each province remained an independent socio-economic region with its own social institutions and internal structure, with its old local laws, customs, traditions, systems of weights and measures, and monetary systems" (ibid., 97). A similar conclusion (i.e. to the second part of Dandamaev and Lukonin's argument), which we should read as a contrast to Hoglund and Fried, is held by Dion ("La Religion," 243–54), who takes for granted that the center of religion in Yehud was the version of Yahwism introduced by the *golah* community (he describes it as the religion defined by the "law of Moses"). Even though he questions the authenticity of the edict of Artaxerxes (Ezra 7:12–26), J. A. Soggin accepts it as historically certain that the "law" Ezra brought to Yehud became the law of Yehud and was "administered with the aid of public powers" (*A History of Israel: From the Beginnings to the Bar Kochba Revolt, AD 135* [London: SCM, 1984], 277).

97. Fried goes so far as to say that Persian judges and officials executed the law in even regional areas within provinces (*Priest and the Great King*, 220). See also Schaper's discussion (throughout his "Jerusalem Temple") of different imperial officials appointed to the temples.

98. If authority was not primarily legitimated by the cult and secondarily by the imperial government we need not explain why the *yhd/h* coins seemed to contradict Jewish law (see, e.g., Rappaport, "Judean Coinage," 1–17).

99. See the lists reconstructed by Avigad, *Bullae and Seals*, 35; Meyers, and Meyers, *Haggai, Zechariah 1–8*, 14. See also the larger discussion in Cataldo, *A Theocratic Yehud*, 90–117.

defense of the law of Moses serving as the functioning social-political law of the province must provide an explanation as to why the only imperially appointed governors of Yehud mentioned are those for whom stories linking them to *golah*-Yahwistic religious tradition have been written. Such a defense must also explain why the religious law is presented in Ezra–Nehemiah in a constructivist sense, to which we look below, rather than a descriptive one.

c. *Constructive Law and the Monotheistic Ideal*

> Thus says the LORD of hosts: Render true judgments, show kindness and mercy to one another; do not oppress the widow, the orphan, the alien, or the poor; and do not devise evil in your hearts against one another. But they refused to listen, and turned a stubborn shoulder, and stopped their ears in order not to hear. They made their hearts adamant in order not to hear the law and the words that the LORD of hosts had sent by his spirit through the former prophets. Therefore great wrath came from the LORD of hosts. Just as, when I called, they would not hear, so, when they called, I would not hear, says the LORD of hosts, and I scattered them with a whirlwind among all the nations that they had not known. Thus the land they left was desolate, so that no one went to and fro, and a pleasant land was made desolate. (Zech 7:9–14)

According to Zechariah's explanation, the general sense of which is shared by the Persian-period biblical texts, of the exilic events, the exiles enjoyed not the consequence of transgressing any political rule of law but the failure to perform expected actions of social justice. Hence the prophetic discourse laments not failed political law but unleashes social-religious commentary on past behaviors. And the envisioned behavioral patterns are framed by prophetic emphasis on religious obedience. Where the passage refers to justice, it is interpreted not as political justice but an action rendered in obedience to Yahweh.

"True judgments," "kindness," and the absence of oppression are certainly qualities every ancient Near Eastern society longed for, and which, subsequently, almost every textual record of ancient laws advertises was the status quo, in glorification of kingly action. But codified law codes of the ancient Near East were not the legal norm.[100] They were categorically ideal in nature, not widely distributed, and law was adjudicated through legal structures or systems more conventional. In kingdoms and empires, judges, officials, and elders cast judgments based on

---

100. Cf. A. Leo Oppenheim, *Ancient Mesopotamia: Portrait of a Dead Civilization* (rev. ed.; Chicago: University of Chicago Press, 1977), 231, see also p. 158; LeFebvre, *Collections, Codes, and Torah*, 1–54.

their interpretation of the general sense of the king's law and on their interpretation of tolerance levels within local communities. In practice, political behavior and courts were not governed by a written code.[101]

While laws certainly existed, and while they were codified, power was expressed in the ability to impose by word or deed patterns of obedient behavior. "A state monopoly for the use of violence," Donnelly reminds us, "is central to the rule of law."[102] But in the case of Yehud, the nature of continued conflicts between groups (*golah* community and the *am ha'aretz*, notably) suggests no power monopoly had been established by the *golah* community.[103] Without one, given its relatively decentralized position, the *golah* community could control neither the rule of law nor its corresponding social-political framework in Yehud. Its theocratic ideals could not govern interaction between social-political agents in Yehud because it had no material basis upon which to justify a set of laws as being politically dominant. Hence it is possible to see the law fulfilling a role within the community as regulating religious behavior but not as a conventional rule of law for the province.

With the scene set, we ourselves must render judgment. The pleasant story about Ezra reading from the law of Moses, lifting the scales of ignorance from the eyes and minds of the people, and dutifully causing wide-scale divorce (and possible subsequent economic meltdown by creating a new class of landless poor),[104] is not even conceivably parallel to a judge adjudicating law.[105] The narrative of Ezra reading from the law portrays a character—whose exact office the author is not entirely certain[106]—who presents an externally produced law as an ideal against which society must be measured.

101. Again see Oppenheim, *Ancient Mesopotamia*, 231, see also p. 158; LeFebvre, *Collections, Codes, and Torah*, 1–54. And note also, Mendenhall, "Ancient Oriental and Biblical Law," 3.

102. Samuel J. M. Donnelly, "Reflecting on the Rule of Law: Its Reciprocal Relation with Rights, Legitimacy, and Other Concepts and Institutions," *The Annals of the American Academy of Political and Social Science* 603 (2006): 42.

103. Smith's work (*Palestinian Parties*) clearly demonstrates that conflict and competition for power were characteristic of Yehud, at least as far as the returnees were concerned.

104. We say this somewhat tongue-in-cheek, but we do so to emphasize that such wide-scale divorce would have had unavoidable economic repercussions. These, however, are never discussed or alluded to in the texts, which might, but not certainly, suggest it never happened.

105. See also LeFebvre's discussion in *Collections, Codes, and Torah*, 129–33.

106. This uncertainly has produced a number of studies on the nature of Ezra's mission. See, for example, Blenkinsopp, "Mission of Udjahorresnet," 409–21; Lester L. Grabbe, "What Was Ezra's Mission?," in *Second Temple Studies, 2. Temple*

If we define Ezra's audience as the *golah* community alone in all its utopian grandeur then our case has been decided: the law of Moses exists solely as the religious law of a community living within a different, already established, provincial rule of law. And perhaps we encounter an identity crisis in the process—even the *golah* community does not appear really to know the law. If the community itself is ignorant of the law, then how may we possibly assume it to have any cultural or material anchor within the province? Do we perhaps see here an instance in which the author is trying to preserve the "face" of the community, despite a general passivity expressed toward the religious law—an attitude that might also be reflected in Haggai's frustration over the lack of progress in building the Jerusalem temple (Hag 1:2–4)? And if so, how could we expect it to have any effectiveness as political law if even those it identifies as its citizens do not know it?

There is an additional problem highlighted by Ezra 7:25–26:

> And you, Ezra, according to the God-given wisdom you possess, appoint magistrates and judges who may judge all the people in the province Beyond the River who know the laws of your God; and you shall teach those who do not know them. All who will obey the law of your God and the law of the king, let judgment be strictly executed on them, whether for death or for banishment or for confiscation of their goods or for imprisonment.

The "law of the king" and the "law of your god" are not entirely compatible. The first is the product of a political structure that legitimates the absolute authority of the king. The second would be the product of a political structure legitimating the absolute authority of the dominant god and by extension the rulers of the religious institution representing the god. As possible political laws, as rules of law, the two are not compatible but seek to distribute and maintain power differently. A law that rejects the presence of foreigners, is in fact based on the total exclusion of foreigners, has no room for the absolute authority of a foreign king. The only possible way to see the two working together is to set the statement "the law of your God and the law of the king," which puts the king's law in a secondary position (note the semantic ordering of the phrase *dt' dy 'lhyk wdt' dy mlk'*), within the context of the Jerusalem temple. In fact, the so-called decree is primarily about the construction of the Jerusalem temple. Thus, the "law of your God" is affirmed as the

Community in the Persian Period (ed. Philip R. Davies and John M. Halligan; JSOTSup 340; Sheffield: Sheffield Academic, 1994), 286–99; David Janzen, "The 'Mission' of Ezra and the Persian-Period Temple Community," *JBL* 119 (2000): 619–43; Fried, "You Shall Appoint Judges," 63–90.

religious law of the cult operating the Jerusalem temple while the "law of the king" is the political regulation within the larger province. The judges and magistrates appointed (possibly) by Ezra could not make legal decisions based on the framework of a law with which society seems to be unfamiliar.[107] Moreover, one can only imagine the consequent problems with legal decisions made based on the superiority of one community and the required exclusion of foreigners within a context largely marked by diversity.

We cannot reach out enthusiastically, as Joel Weinberg, among others, has done, and lionize Yehud as a model situation to which the imperial kings paid especial attention.[108] That it became a model example—in fact, it is his *only* example—of a theocratic community shows his seeming uncritical reliance upon Persian-period texts such as Ezra–Nehemiah. On the international scene, the province was nondescript. It was no oasis, no virginal maiden, no finely sculpted, well-oiled male. It held no status greater than, for example, the city of Babylon, a city and its province that *did* demand personal attention from the imperial government. In addition, there is no pattern showing that the imperial government allowed religious laws to supplant already existing political laws. Neither does, as has been proposed in support of Ezra's law as taking the place of provincial law, the possible transference of the administrative center from Mizpah to Jerusalem in itself suggest the elevation of *golah*-Yahwistic law as the law of the province.[109] Instead, this transference was likely a consequence of Darius' administrative restructuring.[110]

---

107. Fried ("You Shall Appoint Judges"), for example, argues that the judges were, in fact, Persian judges.

108. In fact, it is Weinberg's only example. He writes, "The most well-documented source for the Achaemenid period is the postexilic community of Judah, so this serves as a model for the solution of the task before us. Notably, the postexilic community is an outstanding example of the citizen-temple community, and thus can be referred to for conclusions about this type of 'local administration,' with, however, certain reservations. Furthermore, the sources about the history of the postexilic community allow one to analyze the 200-year evolution of the relationship between 'central' and 'local' administration, which is not possible for other citizen-temple communities" (*Citizen-Temple Community*, 106).

109. On the possibility of Mizpah operating as an administrative center, see Blenkinsopp, *Isaiah 56–66*, 46; André Lemaire, "Nabonidus in Arabia and Judah in the Neo-Babylonian Period," in Lipschits and Blenkinsopp, eds., *Judah and the Judeans in the Neo-Babylonian Period*, 292. Both Lemaire and Ahlström (Ahlström, *The History of Ancient Palestine*, 851, 865) date the transference to 445 B.C.E., around the time of Nehemiah's tenure in Yehud and his rebuilding the walls of Jerusalem. In this case, Yehud's previous governors—we should not follow Alt's now disproved hypothesis that Nehemiah was Yehud's first governor—would have

Likewise, the proposal by Dandamaev and Lukonin that during October 445 B.C.E. Nehemiah declared that the laws collected and codified by Ezra were the basic law code of Judah (Yehud) is without concrete basis.[111] An eager proposal it is; they write, "As a result of [Nehemiah's declaration], Jerusalem was converted into a theocratic state headed by the high priest, and the fundamental principles of self-administration of the Jewish community were laid down within the framework of the supreme authority of the Persian king."[112] If only it were possible to speak of a theocratic state and self-administration functioning within the framework of the Persian empire, as though Yehud could be simultaneously state and non-state, autonomous and governed. Ultimately, however, the religious law of the *golah* community did not constitute a social-political legal code in Persian-period Yehud. Instead, it existed only as a blueprint for "restoration," in which the land as space for restoration was identified, and which required the construction of a new normative order.

---

operated from Mizpah, which might be one reason why the biblical writers of the Persian period do not speak of or perhaps do not know of them. If the authors were confined to the city of Jerusalem, this would explain their seemingly narrow worldview.

110. Edelman's proposal (*The Origins of the "Second" Temple*, 9) is also plausible, though some of her rationale (such as a lacking water source in Mizpah) are not entirely convincing: "The decision to rebuild Jerusalem as the new provincial seat, replacing the long-serving Mizpah, would have been the result of strategic considerations. Jerusalem lay at a major north–south and east–west cross-roads, whereas Mizpah only commanded a position along the main north–south route in the central highlands. It also had a perennial water source on-site, unlike Mizpah."

111. Dandamaev and Lukonin, *Culture and Social Institutions*, 129.

112. Ibid., 129–30.

Chapter 5

CLARIFYING LAND AS THE ARENA FOR RESTORATION

It was Martin Noth who first gave us a clear vision of the Chronicler, whom he determined was responsible for Ezra–Nehemiah, as borrowing from the source material of the Deuteronomistic History.[1] With the benefit of Noth's work, it is not difficult then to see how Ezra–Nehemiah might have adopted the tradition of the Deuteronomistic Historian's (Dtr) tradition of the conquest under Joshua as a model through which to interpret the *golah* community's experience of migration, even though the Joshua tradition did not fully match the experience of the *golah* community.[2] The use of this tradition testifies not only to the perceived difficulties of returning to the land but also to a significant concern that Yahweh—but "Yahweh" as perceived by the *golah* community and not the *am ha'aretz* (note Ezra 4:2)—be validated in a position of authority. As Norman Habel has highlighted, Dtr, to whom the conquest narratives should be attributed, describes Yahweh allocating the land of Israel to the Hebrews as "crucial steps" in the public demonstration of Yahweh's own universal authority.[3] "So acknowledge today and take to heart," writes Dtr, "that the LORD is God in heaven above and on earth beneath; there is no other" (Deut 4:39). In addition, George Coats emphasizes that the conquest as described in Joshua was part of larger narrative frame of wilderness wandering within the Torah that emphasized a divine action the intent of which was establishing divine authority, which was symbolized in the land and the Hebrews that would inhabit it.[4] Both Habel

---

1. Martin Noth, *The Deuteronomistic History* (JSOTSup 15; Sheffield: JSOT, 1981), 2.
2. In addition, whether or not one agrees with his conclusion that the conquest under Joshua was wholly fictional, Liverani (*Israel's History*, 283–87) argues convincingly that the character of Joshua served as a role model for the leaders of the Babylonian returnees.
3. Norman C. Habel, *The Land Is Mine: Six Biblical Land Ideologies* (Minneapolis: Fortress, 1995), 37.
4. George W. Coats, "An Exposition on the Conquest Theme," *CBQ* 47 (1985): 52.

and Coats have highlighted the importance of the connection for the Deuteronomistic History, and consequently for Ezra–Nehemiah, between a public articulation of divine ownership of the land and public demonstration of divine authority. Richard Friedman comes close to this understanding when he writes that Numbers is a unified narrative "recounting a meaningful progression of events, and depicting the incubation and preparation of the people before it becomes a free nation in the land promised to their patriarchs, while also depicting the developing relations between the people and Yahweh."[5] To be sure, the traditions of the wilderness wandering and the land conquest are not important in isolation from the culmination of the processes they begin. Both inaugurate the establishment of "Israel" as a public demonstration of Yahweh's authority.

Because the two traditions do not match up completely, Ezra–Nehemiah interprets and refines the framework of the conquest tradition, which was strongly military in orientation, as one befitting land acquisition and migration within a religious-cultural tradition. The shift from the undeniable presence of a native military component to a dependence upon foreign imperial power and the divine authority of Yahweh also indicates for us the *golah* community's lack of a military. As such, the public demonstration of divine authority could not depend upon any public, material demonstration of authority. In Ezra–Nehemiah's reinterpretation, the exile was represented by the wilderness wandering, the rebuilding of the Jerusalem temple paralleled the Sinai event (in which the relationship between God and people was defined), and the concern for the cultural-religious separation of the Hebrews from the people of the land became even more paranoid in Ezra, who, while employing the same conclusion expressed by Dtr, explained the exile as punishment for not maintaining a rigid boundary between "Israel" and the other peoples in the land. As a cultural metaphor, the wilderness wandering symbolized the initial stages in the process of isolating and defining a new social-political body. Ezra–Nehemiah's emphasis upon geographic displacement as the only event that qualified one as a member of the remnant appeals to this "structuring" process. The Sinai event emphasized not only that divine authority was the absolute authority of the land in question but also that the identity of the people as a social-political body was dependent upon external recognition of this authority.[6] Ezra–Nehemiah interprets the temple as the sacred mountain (a common

---

5. Richard E. Friedman, "Torah (Pentateuch)," *ABD* 6:608.
6. In this sense, Exod 19:1–6 is less a personal, ethical injunction and more a collective obligation meant to emphasize the authority of Yahweh in the land.

interpretation within the ancient Near East following the urbanization of previously [semi-]nomadic groups) and the temple's own state of existence as a reflection or indicator of the future state of the remnant (cf. Ezra 1:2; 3:8–11), whom Ezra identifies as "Israel." The text preserves the distinction between insider and outsider, as codified within the so-called Mosaic Law, but also depends upon the events of the exiles as confirmation that disobedience of divine law entails very real material consequences.

Relatedly, Numbers (26:52–56) describes the apportionment of land according to tribal size. This would suggest a perceived equitable distribution of land insuring that each family had the same or similar amount for inheritance. By equalizing land distribution, it promoted an egalitarian distribution of power in contrast with the early historical class divisions that characterized urban life. In addition, the military organization described in Num 10[7] followed by a "national" census (26:1–4) and an equitable distribution of land as something economically valuable confirms that the driving intent behind the conquest tradition was the creation of a social-political rather than a religious body. Ezra–Nehemiah, on the contrary, views the "conquest" not as an act of creation but one of a restoration that began with the Jerusalem temple (cf. Ezra 1:1–11). In the absence of a strong military component, Ezra–Nehemiah treats the "conquest" as something near to a religious ritual (cf. Ezra 1–3; 6:19–22). This shift in perception from one tradition to the next reflects a shift in the expected power relations that would help constitute the resulting community or collective body. Where Numbers relied upon the confederacy-type model in which authority was, if only ideally, distributed equally among the tribes, Ezra, reflecting actions consistent with a monotheistic nature, emphasized the preeminence of a single community (*golah*) over would-be fellow inheritors (*am ha'aretz*). Ezra's narrative employment of religious ritual instead of a military campaign as metaphor was a consequence of the community's own peripheral status within the structure of Yehud's power relations and its growing conviction that its religious belief system could enforce social solidarity within the province—a conviction that was in full support of the community's pursuit of authority. Where the Numbers tradition focused on the act of establishing the newly defined social-political body, the tradition in Ezra could only focus on restoring authority and moving the *golah* community out from the periphery. Ezra's employment of a religious belief system was made possible by the cult's

---

7. See also Liverani's discussion of this in Liverani, *Israel's History*, 280.

growing confidence that social-political authorities could be judged effectively by religious standards.[8]

1. *Defining Land as the Space for Restoration*

Land as understood within the framework of monotheism is the arena in which the conflict over authority unfolds, which makes it also the eventual space for restoration. Because of this, the biblical descriptions of the physical land of Yehud tend to be oriented toward a utopian vision of a restored Israel. Ezra–Nehemiah's narrative obsession with the geographic space of Jerusalem is a consequence of the text's implicit understanding that "land," defined in either a real or an imaginary (as is the case for later more "mature" monotheisms) sense, is a requisite arena in which the contest for authority must occur in public discourse.[9] This new understanding was a product of the same social-political forces that produced a redefined concept of "Israel" during the Persian Period. As M. Leith writes, "In the Persian period the concept of 'Israel' changed. Before the Babylonian exile, Israel was defined not by worship but by its independent geopolitical existence, by occupying its own land. Exile and Diaspora force a new, evolving, sense of identity. The Persian period (539–332 B.C.E.) constitutes an era of restoration and innovation."[10] According to Ezra–Nehemiah, "Israel" came to identify the "proper" social-political authority, embodied by the *golah* community, in contrast to the prevailing authority in the province.[11] The inherent conflict in re-identifying Yehud's social groups, should the people already in the land acknowledge the *golah* community's authority to redefine them, is aggravated by the community's appeal to its own internal religious system and not to the social system constructed within the relationship of the larger collective of social agents to the land and to each other. Israel

---

8. In stating this we are following R. Bellah (*Beyond Belief: Essays on Religion in a Post-Traditional World* [Berkeley: University of California Press, 1991], 35) who argues that with the rise of historic religions emerged a new religious elite, which also created new forms of conflict as the numbers of participants in the conquest for authority increased.

9. When we employ the term "land" we refer to the real and imagined spaces in which, in the spirit of Deleuze and Guattari, the "productions of desire" occur. Control of the land, therefore, includes authority over the arena of production (as is the inference is Neh 13:15–22).

10. Leith, "Israel Among the Nations," 367.

11. J. Blenkinsopp ("A Jewish Sect of the Persian Period," *CBQ* 52 [1990]: 5–20) has shown us that this redefined meaning can be found in Isa 66:1–5, the four so-called servant songs in Second Isaiah, Mal 3:13–21, and Ezra 9–10.

as a reference to this "proper" authority, we must note further, also identified the geopolitical space, the land, that the community would inhabit. The public exhibition of divine authority required this space in which divine authority could be established and demonstrated through the medium of the *golah* community. In addition, the dissonance of an identity that was not fully anchored in immediate social, political, and material circumstances required the formation of a cultural-religious, institutional dependence upon restoration—the creation of a social order and system that supported a preconceived identity—as necessary.

David Summers' categorical orientation of space, defined principally within the framework of the discipline of art, offers us a starting point for the following discussion.[12] *Real space* is "the space we find ourselves sharing with other peoples and things." *Virtual space* is "space represented on a surface, space we 'seem to see.'" And *personal space* is "articulated by relations of artifacts to the real spatial conditions of our embodied existences, that is, our sizes, uprightness, facing, handedness, vulnerability, temporal finitude, capacities for movement, strengths, reaches and grasps." This tripartite view of space determines his view of, for example, architecture: "Architecture is the art of social space because it both encloses and includes institutions; it is the means by which human groups are set in their actual arrangements."[13] One limitation to this definition, however, is Summers' godfatherly view of architecture, which emphasizes architecture as *the* physical representation of materialist production.[14] Jerusalem's walls cannot be so described. As Pierre Bourdieu has shown, human agents are situated in their "arrangements" within the habitus by the social body's systems of production. Architecture is a *product* of those systems; nevertheless, it is a product that also imposes limitations on the possibilities of action. For the *golah* community, "personal space," in representation of a collective, was determined by the community's monotheistic identity. Boundaries of this

12. David Summers, *Real Spaces: World Art History and the Rise of Western Modernism* (New York: Phaidon, 2003), 43.
13. Ibid.
14. On materialist production as constructive of the distributed relations within a social body, note further, "It is beneath the blows of private property, then of commodity production, that the State witnesses its decline. Land enters into the sphere of private property and into that of commodities. *Classes* appear, inasmuch, as the dominant classes are no longer merged with the State apparatus, but are distinct determinations that make use of this transformed apparatus" (Deleuze, and Guattari, *Anti-Oedipus*, 218). That, however, is only half the tale, because the dismantling of the "State," or more generally the social-political body, and the transforming of its apparatus inaugurates the creation of a rewritten distribution of power.

space can be found, for example, in Ezra: "Shall we break your commandments again and intermarry with the peoples who practice these abominations? Would you not be angry with us until you destroy us without remnant or survivor" (Ezra 9:14)? In addition, while the "real space" in which the community found itself was the province of Yehud, the relevant biblical texts limit our understanding of the "virtual space" it engaged to representations or productions in and immediately surrounding the city of Jerusalem. Note for clarifying example the telescoping view in Zechariah: "The LORD will inherit Judah as his portion in the holy land, and will again choose Jerusalem" (2:12).[15]

Because the need is emphasized by their transition from a dependence upon ideological rather than material conditions for self-definition, the preliminary steps taken by more compact forms of monotheism toward forming an institutional dependence upon restoration, as described above, are deeply encoded within cultural identity and transitioned into fundamental dogmas within the more complex forms of monotheism. Nevertheless, the need for a public demonstration of authority is found in the complex forms as well. To meet this need in part, restoration requires the possession of, and therefore the authority over, real and imagined or virtual space.[16] Moreover, because its intent is a public demonstration of authority, it imposes upon the social world its expectation that the social world will accept its own ultimate rejection from authority in a "restored" world. On account of this, the monotheistic body's resistance to the social body creates an inherent "pariah" quality—the monotheistic member is always in waiting for restoration, the manifestation of divine will. As it is written in the Mishnah, for example, "Whoever does not merit this life is [truly] dead and will not live forever" (*m. Torah* 8:2). Christian and Islamic beliefs and dogmas of paradise can also be found

---

15. The term *nhl* (inherit) refers to receiving property as part of a permanent possession and often as a result of succession (see *TWOT*, s.v.). On the other hand, *bhr* means to "look keenly at" an object as a possible realization of desire. It is often used to denote divine choice of an elect people, as Zech 2:12 shows.

16. These categories also loosely correspond to Edward Soja's "firstspace" and "secondspace." See, for example, Edward W. Soja, *Thirdspace: Journeys to Los Angeles and Other Real-and-Imagined Places* (Oxford: Blackwell, 1996), 1–6, 67. Though Soja bases his work on that of H. Lefebvre (*La production de l'Espace* [Paris: Anthropos, 1974]), Lefebvre's "perceived" and "conceived" spaces, contra Soja, are not independent spaces but are "dialectically connected processes of production" (Christian Schmid, "Henri Lefebvre's Theory of the Production of Space: Towards a Three-Dimensional Dialectic," in *Space, Difference, Everyday Life: Reading Henri Lefebvre* [ed. Henri Lefebvre and Kanishka Goonewardena; New York: Routledge, 2008], 42).

here with striking similarity. While it is without official dogma because of its focus on the present life *'olam hazzeh*, more modern Jewish belief in *'olam haba'* in contrast to *'olam hazzeh* is supported by this passage.[17] This dogma is based on the necessary assumption that divine authority is by nature otherworldly and that it supersedes all possible human authorities in terms of possible rights over and access to the land. One is not hard pressed to accept that that assumption is common to all monotheisms. Ezra's encouragement of the Babylonian exiles to return to Jerusalem is likewise consistent with it:

> Any of those among you who are of his people—may their God be with them!—are now permitted to go up to Jerusalem in Judah, and rebuild the house of the LORD, the God of Israel—*he is the God who is in Jerusalem*... (Ezra 1:3, emphasis mine)[18]

Richard Nelson observes that land, as the exilic redaction of the Deuteronomistic History understands it, was an ambiguous gift. While Dtr presented as it the "Promised Land," the land contained the "seeds of Israel's eventual destruction," which were the elements of previous populations with whom Israel assimilated, which was in turn punished with exile.[19] "It is not surprising," he concludes, "that a return to this land formed no part of his future hope (1 Kgs 8:50)."[20] The idea that the land was linked to a previous disobedience also permeates Ezra–Nehemiah in its concern over the strict regulation and control of community

---

17. For example, "Thus, the Sages of the previous ages declared: 'In the world to come, there is neither eating, drinking, nor sexual relations. Rather, the righteous will sit with their crowns on their heads and delight in the radiance of the Divine Presence'" (*m. Torah* 8:2).

18. Compare also the concept of land expressed here, "Hast thou not seen how thy Lord hath spread the shade—And if He willed He could have made it still—then We have made the sun its pilot; Then We withdraw it unto Us, a gradual withdrawal? And He it is Who maketh night a covering for you, and sleep repose, and maketh day a resurrection. And He it is Who sendeth the winds, glad tidings heralding His mercy, and We send down purifying water from the sky, *that We may give life thereby to a dead land, and We give many beasts and men that We have created to drink thereof*" (Qur'an 25:45–49, emphasis mine). And also, "'Father, glorify your name.' Then a voice came from heaven, 'I have glorified it, and I will glorify it again.' The crowd standing there heard it and said that it was thunder. Others said, 'An angel has spoken to him.' Jesus answered, 'This voice has come for your sake, not for mine. *Now is the judgment of this world; now the ruler of this world will be driven out*'" (John 12:28–31, emphasis mine).

19. Richard D. Nelson, *The Double Redaction of the Deuteronomistic History* (JSOTSup 18; Sheffield: Sheffield Academic, 1981), 124–25.

20. Ibid., 125.

membership. But where, according to Nelson, Dtr appears to have given up hope in the land, the author(s) of Ezra–Nehemiah views the land as the space that Yahweh would bring about restoration. Both view the stability of the land and its representation of divine will linked to the people's obedience of the law.

The immigrating Babylonian Judean returnees viewed Jerusalem constructively; that is, they saw in that space the possibility of a new society. The parameters of that society were regulated by divine law, which was a product of the community itself—the same community that Ezra–Nehemiah identifies as Israel.[21] In order to prevent the "bad seed," as Nelson described it, from destroying the possibility of restoration, the community, drawing upon the divine law, viewed exclusion from the *am ha'aretz* to be its divinely expected obligation. Or as Ezra warns, "The land that you are entering *to possess* is a land unclean with the pollutions of the peoples of the lands, with their abominations. They have filled it from end to end with their uncleanness. Therefore do not give your daughters to their sons, neither take their daughters for your sons, and never seek their peace or prosperity, *so that you may be strong and eat the good of the land and leave it for an inheritance to your children forever*" (Ezra 9:11–12, emphasis mine). In short, either or both real and virtual land is the arena upon which the contest for authority is meted out, an event or process definitive of monotheistic identity.

a. *Inscribing the Land in a Public Display of Divine Authority*
Within the Persian-period biblical literature, the concept of "land" refers to both the city of Jerusalem and its environs as well as a future restored Israel.[22] As material space, the land was the space in which property, and

---

21. Note also Garbini: "The historical process which began at the time of Hezekiah would undergo a phase of intensive acceleration during the exilic period, which certainly would not end with 539 BC. The result was that at that time a completely new view of the history of the Jewish people was established, the main features of which could be summed up in three points: the exiles from Judah affirmed their right to represent all Israel, making their ancestor Abraham the direct ancestor of Jacob and the repository of the divine promise; the institution of the monarchy was repudiated and the sacral figure of the king with his direct relationship with the deity was replaced by the people as a whole, who in this way automatically became a sacred people; and the distant origins of the Jewish people were put in southern Mesopotamia" (*History and Ideology*, 82).

22. Summers writes, "*Land*...is *indefinite* in that it is simply beyond the boundaries of a place. Planarity gives this indefiniteness a new dimension. A notional plane is indefinite in that it may be of any extent, and if land is understood in these planar terms, then it is also understood in terms of the conditions for

subsequently class, could be marked out[23]—to mark the land, to impose taxes upon the body is an act of authority.[24] For the *golah* community, the province of Yehud was the chosen arena for the production of desire—desire as manifest in authority, economic class (control of surplus), and the constituted boundaries, both social and political, that separated member from non-member, or citizen from foreigner.[25] "Your people shall all be righteous; they shall possess the land forever. They are the shoot that I planted, the work of my hands, so that I might be glorified" (Isa 60:21).[26]

measure, which is necessarily the imposition of an *arbitrary unit* of measure. *Whatever may be measured may also be brought under a single rule*" (*Real Spaces*, 202, last emphasis mine).

23. For a related reference on marking out land in confirmation of class and authority note Summers' discussion (ibid., 199) of surveying as a preface to taxation: "Surveying [especially for the purpose of taxation] is a literal and fundamental means by which rule is applied." And further, "'Cadastral' surveying, the establishment of boundaries, is from the Greek meaning 'according to a line, or series,' and perhaps refers to the sighting of landmarks to determine boundaries. Some notion of the significance of such boundaries may be gained by considering that a 'cadaster' may still be a register of taxable property, or that the term for tax in Renaissance Florence was *catasto*, the taxable having changed from land to property, the common term being 'measure'" (ibid.).

24. In this light, the issuance of coins inscribed with *yhd* and either the governor's or the priest's name (or other relevant symbolism) can be seen as an act to demonstrate authority in the land. See, for example, Ya'akov Meshorer, "The Ear of Yahweh on a *Yehud* Coin," in *Eretz-Israel: Archaeological, Historical and Geographical Studies*. Vol. 25, *Joseph Aviram Volume* (ed. Avraham Biran et al.; Jerusalem: Israel Exploration Society, 1996), 434–47; Rappaport, "Judean Coinage," 1–17; Betlyon, "Provincial Government," 633–42; Barag, "Some Notes," 166–68, and "Silver Coin," 4–21.

25. Dozeman ("Geography and History in Herodotus and in Ezra–Nehemiah," 457) argues that not just Yehud but the entirety of *eber naharah* was conceived by Ezra–Nehemiah to be the space in which Yahweh would bring about restoration: "The author of Ezra–Nehemiah also employs the term for ideological and utopian purposes. We will see that Ezra–Nehemiah presents a utopian picture of the Persians ruling over *Abar Naharah* as culturally inclusive monarchs who are constrained by law (conceived space)—an image at odds with Herodotus's critical evaluation of Eastern despots as ethnocentric and lawless. The idealization of Persian rule, grounded in law, fuels the more immediate lived space of the author of Ezra–Nehemiah, in which an emerging form of Yahwism within the territory *Abar Naharah* is presented as a religion of law."

26. This passage from Third Isaiah finds a strong parallel in Second Isaiah, the latter about which Berquist writes, "The comfort of salvation for this prophet points toward Jerusalem. The emphasis is strange, since the audience consists of Babylonian Jews. However, the promise to these exiles is that they will receive the

When we speak of "land," therefore, we refer to those spaces in which desiring production as material production occurs.[27] It is both object and space upon which identity is inscribed and authority imposed. As the arena in which society *produces* it is the singular constant throughout the historical process. And in that we agree with Foucault to a greater degree than Summers: it is better to address the space in which objects emerge and are transformed rather than the permanency, and so "architecture," of objects themselves.[28] In other words, architecture, such as Jerusalem's temple and walls, is an inscription upon the land, where the production of desire and subsequently meaning begin, and is not by itself meaningful. Architectural objects are ephemeral; their values are always contingent upon the meanings that the social-political body provides them. In the case of Jerusalem's walls and temple, however, the Persian-period biblical literature identifies the walls and temple of Jerusalem as a public demonstration of divine authority, which is a meaning provided not by the larger social-political body but by the smaller religious body, or the "remnant," or *golah*, community. This inscription, therefore, remains in a perpetual state of contestation—the meaning attributed to it by the *golah* community competes with the possible range of meanings available within the larger social-political body, the demonstration of whose authority, in contrast, does not require the symbols in question. The value or meaning that such an inscription may receive is based largely upon the mode of production and the perceived relationship of people and land, an issue to which we turn next.

land of Yehud; the audience will be the comfort for Jerusalem. The prophet depicts an emigration from Babylonia to Yehud, so that the exiles can take over a Persian colony. Deutero-Isaiah defines this occupation as good news for Jerusalem (Isaiah 41:27), even though one might reason that the native inhabitants of Yehud would have disagreed" (*Judaism in Persia's Shadow*, 36). In addition, Isa 52:1–2, 7–10 renders Jerusalem fit only for the exiles. The people in the land were regarded as foreigners. "The exiles form an elite to whom God gives the sole right to live in the new Jerusalem" (ibid., 38).

27. Production changes in the process of its own working. It is, as Deleuze and Guattari describe, "interrupted" and redirected, to be interrupted again. The moment it produces, it becomes a product of its own production. Note, for example, "As a machine [the State] no longer determines a social system; it is itself determined by the social system into which it is incorporated in the exercise of its functions" (*Anti-Oedipus*, 221). Berger puts it in terms of a process of externalization, in which actions and relations produce, objectivation, in which the product becomes "fact" to the society, and internalization, in which individuals react and respond to the newly acquired fact (*Sacred Canopy*, 4). Control over those spaces in which such processes occur, in which production *moves*, evokes authority over the social body.

28. Foucault, *Archaeology of Knowledge*, 32.

2. Understanding Production and Perception of the Land in the Process of Restoration

Deleuze and Guattari write, "The earth is the primitive, savage unity of desire and production. For the earth is not merely the multiple and divided object of labor, it is also the unique, indivisible entity, the full body that falls back on the forces of production and appropriates them for its own as the natural or divine precondition."[29] Because the land is always in a state of material production, the nature of social existence is defined first by the human relationship to the system of production that the land makes available. In other words, land must be read within the framework of mode of production, because it is there in the finding of the production of one's means of subsistence that society becomes first self-aware and defines patterns of relationships, of meanings, and of beliefs between and shared among human agents. This point finds agreement with Norman Gottwald, who writes,

> [M]ode of production…refers to the way human capacities and technology are socially organized for the labor necessary to meet basic human needs and to allocate what is produced. In a broader sense, mode of production includes the social ramifications of the labor process in class and status divisions, in political process, in family organization, and in juridical procedures.[30]

A society's mode of production remains always "interrupting" of itself to meet changing needs.[31] One must, for that very reason, view it as part of an ongoing conversation between society and the history of material relations. As modes of interaction—that is, mechanisms and methods of production—with the natural world change, the ways that human agents associate and control, or are controlled, change. And with this latter change, there occurs alterations in the way that individuals think about themselves and each other.[32] Therefore, mode of production is not merely the product of class relations, it resides at their core.

Utopian thinking, on the other hand, treats land as empty space, or more precisely as a canvas for creation or "restoration."[33] It divorces, or sometimes ignores, society's dependence upon the natural world, a

---

29. Deleuze and Guattari, *Anti-Oedipus*, 140.
30. Norman K. Gottwald, "Sociology (Ancient Israel)," *ABD* 6:83.
31. Deleuze and Guattari, *Anti-Oedipus*, 233.
32. My point here is influenced by Gottwald's discussion in *Tribes of Yahweh*, 631.
33. More, *Utopia*, 239.

tendency we see develop within monotheism. In place of that once intimate relationship it imposes its own internally constructed, ideological absolutes of the ethical good and the moral right, concepts whose initial purpose is the preservation of the order that defines a social-political identity. While the reality of which it conceives may boast of an intimate relationship to the natural world, such as in the case of Marx's communism, utopian thinking is not materially grounded; utopian thinking is instead an ideological reaction to very real material circumstances. It exists in the world of transcendent ideas eager and ready to impose themselves upon the material world—and in that there is no difference between restoration and utopian thinking. But utopian discourse is nevertheless chained to a material reality; it cannot shake free of material desire-production. It speaks, therefore, through symbolic reference to its verisimilitude.

Should we not in that sense read the symbolism of the narrative of the land deed in Jeremiah (32:8–15), which finds meaning in a not-yet-realized utopia (restoration)? After all, it carried no *real* authoritative weight in Yehud's economic sphere.[34] As Robert Carroll wrote, "The editors are concerned with the story as a symbolic gesture... The symbolic nature of Jeremiah's action gives hope for the future, and the redactors develop that point in a series of lengthy additions (vv. 16–44)."[35] And in resistance to what is implied in Jeremiah, and also throughout Ezra–Nehemiah, we cannot ignore the wide lack of historical evidence in which a people exiled from any land for seventy years[36] or more had the same rights and properties when they returned as before their absence. After all, every social-political body is animate. Each one moves, changes, adapts, and transforms itself in pursuit of stable forms of authority and order. For this reason, social-political systems cannot be

---

34. According to Carroll, Jeremiah's land transaction prefigures the emergence of future land transactions. Read this way, it becomes a basis for the *future* land claims of the *golah* community (cf. "Textual Strategies," 112–13). It does not, however, confirm the legitimacy of any land claim made by members of the *golah* community.

35. Robert P. Carroll, *From Chaos to Covenant: Prophecy in the Book of Jeremiah* (New York: Crossroad, 1981), 134.

36. As J. Bright notes regarding Jer 25:11, "[Seventy years] seems to be here no more than a round number (i.e., a normal life-span). In Zech i 12 it seems to refer to the interval between the destruction of the temple in 587 and its rebuilding in 520–515. In II Chron xxxvi 20–23 it is made to refer to the period between 587 and Cyrus' edict in 538 (appreciably less than seventy years)" (*Jeremiah* [AB 21; New York: Doubleday, 1965], 160).

"frozen" to preserve forces of production that are inherently contingent upon material and historical circumstances.

Yet the Jeremian narrative of the land deed assumes that the productive flows of society would not be "interrupted," and therefore altered, but would, presumably, enter a hiatus as long as the exiled Judeans remained outside the land. And upon their return, so the presumed assumption goes, the economic flows would be reanimated, re-excited, following the same productive flow or pattern as before the "interruption" of exile. The prophecy's identification of its audience as the exiled Judeans links the activity of economic exchange (which provides the foundation for authority[37]) with specific reference to the land, to the presence of the exiles. According to the text, production of surplus and legitimation of value are generated only when the "correct" inhabitants are present. In part for this reason, we can conclude as Carroll has written, "I suspect therefore that we should read the story of Jeremiah the landowner as a textual strategy helping to enforce the ideological claim to land on the part of those who could trace or claim association with Babylonian Jews."[38]

"Ownership" of the land (Promised Land—a belief reflecting the utopian ideal Yehud/Judah was intended for a specified social body) was confirmation of covenant—a concept that seeking to establish a contractual relationship with the land as a divine "gift" was meaningful only within the religious symbolic system of the *golah* community. Ownership and covenant necessitated Yahweh's presence, which implies that the sanctity of the land depended upon the status of the divine–human relationship. This necessity was perhaps first articulated in the tradition of Abraham, a tradition of which the authors under discussion were likely aware: "On that day the LORD made a covenant with Abram, saying, 'To your descendants I give this land, from the river of Egypt to the great river, the river Euphrates, the land of the Kenites, the Kenizzites, the Kadmonites, the Hittites, the Perizzites, the Rephaim, the Amorites, the Canaanites, the Girgashites, and the Jebusites'" (Gen 15:18–21). The Abrahamic covenant, a concept that seems to support the perception of land rights portrayed in Jeremiah, establishes the parameters of the accessibility of the land as being dependent upon divine election. That this was thought a divine gift of land, and that it was utopian, may be confirmed enough by its described size.

The promise to Abraham expresses two fundamental beliefs: the first that the land of Canaan belonged to Yahweh (and not, by contrast, to any

---

37. Bourdieu, *Practical Reason*, 34.
38. Carroll, "Textual Strategies," 115.

other authority), and the second that the land's inhabitants did not have any legitimate claim to it.[39] "Abram passed through the land to the place at Shechem, to the oak of Moreh. At that time the Canaanites were in the land. Then the LORD appeared to Abram, and said, 'To your offspring I will give this land.' So he built there an altar to the LORD, who had appeared to him" (Gen 12:6–7). In building an altar, Abraham proclaimed that not only was the place a holy site because he had encountered a deity there but also that the site, the space it occupied, was under the jurisdiction of Yahweh. Abraham's actions, while seemingly innocuous, border on a type of imperialism. He does not simply build one altar but continues his constructive act, as though marking out divine territory. "From there he moved on to the hill country on the east of Bethel, and pitched his tent, with Bethel on the west and Ai on the east; and there he built an altar to the LORD and invoked the name of the LORD" (Gen 12:8).

Yet while the paradigmatic ancestor, Abraham, was promised the land as a gift, the Babylonian exiles needed a way to explain their radical removal from the land. To the exiled Judeans Dtr's interpretation of the Mosaic Covenant with its criteria of conditionality offered that explanation. If the land was a gift, and ownership of the land confirmed the divine election of the people, then removal from the land was punishment for disobedience. That this conditional quality of land ownership was known beyond Dtr's circles, and so may reflect a more common idea within the national religious culture, is demonstrated by reference to it in the Holiness Code:

> But if they confess their iniquity and the iniquity of their ancestors, in that they committed treachery against me and, moreover, that they continued hostile to me—so that I, in turn, continued hostile to them and brought them into the land of their enemies; if then their uncircumcised heart is humbled and they make amends for their iniquity, then will I remember my covenant with Jacob; I will remember also my covenant with Isaac and also my covenant with Abraham, and I will remember the land. For the land shall be deserted by them, and enjoy its sabbath years by lying desolate without them, while they shall make amends for their iniquity,

---

39. According to Habel (*The Land is Mine*, 124, 132), the Abrahamic tradition advocates peaceful coexistence with the people already in the land. Relatedly, as Smith (*Palestinian Parties*, as argued throughout, but see pp. 62–81) points out, the Judean returnees could be divided broadly into those of an assimilationist bent and those who advocated an exclusive separation. It is possible to see both traditions within Yehud. And according to Smith, the ideological conflict between the two philosophies was the catalyst for the different perspectives of the Persian-period literature.

because they dared to spurn my ordinances, and they abhorred my statutes. Yet for all that, when they are in the land of their enemies, I will not spurn them, or abhor them so as to destroy them utterly and break my covenant with them; for I am the LORD their God; but I will remember in their favor the covenant with their ancestors whom I brought out of the land of Egypt in the sight of the nations, to be their God: I am the LORD. These are the statutes and ordinances and laws that the LORD established between himself and the people of Israel on Mount Sinai through Moses. (Lev 26:40–46)

It is also true that punishment for disobedience, instead of outright abandonment, implied a desire for a continued relationship on the contingency that inequities were reconciled. "Know then in your heart that as a parent disciplines a child so the LORD your God disciplines you" (Deut 8:5). Only in the possibility of disobedience, in the act of turning away, does one find the concept of return (*swb*).[40] This idea of a return to a restored relationship is a fundamental idea within monotheism generally; within the self-expression of every monotheistic identity there exists an expected "return" in support of divine authority as absolute. It is perhaps most clearly articulated in Judaism's understanding of forgiveness, but it exists in Christianity and in Islam at what might be termed a "primeval level": human beings must "return" to the perfection with which they were created by living obedient lives. And does this concept not also characterize *golah* identity? As Nehemiah recounts, "Remember the word that you commanded your servant Moses, 'If you are unfaithful, I will scatter you among the peoples; but if you *return to me* and keep my commandments and do them, though your outcasts are under the farthest skies, I will gather them from there and bring them to the place at which I have chosen to establish my name'" (1:8–9, emphasis mine). Zechariah expresses a similar understanding, "Therefore say to them, Thus says the LORD of hosts: *Return to me*, says the LORD of hosts, and *I will return to you*, says the LORD of hosts" (1:3, emphasis mine).

Despite Zechariah's lack of an explicit acknowledgment of any *golah–am ha'aretz* distinction, both passages look to those peoples for whom

---

40. For further reference, note Gibbs' discussion (*Why Ethics?*, 308) of the concept from a more modern Jewish perspective. "The Hebrew concept of repentance is linked to the root *sh u v*, which means *turn* and, most often, *return*. The mending of words and of signs and their meanings is a kind of returning. *Teshuvah* is translated as repentance or penitence, but it is not identical to the more familiar Christian concept. Most of all, *teshuvah* signifies a way of return in relationship with God. A baal teshuvah is a Jew who returns from sinful ways to a righteous relation with God, and in contemporary usage it refers to someone who returns to traditional observance from a modern, secular way of life."

the possibility of returning is open. To return to the land and to "possession"[41] of it is simultaneously a return to Yahweh. "Remember the word that you commanded your servant Moses, 'If you are unfaithful, I will scatter you among the peoples; but if you return to me and keep my commandments and do them, though your outcasts are under the farthest skies, I will gather them from there and bring them to the place at which I have chosen to establish my name'" (Neh 1:8–9). Those who remain in the land, so goes this ideology, cannot return because they inhabit that which theoretically has been emptied—a belief that can also be inferred from Leviticus, "[f]or the land shall be deserted by them, and enjoy its sabbath years by lying desolate without them, while they make amends for their iniquity" (quoted at length above). And according to the Chronicler (cf. 1 Chr 9:1–2), the land remained desolate because all of Judah/Israel was taken into exile—although, without a complete purging of the land, social-economic forces and systems would have continued and society's self-preservationist need, or its resistance to disintegration,[42] which would entail the production of economic value, would overrule the value of land deeds held by an absent aristocracy. Importantly, archaeological evidence confirms for us that the land was not empty.[43] And we are safe to assume that not *all* of Judah was taken into exile—to have done so would have overly and unnecessarily taxed the resources of the Babylonian army. Even Ezra–Nehemiah, through its dogged focus on separation, acknowledges that the land was not empty, though it labels the land's residents as foreigners. With relocation constituting the qualifying event for membership, only the *golah* community, among those in Yehud, was capable of enjoying divine election. The people of the land, those who remained, were written off, de-faced and de-identified, specifically in Ezra–Nehemiah, by virtue of their not having participated in the process of definition. This process required geographic movement as a parallel to religious identity. To move out of the space of Judah, the "land," was to flee the state of disobedience. To move into (return to) Yehud, and specifically Jerusalem, was to move into sacred relationship (as denoted by the tithe in Neh 11:1–2). And this was possible, Leviticus tells us, only through divine remembrance: "Yet for all that, when they are in the land of their enemies, I will not spurn

---

41. On an ideological level, the land belonged to Yahweh and Israel was a steward of it. On a material level, the land equaled value and was a basis for class and the distribution of power.

42. Cf. Emile Durkheim, et al., "The Elementary Forms of Religious Life," 19.

43. While he argues for a much more diminished situation, see, for example, Oded ("Where Is the 'Myth'?," 55–74).

them, or abhor them so as to destroy them utterly and break my covenant with them; for I am the LORD their God; but *I will remember in their favor the covenant with their ancestors whom I brought out of the land of Egypt in the sight of the nations, to be their God*" (Lev 26:44–45; cited above, emphasis mine).

The religious tradition of the exodus—the historicity of the event is dubious,[44] but its "truth" was certainly an ideological force in the collective self-definition of the religious community—becomes the shared experience of the Babylonian Judeans and not, in contrast, those who remained in the land. Ezra–Nehemiah follows the so-called National Confession, which maintains through the tradition and imagery of the ancestors that the land was a divine "gift," with a covenant signing in which intercultural mixing (including intermarriage) was expressly forbidden (cf. Neh 10:28–31). To the community, it constitutes a narrative that interfaces self and cultural identity.[45] This, for example, is expressed in Jeremiah, "Cursed be anyone who does not heed the words of this covenant, which I commanded your ancestors when I brought them out of the land of Egypt, from the iron-smelter, saying, Listen to my voice, and do all that I command you. *So shall you be my people, and I will be your God…*" (Jer 11:3–4, emphasis mine). By implication, the people who remained in the land shared a role within the larger exodus–land–conquest narrative; their fate, however, was that of the Canaanites and the like: "Observe what I command you today. See, I will drive out before you the Amorites, the Canaanites, the Hittites, the Perizzites, the Hivites, and the Jebusites" (Exod 34:11). But this narrative tradition cannot shake free the nagging accusation that it dismisses socioeconomic necessities such as reciprocity in favor of utopian constructivism.

Purification of the land required the displacement (from the space of the land) of the people of Yahweh and the routing of the land's inhabitants, followed by a return of the people to the land. Failure to follow this paradigm completely would result in cultural and religious assimilation, interpreted as profanation resulting in punishment and removal from the land.[46] As Exodus states, "I will set your borders from the Red Sea to the sea of the Philistines, and from the wilderness to the Euphrates; for I will hand over to you the inhabitants of the land, and you

---

44. Cf. Niels Peter Lemche, "On the Problems of Reconstructing Pre-Hellenistic Israelite (Palestinian) History," *JHS* 3 (2000): §8.4.

45. Ochs and Capps ("Narrating the Self," 19–43) provide a well-informed discussion on the phenomenon of narrating one's identity.

46. Even the length of time removed from the land, enough for one generation to replace another, is consistent (cf. Josh 5:6).

shall drive them out before you. You shall make no covenant with them and their gods. They shall not live in your land, or they will make you sin against me; for if your worship their gods, it will surely be a snare to you" (Exod 23:31–33). This passage, as one example, provides a basis for understanding the dramatic concern regarding intermarriage in Ezra–Nehemiah. Ezra–Nehemiah's solemn belief (cf. Neh 9:9–37) that Yahweh gave the land to the community's ancestors (and not, in contrast, to the ancestors of the *am ha'aretz*), who were punished in part for assimilating other cultures (cf. Neh 13:26), and so spoiling the land, fuels its paranoia of intermarriage (a paranoia that later would become ritualized in the regulation of marriage in later Judaism). By identifying itself with the Hebrews of the exodus tradition, the *golah* community exploited religious tradition into one supporting its own its claim over the land of Yehud. Liverani notes similarly,

> The "oaths" or "promises" of Yahweh to Abraham and then Moses correspond, at the mythical level, to the legal function of the edicts of the Persian emperors: they provide legitimation for the return and bestow entitlement of property to the land. But at the practical level, the actual return of exiles and their takeover of Palestine required another model. The patriarchal traditions could be used by the returnees as a prefiguration of their presence in the country; but the remainees could equally appeal to them as a model of coexistence between complementary groups. These stories offered the returnees a "weak" yet realistic model of return: in small groups, without direct conflict, by agreement with the residents and surrounding peoples, sharing the land and its resources. The traditions of the conquest offer a "strong" model, preferred by the supporters of violent confrontation and of the exclusion of "extraneous" people. These were logically (or at least narratively) connected to the "exit from Egypt" that marked the liberation of the people from slavery in a foreign land.[47]

Movement, with the events of absence and presence from and within the land constituting a dialectical action capable of defining identity (such as insider versus outsider), presents the core of *golah* identity,[48] which is based on the belief that Yahweh chose those who had been exiled. It lies at the very base of, for example, Jeremiah's "new covenant" (31:31–34) and Ezekiel's "chariot throne" (10:1–22). "Again I will build you, and you shall be built, O virgin Israel" (Jer 31:4)! Virginity implies the absence of that which can shame and profane. "Virgin Israel" can

---

47. Liverani, *Israel's History*, 270.
48. But note also, for further reference, that identity actions, such as struggles, may generate movements—a social movement may involve ideological or ideological and geographic relocation. See Judith A. Howard, "Social Psychology of Identities," *ARS* 26 (2000): 384.

designate only in this case those who, having followed the oracle within the text of Jeremiah, in allowing the land its Sabbaths, thus having endured spatial relocation, were chosen by Yahweh:

> I will let you find me, says the LORD, and I will restore your fortunes and gather you from all the nations and all the places where I have driven you, says the LORD, and I will bring you back to the place from which I sent you into exile. (Jer 29:14)

The final statement in the verse, together with the oracle framing it, offers a direct promise that what was left behind, specifically place (*mqwm*) as space in which institutions may be organized, the people will once again inhabit—there is return (*swb*) to a space-left-behind. Divine selection of a "righteous remnant" marks itself through displacement and re-placement. Jeremiah's letter to the exiles in Babylon says it well, "Thus says the LORD concerning the king who sits on the throne of David, and concerning all the people who live in this city, *your kinsfolk who did not go out with you into exile*: Thus says the LORD of hosts, *I am going to let loose on them sword, famine, and pestilence, and I will make them like rotten figs that are so bad they cannot be eaten...*" (29:16–17, emphasis mine).[49] Not having suffered the displacing act of exile is to lose the possibility of returning, of being a "good fig." Moreover, the land, as the argument goes, can only observe its sabbaths in absence of the remnant, because its previous inhabitants had not given it the freedom to do so—an explanation that is itself an attempt at framing discourses on the issue of land rights within a religious symbolic meaning system: "He took into exile in Babylon those who had escaped from the sword, and they became servants to him and to his sons until the establishment of the kingdom of Persia, to fulfill the word of the LORD by the mouth of Jeremiah, until the land had made up for its sabbaths. *All the days that it lay desolate it kept sabbath*, to fulfill seventy years" (2 Chr 36:20–21, emphasis mine).

In contrast, the biblical authors did not view the people already in the land as occupying space in a materially productive manner with the land—that is, the nature of the people's relationship was not attributed with divine favor, which the biblical author viewed as necessary for a productive relationship (cf. Deut 11:10–12; Ezra 9:7–9; Neh 9:28–30; note also Jer 25:8–11). Instead, they were considered a source of antagonism and a stumbling block to peaceful and productive coexistence with

---

49. The text of Jeremiah seems, in this passage, to suggest exile was a choice, an act of obedience.

the land: "Then the people of the land discouraged the people of Judah, and made them afraid to build ..." (Ezra 4:4). Yet in the larger sense of mode of production, the actions of all social agents in terms of material productivity defines the relationship of the social-political body to the land. This understanding is supported by Gottwald's additional observations made on the issue of mode of production.[50] In his words,

> In a narrower sense, mode of production...refers to the way human capacities and technology are socially organized for the labor necessary to meet basic human needs and to allocate what is produced. In a broader sense, mode of production includes the social ramifications of the labor process in class and status divisions, in political processes, in family organization, and in juridical procedures.[51]

Because they had not permitted the land its sabbaths, and could therefore not "return," the people already in the land according to the Persian-period biblical texts maintained only a superficial existence in the land, as though metaphorically mildew on a garment—that is, any claimed "roots" in the land and therefore also to the land's productive processes (corresponding to surplus production) were rejected by Yahweh: "*I struck you and all the products of your toil with blight and mildew and hail; yet you did not return to me, says the LORD*" (Hag 2:17). Relatedly, Jeremiah's woeful admission, noted above, that kinsfolk of the exiled Judeans would be wiped out confirms for us the existence of Judeans. In fact, it is likely that Jeremiah's "rotten figs" are the same "*am ha'aretz*" vehemently despised in Ezra–Nehemiah.[52] Consequently, the biblical author expects by virtue of the monotheistic argument that the *am ha'aretz* would forfeit any claimed right to the land.[53]

The nature of this ideology, as a sub-set of the *golah* community's monotheistic identity, reflects a utopian view of land as sacred space—space accessible only to those who have atoned through displacement. Or to put it in the words of Jeffrey Alexander,

> To be guilty of sacred-evil did not mean, any more, that one had committed a legal crime. It was about the imputation of a moral one. One cannot defend oneself against an imputed moral crime by pointing to exculpating circumstances or lack of direct involvement. *The issue is one of pollution, guilt by actual association. The solution is not the rational*

---

50. Cf. Gottwald, *Tribes of Yahweh*, 632.
51. Gottwald, "Sociology (Ancient Israel)," 6:83.
52. Porten ("Settlement," 457) also makes this association.
53. See also Ahlström, *The History of Ancient Palestine*, 846; Fried, "The *'am hā'āreṣ*," 125.

demonstration of innocence but ritual cleansing: purification... Retrospection is an effective path toward purification because it provides for catharsis, although of course it doesn't guarantee it. The evidence for having achieved catharsis is confession. If there is neither the acknowledgment of guilt nor sincere apology, punishment in the legal sense may be prevented, *but the symbolic and moral taint will always remain.*[54]

The events of the Babylonian exiles created the possibility of a catharsis for both land and remnant. As acts of dislocation and separation from the land, which were thought to be a divine gift, they encouraged retrospection and confession through the threat of abandonment by the Divine and a subsequent loss of (collective) identity. For the exilic authors the inevitable conclusion was simply this, by nature the land was "good": "[A]nd I have come down to deliver them from the Egyptians, and to bring them up out of that land to *a good and broad land*, a land flowing with milk and honey, to the country of the Canaanites, the Hittites, the Amorites, the Perizzites, the Hivites, and the Jebusites" (Exod 3:8, emphasis mine). The remnant was required to preserve the "goodness" of the land through obedience to Yahweh and Yahweh alone (cf. Lev 18:27–29). However, due to the prevalence of "syncretistic" religious practices (cf. Ezek 7:3), the land was considered to have been polluted and in need of cleansing, a requirement that demanded obedience in two acts: the first, to be removed from the land and faithfully atone for collective sins, and the second, to return and demonstrate Yahweh's intent of restoration. Note Ezekiel's sacrificial metaphor:

> As a pleasing odor I will accept you, when I bring you out from the peoples, and gather you out of the countries where you have been scattered; and I will manifest my holiness among you in the sight of the nations. As a pleasing odor I will accept you, when I bring you out from the peoples, and gather you out of the countries where you have been scattered; and I will manifest my holiness among you in the sight of the nations. (Ezek 20:41–42)

But because the land was never "empty" in a real sense, and because people continued to dwell in the land, the status of the land, and its sabbath observance, could only be directly correlated with the status and dislocation of the "remnant." Otherwise, the association of the exile with Jeremiah's prophecy regarding the land's sabbaths makes little sense (cf. 2 Chr 36:20–21; Jer 25:11–12; 29:10). The "people of Yahweh" can only be described as obedient if the identity of this people was restricted to those who where displaced from the land. What constituted obedience,

---

54. Alexander, *Meanings of Social Life*, 68, emphasis mine.

however, was secondarily defined, or defined in hindsight, in validation of a particular community's already-formed/ing identity.[55] Thus, the *golah* community was credited with obedience *after* displacement—in other words, after "displacement" as an expression of divine will became the basis upon which the identity of the *golah* community would be founded. This definition after the fact, this distinguishing of "self" from "other" for material and ideological gain, clearly articulates the exclusionary tendency within the monotheistic identity. When manifest in physical action, this tendency is daringly close to tyranny, as the glorified recounting of Nehemiah's actions shows (Neh 13:25). And in this can we not hear an echoing parallel between the idealized actions of Nehemiah that dogged champion of the *golah* community, and the words of Thomas More describing aristocratic gain?

> Consequently, in order that one insatiable glutton and accursed plague of his native land may join field to field and surround many thousand acres with one fence, tenants are evicted. Some of them, either circumvented by fraud or overwhelmed by violence, are stripped even of their own property, or else, wearied by unjust acts, are driven to sell. *By hook or crook the poor wretches are compelled to leave their homes—men and women, husbands and wives, orphans and widows, parents with little children...*"[56]

Thus, land plays a critical role in restoration. And when a monotheistic community struggles for control over material space, it appeals to ideological (utopian) space as a superior definition and the basis for an eventual control or authority over "land" in all its possible nuances (namely, real and virtual).

---

55. Even Jeremiah's advice to "build houses and live in them; plant gardens and eat what they produce" (Jer 29:5, see also v. 28) came *after* the first deportation (597 B.C.E.) and a subsequent need to situate it within a meaning system built around obedience to Yahweh. On the historical context for this Bright offers an interesting proposal: "In the midst of unrest in Jerusalem, Jeremiah had learned of similar unrest among the exiles in Babylon. He had also learned that this unrest—again as was true in Jerusalem—had been in good part provoked by prophets who were assuring the exiles that they would soon be going home. Perhaps a rebellion which had broken out in Babylon in the preceding year, and in which elements of the army seem to have been involved...had helped arouse these hopes. The fact that Jeremiah's letter was forwarded (vs. 3) through envoys sent by Zedekiah to Nebuchadnezzar's court fits well with a date in 594, for Zedekiah would have been obliged, after the disturbances that had taken place in Judah, to smooth matters over and assure Nebuchadnezzar of his loyalty" (*Jeremiah*, 210–11).

56. More, *Utopia*, 67, emphasis mine.

a. Monotheism's Ideological Definition of "Land" as an Argument in Support of Authority Over the Land in the Material Sense

As Norman Habel observes, "Just as crucial in the public proving of YHWH as God and ruler over all lands is the process of settling the Israelites in their allocated land (Deut. 4:37–39)… YHWH's identity and authority as ruler are linked to YHWH's capacity to conquer the land allocated to Israel."[57] As the surface upon which surplus as desire is produced, as therefore the field in which class and status, among other material and ideological mechanisms of power are contested and confirmed, land is *the* object of desire—when desire is understood as the lack of need.[58] In other words, this means as the "surface," or material sphere, upon which are inscribed a social-political body's distributions of power—distributions that collectively are the basis for cultural identity.[59] Therein begins the conflict over ownership of the land, because in controlling the land one controls the surplus it produces. And controlling surplus production one directs the exercise of power within a social-political body. It would seem then that for the Persian-period biblical authors this issue is in mind when they advocate that Yahweh's sovereignty is publicly demonstrated by Yahweh's giving the land to the exiled Judeans.[60]

For the immigrating Babylonian Judeans land ownership offered social and economic security. Yet because the visions of eminent domain that the Persian-period biblical authors describe were either not shared by all members of the immigrating community or were rejected out of hand by the landed aristocracy the community leaders turned the ideological exclusivity of the community into the exclusivity of land ownership.[61]

---

57. Habel, *The Land Is Mine*, 38.

58. "[The Earth] is the surface on which the whole process of production is inscribed, on which the forces and means of labor are recorded, and the agents and the products distributed. It appears here as the quasi cause of production and the object of desire (it is on the earth that desire becomes bound to its own repression). The *territorial machine* is therefore the first form of socius, the machine of primitive inscription…" (Deleuze and Guattari, *Anti-Oedipus*, 141).

59. As Habel puts it, "The granting of land has occupation of the land as its goal [cf. Deut. 3:18; 5:31; 12:1; 17:14; 19:1, 14]" (*The Land is Mine*, 40).

60. Cf. ibid., 39. The melding of the land with the collective identity of the people, according to Galambush, is perhaps most poignantly stated in Ezekiel: "The personae of land and people are fused at every level, and the land's welfare is defined exclusively in terms of human needs and desires" (*This Land is My Land*, 83).

61. See also, for example, Ahlström, *The History of Ancient Palestine*, 861; Fried, *Priest and the Great King*, 211; VanderKam, *From Joshua to Caiaphas*, 53–54.

How else but as a political-economic arrangement can we explain the priest Eliashib's relation to Tobiah?[62] "Now before this, the priest Eliashib, who was appointed over the chambers of the house of our God, *and who was related to Tobiah*, prepared for Tobiah a large room where they had previously put the grain offering, the frankincense, the vessels, and the tithes of grain, wine, and oil, which were given by commandment to the Levites, singers, and gatekeepers, and the contributions for the priests" (Neh 13:4–5, emphasis mine). That Eliashib provided a room for Tobiah in the Jerusalem temple suggests that both individuals had entered into a contractual relationship, whether through political or economic relationship. Thus, despite the claim of the biblical texts that power in Yehud was centered in the Jerusalem temple, we have some evidence that members of the *golah* community (and we may presume Eliashib was one based on Neh 7:64 and possibly even Neh 13:28[63]) engaged in social, economic, and political relations with surrounding peoples to, presumably, integrate themselves into the already existing social-economic hierarchy. A further example is provided by one of the sons of Jehoiada, a son of the high priest Eliashib, who married a daughter of Sanballat the governor of Samaria (Neh 13:28).

These events, however, cannot be read in isolation from the exclusionary practices of the *golah* community, nor from the biblical ideology of an "empty" land, an exclusionary ideology par excellence. Both demonstrate how immigrants from the Babylonian diaspora sought to deal with the reality of people already inhabiting the land. They are competing responses to be sure, but they are responses to the same felt need of attending to the social-economic infrastructure. As a response, both the practices of intermarriage and exclusion inscribe upon the

---

62. While the NRSV translates *qrb* as "related" it is not clear family or kin relation is indicated here. It could also, as D. Edelman suggests ("Nehemiah's Adversary, Tobiah the Patron," in *Historie og Konstruktion: Festskrift til Niels Peter Lemchi I Anledning af 60 Års Fødselsdagen den 6. September 2005* [Copenhagen: Københavns Universitet, 2005], 108), indicate a politically contractual relationship. Although if the Eliashib of Neh 13:28 is the same individual, we may see a pattern of intermarriage within the priestly line: "And one of the sons of Jehoiada, son of the high priest Eliashib, was the son-in-law of Sanballat the Horonite..."

63. But note VanderKam, (*From Joshua to Caiaphas*, 51–52) who argues that Eliashib mentioned in Neh 13:4–5 may not have been the high priest. He finds it unlikely that a priest of this position would have engaged relations on this level with a foreigner. However, VanderKam assumes Eliashib's position of authority was both secure and one in which he could not benefit from political alliance. Moreover, VanderKam's assumption of what was likely or unlikely a decision Eliashib might make must remain merely speculative in the absence of supporting evidence.

social-political body a pattern of distributed relations.⁶⁴ This "marking out" is, as a social-economic and political act, identical to that of defining ownership over the land. As Galambush writes in reference to Ezekiel, "To posit a land that is 'devastated,' 'empty,' or both is to posit both need and warrant for the return of the ruling classes and the displacement of those whose control is defined as chaos."⁶⁵ So we must add to our discussion of structured movement the following, the displacement of the righteous remnant must be followed by the displacement of the profane element: "He said, 'This is a basket coming out.' And he said, 'This is their iniquity in all the land.' Then a leaden cover was lifted, and there was a woman sitting in the basket! And he said, 'This is Wickedness'… Then I said to the angel who talked with me, 'Where are they taking the basket?' He said to me, 'To the land of Shinar, to build a house for it…'" (Zech 5:6–7, 10–11). And in the space following displacement there occurs a reconstruction of a social-economic hierarchy, of distributed systems of production, which requires a redistribution of private property. In other words, utopia, or monotheistic restoration, can be found in the present world only after space has been made for it.

b. *The Necessity of (Re)Figured History and (Re)Defined Geography for Restoration*

> In no other way could you have better or more rightly secured this object than by holding up before reasonable mortals themselves that ideal of a commonwealth, that pattern and perfect model of morality, whose equal has never been seen anywhere in the world for the soundness of its constitution, for its perfection, and for its desirability.⁶⁶

---

64. We cannot avoid encountering the very real "mutual interdependence of the individuals among whom the labour is divided" (Marx, "The German Ideology," 160) when we discuss Yehud. But we must also recognize the rather convenient silence on the issue by the biblical texts. Biblical texts would rather see no interdependence. (Habel describes this as the "theocratic ideology" of land [cf. *The Land Is Mine*, 38–43]). In fact, both typically label such a relationship as profane. As Exodus states, "You shall not make a covenant with the inhabitants of the land, for when they prostitute themselves to their gods and sacrifice to their gods, someone among them will invite you, and you will eat of the sacrifice" (34:15). This is repeated almost word-for-word in Ezra, "Therefore do not give your daughters to their sons, neither take their daughters for your sons, and never seek their peace or prosperity, so that you may be strong and eat the good of the land and leave it for an inheritance to your children forever" (9:12).

65. Galambush, *This Land Is My Land*, 92.

66. More, *Utopia*, 35.

As shown by its adoption of the Abrahamic tradition and the Deuteronomistic History, the *golah* community brought with itself reinterpreted visions of the past—visions upon which an idealized future of restoration could be based. In other words, claiming the "heritage of Israel" as its own, the community articulated utopian visions of a future restoration. The process of articulating such visions can be understood, Crouch and Parker point out, as an attempt to restructure the previously established distribution of power: "[I]n seeking to represent alternative futures, groups explicitly draw on history as heritage in order to undermine current structures and practices…"[67] This idea is seen in the redefinition and "repossessing" of land space in Yehud by the immigrating Judeans to the expense of those already in the land. *We the exiled alone are true heirs to Abraham's promise.* As the space of engagement between *golah* and *am ha'aretz*, both geographic and ideological, the land played a central role in the (re)figuring of space for a "restored" society. Upon this medium conflict over social, political, and religious authority was waged as a precursor to the desired restoration. To this end, Jerusalem's walls symbolize, especially for Ezra–Nehemiah, an essential concern for the realization of a theocratic utopia and the confirmation of the community's collective vision. Hence the narrative is never far in its ideological space from the Jerusalem temple, the priesthood, or the *golah* community.

For the purpose of clarification, there is a cross-cultural analogy between what is discussed here and the Diggers350 at St. George's Hill, Surrey, in the United Kingdom.[68] The group occupied the site, which had become a private golf course, in memory of the seventeenth-century Diggers who had claimed the space for "digging," or establishing an early utopian commune as a challenge to land rights under the Cromwellian regime. It did not last. Now private property, a gated community with a golf course, St. George's Hill became contested space when the Diggers350, in the spirit of the original Diggers, set up a memorial stone on top of the hill, a stone that read, "Worke together, Eate bread together." Theirs was a statement against unchecked power, which was expressed through socially legitimated beliefs of land "rights" and their corresponding actions. Moreover, their actions were an attempted "refiguring" of history, an attempt to redefine the nature and purpose of the land or geographic space of George Hill. Theirs was a utopian vision

---

67. D. Crouch and G. Parker, "'Digging Up' Utopia? Space, Practice and Land Use Heritage," *Geoforum* 34 (2003): 396.

68. My awareness of Diggers350 was triggered by the work by Crouch and Parker (ibid., 401–3).

linked to an idealized past. In similar fashion, the Judeans immigrating from Babylon refigured history by linking their interpreted symbolism of Jerusalem's walls and temple to an idealized vision of the past—the ephemeral Mosaic theocracy, or even the "Augustan Age" of the Davidic monarchy—as an attempt to delineate the future.[69]

Likewise, in his vision of a "restored society," Zechariah redefines historical tradition as a plan for the future when he speaks of two crowns, one for the high priest and one either for a Davidic branch or simply for remembrance of days past. The NRSV translates Zech 6:11–14 as reference to a single crown made for Joshua, who in that case must be considered the "branch"; however, the Hebrew *'trwt* is clearly plural. Commentators have struggled to determine both the name of the recipient and the purpose for the second crown.[70] Stephen L. Cook and James VanderKam, for example, both argued that the designation "branch" refers neither to Joshua nor to Zerubbabel but to a future Davidide.[71] Their concern is Zechariah's possible associating of the "branch," a royal epithet, with a Davidic ruler. Both scholars conclude that the crown set aside for remembrance is done so both in remembrance of the Davidic royal line and in waiting for the restoration of it. The proposal is possible, but it remains speculative. Gösta Ahlström, for comparison, argued that the term "branch" was used for Joshua but only after the author either realized Zerubbabel could not get the job done or had abandoned hope in him all together.[72] While this too remains speculative, we can see a common ground in Zerubbabel's dismissal or rejection among the different scholarly proposals.[73] Zerubbabel had previously been entertained as a top contender for leading the restoration (cf. Zech 4:6–7), however, he quickly lost reference in the biblical texts. Nevertheless, his hasty disappearance from the biblical texts, which offer no explanation, cannot simultaneously confirm his rejection by the

---

69. Crouch and Parker (ibid., 405) discuss the past as a means of delineating the future in greater detail.

70. According to Coggins, the plurality of crowns may be due to a later editorial modification (see *Haggai, Zechariah, Malachi*, 14).

71. Cook, *Prophecy and Apocalypticism*, 134–35; VanderKam, *From Joshua to Caiaphas*, 31.

72. Ahlström, *The History of Ancient Palestine*, 820. Fried (*Priest and the Great King*, 204–5) also sees Joshua metaphorically wearing two headpieces symbolizing priestly and secular authority.

73. For further reference, C. C. Torrey (*The Chronicler's History of Israel: Chronicles-Ezra–Nehemiah Restored to Its Original Form* [New Haven ed., 1954; Port Washington: Kennikat, 1973], xxvii) suggests Zech 1–8 was a later interpolation by the Chronicler and was not therefore a genuine prophecy of Zechariah.

imperial government, as Israel Eph'al suggests that it does.[74] There is simply not enough evidence. In addition, if as Frank Cross opines, Zerubbabel and Joshua were politically linked, why would Joshua not be reprimanded in parallel to Zerubbabel?[75] It is more likely that in Zechariah, as is the case in Ezra–Nehemiah, that the individual leaders highlighted retained their importance as long their actions could be related to the Jerusalem temple—a proposal that may be echoed by Tamara Eskenazi, who notes that Ezra speaks of Zerubbabel in reference to restoration of the Jerusalem temple and "proper" worship.[76] In addition, Zechariah's treatment of Zerubbabel may be similar to Ezra–Nehemiah's marginalization of Sheshbazzar, who, while a governor, was largely ignored except for his role in leading a group of returnees and carrying with himself accoutrements intended for the Jerusalem temple.[77] Moreover, Zechariah's focus on Joshua suggests ideological agreement with Ezra–Nehemiah on the "restoration" of a theocratic society—and Zechariah's discussion of the crown(s) is not far from a discussion of the Jerusalem temple (Zech 6:12–13).[78] "Take the silver and gold and make a crown/crowns, and set it on the head of the high priest Joshua son of Jehozadak…" (Zech 6:11).

It would seem then that Ezra–Nehemiah and Zechariah share a happy tendency toward articulating utopian visions regarding a "restored" society. Theirs was a constructive role, an attempt at realizing an ideological blueprint of a "proper" society.[79] It is within that frame that the words of Thomas Dozeman resonate,

> Ezra–Nehemiah presents a utopian picture of the Persians ruling over Abar Naharah as culturally inclusive monarchs who are constrained by law (conceived space)—an image at odds with Herodotus's critical evaluation of Eastern despots as ethnocentric and lawless. The idealization of Persian

---

74. Eph'al, "Syria-Palestine Under Achaemenid Rule," 143.

75. On the possible link between Joshua and Zerubbabel, see Cross, "Reconstruction," 10.

76. Eskenazi, *Ezra–Nehemiah*, 123.

77. See also the discussion regarding Sheshbazzar in Cataldo, *A Theocratic Yehud*, 93–95.

78. And this is not surprising, if, as Cook suggests, Zech 1–8 is a product of the Zadokite priesthood (see *Prophecy and Apocalypticism*, 123).

79. Liverani (*Israel's History*, 274) writes, "The ideological rejection of the right of these other groups to occupy Palestine (connected to the theory of the promise) could not, however, negate their existence. The settlement of returnees was therefore justified by the story of an ancient conquest, set at the time of transition from the Late Bronze Age to the Iron Age, when the tribes became sedentary and the ancient inhabitants were exterminated."

rule, grounded in law, fuels the more immediate lived space of the author of Ezra–Nehemiah, in which an emerging form of Yahwism within the territory Abar Naharah is presented as a religion of law.[80]

At the root of this utopian vision lays the belief that a return would hasten restoration. Zechariah speaks rather poignantly to this:

> In the eighth month, in the second year of Darius, the word of the LORD came to the prophet Zechariah son of Berechiah son of Iddo, saying: The LORD was very angry with your ancestors. Therefore say to them, Thus says the LORD of hosts: *Return to me*, says the LORD of hosts, and *I will return to you*, says the LORD of hosts. Do not be like your ancestors, to whom the former prophets claimed, "Thus says the LORD of hosts, *Return* from your evil ways and from your evil deeds." But they did not hear or heed me, says the LORD. Your ancestors, where are they? (Zech 1:1–5, emphasis mine)

Return, as we have already noted, requires displacement.[81] "Up, up! Flee from the land of the north, says the LORD; for I have spread you abroad like the four winds of heaven, says the LORD. Up! Escape to Zion, you that live with daughter Babylon" (Zech 2:6–7). Return, as a stage in restoration, is both geographic and ideological in the same way that the walls of Jerusalem and Zechariah's crown(s) demand both physical and ideological attention. On one hand, a return is a returning to the geographic space of the land. On the other, it is, according to the biblical authors, a "return" to a "restored" social-political environment. Jerusalem's walls represent in both real and ideological senses the distinction between the *golah* community and the *am ha'aretz*. Zechariah's crown(s) bridge(s) the temporal divide between the previous Judean monarchy and the reestablishment (or restoration) of a political autonomy, while also restricting the definition of citizenship.[82] The very idea of "citizen" is

---

80. Dozeman, "Geography and History in Herodotus and in Ezra–Nehemiah," 457.
81. Drawing upon the work of R. Carroll, Galambush (*This Land Is My Land*, 92) demonstrates the existence of this ideology in Ezekiel.
82. This has led VanderKam (*From Joshua to Caiaphas*, 38–42), for example, to view Zechariah as advocating a royal–priestly diarchy. According to I. Kislev ("The Investiture of Joshua [Numbers 27:12–23] and the Dispute on the Form of the Leadership in Yehud," *VT* 59, no. 3 [2009]: 429–45), a hierocratic ideology developed during this time among members of the priesthood in competition with prevailing sentiments for a monarchy; dreams of a monarchy, however, faded with the disappearance of Zerubbabel (cf. ibid., 444). The investiture of Joshua in Num 27:12–23 contains a Persian-period redaction supporting the political authority of Joshua in Yehud in conjunction with the growing power of the priesthood. While Kislev's suggestion of the existence a hierocratic ideology is not without merit—and

clarified when Zechariah writes, "Thus says the LORD of hosts: I will save my people from the east country and from the west country; and I will bring them to live in Jerusalem. They shall be my people and I will be their God, in faithfulness and righteousness" (Zech 8:7–8). In making this claim, Zechariah draws upon the tradition of the Mosaic Covenant (compare Exod 6:7; 19:6). Fulfillment of both the prophecy and the symbolism of the crown(s) is only possible within the restoration of an autonomous social-political body—a restoration that in Ezra–Nehemiah is symbolized by the construction of Jerusalem's walls (cf. Neh 4:1–23).[83]

A similar notion is expressed in Ezra–Nehemiah where Ezra rejects the aid of others in rebuilding the Jerusalem temple (Ezra 4:1–3). The basis or rationale for the rejection seems to be the perceived election of the *golah* community, despite the claim of people already in the land to also worship Yahweh (4:2).[84] Zerubbabel and Joshua, together with the rest of the heads of families (*r'sy h'bwt*), are identified in their conviction, "You shall have no part with us in building a house to our God, but we alone will build to the LORD, the God of Israel" (4:3). In the Ezra text, the figures of Zerubbabel and Joshua symbolize secular and political authority in Yehud;[85] but they are cast as members of the *golah* community, which was intent on preserving its membership through exclusion. Moreover, access to the temple was restricted; only members of the *golah* community could take part in building it.

This fusion of religion and politics is a product of the monotheistic pursuit of authority. Thus, the term "Israel" in Ezra (cf. again 4:3) is burdened repeatedly with both theological and political nuances. As a theological reference, Israel designates the people of Yahweh, or more

---

it would certainly correspond with M. Smith's emphasis on different developing ideologies in Yehud—his argument for the growing power of the priesthood, and the idea of a hierocracy, tends toward a self-supporting inductive argument based uncritically on the biblical texts.

83. It is important to note that the materials of which the crown is comprised are taken from "the exiles," or members of the immigrant community (Zech 6:10). Thus, the symbols of political authority are kept entirely out of the hands of the *am ha'aretz*.

84. Cf. Torrey, *Chronicler's History*, xxix–xxx.

85. While he concludes that a diarchy existed, which I have shown elsewhere (*A Theocratic Yehud*, 95–109) to be an incorrect description of Yehud's governing structure, Cross ("Reconstruction," 10) links Joshua and Zerubbabel to political authority. Drawing upon the work of Cross, Dyck (*Theocratic Ideology*, 1–2), as well as Meyers and Meyers (*Haggai, Zechariah 1–8*, 352–53), also propose that a diarchy existed in Yehud.

specifically the "remnant."[86] Its political sense is not unrelated to this; it is based on the belief that Yahweh would restore the nation of Israel from the "ground up" with the chosen remnant—a process that would begin in Jerusalem. Yet even the city itself seemed to remain just outside the grasp of *golah* control, much less the entire province. The so-called letter written by Rehum, Shimshai, and associates, which in its presentation seems more like an invention of the biblical author, protests the actions of the *golah* community in rebuilding the city of Jerusalem.[87] The encounter begins with the Jerusalem temple but eventually includes the entire city. What was the city to Samaria? "Then the people of the land discouraged the people of Judah, and made them afraid to build, and they bribed officials to frustrate their plan throughout the reign of King Cyrus of Persia and until the reign of King Darius of Persia" (Ezra 4:4–5).[88] Ezra assumes its reader understands the historical denouement. Restoration, the narrator implies, was in progress. The people of the land petitioned to be a part of that process. But note that according to Ezra–Nehemiah they must approach the *golah* community and its leaders, which infers a recognition on the part of the people of the land that the community stands between the people, who are the "outsiders," and Yahweh. In this case, the community views itself as distinct from the people of the land and as a symbolic wall between that designated social group and Yahweh. In addition, this recognition also infers that all

---

86. As Garbini (*History and Ideology*, 126) puts it, "In Achaemenidean Jerusalem a small group of those who had returned from the Babylonian exile considered themselves the only legitimate 'remnant', not only of the kingdom of Judah which had disappeared but of the whole people of Israel. Jerusalem represented all the tribes because it considered itself, in polemic against the Israelites of Shechem, to be the sole people of God: a sacred people who had the mission of serving God in his temple and in his dwelling, Jerusalem."

87. The number of writers for the letter is impressive: "[T]hen Rehum the royal deputy, Shimshai the scribe, and the rest of their associates, the judges, the envoys, the officials, the Persians, the people of Erech, the Babylonians, the people of Susa, that is, the Elamites, and the rest of the nations whom the great and noble Osnappar deported and settled in the cities of Samaria and in the rest of the province Beyond the River wrote…" (Ezra 3:9–10). It would have been no more impressive to write, "And all the people of the Babylonian Empire raised their voices in one accord and protested the construction of the city of Jerusalem!"

88. It is interesting that despite some assumption in the biblical texts that Yehud (more aptly the Jews in diaspora in Babylonia) held a special place in Cyrus' heart seems in this passage without merit. According to the author the people successfully frustrated the plans of the *golah* community throughout the reign of Cyrus. Had the community or the city of Jerusalem truly been the apple of his eye it seems unlikely he would have permitted this seeming oppression brought about through bribery.

people of Beyond the River recognized Yahweh as the God of the province—certainly a monotheistic ideal!

These sub-narratives of resistance strongly imply a constructivist belief that resistance creates (social-political) reality. Moreover, by explaining the actions of the people of the land as being dependent (i.e. the actions of the *golah* community were the cause that effected the actions of the *am ha'aretz*) upon the actions of the community, they create, in a narrative sense, validation through the response of the people of the land. By arguing that the plan for restoration was thwarted, the author argues that people outside the community, the non-members, recognized that the process of restoration was underway. In other words, the author suggests that the people of the land recognized that a theocratic utopia run by members of the *golah* community was immanently possible and that its arrival would force a radical change in the composition of the social-political body.[89]

3. Brief Remarks on Debt and the Distribution of Land

The abolition of debts, when it takes place, *is a means of maintaining the distribution of land*, and a means of preventing the entry on stage of a new territorial machine, possibly revolutionary and capable of raising and dealing with the agrarian problem in a comprehensive way.[90]

And there were those who said, "We are having to borrow money on our fields and vineyards to pay the king's tax. Now our flesh is the same as that of our kindred; our children are the same as their children; and yet we are forcing our sons and daughters to be slaves, and some of our daughters have been ravished; we are powerless, and our fields and vineyards now belong to others." (Neh 5:4–5)

So I said, "The thing you are doing is not good. Should you not walk in the fear of our God, to prevent the taunts of the nations our enemies?... Restore to them, this very day, their fields, their vineyards, their olive orchards, and their houses, and the interest on money, grain, wine, and oil that you have been exacting from them." (Neh 5:9, 11)

---

89. "The territory of the Utopia that 'is not here' supposes then the courage to create 'another world,' as it should be in the future, as we imagine it in the past or that we presume exists in 'another place.' A determined construction of a counter-image of our immediate reality is necessary for this representation in time and space. *That 'other world,' since it is Utopian, must be 'critical' of this world, must correct it and imposes modifications on the injustices of its structure*" (Fernando Ainsa and Jeanne Ferguson, "Utopia, Promised Lands, Immigration and Exile," *Diogenes* 30, no. 119 [1982]: 50, emphasis mine).

90. Deleuze and Guattari, *Anti-Oedipus*, 196–97, emphasis mine.

5. *Clarifying Land*

This portion of Nehemiah, as is not uncommon of the text as a whole, is more self-aggrandizing than helpful. It is therefore difficult to define with any certainty the economic situation in Yehud as it related to the land, a main source of economic income. It is, however, arguable that an economic strategy is being proposed in the text, in spite of the fact that how the strategy may actually be employed is left to speculation. There are two possible strategies for reading this situation: (1) as an internal, that is, within the *golah* community, series of events; (2) as a criticism of the landed aristocracy, or those who had intermarried or entered into other relations with it for social-economic advancement, seeking to elevate the status of the *golah* community. The latter would be an external–internal conflict looking to legitimate the *golah* community as a ruling class before the people of the land.

a. *First Strategy*
If Nehemiah's actions were restricted to the *golah* community, so that only those members of the *golah* who had fallen on unfortunate circumstances were forgiven their debts, then this event can be interpreted as an attempt to solidify the community as a social-economic class in itself. Debt forgiveness in this situation stops a small number of individuals within the community from controlling the majority of power.[91] It presents the community as a unified front rather than one divided.[92] Moreover, it limits the need community members might have felt to engage in relations of reciprocity with non-members. Nehemiah does not appear concerned to re-imagine a society in which nothing is private but a society in which all have equal access to private property. "I was very angry…and I said to [the nobles and officials], 'As far as we are able, we have bought back our Jewish kindred who had been sold to other nations; but now you are selling your own kin, who must then be bought back by us'" (Neh 5:6, 8)![93] Nehemiah's proposal cannot offer a replacement for

---

91. We may again point to the quote by Deleuze and Guattari (ibid., 196–97) cited above.

92. R. de Vaux (*Ancient Israel*, 173, emphasis mine) describes a similar idea in Israel more generally: "Alienation of family property and the development of lending at interest led to the growth of pauperism and the enslavement of defaulting debtors or their dependents. This destroyed that social equality which had existed at the time of the tribal federation and which still remained as an ideal. *Religious legislation attempted to remedy these evils by two institutions, the sabbatical year and the jubilee year.*"

93. Can we see the essence of this passage, noting also vv. 9–10, reflected also in More's description of Utopia? Verses 9–10 state, "So I said, 'This thing you are doing is not good. Should you not walk in the fear of our God, to prevent the taunts

this social-economic reality and still hope in the viability of its utopian vision. Instead, it must redirect, redefine rather, the nature of the conflict. The division will exist but it cannot be situated in the community, thereby driving it apart. It can only exist in the ideological space between member and non-member. When there, it confirms the separation so much a part of *golah* ideology, separating *golah* and *am ha'aretz*, and affirms the community as a unified body, which is partly what prompts the association of taking interest from fellow community members with disobeying the divine (cf. Neh 5:9). However, the author's understanding of economy, whether subsistence or prestige,[94] either of which may be relevant for the context in question, is not entirely clear. If subsistence, then we would expect some sort of restorative action allowing all families to have access to subsistence means.

On the other hand, prestige ideology—when the community itself must be seen as a unified body—would expect the equalizing of private property within the community. This would occur to the extent that the group could collectively elevate its status in comparison to the landed aristocracy, with which the author sees the *golah* community in competition. In other words, prestige is measured against the community, not the individual, which is especially true if it is to be consistent with any type of utopian vision.[95] Prestige is only a "goal" insofar as the people of

---

of the nations our enemies? Moreover I and my brothers and my servants are lending them money and grain. Let us stop this taking of interests." Compare with More's description (*Utopia*, 245): "[The Utopians] have adopted such institutions of life as have laid the foundations of the commonwealth not only most happily, but also to last forever, as far as human prescience can forecast. At home they have extirpated the roots of ambition and factionalism along with all the other vices. Hence there is no danger of trouble from domestic discord, which has been the only cause of ruin to the well-established prosperity of many cities. As long as harmony is preserved at home and its institutions are in a healthy state, not all the envy of neighboring rulers, though it has rather often attempted it and has always been repelled, can avail to shatter or to shake that nation."

94. W. Bascom's definitions ("Ponapean Prestige Economy," *SJA* 4 [1948]: 211) of the three types are helpful: "[Subsistence economy] concerns food, clothing, and other subsistence commodities which are consumed locally, generally by the household which produces them. [Commercial economy] relates to the commodities produced for export and sold to obtain money with which to purchase clothing, hardware, and a variety of imported goods... The prestige economy involved the goods through which social approval and social status are gained..."

95. The focus on the community over the individual is consistent with the cultures of Israel and Judah generally. H. W. Robinson (*Corporate Personality in Ancient Israel* [Philadelphia: Fortress, 1964], 4, 6) puts this general sense in terms of corporate personality, "There is a similar extension of the living group into the

5. *Clarifying Land*   183

the land react to the community in such a way as to confirm the self-identity and self-perceived status of the community.⁹⁶ In a circumstance such as this, prestige may be best equated with a religious or moral posture upon which the definition of "remnant" is based—but it is one, as in this case, that requires validation in the social-economic context by the people of the land. If the utopian vision remained dormant within the religious-cultural ideology of the community, with no desire being expressly manifest in the material realm or affecting the larger social-economic sphere of the province, than we would not say it required the validation of the people of the land. But the vision was not intended to remain the hidden gem of a small ideological world confined to the religious community alone. Its goal was an outward manifestation, a public demonstration of divine authority.⁹⁷

If we read the situation this way then we can say that prestige, which is an indicator of status, is at the heart of the *golah* monotheistic identity. That is, the separation between member and non-member is what distinguishes between one having access to prestige and one not. By absolving debts within the community, the community as a unified whole presented itself the symbol of prestige, or as the text of Isaiah describes, a light to the nations (Isa 60:3). In most urban-based cultures—in contrast to those not existing in or around urban social systems, therefore containing wholly subsistence-based economies—there is synonymity between prestige and ownership. Private property, which we may read as land, correlated with status, which we may read as a ruling class holding social-economic authority.

---

future as part of its unity. This is best illustrated by the dominant aspiration of the Hebrew to have male children to perpetuate his name, the name that was so much a part of himself that something of him died when his name ceased... Along such lines, then, the corporate personality of the family, the clan, and the people was conceived realistically as a unity, a unity which made possible the all-important doctrine of election, and lent unity to the history itself... The group possesses a consciousness which is distributed amongst its individual members and does not exist simply as a figure of speech or as an ideal."

96. David Riches' definition (in "Hunting, Herding and Potlatching: Towards a Sociological Account of Prestige," *Man* NS 19, no. 2 [1984]: 235) of prestige not as a resource but as a culturally defined value may offer some insight. "As a value, prestige connotes a moral idea, namely that the performance of a certain social activity *merits* a high social regard. It is because prestige is a moral idea that assumptions can be made about information having been conveyed: as a moral idea, prestige embodies an *expectation* that the appropriate information has been passed on."

97. Note for example the description of the city of Jerusalem, which is meant to represent the "restored" exiles, in Isa 60:1–22.

b. *Second Strategy*

The second strategy for reading Nehemiah's revocation of debts is an external-internal model. While similarities between this model and the first exist, the primary difference exists in the relation shared between the *golah* community and the landed aristocracy. According to this model, members of the *golah* community were falling overwhelmingly into debt to the landed aristocracy, which together with intermarriage for social-economic gain was threatening to dissolve communal identity.

Under this strategy, Nehemiah's absolving of debts does several important things. It suggests the loyalty of the provincial governor to the immigrant community and elevates the status of the community over the people of the land. It also undermines the control of the landed aristocracy over the land and the economic sphere. By removing the debt obligations members of the *golah* community had with the landed aristocracy, Nehemiah restructured the distribution of power by reducing the disparity inherent within what Pierre Bourdieu terms the "habitus," or "playing field."[98] Lisbeth Fried suggests something similar,

> Nehemiah endeavored to reduce the power of these large landholders by abrogating the debts of the peasants and returning to them the ownership of their land. The reforms of Nehemiah were an attempt to create a strong peasant class, dependent upon the Persian representative, in opposition to the landed aristocracy.[99]

Like the first, this strategy too speaks to a utopian vision. It is based on the assumption that the provincial governor was doggedly loyal to the *golah* community, even to the possible expense of loyalty to his imperial employer. While possible, it seems unlikely given the relative ease with which inappropriate behavior could have been reported to the imperial authority.[100] It also assumes that the social-economic structures in place in Yehud—we would be naive to assume nothing along these lines existed—could be radically restructured with little to no ill effect on the productive processes within the province. Such structures, however, are not overtly conscious constructions. Nor are they separable from the culture of the society. To replace one structure with another, in a case

---

98. Cf. Pierre Bourdieu, *Méditations Pascaliennes* (Paris: Seuil, 1997), 251.
99. Fried, *Priest and the Great King*, 210.
100. For further reference, see Briant's discussion (*Histoire de l'Empire perse*, 604) of the hierarchy of authority within the Persian empire. Moreover, the existence of "king's eyes and ears," or individuals who monitored local situations and reported back to the imperial government, suggests a political context that would not be overly permissive of actions that would undoubtedly cause noticeable social-economic reactions.

such as this, would necessitate the replacement of an already existing culture, or cultures, with one of an immigrating community. Typically, however, the reverse is true. An immigrating community usually assimilates aspects of a host culture. Host cultures may also take on dominant attributes of a foreign or external culture. But they do not wholly consume it to the expense of their own collective identities. Even Hellenism, an example par excellence, did not overwrite entire local cultures.

This shows the complexity of the discussion we have undertaken. Issues of land, and more generally economic issues, cannot be discussed without taking into account which culture was dominant and which was subordinate. Moreover, we are left without a significant portion of evidence upon which we can better formulate an understanding of economic patterns within Yehud both before and after the arrival, or arrivals plural, of members of the *golah* community. Much is left to theory, and in articulating such a theory we have presented two models. While neither is conclusive, and either is possible, both provide us with an important conclusion. They are utopian. Consequently, the biblical authors condemned those members of the community engaged in intermarriage, for social-economic gain or other reason, as disobedient and a threat to the longevity of the community.[101] Only two actions were possible to such perpetrators, divorcing their "foreign," and also "other," partners or accepting their own exclusion from the community and the "rights" contained in membership.

---

101. This is one reason why Smith (cf. "Politics of Ezra," 72–97), for example, has interpreted the exclusionary posture of the *golah* community as a survival mechanism.

Chapter 6

THE NECESSITY OF AN "OTHER" FOR MONOTHEISTIC IDENTITY

> Every construction of identity inevitably entails a construction of otherness.[1]

As we have been discussing it to this point, the contest for land and authority out of which a monotheistic identity develops is "an antecedent condition of fragmentation and normlessness."[2] For this reason, every monotheistic identity preserves a "carefully cultivated memory,"[3] the intent of which is to preserve the monotheistic identity against dissolution into the social body, which the monotheistic identity perceives as a dissolution into chaos. Restoration is founded upon the preserved identity of those excluded, because it is through a separation from and the rejection of the non-member that the members understand their own identities.[4] Thus, restoration—and also law, as a road map to restoration—requires an identity that embodies multiple discourses of resistance that are themselves reactions to prevailing social-political authorities but that also preserve that identity against irrelevance. Moreover, that identity responds to perceptions of how the world is (the social-political

---

1. Assmann, *The Price of Monotheism*, 23.
2. Jaffee, "One God, One Revelation, One People," 759. Regarding the importance of identity to any normative order, Deleuze (as J. Williams describes in "Deleuze on J. M. W. Turner," in *Deleuze and Philosophy: The Difference Engineer* [ed. Keith Ansell Pearson; Warwick Studies in European Philosophy; New York: Routledge, 1997], 233) emphasizes that the world is committed to identity and representation. Or more specifically, systems of engagement, reciprocity, relation, and other—and so those things that support the structure of any authority—are all dependent upon the presentation and interpretation of identity of and between social agents.
3. I am borrowing the phrase from Jaffee (see "One God, One Revelation, One People," 759).
4. Or, as Davies (*Memories of Ancient Israel*, 106) writes, "individual identity… is meaningless without the existence of other identities from which it can be differentiated."

world) and how it should be (restored "reality"). This response is undertaken in three simultaneous ways: by (1) imposing strict ideological parameters on identity production; by (2) ritualizing and institutionalizing collective identity and agency within a framework supporting divine authority—one that (if only in theory) supplants all "earthly" authorities; and by (3) creating a *discourse of resistance* through symbolic (but sometimes also physical) walls and other expressions of resistance to an external "other."[5] In brief, a monotheistic identity, which demands obedience to its religious law for the purpose of restoration, employs by nature a vocabulary, a discourse, rather, of exclusion in resistance to a perceived threat of its own dissolution into the larger social-political body.[6] In Yehud, for example, *golah* community discourses of resistance—those that have been preserved in biblical texts such as Ezra–Nehemiah—were directed at the prevailing social-political authority in support of the authority of the *golah* community.

Differences between the monotheistic identities themselves lay in how monotheistic religions view the world *as it is in its current state*. Yet monotheistic identities are similar in their view of how the world *should be*. The ideal state—even State—is centralized on divine authority. This idea is easily discernible within the three monotheistic identities of Judaism, Islam, and Christianity. As Hans Küng puts it, "The [Christian] Church must constantly *turn away from the message of the world in metanoia and accept the coming reign of God*..."[7] As John Esposito observes, "[C]ontemporary Islamic movements and societies, *though all in agreement about the ultimate goal of establishing an Islamic state and*

---

5. According to Volf (*Exclusion and Embrace*, 24), solidarity, which is encouraged by shared discourses, is found in active participation within a discourse (which includes struggle) within a community—that is, rather than engaging a discourse on behalf of a community.

6. H. Tajfel and J. C. Turner ("The Social Identity Theory of Intergroup Behavior," in *Psychology of Intergroup Relations* [ed. S. Worchel and W. G. Austin; Chicago: Nelson-Hall, 1986], 7–24) first coined the phrase "social identity theory" to describe the process of identity formation. As T. Ford and G. Tonander describe, "According to social identity theory, a person's social identity is part of the self-concept or identity that is derived from membership in social groups. Esteem for one's group, and thus one's social identity, may be positive or negative depending on how well the in-group compares to relevant out-groups on 'value-laden' dimensions. In addition, it is assumed that people wish to maintain a positive social identity and thus strive to differentiate the in-group favorably from relevant out-groups" ("The Role of Differentiation Between Groups and Social Identity in Stereotype Formation," *Social Psychology Quarterly* 61, no. 4 [1998]: 373; see also Tajfel and Turner, "Social Identity Theory," 16).

7. Küng, *The Church*, 101, emphasis mine.

society, continue to debate about whether evolution or revolution is the appropriate method for its accomplishment and the nature of the state, from caliphate to modern parliamentary governments."[8] And as Eugene Borowitz writes,

> The traditional Jewish attitude toward states is inevitably dialectical. It cannot be categorically propositional for biblical Judaism affirms fundamentally both that God is undisputed Sovereign of all creation and yet he fulfills his sovereignty in human history through individual men and social institutions (without thereby infringing on man's freedom). *The first belief sets limits to the authority of human governments; the second authorizes them.*[9]

These "symbolic parentheses"[10] that emphasize the distinction between insider and outsider[11]—but are not intended to oversimplify the matter—can also be inferred from the following brief examples, the authors of which, while they might represent more "emotionally driven" viewpoints, all share an obvious and propelling concern for the immanent realization of restoration according to their respective traditions:

> Christians cannot complacently abandon so-called *secular* subject areas to non-believers—just so long as they grant us some restricted *sacred* area where we are free to sing hymns and read the Bible. Instead we must identify and critique the dominant intellectual idols, and then construct biblically based alternatives.[12]

> These two verses [Qur'an 4:97–98] urge each Muslim living in an infidel country to leave it and join the Muslim community, unless he is unable. Other verses express the same sense (4:100; 9:20). The purpose of this migration was to protect them from persecution, to weaken the infidel community, and to participate in the effort of war of the new community. Therefore the Qur'an uses together the terms: those who believe, and those who emigrate and strive in the way of Allah (2:218; 8:20, 72, 74, 75; 16:110).[13]

---

8. John L. Esposito and Natana J. De Long-Bas, "Modern Islam," in Neusner, ed., *God's Rule*, 173, emphasis mine.

9. Eugene B. Borowitz, "Judaism and the Secular State," *JR* 48, no. 1 (1968): 22, emphasis mine.

10. I am borrowing the concept from K. T. Erikson (*Wayward Puritans: A Study in the Sociology of Deviance* [New York: Wiley, 1966], 10).

11. Ford and Tonander ("The Role of Differentiation Between Groups and Social Identity in Stereotype Formation," 380) assert that the importance of this distinction is emphasized when the social identity of the in-group is threatened.

12. Küng, *The Church*, 44.

13. Sami A. Aldeeb Abu-Sahlieh, "The Islamic Conception of Migration," *International Migration Review* 30, no. 1 (1996): 38.

> If an Israelite resides in the same courtyard with a heathen or a resident alien, the courtyard does not become a forbidden domain (for carrying) because his sharing a residence with a heathen is not regarded as equivalent in this respect with another Israelite, *but rather is similar to sharing it with cattle.* (*m. Torah* 2.9, emphasis mine)

1. Understanding the Role of Differentiation within the Monotheistic Identity

Monotheistic identity, which emerges in part because a self-identified religious collective, has organized itself through coordinated action for the purpose of its contest over land and authority,[14] rewrites political or other alternative narratives of identity, inscribing them within a "prescribed sphere of action and expectation"[15]—divine action produces the expectation of restoration:

> Then Moses went up to God; the LORD called to him from the mountain, saying, "Thus you shall say to the house of Jacob, and tell the Israelites: You have seen what I did to the Egyptians, and how I bore you on eagles' wings and brought you to myself. *Now therefore, if you obey my voice and keep my covenant, you shall be my treasured possession out of all the peoples. Indeed, the whole earth is mine, but you shall be for me a priestly kingdom and a holy nation.* These are the words that you shall speak to the Israelites." (Exod 19:3–6, emphasis mine)

It is this, what I describe as, "preservationist magnetism," that is, this bringing unto self as a function of identity that defines the parameters of exclusion. The chosen community—self-identified in Yehud not only through self-proclaimed divine election but also through the implication of terms such as "Israel," "kingdom," and "nation"—views itself in radical distinction from the "people of the land." A dependence upon divine rather than natural (i.e. what the social-political body naturally produces) authority, such as what the *golah* community clearly demonstrates, is the consequence of the belief that human collective agency can only occur effectively within parameters first established by divine agency, as though following a previously established archetype.[16] Or as perhaps better stated in Deut 9:3: "Know then today that the LORD your

---

14. On the formation of identities K. Cerulo ("Identity Construction: New Issues, New Directions," *ARS* 23 [1997]: 393) writes, "[G]roup members consciously develop offenses and defenses, consciously insulate, differentiate, and mark, cooperate and compete, persuade and coerce."
15. Ibid., 388.
16. Eliade develops this notion of archetype throughout *The Myth of the Eternal Return*.

God is the one who crosses over before you as a devouring fire; he will defeat them and subdue them before you, so that you may dispossess and destroy them quickly, as the LORD has promised you."

To be clear, divine authority as a central tenet of the monotheistic body is not initially the result of any control over the material productions of the social body. The construction of and initial turn toward divine authority—which is part of the very same process of a monotheistic identity's initial formation—is a reaction to the distributed relations and systems, products of material production. Consequently, the monotheistic agenda common to all monotheistic identities is to "appropriate all the forces and agents of production"[17] from the social body and thereby impose its authority over it. But in part for this reason it cannot exist without the social body upon which its own identity is inscribed. This idea of the necessity of an other against which to define one's self-identity is alluded to in Judges and likely reflects Dtr's attempt to explain the unlikely reality of an "unmixed" population:

> Now these are the nations that the LORD left to test all those in Israel who had no experience of any war in Canaan (it was only that successive generations of Israelites might know war, to teach those who had no experience of it before): the five lords of the Philistines, and all the Canaanites, and the Sidonians, and the Hivites who lived on Mount Lebanon, from Mount Baal-hermon as far as Lebo-hamath. They were for the testing of Israel, to know whether Israel would obey the commandments of the LORD, which he commanded their ancestors by Moses. (Judg 3:1–4)

The example is perhaps made even more clear in Ezra:

> Shecaniah son of Jehiel, of the descendants of Elam, addressed Ezra, saying, "We have broken faith with our God and have married foreign women from the peoples of the land, but even now there is hope for Israel in spite of this. So now let us make a covenant with our God to send away all these wives and their children, according to the counsel of my lord and of those who tremble at the commandment of our God; and let it be done according to the law. (10:2–3)

In Ezra, exclusion of the *am ha'aretz* is necessary in the articulation of the *golah* community's collective identity.[18] Foreign women and children exist for the author as a foil against which the *golah* community defines itself. With this "recategorization" exclusion becomes ritualized in membership, transforming membership into a social ritual and fact upon

---

17. Deleuze and Guattari, *Anti-Oedipus*, 198.
18. Exclusion, as Tajfel and Turner argue ("Social Identity Theory"), is a necessary act in the formation of a social identity.

which a corresponding collective identity is dependent.[19] "[I]f," for example, "you turn back, and join the survivors of these nations left here among you, and intermarry with them, so that you marry their women and they yours, know assuredly that the LORD your God will not continue to drive out these nations before you; but they shall be a snare and a trap for you, a scourge on your sides, and thorns in your eyes, until you perish from this good land that the LORD your God has given you" (Josh 23:12–13). To be clear, however, the act of exclusion is not one of negation but of separation, of *distinction*—a carving out from the social body space for the monotheistic body. As an act of agency it is competitive by nature; and in that it allows for negative reciprocity, which results in yearnings for positions of dominance (thus, a contest for authority) between the monotheistic body and the social body, especially in the area of symbolic power (that is, when monotheism "matures" into its more complex forms).[20]

It is not surprising then that we do not have a fully developed concept of monotheism until after the development of the city: "[M]onotheism, totally ignored by [early agrarian-based] societies...is encountered only in the dominant classes of societies already based on a developed agriculture and a division into classes...in which the advances of the division of labor are accompanied by a correlative division of religious work."[21] Monotheism is less a consequence of polytheism and more a product of an increasingly institutionalized hierarchy of power and organization reflective of a more complex production of surplus. As such, we should note further that a monotheistic identity is not the product of a class in power, which with its dependence upon exclusion would likely result in a social-religious division between victimizer and victimized or a more despotic enforcement of religious law.[22] Instead, it is, in its original form, the consequence of a desire for, including the attempt to direct its production of desire toward, control over the distributed power relationships within the social-political body. It is this idea that undergirds monotheistic ideologies such as that expressed in the text of Jeremiah:

---

19. Cerulo, "Identity Construction," 388.
20. In this sense monotheistic identity reflects what D. Webster describes of hierarchical political identities of early states. He describes negative reciprocity as producing "differential wealth, position, and power" ("On Theocracies," *American Anthropologist* 78 [1976]: 812).
21. Bourdieu, "Genesis and Structure," 8.
22. See also René Girard, "Violence and Religion: Cause Or Effect?," *The Hedgehog Review* 6 (2004): 9.

> This city has aroused my anger and wrath, from the day it was built until this day, so that I will remove it from my sight because of all the evil of the people of Israel and the people of Judah that they did to provoke me to anger—they, their kings and their officials, their priests and their prophets, the citizens of Judah and the inhabitants of Jerusalem. They have turned their backs to me, not their faces; though I have taught them persistently, they would not listen and accept correction. They set up their abominations in the house that bears my name, and defiled it. They built the high places of Baal in the valley of the son of Hinnom, to offer up their sons and daughters to Molech, though I did not command them, nor did it enter my mind that they should do this abomination, causing Judah to sin. Now therefore thus says the LORD, the God of Israel, concerning this city of which you say, "It is being given into the hand of the king of Babylon by the sword, by famine, and by pestilence": See, I am going to gather them from all the lands to which I drove them in my anger and my wrath and in great indignation; I will bring them back to this place, and I will settle them in safety. They shall be my people, and I will be their God (32:31–38).

The monotheistic body's core desire is for a monopoly over power, to which Ezra testifies when it describes the Persian imperial king as a tool of Yahweh (cf. Ezra 1:1–4).[23] By proclaiming its God the supreme, universal authority it symbolically subsumes all earthly power and authority under divine jurisdiction. Or, as Hall, writing from an evangelical Christian perspective, as but one example, puts it,

> [D]ivine grace and sovereignty, while certainly 'other,' work in and through human freedom and responsibility to achieve the fullness of being for which the created order already possesses potentiality. Thus it is not a case of either/or: either divine sovereignty or human willing, either grace or freedom, gospel or law, faith or works. It is a matter of both/and: namely, *a sovereign grace that grasps the human subject and evokes from it the creaturely responsibility for which it has a capacity but which, on account of false pride and sloth, it fails to make good.*"[24]

That responsibility of achieving the "fullness of being" is, according to Christianity generally, a response required of humanity by virtue of its creation, through which human begins were marked with a divine residue or signature. Islam, as Sayyed Hossein Nasr describes it, shares a similar idea:

---

23. Note again Bourdieu, who writes, "Conservation of the monopoly over symbolic power, such as religious authority, depends on the ability of the institution that possesses it to make known to those who are excluded from it the legitimacy of their exclusion, that is, to make them misrecognize the arbitrariness of the monopolization of a power and a competence in principle accessible to anyone" ("Genesis and Structure," 25).

24. Hall, *Imaging God*, 51, emphasis mine.

> Human beings…reflect the Divine Attributes like a mirror, which reflects the light of the Sun. By virtue of being created as this central being in the terrestrial realm, the human being was chosen by God as His viceregent (*khalīfat Allāh*) as well as His servant (*'abd Allāh*). As servants human beings must remain in total obedience to God and in perfect receptivity before what their Creator wills for them. As viceregents they must be active in the world to do God's Will here on earth.[25]

Both ideas, as carefully expressed by their respective authors, reflect a structural-objective quality about the monotheistic body. Human beings, the entire natural order even, were created to reflect publicly divine authority. As social agents, members produce identity when they gather around shared moral values and a "common good," defining themselves as an externally recognizable community of members.[26] Monotheistic identity, therefore, is knowable by the member qua the non-member. The non-member is any individual who has not been, whether through ignorance or conscious refusal or, as in the case of Yehud, wrong "ethnicity," encoded with the culture of the religious community.[27] Moreover, monotheism's inherent distinction expects the existence of an other against which the monotheistic identity is defined. This identity actively resists other relevant, competing identities. In Zechariah, for example, collective identities may be equated with the idols around which they develop: "On that day, says the LORD of hosts, I will cut off the names of the idols from the land, so that they shall be remembered no more; and also I will remove from the land the prophets and the unclean spirit" (Zech 13:2).

As we have been discussing, each monotheistic identity produces itself in part by attempting to subsume, to absorb within itself, political identity—a point perhaps no more clearly made than in the text of Jeremiah.[28]

---

25. Seyyed Hossein Nasr, *The Heart of Islam: Enduring Values for Humanity* (New York: Harper SanFrancisco, 2004), 276.

26. I am drawing in part from Chantal Mouffe's definition of a communitarian view of politics ("Citizenship and Political Identity," *October* 61 [1992]: 29).

27. Ezra–Nehemiah's use of foreign labels is similar to what Ford and Tonander ("The Role of Differentiation Between Groups and Social Identity in Stereotype Formation," 374) describe as an impact of the use of stereotypes: "[W]hen there exist real intergroup differences that negatively distinguish the in-group from some relevant out-group, motivation to attain a positive social identity will influence the structure of emerging stereotypes by biasing the strength with which positively and negatively differentiating attribute dimensions become associated with the in-group and out-group in memory."

28. B. Dauenbauer's description of political identity is important here: "The phenomenon of political identity is troublesome. To have a political identity one must accept as normatively binding a set of claims and practices not wholly of his or

"In those days and at that time I will cause a righteous Branch to spring up for David; and he shall execute justice and righteousness in the land" (Jer 33:15). As the passage suggests, both justice and righteousness necessitate a distinction, a separation, between what is and what is not just or right—concepts that are defined within the dominant meaning system of the corresponding monotheistic identity. And if, as in the case of the *golah* community, divine justice and righteousness are intended for the community itself, both require a clear separation between the member, as one who upholds what is just and right, and the non-member, as one who does not. Or, to offer it differently,

> There will always be a "constitutive outside," an exterior to the community that is the very condition of its existence. It is crucial to recognize that, since to construct a "we" it is necessary to distinguish it from a "them," and since all forms of consensus are based on acts of exclusion, the condition of possibility of the political community is at the same time the condition of impossibility of its full realization.[29]

2. Strategies of (Social) Identity Formation as Relevant for Monotheistic Identity

Based on a multidimensional model of social identity formation, John Berry proposed four strategies for understanding ethnic group affiliation.[30] These strategies (Assimilation, Separation, Integration, and Marginalization[31]) help clarify the structural formation of a social group identity, which for our purpose may clarify the identity struggle among

---

her own determination. And among these claims are those that require the division of humanity into an included 'us' and an excluded 'them'" ("Ricoeur and Political Identity," *Philosophy Today* 39 [1995]: 47).

29. Mouffe, "Citizenship and Political Identity," 30.

30. John Berry, "Immigration, Acculturation, and Adaptation," *Applied Psychology* 46, no. 1 (1997): 5–34.

31. Regarding the four acculturation strategies, he writes, "From the point of view of non-dominant groups, when individuals do not wish to maintain their cultural identity and seek daily interaction with other cultures, the *Assimilation* strategy is defined. In contrast, when individuals place a value on holding to their original culture, and at the same time wish to avoid interaction with others, then the *Separation* alternative is defined. When there is an interest in both maintaining one's original culture, while in daily interactions with other groups, *Integration* is the option; here, there is some degree of cultural integrity maintained, while at the same time seeking to participate as an integral part of the larger social network. Finally, when there is little possibility or interest in cultural maintenance (often for reasons of enforced cultural loss), and little interest in having relations with others (for reasons of exclusion or discrimination) then *Marginalisation* is defined" (ibid., 9).

the returning Judeans in Yehud, as well as the group's self-perceived relationship with the people already in the province. H. Turjeman et al. phrase Berry's strategies in a manner easily accessible to our study. The authors describe Separation as "choosing the heritage over the new culture"; they describe Assimilation as "choosing the new culture over the heritage"; they describe Integration as "adopting both cultures"; and Marginalization they describe as "identifying with neither culture."[32] Of the four strategies, Ezra–Nehemiah clearly employs a Separation strategy but also implies that some returnees adopted strategies of Assimilation or Integration (both of which may be indicated through Ezra–Nehemiah's references to intermarriage as well as Tobiah's office in the temple).[33] As described by Ezra–Nehemiah, the *golah* community rejected the culture in Yehud, choosing instead the *golah*-Yahwistic heritage (or what we might call "remnant heritage") as it identified itself in distinction from the people already in the land. Or as Liverani colorfully describes it, "Having returned from exile, pure and extremely careful to avoid contamination, the returnees found themselves in a country, Palestine, widely contaminated by people, practices, divinities and cults that were impure."[34]

Following any separation strategy, identity must be preserved through a culturally encoding process of ritualization.[35] Otherwise, without a consistent identity pattern, those who have isolated themselves from a dominant culture run the high risk of "significant psychological costs," such as is sometimes expressed through delinquency.[36] Expectations for a ritualized identity include its transference or perseverance from one social-historical context to another, preserved within the life of the group. Turjeman et al. point to two theoretical frameworks for understanding this process: (1) as innate, instinctive, and natural; or (2) a situational perspective in which identity has social boundaries "that are

---

32. Hagit Turjeman, Gustavo Mesch, and Gideon Fishman, "Social Identity, Identity Formation, and Delinquency," *International Journal of Comparative Sociology* 49, no. 2–3 (2008): 113.

33. M. Smith's work (*Palestinian Parties*) has adequately demonstrated that even some of the Persian-period biblical authors developed a strategy of integration.

34. Liverani, *Israel's History*, 357.

35. On the ritualization of identity and behavior, see Richard Davis, "The Ritualization of Behaviour," *Mankind* 13, no. 2 (1981): 103–12; Roger Friedland, "Religious Nationalism and the Problem of Collective Representation," *ARS* 27 (2001): 125–52.

36. For more on acculturation and delinquency, see Berry, "Immigration, Acculturation, and Adaptation," see esp. p. 29; Turjeman, Mesch, and Fishman, "Social Identity, Identity Formation, and Delinquency."

constantly being negotiated..."[37] The first is the more antiquated view of (ethnic) identity, while the second is more self-consciously aware that identity is always in motion, or changing, and must be constantly navigated. In fact, most modern studies on identity formation have rejected any continued viability of the first option.[38]

As we have argued throughout this work, the identity[39] of the *golah* community was ritualized in part through a corresponding ritualization of divine law.[40] In this instance, religion plays a socially constructive role in that it presents a defining force of cultural identity.[41] But this role is not religion's innately; it is given the responsibility within a non-dominant group. In the case of Yehud, it was the *golah* community's anxiety over acculturation that produced an increased dependence upon religion for the construction of the community's identity (cf. Ezra 9:9). This proposal is supported by Davies' observation that, "The stimulus for the ritualization of human behaviour is...the presence of anxiety of some sort."[42]

---

37. Turjeman, Mesch, and Fishman, "Social Identity, Identity Formation, and Delinquency," 112. The authors refer specifically to "ethnic" identity. Because ethnicity is culturally constructed and because Ezra–Nehemiah redefines different ethnic identities (who is "Israelite," who is "foreign"), the theoretical frameworks are not limited in their relevance to our discussion.

38. As Turjeman, Mesch, and Fishman (ibid.) note in their survey of the literature. But see also Henri Tajfel, "Social Psychology of Intergroup Relations," *Annual Review of Psychology* 33, no. 1 (1982): 1–39; Tajfel and Turner, "Social Identity Theory"; Berry, "Immigration, Acculturation, and Adaptation." These authors both offer a survey of relevant literature and also construct effective arguments on identity formation by treating identity from what Turjeman et al. refer to as a "situational perspective" (noted above).

39. According to K. Bhavnani and A. Phoenix, identity is the point where structure and agency meet (*Shifting Identities, Shifting Racisms: A Feminism and Psychology Reader* [London: Sage, 1994], 6).

40. In explaining this we may for the moment possibly assume a heightened sense of awareness regarding social institutions and systems by the biblical authors. This is done to aid in facilitating the argument and to see "below the surface" of what is immediately observable. What this reveals in part are the sometimes unconscious influences that play a role in guiding agency.

41. For instance, note Neusner and Sonn, "In their classical statements, Islam and Judaism agree that the religious regulation of everyday life, extending to acutely detailed dimensions of ordinary conduct, is required to establish a godly society, a people and state formed in accord with God's will. Both stress norms of behavior as much as of belief, emphasis upon the formation, by the faithful, of a state governed by God's law as interpreted and applied by God's representatives" (*Comparing Religions*, 5). In other words, belief patterns are modes of behavior, an act that can in turn become socially constructive as agents engage society.

42. Davis, "The Ritualization of Behaviour," 106.

Thus, what is denoted as *"golah* community" in Ezra–Nehemiah is an identity that reflects a Separation acculturation strategy employed by immigrating Jews from Babylon.

Ritualized obedience resists the anxiety of instability, but it does not always *alleviate* it.[43] It is, in other words, an ever-present threat. Yet an anxiety caused by disorder is typically a *defensive* mechanism and as such does not fully support the production of desire: "To code desire— *and the fear, the anguish of decoded flows*—is the business of the socius."[44] But, by reframing relations of production and distributed power as not naturally social but as religious in nature, that is, as the production of monotheistic desire and not any uniquely social-political desire, the monotheistic community locates its desire, as an object of production, within the divine, who is also the object of ritualized obedience rather than in the material world, for which it must initially compete from the fringes of power.[45] Obedience, therefore, is an act of agency from which expressions of identity are expressed externally.[46] The obvious, heavy emphasis within the Persian-period biblical texts upon obedience to religious law confirms this. Ritualized identity is a collective response to other competing, cultural identities; it is a promise of stability.[47] The *golah* community demonstrates its ritualized identity through obedience to the law, including, for example, observance of the Passover festival, which connects the community with the Hebrews of the Exodus tradition (cf. Ezra 6:19–21).

43. I am reminded of this by ibid.
44. Deleuze and Guattari, *Anti-Oedipus*, 139, emphasis mine.
45. I am drawing in some part from Deleuze and Guattari, who argue that the social field is invested with desire to the point that social production is a production of desire (see ibid., 29). Their argument at this point seems to leave out the material aspect of (social) production and should for this reason not be embraced uncritically. In the situation the *golah* community found itself, that is in their immediate lack of control over material production and the relations of production produced, the community ideology substituted material production with "desiring-production." The religious expression of the *golah* community is emphatically an expression of collective desire.
46. Note also L. Pierre and T. Lawson, who write, "Ritualized behavior is the consequence of the combined elicitation of various systems devised for processing specific materials different from ritual information and it is not the outcome of dedicated ritual mechanisms" ("Evoked Culture, Ritualization and Religious Rituals," *Religion* 38, no. 2 [2008]: 162).
47. This competition Pierre and Lawson (ibid., 158) describe as, "Religious rituals, ideas about those rituals, relevant rules of conduct and habits accompanying those rituals, as cultural items, are transmitted within and among social groups and across generations. In the transmission process, they have to compete with other cultural information for attention."

a. *Resistance (Discourse) as Productive of Identity*

> There can be no *inter*group behavior unless there is some "outside" consensus that the group exists.[48]

The ritualized identity of the *golah* community assumes the advent of restoration and the elevated status of the religious community as the divinely elected community. It necessitates, moreover, external recognition of its existence as an identity. Because of its resistance to the social body, however, the monotheistic identity controls no wholly autonomous basis for social legitimation of its authority.[49] In other words, despite its claim to divine election, and so also its claim to divine structure and legitimation—those things as proposed to be existing autonomously of the social body—religion contains no internal, distinct structure through which to govern society that does not already exist in society. Any existence of a wholly distinct—thus bearing no reflection of the social body's influence—symbolic order, which includes linguistic communication, intersubjective relations, and perhaps more importantly *the acceptance of the law*[50]—is also forfeited. To phrase it somewhat differently, because religions express needs and concerns of a culture, and so are dependent upon the culture itself, the symbolic order to which they lay commanding claim—notably including a universal acceptance of divine law—and which are used in attempts to justify religion's sole access to authority, are produced and reproduced within the culture itself.[51] Wherever an increasing focus on and a drive to assert religion as

---

48. Tajfel, "Social Psychology of Intergroup Relations," 2.

49. Bourdieu describes it in the following manner: "The strictly religious authority and the temporal force that various religious claimants can enlist in their struggle for religious legitimacy is never independent of the weight that laypersons mobilize in the structure of the relations of force between classes. It follows that the structure of objective relations between claimants occupying different positions in the relations of production, reproduction, and distribution of religious goods tends to reproduce the structure of relations of force between groups or classes, but *under the transfigured and disguised form* of a field of relations of force between claimants struggling for the conservation or subversion of the symbolic order" ("Genesis and Structure," 31).

50. For a more detailed discussion of symbolic order, see ibid., 31–33; Paula Murphy, "Jacques, Jacques and Jacks: The Shifting Symbolic in Derrida and Lacan," *Textual Practice* 19, no. 4 [2005]: 509–10.

51. As Friedland ("Religious Nationalism," 125), for example, avers, "religion partakes of the symbolic order of the nation-state." Which should be read in the framework of Weber's statement (*The Sociology of Religion*, 224–25), "The more a religion acquired the aspects of a 'communal religion' (*Gemeinde-Religiosität*), the more political circumstances co-operated to lend a religious transfiguration to the

the dominant institution *above* (and so being universal) society, economy, and politics, can be found within a collective ideology, there too must be found suspicion; religion is not in its primary role a producer of cultural meaning and order but a recipient, a consumer, a cultural product.[52] Instead, we recognize that despite its tendency to, as Green puts it, "totalize, to extend [its] reach to all dimensions of experience,"[53] religion is above all things a culturally *determined* product. Or, as Mary Douglas writes, "Religious beliefs *express society's awareness of itself*; the social structure is credited with punitive powers which maintain it in being."[54]

Within Ezra–Nehemiah, resistance discourse took on the form of a social revisionism, which entailed ignoring or rejecting those things that the author(s) could not explain or that the textual framework could not contain within itself. One notable example, for instance, is the absence of any complete listing of provincial governors. In addition, what constituted the identity of a "citizen" of Yehud according to the text was not one's participation in the symbolic order of the province. One needed to be a member of the *golah* community, from which a restored society would be composed. Thus, we can see that Ezra begins in a rather subversive manner:

> Thus says King Cyrus of Persia: The LORD, the God of heaven, has given me all the kingdoms of the earth, and he has charged me to build him a house at Jerusalem in Judah. Any of those among you who are of his people—may their God be with them!—are now permitted to go up to Jerusalem in Judah, and rebuild the house of the LORD, the God of Israel— he is the God who is in Jerusalem; and let all survivors, in whatever place

---

ethic of the subjugated. Thus, Jewish prophecy, in a realistic recognition of the external political situation, preached resignation to the dominion of the great powers, as a fate apparently desired by God."

52. In saying that, I agree with and employ the caveat first articulated by Berger (*Sacred Canopy*, 47–48), who cautions, "It must be stressed very strongly that what is being said here does not imply a sociologically deterministic theory of religion. It is not implied that any particular religious system is nothing but the effect or 'reflection' of social processes. Rather, the point is that the *same* human activity that produces society also produces religion, with the relation between the two products always being a dialectical one. Thus it is just as possible that, in a particular historical development, a social product is the effect of religious ideation, while in another development the reverse may be the case. The implication of the rootage of religion in human activity is *not* that religion is always a dependent variable in the history of a society, but rather that it derives its objective and subjective reality from human beings, who produce and reproduce it in their ongoing lives."
53. Green, "Religion and Politics," 2.
54. Douglas, *Purity and Danger*, 126, emphasis mine.

they reside, be assisted by the people of their place with silver and gold, with goods and with animals, besides freewill offerings for the house of God in Jerusalem. (Ezra 1:1–4)

The intent of the decree, the authenticity of which we may consider somewhat suspect following the pattern of Ezra 7:11–26,[55] was to place imperial authority behind the actions of the *golah* community in Yehud. Casting Cyrus as the tool of Yahweh for the benefit of the exiles was intended as a revision of the social-political narrative. In other words, according to what seems to be the stance of Ezra–Nehemiah, if the Persian empire acted solely at the behest of Yahweh, Yahwistic religion could embody the framework through which imperial actions must be interpreted. Such is the authorial intent to refocus one's view of the social world into something governed and controlled by the divine, which is done only through the divine's chosen people. For example, "So the elders of the Jews built and prospered, through the prophesying of the prophet Haggai and Zechariah son of Iddo. They finished their building by command of the God of Israel and by decree of Cyrus, Darius, and King Artaxerxes of Persia…" (Ezra 6:14).

What is more, the appeal to the religious tradition of the exodus is unavoidable (compare Exod 12:35–36).[56] Just as the Egyptians provided the Hebrews with jewelry and clothing, which the narrator describes as "plundering," the people of possibly both Babylonia and Yehud are commanded to provide like materials for the immigrants (*golah* community) and for sacrifices to be conducted at the Jerusalem temple (Ezra 1:4; 7:14–18). In short, the description *wkl-tns 'r mkl-hmqmwt 'sr hw' gr-sm* is not temporally or spatially located. One may feasibly interpret "his place" as the space occupied whether before or after the journey—that is, whether a present or an intended future sense. With the evocative power

---

55. Cf. Wilhelm Rudolph, *Esra Und Nehemia Samt 3. Esra* (Handbuch Zum Alten Testament 20; Tübingen: J. C. B. Mohr, 1949), 73–77; Jacob Myers, *Ezra, Nehemiah* (ABD 14; Garden City: Doubleday, 1965), 57–63; David J. A. Clines, *Ezra, Nehemiah and Esther* (New Century Bible; Grand Rapids: Eerdmans, 1984), 10–16; H. G. M. Williamson, *Ezra, Nehemiah* (WBC 16; Waco: Word, 1985), 97–105; Hoglund, *Achaemenid Imperial Administration*, 226–27.

56. Note also Zech 10:9–12: "Though I scattered them among the nations, yet in far countries they shall remember me, and they shall rear their children and return. I will bring them home from the land of Egypt, and gather them from Assyria; I will bring them to the land of Gilead and to Lebanon, until there is no room for them. They shall pass through the sea of distress, and the waves of the sea shall be struck down, and all the depths of the Nile dried up. The pride of Assyria shall be laid low, and the scepter of Egypt shall depart."

of imperial decree, so goes the text's ideology, preexisting social structures must bow to the *golah* community's social-religious blueprint: "And you, Ezra, according to the God-given wisdom you possess, appoint magistrates and judges who may judge all the people in the province Beyond the River who know the laws of your God; and you shall teach those who do not know them" (Ezra 7:25). Note also Liverani's clarification:

> The "oaths" or "promises" of Yahweh to Abraham and then Moses correspond, at the mythical level, to the legal function of the edicts of the Persian emperors: they provide legitimation for the return and bestow entitlement of property to the land.[57]

That the *golah* community seems to have seen in itself a parallel to the the Hebrews of the exodus tradition implies a collectively perceived connection of Yehud with a pre-conquest Canaan. As Liverani writes, "The traditions of the conquest [found in Joshua and Judges] offer a 'strong' model, preferred by the supporters of violent confrontation and of the exclusion of 'extraneous' people. These were logically (or at least narratively) connected to the 'exit from Egypt' that marked the liberation of the people from slavery in a foreign land."[58] As the property of Yahweh, the land was deeded, mythically, to the divine remnant (Neh 9:23). As was the case with the Canaanites, the landed inhabitants of Yehud were re-identified subsequently as profane, foreign, being without any legitimate stake in or claim to the land—in other words, the losers of the contest.

In a structural sense, the *golah* community appealed to the monotheistic body, in contrast to the social body, as the productive source for its collective identity. This appeal, in this situation, reflects also a defense of the monotheistic identity—that is, in the sense that monotheism assumes itself, especially its symbolic order, universal and absolute—against a panoply of alternatives. Regarding the structure of this defensive posturing, Daniel Smith writes, "The preservation of an identity under threat calls for 'defensive structure.' If, as we have suggested, 'ethnic identity' is preserved by conscious choice in circumstances of intercultural contact (Barth), then an analysis of the social mechanisms of the Judean exiles in Babylon ought to reveal creatively structured identities in order to be 'the people of God' in a foreign land."[59] Categorical exclusion, between sacred and profane, which in Ezra–Nehemiah,

---

57. Liverani, *Israel's History*, 270.
58. Ibid.
59. Smith, *Religion of the Landless*, 63.

and relatedly in Ezekiel, become translated into such social terms as citizen and foreign, is an extension of this proposed revision of social identity.[60] By rewriting the definition of "citizen," a social identity constructed in contrast to "foreigner," the biblical text restricts the identity definition of "citizen" to the immigrating community, to which the so-called *Golah* Lists (Ezra 2:1–67; Neh 7:4–69) attest, and confirms for us the continued role that a contest for land and authority has upon the social identity of the community.

3. *Discourses of Resistance on Land and Authority*

> While Ezra prayed and made confession, weeping and throwing himself down before the house of God, a very great assembly of men, women, and children gathered to him out of Israel; the people also wept bitterly. Shecaniah son of Jehiel, of the descendants of Elam, addressed Ezra saying, "We have broken faith with our God and have married foreign women from the peoples of the land, but even now there is hope for Israel is spite of this (Ezra 10:1–2).

According to Karen Cerulo, "[C]ollective agency includes a conscious sense of group as agent. [It] is enacted in a moral space."[61] That sense of collective agency, as a cornerstone for social identity, especially with its focus on the importance of *moral* space resonates in the words of Shecaniah and the descendants of Elam, "We have broken faith with our God and married foreign women from the peoples of the land" (cited in the passage above). Identities, as the places where structure and agency meet,[62] are subject to both external and internal interpretations. For Ezra, this "conscious sense," as Cerulo phrases it, begins with a recognition of the group's relationship to the divine—the identity of the *golah* community is based on the existence of Yahweh and Yahweh's exclusive election of the group. For this reason, members of the group must see themselves in separation from the so-called peoples of the land. And it is in that separation that is articulated the group's political imagination as

---

60. Note further Garbini (*History and Ideology*, 126), who writes, "In Achaemenidean Jerusalem a small group of those who had returned from the Babylonian exile considered themselves the only legitimate 'remnant', not only of the kingdom of Judah which had disappeared but of the whole people of Israel. Jerusalem represented all the tribes because it considered itself, in polemic against the Israelites of Shechem, to be the sole people of God: a sacred people who had the mission of serving God in his temple and in his dwelling, Jerusalem."
61. Cerulo, "Identity Construction," 393.
62. Again see Bhavnani and Phoenix, *Shifting Identities, Shifting Racisms*, 6.

an outward projection of self-perceived agency, which as we have seen makes little room for including the *am ha'aretz* within the constitutive definition of Yehud's "political community." And it is in this community, according to Schimmelfennig, where the basic qualities of what is considered normative are identified:

> All polities have institutionalized a standard of political legitimacy that is based on the collective identity, the ideology, and the constitutive values and norms of the political community. *The standard of legitimacy defines who belongs to the polity as well as the rights and duties of its members. It distinguishes rightful and improper ways of acquiring, transferring, and exercising political power*, and it determines which political purposes and programs are desirable and permissible.[63]

In its description of Yehud's social context, however, Ezra–Nehemiah says next to nothing about how power and knowledge, the exercise of which is usually determined by the political community, were legitimated or deployed outside of the community in the larger social-political context.[64] That is, it contains no reference to the material production of power, and seemingly assumes that ideologies based on an isolation of Yahweh as the only true authority were enough to support the demands of the social-political body. Moreover, the text remains suspiciously silent on the actual material conditions of production upon which the appropriation of power in a collective is based.[65] If the land were empty and so a blank canvas upon which the creative process of society building could occur, this would not pose for us the same problem. Yet the paranoid focus on the construction and maintenance of a social identity, including especially the text's expressed passion against intermarriage,

---

63. Schimmelfennig, "The Community Trap," 62, emphasis mine.

64. I am reminded of the importance of this by Berquist ("Constructions of Identity," 59–60) who himself was making an observation of Foucault: "Michel Foucault pointed out the ways that social systems must deploy power and knowledge as tools toward constructing and controlling themselves as systems so that they maintain some semblance of coerced stability even in the midst of their inherent dissolution (Foucault, *Archaeology of Knowledge*; Michel Foucault, *Power/Knowledge: Selected Interviews and Other Writings, 1972–77* [trans. Colin Gordon et al.; New York: Pantheon, 1980]). There is a heuristic principle here: one studies the places where society is about to fall apart in order to recognize the uses of power to stabilize the society. Thus, Foucault studied prisons, mental hospitals, and other such heterotopia."

65. Deleuze and Guattari's discussion (see *Anti-Oedipus*, 194) of the original materiality of (desire) production demonstrates the importance of understanding the material conditions in which (social-political) production takes place.

can do not but confirm for us that the land was *not* empty.[66] We do not, in other words, have before us a blank canvas upon which a utopian society could be drawn. Yehud was not, if we invoke the spirit of Thomas More, an island pure and unadulterated from the travails of society. It was not a geographic space devoid of any social-political body or its corresponding institutions, waiting to be cultivated; otherwise, statements such as the following, which we have mentioned before but which continues to bear relevance, would have no relevant basis: "So now let us make a covenant with our God to send away all these [foreign] wives and their children, according to the counsel of my lord and those who tremble at the commandment of our God; and let it be done according to the law" (Ezra 10:3).[67] Such wide scale divorce and abandonment of children would impose an economic strain upon society.[68] In doing so it would either create or aggrandize a landless, unemployable class of poor and presumably force a "marriage rush" as families vied for higher social-economic positions by marrying upward. Such an action could only be tolerated in a society wherein the immigrating exiles (*golah* community) were already the social majority, and in which the community already controlled the material power to enforce social-political division. But as a minority,[69] any such overtures would likely be restrained by the dominant majority. Or to put it differently, the self-regulation of society, the regulated and regulating systems of the larger provincial culture, would not have permitted such structurally altering, and therefore chaotic, acts.

For that reason, in part, any proposed change of this magnitude could only be ideological. Based alone on the religious ideology of an immigrating community, the utopian vision of the *golah* community was without the ability—it was restricted to being a vision and not a reality—actively to direct the material forces of production. Consequently, the

---

66. For further reference, see Carroll, "Exile! What Exile?"; Galambush, *This Land Is My Land*; Barstad, "After the 'Myth'"; Oded, "Where Is the 'Myth'?"

67. On "those who tremble," see Blenkinsopp, "A Jewish Sect of the Persian Period."

68. But compare to Riches ("Hunting, Herding and Potlatching: Towards a Sociological Account of Prestige," 238–39), who argues that divorce rates could be higher in nomadic societies because access to land and wild resources was not contingent upon marriage or filial relation. His conclusion, along with the contrast of our own, emphasizes that an awareness of the economic effect of marriage must be acknowledged in any study of social-economic identity.

69. On both the Babylonian Judeans and those that "returned" to Yehud as minority groups, see also Smith (*Religion of the Landless*, 58–63) who argues that the focus on ethnic boundaries was a defense mechanism of a minority group coming into contact with a majority culture.

community's social identity appealed to a divine usurpation or rejection of those forces it did not control, symbolized in the radical distinction between member and non-member as one that mirrors the division between sacred and profane. "Member," in that instance, was one who had been (re)encoded with the religious culture of the *golah* community. Everyone and everything else was both non-member and unavoidably profane, existing without the possibility of contractual relationship—a criteria necessary for enjoying the benefits of restoration—with the divine.[70]

We can conclude then that the collective identity of the *golah* community, as D. Smith noted above, was reactionary and not initially productive, and depended upon the preexistence of a society and its social agents. By that we mean that *golah* community identity would have looked noticeably different had the people of the land, the foil against which it could project its notion and definition of self and also its understanding of what was sacred could be cast, had been absent. In other words, an empty land, devoid of those forces against which the *golah* community reacted to construct its identity, would have produced a different result. The absence of a contest for authority, I propose, would not have resulted in the development of a monotheistic identity.

Nehemiah, for instance, states, "When the people heard the law, they separated from Israel all those of foreign descent" (13:3). The term *'rb* translated by the NRSV as "foreign descent" refers generally to "mixed company." It is used also in Exod 12:38 to refer to those who were "not Israelite." In Nehemiah it provides us with a contextual understanding that the primary perception of society was that of a separation between those considered Israelite and those not so considered. Or to put it differently, the primary distinction as perceived by the biblical authors was between member and non-member, those categories projected by the *golah* community and based on the identity of the community and its culture. Zechariah confirms this distinction with its description of Yahweh as a wall of fire around Jerusalem (2:5). There, fire symbolizes both defense and purification, both of which are divine actions. The metaphor of fire represents exclusionary distinction, a distinction which defined the collective identity of the community and was codified within the community's religious law: "On that day they read from the book of

---

70. Berger describes this basic trend in the following manner: "The concentration of religious activities and symbols in one institutional sphere, however, *ipso facto* defines the rest of society as 'the world,' as a profane realm at least relatively removed from the jurisdiction of the sacred" (*Sacred Canopy*, 123).

Moses [see Ezra 7:6; Neh 8:1] in the hearing of the people; and it was found written that no Ammonite or Moabite should ever enter the assembly of God..." (Neh 13:1).

Reading the passages from Zechariah and Nehemiah together highlights an underlying emphasis on purified space and on maintaining a distinction between what has been purified and what has not, or what remains profane. A perception of this type is not concerned with the population density or the production capacity, both of which speak to economic strength, of the city. It is not concerned with whether the city is, as discussed previously, bureaucratic, industrial, or ceremonial.[71] And we should not forget that these descriptions are about a city, not a province. One cannot help but feel that the authorial obsession with the purification and distinction of a single city (Jerusalem) betrays the *golah* community's lack of authority over the province. We have already noted that in their revision of space, the authors assume a religious-ceremonial status for Jerusalem and elevate its status based on their belief Yahweh has chosen the city. As a reminder, "The *ceremonial city* is a center for the regulation of the symbols that undergird and constitute a society. Various scholars refer to this type as the royal-ritual city, and much of the work of the biblical city would involve the central reality of kingship..."[72] It is clear the *golah* community viewed Jerusalem as the "center for the regulation of the symbols that undergird and constitute a society." Yet in the absence of any kingship functions (despite their prophesied possibilities) Jerusalem's ceremonialism is reduced to having meaning only within a *golah*-Yahwistic, religious symbolic system. And since the *golah* community was a minority within the larger society, no *golah*-Yahwistic perception would have been reason enough to transfer provincial center of power from Mizpah to Jerusalem.[73] We must look

---

71. O'Connor, "The Biblical Notion of the City," 30–32.
72. Ibid., 32.
73. Lemaire ("Nabonidus," 292) suggests that Mizpah was "very likely" the capital of Judah from 587 to 445 B.C.E. As Blenkinsopp (*Isaiah 56–66*, 46) notes, after the Babylonian conquest, the administrative center for what would be Yehud moved to Mizpah. It is probable that a temple was set up in Bethel to correspond to this move, to be in close proximity to Mizpah. He also writes ("Bethel in the Neo-Babylonian Period," in Lipschits and Blenkinsopp, eds., *Judah and the Judeans in the Neo-Babylonian Period*, 99), "[T]he old Bethel sanctuary, having survived the Assyrian conquest and the reforming zeal of Josiah, obtained a new lease on life by virtue of the favored status of the Benjamin region and the proximity of Bethel to the administrative center at Mizpah: hence, the juxtaposition of Mizpah and Bethel in Judges 20–21." This tradition would suggest less that the administrative center followed the temple but that the temple followed the administrative center. This

beyond the ceremonialism embraced by Ezra–Nehemiah (and also Haggai, Zechariah, and Ezekiel) to find any reason for this transference, and find it instead as a result of a coercing, regulating imperial power confirming its control over conquered territories.[74]

An exclusivist posture is at the heart of any monotheistic identity. After all, is it not ultimately the goal of every monotheistic religion to make way for a "new" world wherein the righteous, purified community may exist without fear of corruption? That fear of corruption and dissolution rattles the biblical authors as they usher before us their perspectives on Yehud. Or, as Liverani describes similarly,

> Once back in Judea, the returnees used the expression "people of the land" to define the people who lived there: Judeans who had neither been deported nor emigrated, and non-deported Israelites of the north. All of them were Yahwists and members, broadly speaking, of the 'Israelite' community which was to be reconstructed. They lacked, however, all the cultic and ideological ideas elaborated during the exile. Thus the term "people" began to acquire a connotation of exclusion, opposed to its traditional meaning, which had always indicated belonging...[75]

This posture, as described by Liverani, is reactionary; it requires the existence of an externalized "other," cast outside the body and memorialized there through (re)defined identity boundaries regulated through religious law. Inherent within the monotheistic identity is the desire to claim owned power over this other. By "owned power" we mean the authority to name the other, to categorize them as something less than a free citizen. But is Bausani correct, "The ethics of primary monotheisms is [sic] an ethic of power and will"?[76] The free citizen, the culturally encoded member, receives citizenship as the fruit of their labor, which is defined initially as resistance to the "power" of the other. Perhaps Bernard Dauenhauer's statement on political society is appropriate here: "To preserve a political society, its members must shape the character of

---

theory would correspond to the re-centralization of Jerusalem which seemed to have been followed by a lagging completion time for rebuilding the Jerusalem temple (although if Edelman's argument [in *The Origins of the 'Second' Temple*] is correct, though it has yet to receive scholarly consensus, the completion time must be moved up substantially).

74. Moreover, the community could not, therefore, have afforded economically to exercise total exclusion. And we see hints of this (as suggested by Liverani [*Israel's History*, 358–59]) in Neh 13:15–16. There, Phoenicians appear to have been very much a part of the society, possibly offering it financial strength.

75. Ibid., 257.

76. Alessandro Bausani, "Can Monotheism Be Taught?," *Numen: International Review for the History of Religions* 10, no. 1 (1963): 169.

newcomers in their midst by instilling within them a particular set of identifications. A crucial part of this set is the conviction that one is obligated to perpetuate the society."[77] Monotheism *desires* authority. Yet while authority over the social body may be monotheistic identity's fundamental desire, the identity's law-based ethics are initially concerned with exclusion for the purpose of distinction, of defining collective identity.

According to texts such as Ezra–Nehemiah, Haggai, Zechariah, and Ezekiel, the final product of individual (desire) production, is a "restored" utopia, in which the member exists in resistance to the excluded "other." This other exists simultaneously there and not there. Zechariah's wall of fire must have a reason to exist, to purify space by removing profane; but without this other the fire is constrictive, an oppressor. What is socially "real" is offered through divine perspective, itself a perspective of the self-proclaimed righteous community. Thus, the words of God are the manifest desires of the corresponding monotheistic identity—and that is the reason why each monotheistic identity must reject the existence of others; the words of God cannot compete. Divine favor cannot be shared among communities defined in distinction from others. Moreover, divine intent must make sense within the religious culture of the community. In this way, divine intent is restricted to, and in fact simply *is* the perspective or intent of the community (an example of which we saw in Ezra 4:1–2). By petitioning the permission of Zerubbabel and the heads of families (presumably of the *golah* community) the "adversaries" described are presented as validating the authority of the *golah* community over the Jerusalem temple and even of their divine election. In other words, they are presented as "buying in" to the monotheistic identity expressed by the *golah* community.

Zerubbabel's attachment to the heads of families is important in Ezra–Nehemiah because Ezra–Nehemiah makes little fuss over his role as governor.[78] Based on the way the biblical texts treat him, he is important only so long as his activities can be connected to the Jerusalem temple or, temporarily for Zechariah, the hoped-for Davidic throne.[79] Note, for

77. Dauenhauer, "Ricoeur and Political Identity," 51.
78. S. Japhet proposes that Ezra was written from a considerable historical distance from Zerubbabel, about 100–150 years. If true, the author's treatment of Zerubbabel would reflect a highly ideological agenda. Garbini (*Myth and History*, 101), for reference, suggests that Ezra was composed toward the end of the fourth century in order to justify the temple in Jerusalem over the temple in Gerizim.
79. Eph'al ("Syria-Palestine Under Achaemenid Rule," 143) posits that Zerubbabel's disappearance was due to his deposition by the Persian authorities. However, there is no corroborating evidence for this hypothesis and it is not more feasible than

example: "But Zerubbabel, Jeshua, and the rest of the heads of families in Israel said to them, 'You shall have no part with us in building a house to our God; but we alone will build to the LORD, the God of Israel, as King Cyrus of Persia has commanded us'" (4:3). The focus is clearly on the Jerusalem temple and its role in the development of a religious symbolic order that seems to be intended as the dominant order, in which was also given meaning the identity "Israel"—a term that unavoidably carries with itself a complex history.[80] Note also a similar observation by Leith, who writes,

> According to the theology of the exiles, bluntly expressed in Ezekiel 11, Yahweh had deserted Judah and joined the people in exile. According to Ezekiel, God has no patience with "inhabitants of Jerusalem"—in other words, nonexiled Jews who make the counterclaim that the land is theirs because God was punishing the exiles. Ezekiel speaks for his constituency and promises that once the returnees have cleansed the land of the supposedly syncretistic practices of the indigenous Judahites, Yahweh will restore their lands to the true people of Israel—the exiles—whether those remaining liked it or not.[81]

a. *Walls, Social Identities, and Authority: Components of Monotheism's Discourse of Resistance*

> [T]he emphasis on Nehemiah's actions serves a structural purpose in the composition as a whole. This purpose is to focus attention on the formation of a holy community *through the process of separating the community*

---

our hypothesis that Zerubbabel's disappearance was due to the changing agenda or favor of the biblical author.

80. One should also see Davies' discussion (in *Memories of Ancient Israel*, 47–57) of the multiple uses and meanings of the term "Israel." For example, he writes, "Let's briefly list the various biblical Israels, from the broadest to the narrowest. The broadest is the Israel of twelve tribes. In Genesis, this Israel is a family, part of the Abrahamic clan and related to other Abrahamic families. It is part of a group including Aram, Moab, Ammon, Edom, and Ishmael. From Exodus onward this family becomes a nation and markedly more detached from even its Abrahamic neighbors. In Chronicles it becomes a single kingdom based in Jerusalem and constituting the whole territory of the kingdom of David, which in fact includes much of the land occupied by the Abrahamic nations. In the books of Samuel Israel seems to mean territory—probably Benjamin, Ephraim, and Manasseh, the tribes descended, according to Genesis, from Rachel—ruled by Saul, but excluding Judah. In Kings Israel is used almost exclusively for the kingdom of the ten tribes, but at the end this kingdom no longer forms part of Israel, but only Judah. In Ezra and Nehemiah Israel is restricted not only to Judah but to those Judeans who returned from exile" (ibid., 54–55).

81. Leith, "Israel Among the Nations," 397.

from the peoples around it, physically by rebuilding the walls of Jerusalem and religiously by the reinforcement of cultic regulations such as the observance of the Sabbath.[82]

In Nehemiah it is written, "So the king [Artaxerxes] asked me, 'Why are you so sad? You aren't sick, are you? You look like a man deep with troubles.' Then I was badly frightened, but I replied, 'Long live the king! Why shouldn't I be sad? For the city where my ancestors are buried is in ruins, and the gates have been burned down'" (Neh 2:2–3). Nehemiah's appointment as governor, the author suggests, was motivated by Nehemiah's concern for Jerusalem in addition to the king's concern for Nehemiah. And in making this connection the author reduces the field of political action to the city of Jerusalem, which becomes within the narrative the central symbol for *golah* monotheistic identity. Since this is our only "evidence" of the event, it creates, as Pierre Briant describes it, an "optical illusion," the result of an uneven distribution of the evidence.[83] That is to say, the king's fondness for Nehemiah becoming translated into a relative fondness for Jerusalem is a pleasing sentiment, but it is one that should not be taken uncritically:

> Then I said to them, "You see the trouble we are in, how Jerusalem lies in ruins with its gates burned. Come, let us rebuild the wall of Jerusalem, so that we may no longer suffer disgrace." (Neh 2:17)

To speak of gates is to speak simultaneously of walls; gates are portals through walls, the control mechanisms controlling access to enclosed space.[84] What Nehemiah mourns is not as much the lack of gates as it is

---

82. Hoglund, *Achaemenid Imperial Administration*, 208, emphasis mine. Compare also Brevard S. Childs, *Introduction to the Old Testament as Scripture* (Philadelphia: Fortress, 1979), 632–34; Tamara C. Eskenazi, "The Structure of Ezra–Nehemiah and the Integrity of the Book," *JBL* 107, no. 4 (1988): 80–81.

83. Pierre Briant, *From Cyrus to Alexander: A History of the Persian Empire* (trans. Peter T. Daniels; Winona Lake: Eisenbrauns, 2002), 585–86.

84. M. Moore ("On the Signification of Walls in Verbal and Visual Art," *Leonardo* 12, no. 4 [1979]: 311) puts it colorfully, "Second in importance only to the separation function is another theme associated with walls, referred to by dictionaries as the 'prevention of free entry or egress.' While birth separation has profound individual or ontogenetic significance, the impenetrability of walls, hence their *defensive* function, is endowed with group or phylogenetic meaning. Whether naturally formed or an artifact, whether in a cave, a castle or a city, walls offer security and protection to those dwelling behind them. This need for protection was demonstrated on the most grandiose scale by the emperor Shih Huang Ti who, following his predecessors' custom, built a 2400 km long wall on the western frontier to defend China. Long before him, in 7000 B.C., the neolithic people inhabiting Jericho surrounded it with a massive wall against invaders."

the lack of a wall–gate control mechanism surrounding a reconstituted Jerusalem.[85] Better stated, he mourns the lack of defined space as the property of Yahweh and over which the *golah* community would, in theory as the divine remnant, have authority: "Ezra–Nehemiah focuses its account on three stages of response to the edict… The third, under Nehemiah, rebuilt the walls of Jerusalem, *thereby enclosing the community with a solid and secure boundary—both physically and metaphorically* (Nehemiah 1–7)."[86] Nehemiah mourns Jerusalem not as a social-economic center, one existed already at Mizpah,[87] but as the central symbol of the *golah* community.[88] Nehemiah's (delayed) action on his arrival in Jerusalem is telling:

---

85. According to D. Ussishkin, this idealized reconstruction was never fulfilled. "Nehemiah found the city largely abandoned with its old, massive city walls still standing but partly damaged or destroyed. In an effort to revive Jerusalem, he first turned to restoring the city walls. This action (as pointed out to me by Axel Knauf) was first and foremost a symbolic, national, political act rather than a purely military act. Following this, attempts were made to settle the vast intramural areas, but these attempts largely failed. Large regions of the walled city remained uninhabited, while the population concentrated around the City of David and the area of the Temple Mount. This was probably the appearance of the city encountered by Alexander the Great in 332 B.C.E., and it remained so until its period of renewed prosperity, which began in the Late Hellenistic Period, in the second century B.C.E." ("The Borders and De Facto Size of Jerusalem," in Lipschits and Oeming, eds., *Judah and the Judeans in the Persian Period*, 164).

86. Eskenazi, *Ezra–Nehemiah*, 123, emphasis mine.

87. Cf. J. Zorn, *Nabeh, Tell En* (New Encyclopedia of Archaeological Excavations in the Holy Land 3; Jerusalem: Israel Exploration Society, 1993); Israel Finkelstein and Neil Asher Silberman, *The Bible Unearthed: Archaeology's New Vision of Ancient Israel and the Origin of Its Sacred Texts* (New York: Free Press, 2001), 307; Blenkinsopp, *Isaiah 56–66*, 46; Lemaire, "Nabonidus," 92; Edelman, *The Origins of the "Second" Temple*, 58.

88. In this sense, the walls may be considered to fulfill a purpose described in a general sense by Summers: "The walls of cities provide an instructive example of boundaries. Walls may keep others out, but they also define the extent of the protection of a god, or of the jurisdiction of a ruler. The walls of institutions as different as ancient Near Eastern cities and traditional African settlements and cities were understood in this way. This being so, the defense of a city is more than self-preservation. The walled city is not only secure but sacred, a precinct within which protection is afforded by tutelary deities, who must in their turn be respected and defended. City gates may also have a double value; they are typically fortified, but they are also conspicuous and distinguished, and mark passage from one kind of space to another" (*Real Spaces*, 154).

> Three days after my arrival at Jerusalem, I slipped out during the night, taking only a few others with me. I had not told anyone about the plans God had put in my heart for Jerusalem. We took no pack animals with us, except the donkey that I myself was riding. I went out through the Valley Gate, past the Jackal's Well, and over to the Dung Gate to inspect the broken walls and burned gates. (Neh 2:11–13)

Why does he go out under the cover of darkness? The narrator suggests something illicit may be going on, something outside Nehemiah's jurisdiction as governor.[89] Moreover, Nehemiah operates in reaction to Sanballat and Tobiah's anger about someone "who was interested in helping Israel" (2:10). The narrator casts the relationship between Sanballat and Tobiah and Nehemiah into one defined by a competition for space. But in this situation Nehemiah has been re-figured by the author; he is not the governor but the vanguard of the *golah* monotheistic identity.

In all of this, we might hear an echo in the words of Susan Kenzle, who writes, "The delineation of territory is a defensive mechanism and communicates both ownership and personalization of space."[90] The construction of and focus on Jerusalem's walls is a focus on ownership and personalization of space by the *golah* community. Nehemiah's fight, as the text defines it, was not for the stability of the province, as one might expect of a governor, there is hardly any expressed awareness of a world outside Jerusalem. His fight was over the ownership and definition of space. "But now I said to [the city officials], 'You know full well the tragedy of our city. It lies in ruins, and its gates are burned. Let us rebuild the wall of Jerusalem and rid ourselves of this disgrace!'... But when Sanballat, Tobiah, and Geshem the Arab heard of our plan, they scoffed contemptuously. 'What are you doing, rebelling against the king like this?' they asked. But I replied, 'The God of heaven will help us succeed. We his servants will start rebuilding this wall. But you have no stake or claim in Jerusalem'" (Neh 2:16–17, 19–20). The protest is framed in the form of rebellion but the response appeals to *golah* religious ideology. This response is the result of authorial reconfiguring of

---

89. It would be difficult to conclude any argument regarding whether or not Nehemiah actually did as described. The main issue at stake is the perspective the author uses to frame any discussion of Nehemiah. In other words, Nehemiah and his actions are both given meaning based on the cultural meaning system of the *golah* community.

90. Susan C. Kenzle, "Enclosing Walls in the Northern San Juan: Sociophysical Boundaries and Defensive Fortifications in the American Southwest," *Journal of Field Archaeology* 24, no. 2 (1997): 199.

the distribution of power, making the imperial king the tool of Yahweh. Sanballat et al.'s warning of going "straight to the top" is trumped by Nehemiah et al.'s response of going above the imperial king.[91]

Ezra–Nehemiah's vision for the wall of stone parallels Zechariah's vision of a wall of fire. Both symbolize a demarcation between the righteous community and the profane.[92] The excitement of Zechariah's vision may be emphasized by the statement in Neh 1:3 that the walls of Jerusalem themselves had been destroyed by fire. In its destructive capacity, fire may represent judgment (cf. Isa 66:16; Ezek 30:14; 38:22; Dan 7:10). Yet it is also a judgment that may result in purification, especially, "For I will be a wall of fire all around it, says the LORD, and I will be the glory within it" (Zech 2:5). Where fire was previously connected with destruction, it is now associated with exclusive demarcation and sanctification; the glory of Yahweh must sanctify lest it be profaned. But what is this glory if it is not the desiring-production of the community externally expressed as a public demonstration of divine authority? In every religion, gods are the objectivated expression of the religious identity, and the divine world is a reflection of an idealized world.[93] Zechariah's desire for the imminence of this vision leads to his blending of divine and human worlds. Jerusalem becomes not simply an archetype but the physical abode of Yahweh. And while Zechariah does not contain reference to the *golah–am ha'aretz* divide that makes Ezra–Nehemiah so colorful, his vision of Jerusalem as the center of symbolic and social order is very much the same. Restoration begins with exclusion and ends

---

91. That Yahweh "controlled" Cyrus seems to have been a common theme shared by a number of Persian-period biblical texts (cf. Isa 44:28; 45:1; Ezra 1:1).

92. One might also note the statement by Oppenheim (*Ancient Mesopotamia*, 128), "The walls of the cities in the ancient Near East were, in fact, more than a demarcation line between the city and the open fields, more than a prepared line of defence. They were the dominant feature of urban architecture. Their size and arrangement proclaimed the importance and might of the city, their gateways displayed its wealth with monumentality intended to impress the visitor and ward off the enemy. The carefully maintained walls were placed under the protection of deities and given long and propitious names."

93. While she disagrees in part with Durkheim, Douglas' summary of part of his argument is apropos here: "[Religious deities] are merely ideas awakened by the experience of society, merely collective ideas projected outwards, mere expressions of morality. So they have no fixed material point of reference. Even the graven images of gods are only material emblems of immaterial forces generated by the social process. Therefore they are ultimately rootless, fluid, liable to become unfocused and to flow into other experiences. It is their nature always to be in danger of losing their distinctive and necessary character. The sacred needs to be continually hedged in with prohibitions" (*Purity and Danger*, 26–27).

in utopia. With the power of the Persian empire in the hands of its god, the righteous remnant, the *golah* community, patterns an image of society based on a projected archetype of its god and divine will.[94] The

---

94. S. Japhet's argument ("The Concept of the "Remnant" in the Restoration Period: On the Vocabulary of Self-Definition," in *From the Rivers of Babylon*, 432–49) that Haggai and Zechariah refer to the people who remained in the land as the remnant is intriguing but not entirely convincing. Her focus, the term *s'r*, is ambiguous enough to be possibly defined via two meaning systems, that of, for the sake of simplicity, the *golah* and that of the *am ha'aretz*. The cultural meaning behind this self-definition must stem from a unified community culture. While the *golah* community was certainly not the only defined collective, the parameters of other such collectives are difficult to assess. That said, if she is correct that the employment of the idea of remnant is still quite similar to the manner in which the *golah* community adopted the term. It uses religious belief to isolate and define a particular collective of individuals from others and presents this collective as divinely elected. What is interesting is the lack of perceivable conflict between the *golah* community and the Judeans who remained who both claimed the unique status of "remnant." Such a conflict would undoubtedly have had several fronts, religious, social, and economic, the latter especially so if we accept that the Babylonian exiles were of the aristocratic class. Japhet hopes to avoid any such criticism by arguing that Nehemiah in fact recognized as remnant survivors in Judah those who had escaped captivity (see ibid., 439). Note also, "Accordingly, 'the remnant' referred to in Neh 1:2, those 'who remained from the captivity,' would be the people who survived after all the others were taken captive—that is, those who did not go into Exile. This conclusion raises some serious historical questions. Nehemiah's definition may imply that in his time there was as yet no major return of Jews from Babylon to Judah" (ibid., 438–39). It is possible to read *s'r* in conjunction with the exiles as punishment (on "punishment" cf. Jer 13:1–27). Thus, the remnant would refer to those who had survived the purification process of exile. In this way, we could translate the statement *'l-hyhwdym hplyth 'sr-ns'rw mn-hsby w'l-yrwslm* as "about the Judeans that were delivered, those who were made a remnant from (the event of) the captivity and about Jerusalem." If this reading is permissible then we would expect that by the time Nehemiah spoke with Hanai and entourage, some of the exiled Judeans had returned to Yehud (compare also Ezekiel's definition of remnant in Ezek 11:1–20). Japhet's argument seems to be based on the belief that none had yet returned. Oded offers an argument similar to that of Japhet, but it too must make rather weak connections. "In the list of returnees (Ezra 2; Nehemiah 7) many settlements were in the territory of Benjamin. This means that the author of Ezra–Nehemiah considered all the people of Judah and Benjamin to be returnees, whether or not they went into exile" ("Where Is the 'Myth'?," 63). The inhabitation of territories within Benjamin does not equate going into exile, as even Ezra–Nehemiah suggests that members of the *golah* community lived in areas outside Jerusalem (references to Judah may have been made in an inclusive manner and not as a way to exclude Benjamin, a tribe that had previously collapsed into Judah; cf. Neh 7:6; 11:3; Ezra 1:5; 4:1; 10:9; note also the contrast between Israel and Judah and Benjamin in 2 Chr 34:9).

remnant, in whose midst Yahweh will dwell, will become like a magnet that reorients all other peoples toward Yahweh. "Many nations shall join themselves to the LORD on that day, and shall be my people; and I will dwell in your midst. And you shall know that the LORD of hosts has sent me to you. The LORD will inherit Judah as his portion in the holy land, and will again choose Jerusalem" (Zech 2:11–12).

It is worth noting that the list of returnees, members of the *golah* community, is provided in Nehemiah after the narrated completion of Jerusalem's wall: "Now when the wall had been built and I had set up the doors… These are the people of the province who came out of the captivity of those exiles whom King Nebuchadnezzar of Babylon had carried into exile…" (Neh 7:1, 6). The walls symbolize what the so-called Golah List delineates, the identification and separation of the *golah* community. It was only after the completion of the walls symbolizing the demarcation of Jerusalem that the author has Nehemiah "enroll the people by genealogy" (7:5). This codifying of citizenship confirms loyalty, and in itself represents a metaphorical wall excluding from membership those whose names are not listed. It is presumably also the list from which individuals and families were selected as "tithes" to populate the city of Jerusalem (see Neh 11:1–2). More importantly, it patterns the exclusionary posture of the community by imposing the community's monotheistic identity as a social framework. We can be fairly confident that this categorization of the social body was not accepted by those outside the community. This acceptance would require an acceptance and a legitimation of their own rejection with the simultaneous legitimation of the *golah* community as the divinely elected. This acceptance could occur only at their own expense.

A similar sentiment is expressed in Ezek 11 (see vv. 16, 22–24) where the prophet describes Yahweh as deserting Judah and joining the people in exile.[95] It is a dramatic argument but we must note an entirely religious one. In it we see a proposed exclusion separating member from nonmember, and also a defining of space as the property of Yahweh and so always susceptible to a divine re-imaging of space. Distributed relations

---

95. Leith ("Israel Among the Nations," 397) puts it poignantly, "According to Ezekiel, God has no patience with the 'inhabitants of Jerusalem'—in other words, nonexiled Jews who make the counterclaim that the land is theirs because God was punishing the exiles. Ezekiel speaks for his constituency and promises that once the returnees have cleansed the land of the supposedly syncretistic practices of the indigenous Judahites, Yahweh will restore their lands to the true people of Israel—the exiles—whether those remaining liked it or not."

among social agents were rewritten not as the results of real material (and ideological) processes but as the creation and manifestation of divine will. Or, as Liverani puts it, "The returnees, during their exile, had built up a 'strong' ideology, based on the new covenant, on Yahweh's exclusiveness, on the 'remnant that shall return'...."[96] Moreover, Ezra's prayer (Ezra 9:1–15) makes several poignant claims: that Yahweh was the community's god, that the *golah* community had been divinely preserved, and that the community had been given a stake in the holy place of Yahweh (see v. 8). The obligation of the community, therefore, was to rebuild the Jerusalem temple and to construct a wall around the city of Jerusalem.[97]

The connection between the wall and the temple seems unavoidable. The temple symbolizes divine authority. The reconstructed walls were likely part of an imperial refortification policy, evidence for which we must find in archaeology rather than in the biblical text.[98] Yet in Ezra–Nehemiah they symbolize an enforced separation of the remnant from the people of the land. With the rebuilding of Jerusalem's walls and temple, the community inaugurates the process of divine restoration. And the separation produced by the walls, the exclusion it represents must be mirrored in the community before the security of the walls, the divine protection it represents, can be manifest. It is not surprising, then, that a condemnation follows immediately this connection made between God, people, and wall: "[S]hall we break your commandments again and intermarry with the peoples who practice these abominations? Would you not be angry with us until you destroy us without remnant or survivor" (Ezra 9:14)? Ezra's prayer, with its concern over intermarriage between the *golah* and the *am ha'aretz*, expresses his fear that the community will lose its distinctive identity and become like everyone else—that is, like the *am ha'aretz*.[99] Ultimately, then, the sociological problem of conflict between the immigrating community (*golah*) and the people already in the land (*am ha'artez*), and so also the "problem" of territorialization,

---

96. Liverani, *Israel's History*, 256.

97. G. Ravasi (*Antico Testamento: Introduzione* [Milan: Mondadori, 1991], 160) notes with perhaps too much enthusiasm, "La prima dimensione che appare evident nell'opera di riforma di Esdra e Neemia è quella della sacralità e dela separatezza della communità. Il centro è il tempio la cui santità si distende progressivamente a tutte le altre strutture sociali e politiche."

98. Cf. H. G. M. Williamson, "Nehemiah's Walls Revisited," *PEQ* 116 (1984): 81–88; Hoglund, *Achaemenid Imperial Administration*, 210.

99. See also Blenkinsopp ("A Jewish Sect of the Persian Period") who discusses Ezra's prayer in relation to a dissident group in Yehud.

both of which are identified by the nature of discourses of resistance within the biblical texts, was a conflict created by the *golah* monotheistic identity.[100]

---

100. This "clash," as Ahlström notes (*The History of Ancient Palestine*, 846), was not simply religious but was in a very real sense sociological. However, because of the community's lack of true authority in the social sphere the biblical authors redefine the problem as a religious one with a vocabulary whose meaning is drawn from the religious culture of *golah* Yahwism.

Chapter 7

THE MONOTHEISTIC BODY WITHIN VIEW:
UNDERSTANDING THE PARAMETERS OF THE MODEL

As this work has sought to show, a material-based conflict over land and authority was the *initial* catalyst for the development of monotheism. The failure to acquire absolute control over land and authority resulted in the "maturation" of monotheism into what would offer a structured basis for its more complex forms (i.e. Judaism, Islam, and Christianity), which entailed a transition from a dependence upon material conditions to the construction and institutionalized preservation of ideological conditions (belief systems, values, truths, doctrines) as a legitimating base for its claim to authority.[1] Despite this transition, however, monotheism cannot escape the influence of immanent historical and material conditions. It remains in a perpetual state of reaction (and often resistance) to the historical conditions of the material world.

All forms of (strict) monotheism, or monotheistic identities, share "genetic qualities," or the structural qualities of the monotheistic body; consequently, each identity is both interrelated and distinct from the others. In other words, while the different forms of monotheistic identity are contingent upon distinct historical and material circumstances, leading to their differences, all share basic structural qualities upon which their unique identities are built. This study of the *golah* community highlighted some of those qualities. The possession of land, which in the social environment of Yehud (and also the larger ancient Near Eastern context) is equivalent to the attainment of value and consequently

    1. The related development of the divine into an exclusive and solitary deity was preceded by what M. Smith describes as a "depersonalization" of the divine, which the "birth" of monotheism required before divinity could become tantamount to identity (see *Origins of Biblical Monotheism*, 164). He states further (ibid., 164, see also 67–80) that the single deity resulted in part from the familial structure superimposed upon the divine realm. Thus, the "patriarchal" deity becomes the authority. But when divinity supersedes identity, the divine family and court are blended into aspects of a singular concept of divinity. While I agree this is a logical development, I would add that emphasis needs to be placed on conflict or struggle as the final push from identity into divinity as being tantamount.

authority, is a desire expressed by monotheism in both its compact and its more complex forms. For the latter, the idea of land as value is no longer tied to the material world but is contingent upon a successful restoration—an event that will overturn or replace any existing material reality. At its core, monotheism pursues authority, which entails control over the forces of production. Control over those forces permits the power to identify, categorize, and define the nature of the social body. Because of monotheism's initial failure to establish a basis of authority in the material world, which occurred under its more compact forms, it constructed and subsequently depends upon the three pillars (revelation, law, and restoration) to support the absolute nature of divine authority. While revelation interrupts the normative order, within which material bases for authority are defined, (divine) law rewrites the permitted behavior of the monotheistic member (though the intent is to do so for the larger social body) in support of the coming restoration.

Divine law, to be clear, which is always a consequence or product of revelation in monotheism, proffers a blueprint for restoration and preserves the transition—the intent is both ideological and material— from revelation to restoration. Because restoration requires an absolute overturning of material authority, the force of the law must void the legitimacy of that authority by rigidly enforcing a separation between insider and outsider, or member and non-member. It must, in other words, become the mechanism through which a re-institutionalization of authority, and the systems through which it is exercised, is radically imposed upon the social-political body.

As our discussion of monotheism within this work progressed two related processes, for lack of a better term, became apparent.[2] The first comprises the material conditions contributing to the formation of the "objective structures" of monotheism, which our case study of Yehud has shown us. The second comprises the ideological and the *distinct* material conditions that condition the reception of and response to the monotheistic body by individual monotheistic identities—that is, specifically those of a more "complex" form (Islam, Judaism, and Christianity).[3] In its more nascent, or compact, form, monotheism entailed a response to immediate material conditions. As it matured, becoming

---

2. I owe a great deal to Charles Pazdernik, who helped me clarify the specifics of the following issue.

3. I am not using this term with the sense that it is normally given when contrasted with the term "primitive." Instead, I am contrasting compact with complex to emphasize that monotheism's complex forms are reiterations, reinterpretations, and expansions upon the compact form that most closely reflects the monotheistic body.

increasingly "complex," its development within different monotheistic identities entailed (1) an ideological response to its original material circumstances, (2) an ideological response to the lack of a perceivable immediate restoration within the material world, and also (3) a reaction to the historical and material circumstances of the context specific to the monotheistic identity. The third point addresses the catalyst for the formation of a new monotheistic identity. Furthermore, monotheism, as a general pattern, will only continue to develop as long as there remains a relevant contest within which it is engaged with the social and material world.[4] We should also emphasize that the simultaneous existence of multiple monotheistic identities results in an additional contest for authority between these identities themselves (i.e. in addition to the general contest that monotheism has with society). Each identity defines itself under the dogmatic belief that there can be only one "face," or one identity, upon the body and only one law, thus, one restoration and one (perception of) God. Understanding that ideological framework allows us to understand better extreme statements such as the following, which connects the possession of land with the truest expression of monotheistic identity:

4. This is as true in its origin as it is in its later stages. For example, early Judean "monotheistic" discourse in the seventh and sixth centuries B.C.E. was in large part a reaction to the social-political situation, and the subsequent loss of national authority through the exiles. Smith writes (ibid., 165), "The loss of identity as a nation changed Israel's understanding of the national god. Looming empires made the model of a national god obsolete. Moreover, the rise of supra-national empires suggested the model of a supra-national god... As Judah's situation on the mundane level deteriorated in history, the cosmic status of its deity soared in its literature." While there is some truth to his argument, relegating the development of monotheism to a survival mechanism is not alone sufficient to explain the continuing existence of a monotheistic structure. Moreover, it appears to depend upon a general intellectual shift, which Jaspers and Eisenstadt have referred to as the Axial Age. What drives the formation of a monotheistic identity is a desire for authority, not merely a need to survive. As Jeffrey Tigay notes, "The need to emphasize the monotheistic idea in this period was probably due to the increased exposure of Israel to the triumphant Assyrian and Babylonian empires, which attributed their victories, including victories over Israel, to their gods" (*Deuteronomy: The JPS Torah Commentary* [Philadelphia: Jewish Publication Society, 1996], 433). Thus, a model of resistance was established prior to the exposure of Yehud to the *golah* community. The reduction of the normative political authority created a vacuum the monotheistic body sought to fill. But note further that with later Rabbinic Judaism and early Christianity it was the desire for a reduction in the social-political authority of the Roman Empire that perpetuated the monotheistic ideal. A similar development can be observed in Medina, where monotheistic sentiments developed in conjunction with Muhammad's solidification of social-political authority.

> A person should always live in the Land of Israel, even in a city with an idolatrous majority, and should not live outside the Land, even in a city with a Jewish majority, for whoever lives in the Land of Israel resembles one who has God, and whoever lives outside the Land resembles one who has no God. (*b. Ket.* 100b)[5]

Along those lines, it is also important to note that discourses of resistance are necessary for a monotheistic identity. Such discourses are the means by which the boundaries of identity are distinguished. Resistance, in this regard, is an act that reflects a position outside of authority. It is effective (perhaps even affective) for restoration in that it defines a monotheistic identity in relation to the process of its desired restoration. This motivation for resistance is codified within divine law, which is itself constructed as a form of resistance to a more dominant law that is more naturally the product of the larger social body. The goal of resistance, then, is the successful contest for authority by the monotheistic community.

1. *Authority, Law, and an Apparatus of Control*

Each monotheistic identity understands the divine restoration of authority to be specific to it; each asserts, in other words, a "privatizing claim" over that authority and the processes (of restoration) toward that end. There can be no acceptance of any other (monotheistic) claim to authority; otherwise, the certainty of restoration, which requires both a community and its god defined through exclusion, dissipates. Divine law uniquely supports that claim through its intermediation between revelation and restoration as well as its regulation of individual and collective behavior as a mechanism through which the identity of the member, or insider, is defined in contrast to the outsider; but its continued relevance depends upon the successful establishment by the law's respective monotheistic identity of an apparatus of control through which the law itself is enforced. In the more mature forms of monotheism, this ideological *fait accompli* no longer depends upon specific material circumstances; such forms have already transitioned into an institutionalized dependence upon ideological "truths." For example, the Qur'an assumes divine authority to be self-evident by virtue of the existence of the material world. That is, material circumstances are no longer the source or basis of truth; to the contrary, they testify to a "greater truth" upon which the laws of the natural world depend:

---

5. Cited in Raphael Jospe, *Jewish Philosophy*, vol. 1 (Lanham: University Press of America, 2008), 215 n. 8.

> Your Guardian-Lord is Allah, Who created the heavens and the earth in six days, and is firmly established on the throne (of authority): He draweth the night as a veil o'er the day, each seeking the other in rapid succession: He created the sun, the moon, and the stars, (all) governed by laws under His command. Is it not His to create and to govern? Blessed be Allah, the Cherisher and Sustainer of the worlds! (Qur'an 7:54 [Yusuf Ali])[6]

As we saw with the *golah* community, the apparatus of control, through which divine authority over the material world is ideally preserved, took the form of threatened divine punishment, specifically the possession of or dispossession from the land (cf. Neh 9:22–27; compare Deut 15:28–37). This appeal to divine authority was not unique to religion. Within the historical ancient Near Eastern context, an appeal to the punishing power of a higher order, specifically a divine order, was commonplace. Hammurabi, for a related political example from the ancient Near East, opens and closes his laws by proclaiming divine favor upon his "creation" of a law code. Similar, as the above example testifies, is true for each monotheistic identities; each maintains that its law is authoritative not simply for the sake of the religious community alone but also unequivocally for the whole of the natural world. Consequently, divine punishment of transgression of the divine law further separates the member from the non-member. The power of this separation depends upon the member preserving within the religious symbolic order the fear of the consequences of non-membership through her actions and choices, which entails, or from which can be inferred, a rejection of the truth claim of monotheism. Or, as R. Albert Mohler writes fearfully from the Christian tradition, "the abdication of the universal truth claim [of Christianity] and the retreat into the notion of truth as communal, defined within a given cultural-linguistic system, is a massive concession *fatal to any evangelical theology*."[7] We saw something similar in the case of the *golah* community. Ezra's Mosaic Law offered the framework for a regulated, monotheistic identity to the community. And belief in its possible imposition over the social body—constituting the apparatus by which the

---

6. A similar idea of dominion over the natural world is expressed in a quranic reference to a final restoration, which entails the final victory of monotheistic authority over the material world: "The Event (the Hour or the punishment of disbelievers and polytheists or the Islamic laws or commandments), ordained by Allah will come to pass, so seek not to hasten it. Glorified and Exalted be He above all that they associate as partners with Him" (Qur'an 16:1 [Muhsin Khan]).

7. R. Albert Mohler, "The Integrity of the Evangelical Tradition and the Challenge of the Postmodern Paradigm," in *The Challenge of Postmodernism: An Evangelical Engagement* (ed. David S. Dockery; Grand Rapids: Baker, 1995), 81, emphasis mine.

distinction between member and non-member was legitimated and enforced—was supported by the community's belief that its religious law was universally authoritative.

Yet this universal and absolute authority, and so also monotheism's apparatus of punishment, depends ultimately on monotheism's successful (re)presentation of the encompassing social body to the social body itself as a body external—that is, as a body whose own rejection is necessary for monotheistic restoration. In other words, members of the social body must accept their statuses as outsiders. The rejection of those "foreign," for example, in Ezra–Nehemiah by the *golah* community was simultaneously an exclusion of the "foreign" element and an articulation of monotheistic self-identity. "All these had married foreign women, and they sent them away with their children" (Ezra 10:44). Similarly, it is through a rejection of any alternative authority or law that divine authority and law may be proclaimed *the* authority. An implication of this can be found in the Covenant Code, "I am the LORD your God…you shall have no other gods before me" (Exod 20:2–3).

Likewise, monotheism in its more complex adaptations has depended less upon an immediate demonstration of physical or material power by the divine (compare the Day of Yahweh as described in Mal 4:1 and Joel 2:1–17). It has depended more upon the supremacy of divine knowledge itself as the source by which "right," "good," and "truth"—ideas, Nietzsche pointed out, that are often enforced by those in a position of authority[8]—are defined with universal implication in confirmation of divine authority. For monotheism, this objectifying of ideological rationale insulates the community-given, absolute nature of "right," "truth," and "good" from any possible contestation proffered by the social body. And as monotheism moves away from any overt or immediate dependence upon a material confirmation of its symbolic system, it relies increasingly upon a self-perpetuating truth: the *idea* of revelation as confirmation of divine authority and existence is the rationale for the truth of promised restoration and the inarguable basis for divine authority.[9] This transition from a material dependence to an ideological one, for lack of a better description, reflects also a revision of the "rules of the

---

8. Cf. his essay on Good and Evil: "Good and Bad," in Nietzsche, *Genealogy of Morals*, 24–56.

9. By extension, Louay Safi writes of Islam, although his comments are true for all monotheistic religions, "The natural order is the way it is because it reflects God's will and design, *and the social order is the way it is because it responds to God's order and command* (*The Qur'anic Narrative: The Journey of Life as Told in the Qur'an* [Westport: Praeger, 2008], 37, emphasis mine).

contest." With its identity no longer dependent solely upon material production, monotheism proclaims that absolute power is found in absolute knowledge, exists beyond creation, therefore is infinite in contrast to material (which is ephemeral), and so divine.[10]

For monotheism, God's omniscience and omnipotence are not theological abstracts but explicit, absolute truths. The *golah* community first demonstrated this for us through its claimed right over the land and Jerusalem temple—a right the community believed genuine based on its privatizing claim over the divine ("the deity with absolute power is *our* god").

It can be said then—and the following sources offer both a clarification and a confirmation of this proposal—that the meaning of law within the monotheistic body transcends any codified system of behavior, although it includes that. It includes the very order of creation, which is of divine design, as the very core upon which secondary, and so subservient, laws are based (notably political laws). Or, as Francis Schaeffer, who built a career on identifying issues where Christians should not compromise with society,[11] puts it, "The base for law is not divided, and *no one has the right to place anything, including king, state or church, above the content of God's Law.*"[12] The Hebrew and Christian Bibles

---

10. It is in this sense that the hadith narrated by Abu Hurayra, for Islamic example, can assume not only divine creation but the absolute nature of divine order within creation: "Adam and Moses argued, and Moses said, 'O Adam, you whom God created with His hands and breathed His spirit into have led the people astray and exiled them from Paradise.' Adam replied, 'And you, O Moses, whom God purified with His own speech, do you blame me for committing an act which God had fated for me before the creation of the heavens and the earth?' So Adam bested Moses in the argument" (from the *Jāmi'* of al-Tirmidhī, cited in Jonathon A. C. Brown, *Hadith: Muhammad's Legacy in the Medieval and Modern World* [Oxford: Oneworld, 2009], 176). And further, from the Qur'an, "With Him are the keys of the unseen, the treasures that none knoweth but He. He knoweth whatever there is on the earth and in the sea. Not a leaf doth fall but with His knowledge: there is not a grain in the darkness (or depths) of the earth, nor anything fresh or dry (green or withered), but is (inscribed) in a record clear (to those who can read) (Qur'an 6:59)."

11. In addition to his volumous work, one should see the L'Abri Consensus of Faith, which was never published but is available online at http://www.labri.org/statements/The-LAbri-Statements.pdf.

12. Francis A. Schaeffer, *A Christian Manifesto* (rev. ed.; Westchester: Crossway, 1982), 29–30, emphasis mine. Focusing on humanism because of its operation outside the constraints or parameters of divine law, he writes further, "Humanism, with its lack of *any* final base for values or law, always leads to some form of authoritarianism to control the chaos… With its mistaken concept of final reality, it has no intrinsic reason to be interested in the individual, the human being. Its natural interest is the two collectives: the state and society."

likewise confirm this in their shared opening salvo, "In (the) beginning God created the heavens and the earth" (Gen 1:1, translation mine). And Thomas Aquinas, a proponent of natural theology—that is, inquiry into the existence of God using reason and experience by bracketing out sacred writings or traditions—argued that "natural" laws were really tempered reflections of a greater divine law. According to Aquinas, reason testified to the existence of a truth beyond human comprehension, which would consequently confirm the existence of an authority higher than that which animates human institutions. Ultimately, then, one who acts according to a natural law, when it is the rational way of things, acts according to the eternal law which has imprinted itself upon every natural law. Note, as an elucidating example, the following words by Aquinas:

> [S]ince all things subject to Divine providence are ruled and measured by the eternal law…it is evident that all things partake somewhat of the eternal law, in so far as, namely, from its being imprinted on them, they derive their respective inclinations to their proper acts and ends. Now among all others, the rational creature is subject to Divine providence in the most excellent way, in so far as it partakes of a share of providence, by being provident both for itself and for others. Wherefore it has a share of the Eternal Reason, whereby it has a natural inclination to its proper act and end: *and this participation of the eternal law in the rational creature is called the natural law.* (*Sum.Theo.* Question 91, Article 2, emphasis mine)

Despite its "rational" approach, Aquinas' theory depends upon the monotheistic presupposition of a supernatural authority and its absolute superiority over all forms of human authority. Moreover, it is consistent with monotheism's contest for authority. That is, by making "natural law," and therefore also the institutionalized authority it supports, subservient to divine law and authority, the authority of the monotheistic body over the social body is presupposed. But, in more general terms, the act of realizing, the making objectively manifest of that authority, is what frames a monotheistic identity's struggle within the material world. This ever-present struggle frames not only a monotheistic identity's internal discourse but also its discourses with competing forms of monotheism.

As a whole, and apart from more recent trends among some Orthodox Jewish sects residing in the nation of Israel, Judaism after the Diaspora of the first century C.E. has absorbed this struggle, or contest, by accepting the public, political authority of the society in which the Jewish community exists, while internally regulating itself on the basis of a presupposed divine authority. This has been for Jewish communities a mechanism of self-preservation—that is, a preserving of self by "flying under the radar."[13] To be sure, however, this tendency reflects not only the unique circumstances in which Jewish monotheism developed but also the general tendency of more mature forms of monotheism to wait patiently on divine restoration. Human attempts to bring about restoration, which would ultimately confirm the superiority of human authority, are promised always to end in failure. For example,

> R. Helbo said that there were four oaths: God made Israel swear that they would not rebel against the worldly kingdoms [*malkhiyot*]; that they would not force the end; they would not reveal their secret [*mystirin*] to the nations of the world; and that they would not ascend the wall from the Diaspora [*min ha-golah*]... R. Onia said that God made them swear four oaths because of [what happened] in four generations that forced the end and failed [*ve-nikshalu*]... one of them was in the days of *Koziba*... Why was this? Because they did not have faith [*she-l'o he'eminu*] in the Lord and they did not trust in his salvation...and they violated [*she'avru al*] the oath. (*Shir ha-Shirim Rabbah* 2.18)

And for further example, the Christian book of Revelation, which while written for the Christian community under the Roman Empire has since been interpreted by Christians generally as diachronically relevant, advocates that the religious community patiently endure the trials and

---

13. Note also D. Novak, who writes of Jewish history, "When it [i.e. political subordination] has been the result of conquest pure and simple, the only moral significance it has for the Jews is to find the means by which to be freed from such involuntary slavery. *Minimally, Jews have done this by secretly subverting the authority of their conquerors while paying lip service to them in public. Maximally, Jews have been able to flee their conquerors in order to settle in places affording them more communal independence and personal freedom.* Most radically, Jews have attempted revolution against their conquerors as was the case in 66 CE before the destruction of the Second Temple, and again in 135 CE about three generations after the destruction of the Second Temple in 70 CE" (*The Jewish Social Contract: An Essay in Political Theology* [Princeton: Princeton University Press, 2005], 94–95, emphasis mine). Compare with Borowitz's comment, "What Judaism seeks in non-Jewish governments is obviously God's righteousness fulfilled. According to Jewish law, the sons of Noah (that is, all men) are commanded by God to be just to one another. Thus the non-Jewish king is obligated to establish justice and authorized when he does so. Therefore, the Jew has a religious basis for his civil responsibility to such a non-Jewish king. The fuller obedience to God would, of course, be for Israel to live as a community whose life was structured by God's Torah. The non-Jewish world is not commanded and does not observe the fuller law. Hence life for the Jew in the midst of such a non-observant people can never have the same quality of sanctity that independent life on its own land might have. That is the source of the negative religious attitudes toward non-Jewish states, and they may best be analyzed in terms of the concept galut" ("Judaism," 28–29).

tribulations of the secular world. Yet in doing so, the community must consistently function in a manner condoning divine authority above any earthly one (cf. Rev 2:26). A similar position is found in the hadith *Kitab al-Hajj*, "Ibn 'Umar (Allah be pleased with them) reported Allah's Messenger (may peace be upon him) as saying: He who patiently endures the hardships of it (of this city of Medina), I would be an intercessor or a witness on his behalf on the Day of Resurrection" (7:3180 [Sahih Muslim]). Endurance, perseverance, patience, all are terms that not only reflect the transition from expectations based on material conditions to ideological conditions as a basis for authority but also enjoin the religious community to not hasten the final accomplishment of divine authority, which comes only through restoration. Yet they equally request that the community internally construct the foundation upon which divine authority will at some future point finally supplant every natural, political authority. In other words, just as the *golah* community saw itself as the "seed" from which a restored nation would arise—that is, the parameters of the community's own identity became the "space" within which restoration would occur—more complex forms of monotheism continue to depend upon the identity of the community as the identifiable base for the process of restoration. In short, the qualitative natures of restoration and authority are consistent with the self-perception of the monotheistic community.

2. Deviance as a Threat to Monotheistic Identity

> One lives in a community, one enjoys the advantages of a communality...one dwells protected, cared for, in peace and trustfulness, without fear of certain injuries and hostile acts to which the man *outside*, the "man without peace," is exposed...[14]

As our study of the *golah* community demonstrated, the stability of the monotheistic identity is contingent upon a rigid maintenance of boundaries. In the more compact forms of monotheism the conditions that define these boundaries are both ethnic and moral, the former which should be understood as a constituted identity based in part on historical and material circumstances. And while sects of later Judaism still maintain those boundaries, Christianity and Islam both generally emphasize moral conditions over ethnic ones.[15] In other words, a *monotheistic* people, a

---

14. Nietzsche, *Genealogy of Morals*, 71.
15. Regarding Islam, see, for example, Esposito and De Long-Bas, "Classical Islam," 143. But compare to A. Ahmed (*Journey into Islam: The Crisis of Globalization* [Washington, D.C.: Brookings Institution, 2007], 86) who argues that the

people whose identity is defined in contrast to all others as the only *true* identity, and the nature upon which the concept of a monotheistic God is based, exists by rejecting the legitimacy of other identities. Ezra–Nehemiah poignantly portrays this by its labeling of all peoples outside the *golah* community as foreign—a label that reduces all people into a single analyzable bloc of non-member, or outsider. This exclusionary focus results in part in a privatizing of the three pillars of the monotheistic body—*divine revelation was to us, to be interpreted by us, identifies us as an elected community, etc.*—note also, the competing claim by each monotheistic identity to the same pillars exaggerates the contest between the identities themselves over that which occurs between monotheism and the social body generally. Instability, then, is perceived or defined either as anything that contests a monotheistic identity's claim of "ownership" over the three pillars or that threatens the exclusivity that is a cornerstone of its own collective identity.

Sources of instability can be either internal or external to a monotheistic community. Deviance, as an internal example, threatens the perceived unquestionability of the community's identity as *the* community of divine election. It threatens to reveal the fragility of the power—which, as monotheism mutates into more complex forms, becomes increasingly based within the ideological rather than the material realm—that holds a monotheistic identity together. An unfortunate, but not *only*, defensive reaction within monotheistic communities has been one of violence, whether rhetorical or real, which appeals to a material or physical force in support of an ideologically based power.[16]

In an attempt to identify reason for what he perceives to be monotheism's vehement reaction to deviance, Maaike de Haardt asserts that monotheism by nature promotes violent behavior because it "knows no tolerance" and therefore strives to "eliminate the other."[17] His proposal, however, is too simplistic, if not overly reductive, in that it overlooks tolerable deviance. Moreover, despite its protest of the "other," monotheism cannot afford to eliminate fully this other—something that while monotheistic identities may be consciously unaware the monotheistic

---

distinctions characteristic of tribalism are one of the biggest stumbling blocks in Islam's attempt to deal with globalization. Regarding Christianity, see for example Volf, *Exclusion and Embrace*, 66.

16. See also Maike de Haardt, "The Whole Life: Beyond the Boundaries of Monotheism?," in *The Boundaries of Monotheism: Interdisciplinary Explorations Into the Foundations of Western Monotheism* (ed. Anne-Marie Korte and Maaike de Haardt; Leiden: Brill, 2009), 135.

17. Ibid.

body itself knows implicitly. Monotheistic desire[18] is in fact a desire for authority over the very subject some suggest it wants to eliminate. Violence certainly has occurred within the history of monotheism, but it alone is no less driven by a competition for authority—in contrast to superiority through elimination—than the violence of any other social-political collective within the social body.

While a monotheistic identity regulates internal group behavior toward the final realization of absolute, divine authority, deviance itself threatens the very foundation upon which divine authority must be constructed. Permitting or embracing perilous deviance—that is, deviance beyond community-defined, tolerable limits—threatens the fabric of a monotheistic identity. As the Jewish scholar Donniel Hartman writes,

> Marginalization is permitted not only on the merits of the inherent deviance in question, but also on the basis of its potential consequences. In a certain sense, a very broad measure of deviance that hitherto was deemed tolerable, can, under these conditions, be classified as intolerable. The significant criterion ceases to be the nature of the actual deviance and its correlation to the core features of a community's shared cultural space, but rather the society's degree of comfort or fear regarding the stability of this space.[19]

Our study of the *golah* community showed that the community's tendency toward a defensive structuring promoted a heightened concern for intolerable deviance. Intermarriage, Ezra–Nehemiah's most colorful example of this, was deemed intolerable because it threatened the exclusive nature of the community's identity and opened the possibility that the benefits of membership could be enjoyed by those who were traditionally considered to be outsiders. The member could only retain the benefits of membership if he divorced his "foreign"—a term, again, whose sole purpose was to emphasize the boundary between the *golah* community and everyone else—wives and children. The focus in that situation, as it is within monotheism generally, was upon internally preserving the rigid boundary between member and non-member. This focus continues to be shared in more modern forms of monotheism such as Judaism. As Hartman, again, writes,

> By definition, marginalization affects the various manifestations of membership. Being classified as an insider is accompanied by various consequences, rights and benefits, all of which may be called into question

---

18. In terms of its desire production, to borrow again from Deleuze and Guattari (*Anti-Oedipus*, 139–45).
19. Hartman, *Boundaries of Judaism*, 74–75.

when one's basic status is being redefined. In its most radical form…the process of marginalization affects the intolerable deviant's standing in the sphere of basic membership. The sphere of basic membership is that sphere which grants the first and most fundamental good distributed by society: membership itself. It serves to delineate and encompass all those who are members or insiders, distinguishing between citizen and non-citizen. Marginalization in this sphere leads to expulsion and to the intolerable deviant being designated as an outsider.[20]

It is through the very process of defining the deviant outsider that the community confirms the boundaries of its own identity. As Ezra–Nehemiah showed, the identity of the *golah* community necessitated the *am ha'aretz*. Core monotheistic doctrines, which depend upon a boundary between acceptance and non-acceptance, mark the division between what is tolerable and what is intolerable in deviance—but the very definition of deviance always begins in tension with what the law has deemed to be the process of restoration. The limit of what is tolerable deviance depends upon what the community believes to be "absorbable," or that which does not threaten restoration. Within Christianity, for example, a momentary "lapse" into sin, such as the brief pursuit of earthly desires, is tolerable while the rejection of the authority of the Holy Spirit is not, neither is a rejection of Jesus as God. Similarly in Islam, one must not reject Muhammad as God's prophet nor the absolute authority of the Divine, both of which constitute the fundamental components of the *shahadah*. And in Judaism, rejecting the framework of divine law, covenant, and divine authority is intolerable. One who does so is categorized as *meshumad*, or one who has separated oneself from the community.[21]

To give an Islamic example, the Hadith of the Slave Girl (*hadīth al-jāriya*) addresses the importance of discerning between member and non-member as a starting point for identifying what is tolerable in terms of membership. In this hadith, the Prophet tests a slave girl by asking her if he was a prophet and where God was, two questions whose answers constitute the fundamental components of the *shahadah*. Her response that yes, Muhammad was a prophet, and that God was "in the sky"

---

20. Ibid., 22.
21. Note also D. Hartman, who writes, "By *meshumad*, the text is referring not to an individual who has simply deviated from one or some of the *mitzvot* or principles of Judaism, but rather an individual who has completely exited the social and religious framework of both Judaism and the Jewish people. While formally a Jew through conversion, he warrants *meshumad* classification by choosing to return to his non-Jewish status, with all its ideological and social commitments" (ibid., 37).

(*fī al-samā*) the Prophet deemed as a correct profession of faith.[22] The Qur'an itself also emphasizes the importance of this discernment, upon which the identity of the monotheistic community depends (cf. 2:9; 63:4).

In fact, for all forms of monotheism, rejection of divine authority, which is simultaneously a rejection of the respective monotheistic identity, is always intolerable and is that which the religious community must hate and consequently destroy. Maimonides, whose views emphasize the monotheistic distinction between member and non-member, makes this abundantly clear:

> Whoever repudiates the Oral Torah is not the rebellious elder mentioned in the Torah, but rather is one of the *minim*, who any person has a right to put to death. Once it is made clear that he indeed repudiates the Oral Torah, he is cast into [a pit] and not rescued from it (*moridin ve-lo ma-alin*), similar to the other *minim, apikorsim*, those who say that the Torah is not from heaven, informers and *meshumadim*. All of the above are not a part of Israel, and do not require witnesses, prior warning, or judges [before being put to death]. Rather anyone who kills one of them has fulfilled a great *mitzvah* and removed a stumbling block. (*m. Torah*, Hilkhot Mamrim 3.1)

And the term *min* refers either to one who is an idolater or who has rejected Judaism through a blending of categories (such as might occur with a "Jewish Christian").[23] According to the midrash *Seder Olam Rabbah*, both the *meshumadim* and the *min* are locked for eternity in Gehenom (ch. 3).[24] Importantly, a *min* will be known by his response to core doctrines, and thus confirm what is intolerable:

> And God said, "Let us make man." (Gen 1.26). The *minim* asked R. Simlai: How many deities created the world? (*Gen. Rab.* 8.9)

> *Minim* asked Rabban Gamliel: How do we know that God will resurrect the dead? He responded [with proof] from the Torah, the Prophets and the Writings, and they did not accept it. (*b. Sanh.* 90b)[25]

---

22. Note also Brown (*Hadith*, 181), who discusses in more detail the importance and the traditional interpretations of this hadith.

23. According to Maimonides there exists five classes of *minim*: "one who says there is no God and the world has no ruler; one who says that there is a ruling power but that it is vested in two or more persons; one who says there is one ruler, but he is a body and has form; one who denies that God alone is the First Cause and Rock of the Universe; likewise, one who worships any one besides God, to serve as a mediator between the human being and the Lord of the Universe. Whoever belongs to any of these five classes is termed a *min*" (*m. Torah*, Hilkhot Teshuvah 3.7).

24. As noted by Hartman, *Boundaries of Judaism*, 38.

25. Cited in ibid., 44.

There is a parallel to the prescribed treatment of a *min* in the hadith tradition. "Whoever changes their religion [from Islam], kill them" (*Saḥīḥ al-Bukhārī: kitāb al-jihād, bāb* 149).[26] However, the following is of equal note, "The fact that neither the Prophet nor the early caliphs actually implemented these rulings when individuals left Islam means that these hadiths addressed the issue of *treason to the Muslim community* and not a person's individual choice of belief."[27] That focus on cutting out the deviant is found also in the Christian tradition: "And if your right hand causes you to sin, cut it off and throw it away; it is better for you to lose one of your members than for your whole body to go into hell" (Matt 5:30). Each of the examples expresses monotheism's general concern for that which threatens the stability and definition of the monotheistic identity; consequently, that which represents treasonous opposition must be driven outside of the community and maintained there in perpetuity.

In short, deviance and the threat it poses to any eventual restoration emphasize the perpetual need for boundary maintenance within monotheism.[28] Exclusion, as we have been discussing it, is a mechanism by which a monotheistic identity protects and preserves its boundaries.

3. *Discourses of Resistance*

Our study of the *golah* community has shown us that within monotheism the process of identity production, while tied initially to the material world, becomes increasingly dependent upon ideological "truths" (beliefs, dogmas, laws, traditions, etc.). Such truths are defined individually within the symbolic order unique to each unique monotheistic identity. For example, the *golah* community's claim to the land of Yehud, and consequently authority, rested upon its self-expressed identity as *the* remnant.

---

26. Cited in Brown, *Hadith*, 263. But note also there are two general categories of member/non-member: "*[I]man* and *kufr*, or faith and infidelity, cannot, and must not, be reduced to a question of affiliation and formal association with a particular religion or religious group. They signify two opposing attitudes and moral commitments, that separate individuals with remarkable compassion and strong commitment to the common good from those given to selfishness, greed, and callousness" (Safi, *The Qur'anic Narrative*, 62).

27. Brown, *Hadith*, 263, emphasis mine.

28. On boundary maintenance note also Hartman: "A boundary policy is more than the demarcation of the line between tolerance and deviance and between tolerable and intolerable deviance. One of its most significant features involved the varying ways that it treats whatever or whoever it classifies as intolerable" (*Boundaries of Judaism*, 48).

It was not based on the community's actual control over the land or over the existing systems of production that depended upon the land. It was instead based on the assumed inevitability of restoration, of which only the community alone would be the intended beneficiaries. As a group on the periphery of social-economic power, the community wholly embraced and codified as law an attitude of separation from and resistance to the social-political systems and authorities that were beyond its control. This process of identity formation as expressed through discourses of resistance, whether by offering lip service or through outright active rejection, is a critical component of all monotheism. It is always present in monotheism's different forms, from the "compact" (as we might describe the monotheism of the *golah* community) to the more "complex" (as we might describe later monotheisms—Judaism, Islam, and Christianity—that have adapted to a necessary dependence upon the ideological realm rather than the material realm). Divine law, as we discussed previously, sustains the structure by and through which such discourses may be appropriately engaged. Thus, while there are unique qualities to the manners in which different monotheisms respond to their immediate social-political contexts, the nature of the response itself, as first demonstrated by the *golah* community, is a fundamental component of monotheistic identity formation common within the monotheistic body.

Resistance to a normative order gives way to revision or reinterpretation—these are consequences of revelation's interruption of a normative social-political order and restoration as a consequence of revelation. The author of Revelation, for example, writes that for Christians new names, thus new identities—those defined external to the material world—will be given to the faithful community (2:17). Providing members with new names presupposes that the very possibility of restoration depends upon the formation of a community identity that is not dependent upon the material, created world. That is because the current state of created existence does not, according to monotheism generally, reflect its original intent; in other words, a natural political authority is not wholly divine authority. Instead, divine intent, which must separate itself from a world governed by human will, is a restored world in which every act or response is directed toward the infinite and absolute nature of divine authority.[29]

---

29. For further reference, note also Esposito and de Long-Bas ("Classical Islam," 132), who writes of Islam, "Central to Islam is the doctrine of *tawhid*, or absolute monotheism, in which God is the creator, sustainer, judge, and sovereign of the universe. God's will, as expressed in Islamic law, and rule are therefore comprehensive and applicable to all creatures and aspects of life."

Before the advent of restoration and its inauguration of a new world order, however, monotheism cannot avoid a dependency upon the material realities of the natural world for its own existence.[30] That is why monotheistic identity necessitates the existence of an "other" against which it defines itself through exclusion and resistance. For the *golah* community this was the *am ha'aretz*. For later Judaism it is the Gentiles or "goyim." For Christianity and Islam, it is generally the non-believer, although other terms (such as "sinner" and "infidel") may be used to designate the same concept. Parameters of behavior, which define the identity of the monotheistic community, are uniquely regulated by the community's divine law.

To truly understand the consequences of monotheism's fundamental contest, through which one is either rewarded with or loses out on the "fruit" of restoration, one must first recognize and accept the absolute authority of the divine.[31] The necessity of this choice was made clear, for example, in Zechariah's apparent abandonment of Zerubbabel as part of divine restoration. This choice was also demonstrated by the community's

---

30. Even monotheistic descriptions of the afterlife find their equivalents in the material world. Note, for example, "The Garden and the Fire may have been articles of faith, but within hadiths they were ultimately represented as spaces. These spaces are not abstract worlds characterized by platonic ideals or God's love. Instead, the Islamic afterworld is a designed realm with an orderly nature and an urban setting. The Fire is not just heat and flame, but also individualized cells that constitute an intricate world of punishment. The Garden is not just lush flora and abundant water, but also a multitiered world filled with tents, pavilions, and marketplaces. Neither realm is primordial. The Fire is not related to the first worldly fires, and the Garden is not the first cosmic Garden of Eden as much as it is the final aspiration for living… More significant, both the Garden and the Fire can be understood through earthly landscapes. The Garden is the idealized landscape that is temperate, green, filled with rivers, and, as a result, fruitful. As a landscape it is like a beautiful garden on earth; however, it exceeds earthly limitations because trees can both flower and provide fruit simultaneously—a biological process that is impossible. If the Garden is the idealized green, then the Fire is the desert intensified. It is arid, dry, barren, and intensely hotter than the purest part of flame. The Garden and the Fire, then, are based on and ultimately exceed earthly parameters" (Nerina Rustomji, *The Garden and the Fire: Heaven and Hell in Islamic Culture* [New York: Columbia University Press, 2009], 63–64).

31. According to Nasr, the cosmos testifies to the absolute authority of a Creator God: "[A]ccording to Islamic teachings the cosmos is itself the first revelation of God. In such a sacralized cosmos phenomena are at once veils of spiritual realities and symbols that reveal those realities. In the Abrahamic world the world of nature is itself a book to be deciphered but only by virtue of access to prophecy as the Abrahamic religions understand it" (Nasr, *Islamic Philosophy*, 231).

recognition that to preserve itself it must be able to respond effectively to a social-political world in flux. Monotheistic communities must continue to do so until which time divine restoration "stabilizes" the order of the world. The tension that we saw in Zechariah continues to exist in later monotheisms. For example, Novak writes of Judaism—note that his statement shows a Jewish adaptation to historical disappointments as it waits for the restorative actions of the Messiah,

> The result of the great historical disappointment in Bar Kokhba's defeat might very well have led to a more apocalyptic messianism than that previously promoted by Bar Kokhba's rabbinical sponsors. It also seems to have led to a more modest Jewish realpolitik. The messiah would not be brought *by* the Jews; rather, he would be directly sent *to* the Jews from God. The Jews would not have to wait for any future verification. The Messiah would come at once totally or not at all. Full redemption would be immediate. The kingdom of God would descend from heaven wholly intact and complete. *In the meantime, the Jews would have to make what are in essence temporary political arrangements... Thus the messianic restoration of the full covenant would not involve any temporally conditioned negotiations with gentile nations, because in the end of days, God would be ruling the whole world from Jerusalem through the Messiah as his regent on earth.*[32]

Monotheistic identities produce and preserve boundaries between member and non-member through a ritualization of identity, a process that for the *golah* community was framed by Ezra's version of the so-called Mosaic Law. In part, this ritualization, which preserves a *contradistinctive* identity,[33] takes place through a discourse of resistance, a discourse that is codified within divine law (cf. Neh 13:1). And because the reality after which the monotheistic body, upon which a monotheistic identity is based, patterns its own production of desire is utopian in its unrealized state, land symbolizes not only (material) authority, through ownership, but also geographic space as testimony to the future realization of utopia. Consequently, divine law, which codifies acts of resistance, is a dominating discourse through which monotheism asserts its authority over the social body. In other words, it both constructs and regulates the monotheistic community toward the goal and reality of restoration. And it is this very discourse that defines its monotheistic, religious identity as an identity wholly distinct from anything else within the created order.

---

32. Novak, *The Jewish Social Contract*, 98–99, emphasis mine.
33. In Ezra 6:19-21, for example, the Passover celebration ritualizes the distinction between the *golah* community and the *am ha'aretz*.

Where we saw in our study that Yehud offered a "compact" form of monotheism, for which material authority was still a viable goal, monotheistic development into its more complex forms shows a shift from a dependence upon material authority to an authority grounded in the sacred realm. Tracing out this shift and its impact upon later forms of monotheism demands a focused study dedicated to each form of monotheism. Such projects should construct themselves upon the basic structures of the model developed within this work, testing its limits and relevance. Their applications of this model should treat the model as a skeletal structure, thereby making room for historical (and material) particularities, upon which their driving theories may be constructed. Moreover, each must begin its methodological inquiry with the assumption that at the *origin* of every monotheism there is a reaction to a profound event—such as the exiles for the *golah* community—within an identifiable material-historical context, producing a contest over land and authority. Should the analysis not begin in this way, it runs the risk of excusing the very human origins of the institution of monotheism and of a monotheistic God.

BIBLIOGRAPHY

Abrahamian, Ervand. *Khomeinism: Essays on the Islamic Republic*. Berkeley: University of California Press, 1993.

———. "The Making of the Modern Iranian State." Pages 693–719 in *Comparative Politics at the Crossroads*. Edited by Mark Kesselman, Joel Krieger, and William A. Joseph. Lexington, Mass.: D. C. Heath & Co., 1995.

Abu-Sahlieh, Sami A. Aldeeb. "The Islamic Conception of Migration." *International Migration Review* 30, no. 1 (1996): 37–57.

Ahlström, Gösta W. *The History of Ancient Palestine*. Minneapolis: Fortress, 1993.

Ahmed, Akbar S. *Journey into Islam: The Crisis of Globalization*. Washington, D.C.: Brookings Institution, 2007.

Ainsa, Fernando, and Jeanne Ferguson. "Utopia, Promised Lands, Immigration and Exile." *Diogenes* 30, no. 119 (1982): 49–64.

Ake, Claude. "A Definition of Political Stability." *Comparative Politics* 7, no. 2 (1975): 271–83.

Albright, William Foxwell. *From the Stone Age to Christianity: Monotheism and the Historical Process*. 2d ed. Garden City, N.Y.: Doubleday, 1957.

Alexander, Jeffrey C. *The Meanings of Social Life: A Cultural Sociology*. Oxford: Oxford University Press, 2003.

Alt, Albrecht."Die Landnahme der Israeliten in Palästina." Pages 89–125 in *Kleine Schriften zur Geschichte des Volkes Israel*. Munich: Beck, 1953. Published in English as "The Settlement of the Israelites in Palestine." Pages 135–69 in *Essays on Old Testament History and Religion.* Oxford: Blackwell, 1966.

———. "Die Rolle Samarias Bei Der Entstehung Des Judentums." Pages 5–28 in *Festschrift Otto Procksch zum sechzigsten Geburtstag*. Leipzig: A. Deichert & J. C. Hinrichs, 1934. Repr. Pages 316–37 in *Kleine Schriften zur Geschichte des Volkes Israel, I.* Munich: Beck, 1953.

Amjad, Mohammed. *Iran: From Royal Dictatorship to Theocracy*. New York: Greenwood, 1989.

Armstrong, David. "Bodies of Knowledge / Knowledge of Bodies." Pages 17–27 in Jones and Porter, eds., *Reassessing Foucault*.

Árnason, Jóhann Páll, S. N. Eisenstadt, and Björn. Wittrock, eds. *Axial Civilizations and World History*. Jerusalem Studies in Religion and Culture 4. Leiden: Brill, 2005.

Assmann, Jan. *Moses the Egyptian: The Memory of Egypt in Western Monotheism*. Cambridge: Harvard University Press, 1997.

———. *The Price of Monotheism*. Stanford, Calif.: Stanford University Press, 2010.

Avigad, Nahman. *Bullae and Seals from a Post-Exilic Judean Archive*. Qedem 4. Jerusalem: Hebrew University, 1976.

Balcer, Jack Martin. "The Athenian Episkopos and the Achaemenid 'King's Eye'." *AJP* 98 (1977): 252–63.

———. *Sparda By the Bitter Sea: Imperial Interaction in Western Anatolia.* Brown Judaic Studies 52. Chico, Calif.: Scholars Press, 1984.
Barag, Dan P. "A Silver Coin of Yohanan the High Priest and the Coinage of Judea in the Fourth Century B.C." *INJ* 9 (1986): 4–21.
———. "Some Notes on a Silver Coin of Johanan the High Priest." *BA* 48 (1985): 166–68.
Barkin, J. Samuel. "Realist Constructivism." *International Studies Review* 5, no. 3 (2003): 325–42.
Barstad, Hans M. "After the 'Myth of the Empty Land': Major Challenges in the Study of Neo-Babylonian Judah." Pages 3–20 in Lipschits and Blenkinsopp, eds., *Judah and the Judeans in the Neo-Babylonian Period.*
Bascom, William R. "Ponapean Prestige Economy." *SJA* 4 (1948): 211–21.
Baskauskas, Liucija. "The Lithuanian Refugee Experience and Grief." *International Migration Review* 15 (1981): 276–91.
Bausani, Alessandro. "Can Monotheism Be Taught?" *Numen: International Review for the History of Religions* 10, no. 1 (1963): 167–201.
Becking, Bob. "'We All Returned as One!': Critical Notes on the Myth of the Mass Return." Pages 3–18 in Lipschits and Oeming, eds., *Judah and the Judeans in the Persian Period.*
Bedford, Peter R. "Diaspora: Homeland Relations in Ezra–Nehemiah." *VT* 52 (2001): 147–65.
Bellah, Robert Neelly. *Beyond Belief: Essays on Religion in a Post-Traditional World.* Berkeley: University of California Press, 1991.
———. "Religious Evolution." Pages 36–50 in *Reader in Comparative Religion: An Anthropological Approach.* Edited by William A. Lessa and Evon Z. Vogt. New York: Harper & Row, 1972.
———. "What is Axial About the Axial Age?" *EJS* 46, no. 1 (2005): 69–69.
Berger, Peter L. *The Sacred Canopy: Elements of a Sociological Theory of Religion.* 1967. New York: Anchor, 1990.
Berquist, Jon L. "Constructions of Identity in Postcolonial Yehud." Pages 53–66 in Lipschits and Oeming, eds., *Judah and the Judeans in the Persian Period.*
———. *Judaism in Persia's Shadow: A Social and Historical Approach.* Minneapolis: Fortress, 1995.
Berry, John. "Immigration, Acculturation, and Adaptation." *Applied Psychology* 46, no. 1 (1997): 5–34.
Betlyon, John W. "The Provincial Government of Persian Period Judea and the Yehud Coins." *JBL* 105 (1986): 633–42.
Bhavnani, Kum-Kum, and Ann Phoenix. *Shifting Identities, Shifting Racisms: A Feminism and Psychology Reader.* London: Sage, 1994.
Blenkinsopp, Joseph. "Bethel in the Neo-Babylonian Period." Pages 93–107 in Lipschits and Blenkinsopp, eds., *Judah and the Judeans in the Neo-Babylonian Period.*
———. *Isaiah 56–66: A New Translation With Introduction and Commentary.* New York: Doubleday, 2003.
———. "A Jewish Sect of the Persian Period." *CBQ* 52 (1990): 5–20.
———. "The Mission of Udjahorresnet and Those of Ezra and Nehemiah." *JBL* 106 (1987): 409–21.
Boer, Roland. *Jameson and Jeroboam.* Atlanta: Scholars Press, 1996.

Borowitz, Eugene B. "Judaism and the Secular State." *JR* 48, no. 1 (1968): 22–34.
Bourdieu, Pierre. "Genesis and Structure of the Religious Field." *Comparative Social Research* 13 (1991): 1–44.
———. *In Other Words: Essays Toward a Reflexive Sociology*. Translated by Matthew Adamson. Stanford, Calif.: Stanford University Press, 1990.
———. *Méditations Pascaliennes*. Paris: Seuil, 1997.
———. *Practical Reason: On the Theory of Action*. Stanford, Calif.: Stanford University Press, 1998.
Briant, Pierre. *From Cyrus to Alexander: A History of the Persian Empire*. Translated by Peter T. Daniels. Winona Lake, Ind.: Eisenbrauns, 2002.
———. *Histoire de l'Empire perse de Cyrus à Alexandre*. Paris: Fayard, 1998.
Bright, John. *A History of Israel*. 2d ed. Philadelphia: Westminster, 1972.
———. *Jeremiah*. Edited by William Foxwell Albright, and David Noel Freedman. Anchor Bible 21. New York: Doubleday, 1965.
Brown, Jonathon A. C. *Hadith: Muhammad's Legacy in the Medieval and Modern World*. Oxford: Oneworld, 2009.
Burns, Gene. "Ideology, Culture, and Ambiguity: The Revolutionary Process in Iran." *Theory and Society* 25 (1996): 349–88.
Carr, Edward Hallett. *The Twenty Years' Crisis, 1919–1939: An Introduction to the Study of International Relations*. Houndmills: Palgrave, 2001.
Carrier, Nicolas. "Speech for the Defense of a Radically Constructivist Sociology of (Criminal) Law." *International Journal of Law, Crime and Justice* 36, no. 3 (2008): 168–83.
Carroll, Robert P. "Ancient Israelite Prophecy and Dissonance Theory." *Numen: International Review for the History of Religions* 24 (1977): 135–51.
———. "Exile! What Exile? Deportation and the Discourse of Diaspora." Pages 62–79 in Grabbe, ed., *Leading Captivity Captive*.
———. *From Chaos to Covenant: Prophecy in the Book of Jeremiah*. New York: Crossroad, 1981.
———. "Textual Strategies and Ideology in the Second Temple Period." Pages in Davies, ed., *Second Temple Studies, 1*, 108–24.
Carter, Charles E. *The Emergence of Yehud in the Persian Period: A Social and Demographic Study*. JSOTSup 294. Sheffield: Sheffield Academic, 1999.
Cataldo, Jeremiah W. "The Crippled *Ummah*: Toward Redefining *Golah* in Ezra–Nehemiah." *The Bible and Critical Theory* 4, no. 1 (2008): 6.1–6.17.
———. "Persian Policy and the Yehud Community During Nehemiah." *JSOT* 28 (2003): 240–52.
———. *A Theocratic Yehud? Issues of Government in Yehud*. LBHOTS 498. London: T&T Clark International, 2009.
———. "Whispered Utopia: Dreams, Agendas, and Theocratic Aspirations in Persian-Period Yehud." *SJOT* 24, no. 1 (2010): 53–70.
Cerulo, Karen A. "Identity Construction: New Issues, New Directions." *ARS* 23 (1997): 385–409.
Childs, Brevard S. *Introduction to the Old Testament as Scripture*. Philadelphia: Fortress, 1979.
Clines, David J. A. *Ezra, Nehemiah and Esther*. New Century Bible. Grand Rapids: Eerdmans, 1984.
Coats, George W. "An Exposition on the Conquest Theme." *CBQ* 47 (1985): 47–54.

Coggins, R. J. *Haggai, Zechariah, Malachi*. Sheffield: JSOT, 1987.
Cook, Stephen L. *Prophecy and Apocalypticism: The Postexilic Social Setting*. Minneapolis: Fortress, 1995.
Cross, Frank Moore, Jr. "A Reconstruction of the Judean Restoration." *JBL* 94 (1975): 4–18.
Crouch, D., and G. Parker. "'Digging Up' Utopia? Space, Practice and Land Use Heritage." *Geoforum* 34 (2003): 395–408.
Dandamaev, Muhammad A., and Vladimir G. Lukonin. *The Culture and Social Institutions of Ancient Iran*. Translated by Philip L. Kohl. Cambridge: Cambridge University Press, 1989.
Dandamayev, M. A. "Achaemenid Imperial Policies and Provincial Governments." *Iranica Antiqua* 34 (1999): 269–82.
Dauenhauer, Bernard P. "Ricoeur and Political Identity." *Philosophy Today* 39 (1995): 47–55.
Davies, Philip R. "Exile! What Exile? Whose Exile?" Pages 128–38 in Grabbe, ed., *Leading Captivity Captive*.
———. "'Law' in Early Judaism." Pages 3–33 in *Judaism in Late Antiquity*. Vol. 3. *Where We Stand: Issues and Debates in Ancient Judaism*. Edited by Jacob Neusner and A. J. Avery-Peck. Leiden: Brill, 1999.
———. *Memories of Ancient Israel: An Introduction to Biblical History—Ancient and Modern*. Louisville: Westminster John Knox, 2008.
———, ed. *Second Temple Studies, 1: Persian Period*. Sheffield: Sheffield Academic, 1991.
———. "What Separates a Minimalist from a Maximalist? Not Much." *Biblical Archaeology Review* 26 (2000): 24–27, 72–73.
Davis, Richard. "The Ritualization of Behaviour." *Mankind* 13, no. 2 (1981): 103–12.
De Bremond, Ariane. "The Politics of Peace and Resettlement Through El Salvador's Land Transfer Programme: Caught Between the State and the Market." *Third World Quarterly* 28, no. 8 (2007): 1537–56.
de Haardt, Maike. "The Whole Life. Beyond the Boundaries of Monotheism?" Pages 129–53 in *The Boundaries of Monotheism: Interdisciplinary Explorations into the Foundations of Western Monotheism*. Edited by Anne-Marie Korte and Maaike de Haardt. Leiden; Boston: Brill, 2009.
de Vaux, Roland. *Ancient Israel: Its Life and Institutions*. Translated by John McHugh. New York: McGraw-Hill, 1961.
Deleuze, Gilles, and Félix Guattari. *Anti-Oedipus: Capitalism and Schizophrenia*. Minneapolis: University of Minnesota Press, 2005.
———. *A Thousand Plateaus: Capitalism and Schizophrenia*. Minneapolis: University of Minnesota Press, 1987.
Dever, William G. "Archaeology and the 'Age of Solomon': A Case-Study in Archaeology and Historiography." Pages 217–51 in *The Age of Solomon: Scholarship at the Turn of the Millennium*. Edited by Lowell K. Handy. Leiden: Brill, 1997.
Dion, Paul-Eugène. "The Civic-and-Temple Community of Persian Period Judaea: Neglected Insights from Eastern Europe." *JNES* 50 (1991): 281–87.
———. "La Religion des Papyrus d'Éléphantine: Un Reflet du Juda d'avant l'Exil." Pages 243–54 in *Kein Land für sich allein: Studien zum Kulturkontakt in Kanaan, Israel/Palästina und Ebirnâri für Manfred Weippert zum 65. Geburtstag*. Edited by Ulrich Hübner and Ernst Axel Knauf. Göttingen: Vandenhoeck & Ruprecht, 2002.

Donald, Merlin. *Origins of the Modern Mind: Three Stages in the Evolution of Culture and Cognition*. Cambridge, Mass.: Harvard University Press, 1991.

Donnelly, Samuel J. M. "Reflecting on the Rule of Law: Its Reciprocal Relation With Rights, Legitimacy, and Other Concepts and Institutions." *The Annals of the American Academy of Political and Social Science* 603 (2006): 37–53.

Douglas, Mary. *Purity and Danger: An Analysis of Concepts of Pollution and Taboo*. London: Routledge & Kegan Paul, 1966.

———. *Purity and Danger: An Analysis of Concept of Pollution and Taboo*. Routledge Classics. London; New York: Routledge, 2006.

———. "Responding to Ezra: The Priests and the Foreign Wives." *Biblical Interpretation* 10 (2002): 1–23.

Dozeman, Thomas B. "Geography and History in Herodotus and in Ezra–Nehemiah." *JBL* 122, no. 3 (2003): 449–66.

Driver, Felix. "Bodies in Space: Foucault's Account of Disciplinary Power." Pages 113–31 in Jones and Porter, eds., *Reassessing Foucault*.

Durkheim, Émile. *The Elementary Forms of the Religious Life*. Translated by Karen E. Fields. New York: Free Press, 1995.

Durkheim, Emile, Carol Cosman and Mark Sydney Cladis. "The Elementary Forms of Religious Life." (2008): xli, 358.

Dyck, Jonathan E. *The Theocratic Ideology of the Chronicler*. Biblical Interpretation Series 33. Leiden: Brill, 1998.

Earle, Timothy K. "Chiefdoms in Archaeological and Ethnohistorical Perspective." *Annual Review of Anthropology* 16 (1987): 279–308.

Easterly, William. "Debt Relief." *Foreign policy* 127 (2001): 20–26.

Edelman, Diana. "Nehemiah's Adversary, Tobiah the Patron." Pages 106–14 in *Historie og Konstruktion: Festskrift til Niels Peter Lemchi I Anledning af 60 Års Fødselsdagen den 6. September 2005*. Edited by Mogens Müller and Thomas L. Thompson. Københavns Universitet, 2005.

———. *The Origins of the "Second" Temple: Persian Imperial Policy and the Rebuilding of Jerusalem*. London: Equinox, 2005.

———. What's in a Date? The Unreliable Nature of the Dates in Haggai and Zechariah." Pages 80–150 in *The Origins of the "Second" Temple*.

Eisenstadt, S. N. "The Axial Age Breakthrough in Ancient Israel." Pages 127–34 in Eisenstadt, ed., *The Origins and Diversity of Axial Age Civilizations*.

———. "Axial Civilizations and the Axial Age Reconsidered." Pages 531–74 in Árnason, Eisenstadt, and Wittrock, eds., *Axial Civilizations and World History*.

———. "The Expansion of Religions: Some Comparative Observations on Different Modes." *Comparative Social Research* 13 (1991): 45–73.

———. "Introduction." Pages 1–28 in *The Origins and Diversity of Axial Age Civilizations*. Albany: State University of New York Press, 1986.

———, ed. *The Origins and Diversity of Axial Age Civilizations*. Albany: State University of New York Press, 1986.

Eliade, Mircea. *The Myth of the Eternal Return: Cosmos and History*. Translated by Willard R. Trask. Bollingen. Princeton: Princeton University Press, 2005. Repr., New York: Bollingen, 1954.

Elkana, Yehuda. "The Emergence of Second-Order Thinking in Classical Greece." Pages 40–64 in Eisenstadt, ed., *The Origins and Diversity of Axial Age Civilizations*.

Elvin, Mark. "Was There a Transcendental Break-Through in China?" Pages 325–59 in Eisenstadt, ed., *The Origins and Diversity of Axial Age Civilizations*.

Eph'al, Israel. "Syria-Palestine Under Achaemenid Rule." Pages 139–64 in *Cambridge Ancient History*. Vol. 4, *Persia, Greece and the Western Mediterranean, C. 525 to 479 B.C.* Edited by John Boardman, N. G. L. Hammond, D. M. Lewis, and M. Ostwald. Cambridge: Cambridge University Press, 1988.

Erikson, Kai. *Wayward Puritans: A Study in the Sociology of Deviance*. New York: Wiley, 1966.

Eskenazi, Tamara C. *Ezra–Nehemiah*. Women's Bible Commentary, Expanded Edition with Apocrypha. Louisville: Westminster John Knox, 1998.

———. *In an Age of Prose: A Literary Approach to Ezra–Nehemiah*. Atlanta: Scholars Press, 1988.

———. "Nehemiah 9–10: Structure and Significance." *JHS* 3 (2001): Article 9.

———. "The Structure of Ezra–Nehemiah and the Integrity of the Book." *JBL* 107, no. 4 (1988): 641–56.

Esposito, John L., and Natana J. De Long-Bas. "Classical Islam." Pages 131–57 in Neusner, ed., *God's Rule*.

———. "Modern Islam." Pages 159–84 in Neusner, ed., *God's Rule*.

Finkelstein, Israel, and Neil Asher Silberman. *The Bible Unearthed: Archaeology's New Vision of Ancient Israel and the Origin of Its Sacred Texts*. New York: Free Press, 2001.

Flood, Gavin D. *An Introduction to Hinduism*. New York: Cambridge University Press, 1999.

Ford, Thomas; Tonander, George. "The Role of Differentiation Between Groups and Social Identity in Stereotype Formation." *Social Psychology Quarterly* 61, no. 4 (1998): 372–84.

Foucault, Michel. *The Archaeology of Knowledge and the Discourse on Language*. Translated by A. M. Sheridan Smith. New York: Pantheon, 1972.

———. *Discipline and Punish: The Birth of the Prison*. Translated by Alan Sheridan. New York: Vintage, 1995.

———. *Power/Knowledge: Selected Interviews and Other Writings, 1972–77*. Translated by Colin Gordon, Leo Marshall, John Mepham, and Kate Soper. New York: Pantheon, 1980.

Freedman, David N. "Son of Man, Can These Bones Live?" *Interpretation* 29 (1975): 171–86.

Fried, Lisbeth S. "The *'Am Hā'āreṣ* in Ezra 4:4." Pages 123–45 in Lipschits and Oeming, eds., *Judah and the Judeans in the Persian Period*.

———. *The Priest and the Great King: Temple–Palace Relations in the Persian Empire*. Biblical and Judaic Studies. Winona Lake: Eisenbrauns, 2004.

———. "'You Shall Appoint Judges': Ezra's Mission and the Rescript of Artaxerxes." Pages 63–90 in *Persia and Torah: The Theory of Imperial Authorization of the Pentateuch*. Edited by James W. Watts. Atlanta: Society of Biblical Literature, 2001.

Friedland, Roger. "Religious Nationalism and the Problem of Collective Representation." *ARS* 27 (2001): 125–52.

Friedman, Richard E. "Torah (Pentateuch)." *ABD* 6:05–22.

Galambush, Julie. "This Land Is My Land: On Nature as Property in the Book of Ezekiel." Pages 71–94 in *"Every City Shall Be Forsaken": Urbanism and Prophecy in Ancient Israel and the Near East.* Edited by Lester L. Grabbe and Robert D. Haak. Sheffield: Sheffield Academic, 2001.

Garbini, Giovanni. *History and Ideology in Ancient Israel.* Translated by John Bowden. New York: Crossroad, 1988.

———. *Myth and History in the Bible.* Translated by Chiara Peri. JSOTSup 362. Sheffield: Sheffield Academic, 2003.

Gibbs, Robert. *Why Ethics?* Princeton: Princeton University, 2000.

Girard, René. "Violence and Religion: Cause Or Effect?" *The Hedgehog Review* 6 (2004): 8–20.

Glasersfeld, Ernst von. *Radical Constructivism: A Way of Knowing and Learning.* London: Falmer, 1995.

Gnuse, Robert Karl. "Breakthrough Or Tyranny: Monotheism's Contested Implications." *Horizons* 34, no. 1 (2007): 78–95.

———. *No Other Gods: Emergent Monotheism in Israel.* JSOTSup 241. Sheffield: Sheffield Academic, 1997.

Gottwald, Norman K. "Social Class as an Analytic and Hermeneutical Category in Biblical Studies." *JBL* 112, no. 1 (1993): 3–22.

———. "Sociology (Ancient Israel)." *ABD* 6:79–89.

———. *The Tribes of Yahweh: A Sociology of the Religion of Liberated Israel 1250–1050 B.C.E.* Maryknoll: Orbis, 1979.

———. "Two Models for the Origins of Ancient Israel: Social Revolution Or Frontier Development." Pages 5–24 in Huffmon, Spina, and Green, eds., *The Quest for the Kingdom of God.*

Grabbe Lester L., ed., *Leading Captivity Captive: "The Exile" as History and Ideology.* JSOTSup 278. Sheffield: Sheffield Academic, 1998.

———. "The 'Persian Documents' in the Book of Ezra: Are They Authentic?" Pages 531–70 in Lipschits and Oeming, eds., *Judah and the Judeans in the Persian Period.*

———. *What Was Ezra's Mission?* Pages 286–99 in *Second Temple Studies, 2: Temple Community in the Persian Period.* Edited by Tamara C. Eskenazi and Kent H. Richards. Sheffield: Sheffield Academic, 1994.

Green, William Scott. "Religion and Politics—a Volatile Mix." Pages 1–9 in Neusner, ed., *God's Rule.*

Gropp, Douglas M. "The Samaria Papyri from Wadi Daliyeh: Introduction." In *Wadi Daliyeh II and Qumran Cave 4: The Samaria Papyri From Wadi Daliyeh 28/ Miscellanea, Part 2.* Edited by Emanuel Tov, Douglas M. Gropp, Moshe J. Bernstein, Monica Brady, James Charlesworth, Peter W. Flint, Haggai Misgav, Stephen Pfann, Eileen Schuller, Eibert J. C. Tigchelaar, and James C. VanderKam. Oxford: Clarendon, 2001.

Habel, Norman C. *The Land Is Mine: Six Biblical Land Ideologies.* Minneapolis: Fortress, 1995.

Hall, Douglas John. *Imaging God: Dominion as Stewardship.* Grand Rapids: Eerdmans. New York: Friendship, 1986.

Hall, Rodney Bruce. "Moral Authority as a Power Resource." *International Organization* 51 (1997): 591–622.

Hanson, Paul. *The Dawn of Apocalyptic: The Historical and Sociological Roots of Jewish Apocalyptic Eschatology.* Philadelphia: Fortress, 1979.

Harris, Marvin. *Cows, Pigs, Wars, and Witches: The Riddles of Culture.* New York: Vintage, 1974.

Hart, H. L. A. *The Concept of Law.* 2d ed Oxford: Clarendon, 1994.

Hartman, Donniel. *Boundaries of Judaism.* London: Continuum, 2007.

Harvey, Barry A. "Insanity, Theocracy, and the Public Realm: Public Theology, the Church, and the Politics of Liberal Democracy." *Modern Theology* 10 (1994): 27–57.

Hocart, A., M. "The Origin of Monotheism." *Folklore* 33, no. 3 (1922): 282–93.

Hoglund, Kenneth G. "The Achaemenid Context." Pages 54–72 in Davies, ed., *Second Temple Studies, 1: Persian Period.*

———. *Achaemenid Imperial Administration in Syria-Palestine and the Missions of Ezra and Nehemiah.* SBL Dissertation Series 125. Atlanta: Scholars Press, 1992.

Hornblower, Simon. *The Greek World 479–323 BC.* New York: Routledge, 1991.

Howard, Judith A. "Social Psychology of Identities." *ARS* 26 (2000): 367–93.

Huffmon, H. B., F. A. Spina, and Alberto Ravinell Whitney Green, eds. *The Quest for the Kingdom of God: Studies in Honor of George E. Mendenhall.* Winona Lake. Ind.: Eisenbrauns, 1983.

Hurtado, L., W. "First-Century Jewish Monotheism." *JSNT* 21, no. 71 (1999): 3–26.

Jackson, Bernard S. *Studies in the Semiotics of Biblical Law.* JSOTSup 314. Sheffield: Sheffield Academic, 2000.

Jaffee, Martin S. "One God, One Revelation, One People: On the Symbolic Structure of Elective Monotheism." *JAAR* 69, no. 4 (2001): 753–75.

James, E. O. "Primitive Monotheism." *Sociological Review* 27 (1935): 328.

Janzen, David. "The 'Mission' of Ezra and the Persian-Period Temple Community." *JBL* 119 (2000): 619–43.

Japhet, Sara. "The Concept of the 'Remnant' in the Restoration Period: On the Vocabulary of Self-Definition." Pages 432–49 in *From the Rivers of Babylon.*

———. *From the Rivers of Babylon to the Highlands of Judah: Collected Studies on the Restoration Period.* Winona Lake, Ind.: Eisenbrauns, 2006.

———. "Sheshbazzar and Zerubbabel Against the Background of the Historical and Religious Tendencies of Ezra–Nehemiah: Part 1." Pages 53–84 in *From the Rivers of Babylon.*

Jaspers, Karl. "The Axial Age of Human History." *Commentary (New York)* 6 (1948): 430.

———. *The Origin and Goal of History.* London: Routledge & Kegan Paul, 1953.

Joannès, F., and André Lemaire. "Trois Tablettes cunéiformes à l'Onomastique ouest-sémitique." *Transeuphratène* 17 (1999): 17–33.

Jones, Colin, and Roy Porter, eds. *Reassessing Foucault: Power, Medicine, and the Body.* London: Routledge, 1994.

Jospe, Raphael. *Jewish Philosophy,* vol. 1. Lanham: University Press of America, 2008.

Karen, Robert. "Two Faces of Monotheism." *Contemporary Psychoanalysis* 39, no. 4 (2003): 637–63.

Karp, David Jason. "The Utopia and Reality of Sovereignty: Social Reality, Normative Ir and 'Organized Hypocrisy'." *Review of International Studies* 34 (2008): 313–34.

Kenzle, Susan C. "Enclosing Walls in the Northern San Juan: Sociophysical Boundaries and Defensive Fortifications in the American Southwest." *Journal of Field Archaeology* 24, no. 2 (1997): 195–210.

Kessler, John. *The Book of Haggai: Prophecy and Society in Early Persian Yehud*. Atlanta: Society of Biblical Literature, 2007.

———. "Persia's Loyal Yahwists: Power, Identity, and Ethnicity in Achaemenid Yehud." Pages 91–121 in Lipschits and Oeming, eds., *Judah and the Judeans in the Persian Period*.

Khaldun, Ibn. *The Muqaddimah: An Introduction to History*, vol. 1. Translated by Franz Rosenthal. New York: Pantheon, 1958.

Khomeini, Ruhollah. *Islam and Revolution: Writings and Declarations of Imam Khomeini*. Translated by Hamid Algar. Berkeley, Calif.: Mizan, 1981.

King, Richard. "Orientalism and the Modern Myth of 'Hinduism'." *Numen: International Review for the History of Religions* 46, no. 2 (1999): 146–85.

Kislev, Itamar. "The Investiture of Joshua (Numbers 27:12–23) and the Dispute on the Form of the Leadership in Yehud." *VT* 59, no. 3 (2009): 429–45.

Kollock, Peter. "Social Dilemmas: The Anatomy of Cooperation." *ARS* 24 (1998): 183–214.

Krisciunas, Raymond G. "The Emigrant Experience: The Decision of Lithuanian Refugees to Emigrate, 1945–1950." *Lithuanian Quarterly Journal of Arts and Sciences* 29 (1983).

Küng, Hans. *The Church*. Translated by Ray Ockenden and Rosaleen Ockenden. New York: Sheed & Ward, 1967.

Lefebvre, Henri. *La Production de l'Espace*. Paris: Anthropos, 1974.

LeFebvre, Michael. *Collections, Codes, and Torah: The Re-Characterization of Israel's Written Law*. LBHOTS 451. New York: T&T Clark International, 2006.

Leith, Mary J. W. "Israel Among the Nations: The Persian Period." Pages in *The Oxford History of the Biblical World*. Edited by Michael D. Coogan, 367–419. Oxford: Oxford University Press, 1998.

———. *Wadi Daliyeh: The Wadi Daliyeh Seal Impressions*. Discoveries in the Judaean Desert 24. Oxford: Clarendon, 1997.

Lemaire, André. "Nabonidus in Arabia and Judah in the Neo-Babylonian Period." Pages 285–98 in Lipschits and Blenkinsopp, eds., *Judah and the Judeans in the Neo-Babylonian Period*.

———. "Populations et Territoires de Palestine à l'Époque perse." *Transeuphratène* 3 (1990): 31–74.

Lemche, Niels Peter. "On the Problems of Reconstructing Pre-Hellenistic Israelite (Palestinian) History." *JHS* 3 (2000).

Lipschits, Oded. "Achaemenid Imperial Policy, Settlement Processes in Palestine, and the Status of Jerusalem in the Middle of the Fifth Century B.C.E." Pages 19–52 in Lipschits and Oeming, eds., *Judah and the Judeans in the Persian Period*.

———. *The Fall and Rise of Jerusalem: The History of Judah Under Babylonian Rule*. Winona Lake, Ind.: Eisenbrauns, 2005.

Lipschits, Oded, and Joseph Blenkinsopp, eds. *Judah and the Judeans in the Neo-Babylonian Period*. Winona Lake, Ind.: Eisenbrauns, 2003.

Lipschits, Oded, and Manfred Oeming, eds. *Judah and the Judeans in the Persian Period*. Winona Lake, Ind.: Eisenbrauns, 2006.

Liverani, Mario. *Israel's History and the History of Israel*. Translated by Chiara Peri and Philip R. Davies. London: Equinox, 2005.

Luhmann, N., and W. Rasch. *Theories of Distinction: Redescribing the Descriptions of Modernity*. Palo Alto, Calif.: Stanford University Press, 2002.

Macnicol, Nicol. *Indian Theism, from the Vedic to the Muhammadan Period*. London: Milford, Oxford University Press, 1915.

Mannheim, K. *Ideology and Utopia: An Introduction to the Sociology of Knowledge*. Translated by Louis Wirth, and Edward Shils. New York: Harcourt Brace Jovanovich, 1936.

Margalith, Othniel. "The Political Background of Zerubbabel's Mission and the Samaritan Schism." *VT* 41 (1991): 312–23.

Marx, Karl. "Alienation and Social Classes." Pages 133–42 in Tucker, ed., *The Marx–Engels Reader*.

———. "The German Ideology." Pages 146–200 in Tucker, ed., *The Marx-Engels Reader*.

Matar, Anat. *Modernism and the Language of Philosophy*. London: Routledge, 2006.

McEvenue, Sean. "The Political Structure in Judah From Cyrus to Nehemiah." *CBQ* 43 (1981): 353–64.

McKenzie, John L. *Second Isaiah*. Edited by William Foxwell Albright and David Noel Freedman. Anchor Bible 20. New York: Doubleday, 1968.

Mendenhall, George. "Ancient Oriental and Biblical Law." Pages 3–24 in *The Biblical Archaeologist Reader*, vol. 3. Edited by Edward F. Campbell and David N. Freedman. Garden City, N.Y.: Anchor, 1970.

———. *The Tenth Generation*. Baltimore: Johns Hopkins University Press, 1973.

Merry, Sally Engle. "Spatial Governmentality and the New Urban Social Order: Controlling Gender Violence Through Law." *American Anthropologist* NS 103, no. 1 (2001): 16–29.

Meshorer, Ya'akov. "The Ear of Yahweh on a *Yehud* Coin." Pages 434–47 in *Eretz-Israel*, vol. 25. *Archaeological, Historical and Geographical Studies: Joseph Aviram Volume*. Edited by Avraham Biran, A. Ben-Tor, G. Foerster, A. Malamat, and David Ussishkin. Jerusalem: Israel Exploration Society, 1996.

Meyers, Carol L., and Eric M. Meyers. *Haggai, Zechariah 1–8*. Anchor Bible 25B. Garden City, N.Y.: Doubleday, 1987.

Mohler, R. Albert. "The Integrity of the Evangelical Tradition and the Challenge of the Postmodern Paradigm." Pages 67–88 in *The Challenge of Postmodernism: An Evangelical Engagement*. Edited by David S. Dockery. Grand Rapids: Baker, 1995.

Momigliano, Arnaldo. *Alien Wisdom: The Limits of Hellenization*. Cambridge: Cambridge University Press, 1975.

Moore, Michael. "On the Signification of Walls in Verbal and Visual Art." *Leonardo* 12, no. 4 (1979): 311–13.

More, Thomas. *Utopia*. Edited by Edward Surtz and J. H. Hexter. Yale edition of the Complete Works of St. Thomas More edition. Complete Works of St. Thomas More 4. New Haven: Yale University Press, 1965.

Morgenstern, Julian. "Jerusalem—485 BC." *Hebrew Union College Annual* 27 (1956): 101–79.

Mouffe, Chantal. "Citizenship and Political Identity." *October* 61 (1992): 28–32.

Murphy, Paula. "Jacques, Jacques and Jacks: The Shifting Symbolic in Derrida and Lacan." *Textual practice* 19, no. 4 (2005): 509–27.

Myers, Jacob. *Ezra. Nehemiah*. Anchor Bible 14. Garden City, N.Y.: Doubleday, 1965.
Nasr, Seyyed Hossein. *The Heart of Islam: Enduring Values for Humanity*. New York: Harper SanFrancisco, 2004.
———. *Islamic Philosophy from Its Origin to the Present: Philosophy in the Land of Prophecy*. SUNY series in Islam, Albany: State University of New York Press, 2009.
Nelson, Richard D. *The Double Redaction of the Deuteronomistic History*. JSOTSup 18. Sheffield: Sheffield Academic, 1981.
Neusner, Jacob, ed. *God's Rule: The Politics of World Religions*. Washington, D.C.: Georgetown University Press, 2003.
Neusner, Jacob, and Tamara Sonn. *Comparing Religions Through Law: Judaism and Islam*. London: Routledge, 1999.
Nicholson, Ernest. *The Pentateuch in the Twentieth Century: The Legacy of Julius Wellhausen*. Oxford: Clarendon, 1998.
Nietzsche, Friedrich Wilhelm. *On the Genealogy of Morals; Ecce Homo*. Translated by Walter Arnold Kaufmann and R. J. Hollingdale. New York: Vintage, 1989.
Nikiprowetzky, V. "Ethical Monotheism." *Daedalus* 104, no. 2 (1975): 69–89.
Niogosian, S. A. "The Religions in Achaemenid Persia." *Studies in Religion* 4, no. 4 (1974): 378.
Noth, Martin. *The Deuteronomistic History*. JSOTSup 15. Sheffield: JSOT, 1981.
Novak, David. *The Jewish Social Contract: An Essay in Political Theology*. Princeton, N.J.: Princeton University Press, 2005.
O'Connor, Michael Patrick. "The Biblical Notion of the City." Pages 18–39 in *Constructions of Space II: The Biblical City and Other Imagined Spaces*. Edited by Jon L. Berquist and Claudia V. Camp. LHBOTS 490. New York: T&T Clark International, 2008.
Obama, Barack. *The Audacity of Hope: Thoughts on Reclaiming the American Dream*. New York: Vintage, 2008.
Ochs, Elinor, and Lisa Capps. "Narrating the Self." *Annual Reviews in Anthropology* 25 (1996): 19–43.
Oded, B. "Where is the 'Myth of the Empty Land' to Be Found? History Versus Myth." Pages 55–74 in Lipschits and Blenkinsopp, eds., *Judah and the Judeans in the Neo-Babylonian Period*.
Oppenheim, A. Leo. *Ancient Mesopotamia: Portrait of a Dead Civilization*. Rev. ed. Chicago: University of Chicago Press, 1977.
Otto, Rudolph. *The Idea of the Holy: An Inquiry into the Non-Rational Factor in the Idea of the Divine and Its Relation to the Rational*. New York: Oxford University Press, 1958.
———. "The 'Idea of the Holy': Mysterium Tremendum." *Parabola* 23 (1998): 72–76.
Pakkala, Juha. "The Monotheism of the Deuteronomistic History." *SJOT* 21, no. 2 (2007): 159–78.
Pearce, Laurie. "New Evidence for Jews in Babylonia." Pages 399–411 in Lipschits and Oeming, eds., *Judah and the Judeans in the Persian Period*.
Peri, Chiara. "The Construction of Biblical Monotheism: An Unfinished Task." *SJOT m* 19, no. 1 (2005): 135–42.
Pierre, Liénard, and E., Thomas Lawson. "Evoked Culture, Ritualization and Religious Rituals." *Religion* 38, no. 2 (2008): 157–71.

Pinsky, Robert, ed. and trans. *The Inferno of Dante*. New York: Farrar, Straus & Giroux.
Plöger, Otto. *Theocracy and Eschatology*. Translated by S. Rudman. Oxford: Blackwell, 1968.
Porten, Bezalel. "Settlement of the Jews At Elephantine and the Arameans at Syene." Pages 451–70 in Lipschits and Blenkinsopp, eds., *Judah and the Judeans in the Neo-Babylonian Period*.
Radin, Paul. *Monotheism Among Primitive Peoples*. London: G. Allen & Unwin, 1924.
Rappaport, Uriel. "The First Judean Coinage." *Journal of Jewish Studies* 32 (1981): 1–17.
Ravasi, Gianfranco. *Antico Testamento: Introduzione*. Italia: Mondadori, 1991.
Reay, Diane. "Rethinking Social Class: Qualitative Perspectives on Class and Gender." *Sociology (Oxford)* 32, no. 2 (1998): 259–75.
Riches, David. "Hunting, Herding and Potlatching: Towards a Sociological Account of Prestige." *Man, New Series* 19, no. 2 (1984): 234–51.
Robinson, H. Wheeler. *Corporate Personality in Ancient Israel*. Philadelphia: Fortress, 1964.
Rudolph, Wilhelm. *Esra und Nehemia samt 3. Esra*. Handbuch zum Alten Testament 20. Tübingen: J. C. B. Mohr, 1949.
Rustomji, Nerina. *The Garden and the Fire: Heaven and Hell in Islamic Culture*. New York: Columbia University Press, 2009.
Safi, Louay M. *The Qur'anic Narrative: The Journey of Life as Told in the Qur'an*. Westport, Conn.: Praeger, 2008.
Said, Edward W. *Orientalism*. New York: Vintage, 1994. Repr., 1979.
Schaeffer, Francis A. *A Christian Manifesto*. Rev. ed. Westchester, Ill.: Crossway, 1982.
Schaper, Joachim. "The Jerusalem Temple as an Instrument of the Achaemenid Fiscal Administration." *VT* 45 (1995): 528–39.
———. "The Temple Treasury Committee in the Times of Nehemiah and Ezra." *VT* 47 (1997): 200–206.
Schiffrin, Deborah. "Narrative as Self-Portrait: Sociolinguistic Constructions of Identity." *Language in Society* 25, no. 2 (1996): 167–203.
Schimmelfennig, Frank. "The Community Trap: Liberal Norms, Rhetorical Action, and the Eastern Enlargement of the European Union." *International Organization* 55, no. 1 (2001): 47–80.
Schmid, Christian. "Henri Lefebvre's Theory of the Production of Space: Towards a Three-Dimensional Dialectic." Pages 27–45 in *Space, Difference, Everyday Life: Reading Henri Lefebvre*. Edited by Henri Lefebvre and Kanishka Goonewardena. New York: Routledge, 2008.
Schwartz, Benjamin I. "The Age of Transcendence." *Dædalus*, 104, no. 2 (1975): 1–7.
Smith, Daniel L. "The Politics of Ezra: Sociological Indicators of Postexilic Judaean Society." Pages 72–97 in Davies, ed., *Second Temple Studies, 1*.
———. *The Religion of the Landless: A Sociology of the Babylonian Exile*. Bloomington: Meyer-Stone, 1989.
Smith, Mark S. *The Origins of Biblical Monotheism: Israel's Polytheistic Background and the Ugaritic Texts*. New York: Oxford University Press, 2001.
Smith, Morton. *Palestinian Parties and Politics That Shaped the Old Testament*. 2d ed. London: SCM, 1987.
Smith, Roger W. "The Economy of Guilt." *Political Theory* 3, no. 2 (1975): 198–215.

Soggin, J. Alberto. *A History of Israel: From the Beginnings to the Bar Kochba Revolt, Ad 135*. London: SCM, 1984.
———. *Introduction to the History of Israel and Judah*. Translated by John Bowden. London: SCM, 1993.
Soja, Edward W. *Thirdspace: Journeys to Los Angeles and Other Real-and-Imagined Places*. Oxford: Blackwell, 1996.
Steinberg, Naomi. "The Deuteronomic Law Code and the Politics of State Centralization." Pages 161–70 in *The Bible and the Politics of Exegesis*. Edited by David Jobling, Peggy L. Day, and Gerald T. Sheppard. Cleveland: Pilgrim, 1991.
Stolper, Matthew W. *Entrepreneurs and Empire: The Murašû Archive, the Murašû Firm, and Persian Rule in Babylonia*. Publications de l'Institut historique et archéologique Néerlandais de Stamboul. Leiden: Nederlands Historisch-Archaeologisch Instituut te Istanbul, 1985.
Summers, David. *Real Spaces: World Art History and the Rise of Western Modernism*. New York: Phaidon, 2003.
Swaine, Lucas A. "How Ought Liberal Democracies to Treat Theocratic Communities?" *Ethics* 111, no. 2 (2001): 302–43.
Sweeney, Marvin A. *Reading the Hebrew Bible After the Shoah: Engaging Holocaust Theology*. Minneapolis: Fortress, 2008.
Tajfel, Henri. "Social Psychology of Intergroup Relations." *Annual Review of Psychology* 33, no. 1 (1982): 1–39.
Tajfel, Henri, and John C. Turner. "The Social Identity Theory of Intergroup Behavior." Pages 7–24 in *Psychology of Intergroup Relations*. Edited by S. Worchel and W. G. Austin. Chicago: Nelson-Hall, 1986.
Teubner, Gunther. "How the Law Thinks: Toward a Constructivist Epistemology of Law." *Law & Society Review* 23, no. 5 (1989): 727–58.
Thompson, Thomas L. *The Historicity of the Patriarchal Narratives: The Quest for the Historical Abraham*. Harrisburg, Pa.: Trinity Press International, 2002.
Tigay, Jeffrey H. *Deuteronomy: The JPS Torah Commentary*. Philadelphia: Jewish Publication Society, 1996.
Tillich, Paul. *Systematic Theology*. 3 vols. Chicago: University of Chicago Press, 1951.
Torrey, Charles C. *The Chronicler's History of Israel: Chronicles–Ezra–Nehemiah Restored to Its Original Form*. New Haven ed. 1954. Port Washington, N.Y.: Kennikat, 1973.
———. "The Exile and Restoration." Pages 285–335 in *Ezra Studies*. New York: Ktav, 1970.
Tozer, Aiden W. *The Knowledge of the Holy: The Attributes of God: Their Meaning in the Christian Life*. New York: HarperSanFrancisco, 1961.
Trible, Phyllis. *Texts of Terror: Literary-Feminist Readings of Biblical Narratives*. Philadelphia: Fortress, 1984.
Tucker, Kenneth H. *Classical Sociological Theory: A Contemporary Approach*. Malden, Mass.: Blackwell, 2002.
Tucker, Robert C., ed. *The Marx-Engels Reader*. New York: Norton, 1978.
Turjeman, Hagit, Gustavo Mesch, and Gideon Fishman. "Social Identity, Identity Formation, and Delinquency." *International Journal of Comparative Sociology* 49, no. 2–3 (2008): 111–26.
Ussishkin, David. "The Borders and *De Facto* Size of Jerusalem." Pages in Lipschits and Oeming, eds., *Judah and the Judeans in the Persian Period*, 147–66.

Valliere, Paul. *Modern Russian Theology: Bukharev, Soloviev, Bulgakov—Orthodox Theology in a New Key*. Grand Rapids: Eerdmans, 2000.
Van de Mieroop, Marc. *The Ancient Mesopotamian City*. Oxford: Oxford University Press, 1997.
Van, Seters, John. *Abraham in History and Tradition*. New Haven: Yale University Press, 1975.
———. *Prologue to History: The Yahwist as Historian in Genesis*. Louisville: Westminster John Knox, 1992.
VanderKam, James C. *From Joshua to Caiaphas: High Priests After the Exile*. Minneapolis: Fortress, 2004.
Verhey, Allen. *Remembering Jesus: Christian Community, Scripture, and the Moral Life*. Grand Rapids: Eerdmans, 2002.
Volf, Miroslav. *Exclusion and Embrace: A Theological Exploration of Identity, Otherness, and Reconciliation*. Nashville: Abingdon, 1996.
Weber, Max. *The Agrarian Sociology of Ancient Civilizations*. Translated by R. I. Frank. Foundations of History Library. London: NLB, 1976.
———. *Ancient Judaism*. Edited and translated by Hans H. Gerth and Don Martindale. New York: Free Press, 1952.
———. *Economy and Society: An Outline of Interpretive Sociology*. Translated by Ephraim Fischoff, Hans H. Gerth, A. M. Henderson, Ferdinand Kolegar, C. Wright Mills, Talcott Parsons, Max Rheinstein, Guenther Roth, Edward Shils, and Claus Wittich. Edited by Guenther Roth and Claus Wittich. New York: Bedminster, 1968.
———. "Politics as a Vocation." Pages 77–128 in *From Max Weber: Essays in Sociology*. Edited by Hans H. Gerth, and C. Wright Mills. New York: Oxford University Press, 1958.
———. *The Sociology of Religion*. Translated by Ephraim Fischoff. Boston: Beacon, 1993.
Webster, David L. *The Fall of the Ancient Maya: Solving the Mystery of the Maya Collapse*. London: Thames & Hudson, 2002.
———. "On Theocracies." *American Anthropologist* 78 (1976): 812–28.
Weinberg, Joel. *The Citizen–Temple Community*. Translated by Daniel L. Smith-Christopher. JSOTSup 151. Sheffield: JSOT, 1992.
Wellhausen, Julius. *Prolegomena to the History of Israel*. Scholars Press Reprints and Translations Series. Atlanta: Scholars Press, 1994.
Westbrook, Raymond. "Biblical and Cuneiform Law Codes." *RB* 92, no. 2 (1985): 247–64.
———. "Biblical Law." Pages 1–17 in *An Introduction to the History and Sources of Jewish Law*. Edited by Neil S. Hecht, B. S. Jackson, S. M. Passamaneck, and D. Piattelli. Oxford: Clarendon, 1996.
———. "Cuneiform Law Codes and the Origins of Legislation." *Zeitschrift für Assyriologie* 79 (1989): 201–22.
———. *Studies in Biblical and Cuneiform Law*. Cahiers de Revue Biblique 26. Paris: Gabalda, 1988.
Williams, James. "Deleuze on J. M. W. Turner." Pages 233–46 in *Deleuze and Philosophy: The Difference Engineer*. Edited by Keith Ansell Pearson. New York: Routledge, 1997.
Williamson, Hugh G. M. *Ezra, Nehemiah*. WBC 16. Waco: Word, 1985.
———. "Nehemiah's Walls Revisited." *PEQ* 116 (1984): 81–88.

Wilson, Robert R. "The Mechanisms of Judicial Authority in Early Israel." Pages 59–75 in Huffmon, Spina, and Green, eds., *The Quest for the Kingdom of God.*
———. *Prophecy and Society in Ancient Israel.* Philadelphia: Fortress, 1980.
Zayani, Mohamed. "Gilles Deleuze, Félix Guattari and the Total System." *Philosophy and Social Criticism* 26, no. 1 (2000): 93–114.
Zertal, Adam. "The Province of Samaria (Assyrian *Samerina*) in the Late Iron Age (Iron Age III)." Pages 377–412 in Lipschits and Blenkinsopp, eds., *Judah and the Judeans in the Neo-Babylonian Period.*
Zorn, J. *Nabeh, Tell En.* Edited by Ephraim Stern. New Encyclopedia of Archaeological Excavations in the Holy Land 3. Jerusalem: Israel Exploration Society, 1993.

INDEXES

INDEX OF REFERENCES

HEBREW BIBLE/ OLD TESTAMENT

Genesis
1:26	231
12:6–7	162
12:8	162
12:50	104
15:18–21	161
45:7–8	104

Exodus
1:7	59
3:8	169
6:7	178
12:35–36	200
12:38	205
16:29–31	66
19:1–6	150
19:2	83
19:3–6	189
19:5–6	131
19:6	178
20:2–3	223
20:3	7
20:8	92
23:31–33	166
32:32–33	112
34:11	165
34:15	173

Leviticus
18:27–29	169
26:40–46	163
26:44–45	165

Numbers
2:2	94
10	151
26:1–4	151
26:52–56	151
27:12–23	177

Deuteronomy
3:18	171
4:37–39	171
4:39	149
5:7	7
5:31	171
7:1–4	136
7:1–2	140
8:5	163
9:3	189
11:10–12	167
11:13–15	41
11:18–23	41
12:1	171
12:27	137
15:28–37	222
16:12–13	74
17:14	171
19:1	171
19:14	171
27:5–6	137
30:16	120

Joshua
5:6	165
23:12–13	191

Judges
3:1–4	190
20–21	206

1 Samuel
8:5	65
17:45	71

2 Samuel
7:6	106

1 Kings
8:50	155
11:1	136
11:3–4	136
11:13	58
11:32	58
11:36	58

2 Kings
19:30–31	71, 105
21:1–2	76
21:8–12	58
25:12	61
25:22	47, 61
25:24–26	63
25:25–26	64

1 Chronicles
4:43	105
9:1–2	164

2 Chronicles
34:9	214
36:20–23	160
36:20–21	167, 169

Ezra
1–3	151
1:1–11	151
1:1–4	192, 200
1:1–2	49
1:1	213
1:2	151
1:3	102, 155
1:4	200

Index of References

1:5	214	9:7	16	5:11	180	
1:8	73	9:8	216	5:12–13	134	
1:11	73	9:9	16, 196	5:12	95	
2	214	9:11–12	156	5:15	126	
2:1–67	202	9:12	173	7	214	
2:2	74	9:14	154, 216	7:1–18	143	
3:2	74, 104, 134, 137	9:24	49	7:1	215	
3:8–11	151	10:1–14	100	7:4–69	202	
3:8	75	10:1–12	66	7:5	215	
3:9–10	179	10:1–2	202	7:6	214, 215	
4:1–3	75, 178	10:2–5	90	7:64	172	
4:1–2	55, 208	10:2–3	190	8:1	134, 206	
4:1	214	10:3	204	8:8	131	
4:2–3	127	10:9	214	8:9	142	
4:2	149, 178	10:10	89	8:13–18	137	
4:3	75, 178	10:12	142	8:14	134	
4:4–5	179	10:18–44	90	9:1–37	53	
4:4	168	10:18	89	9:7–8	136	
4:7–23	141	10:44	89, 223	9:9–37	166	
5:2	75			9:22–27	222	
5:14	73	*Nehemiah*		9:23	201	
6:14	200	1–7	211	9:24	30	
6:19–22	151	1:2	214	9:28–30	138, 167	
6:19–21	197, 235	1:3	163, 213	9:36	30, 53	
7:6	134, 206	1:8–9	163, 164	10:28–31	165	
7:10	143	2:2–3	210	10:29	134	
7:11–28	49, 51	2:3–5	141	11:1–2	164, 215	
7:11–26	79, 128, 200	2:10	212	11:1	80	
		2:11–13	212	11:3	214	
7:12–28	32	2:16–17	212	12:22	51	
7:12–26	143	2:17	210	12:47	75	
7:12–14	141	2:19–20	212	13	100, 135	
7:14–18	200	2:20	55	13:1–3	83	
7:20	49	3:7	126	13:1	135, 206, 235	
7:21	142	4:1–23	178			
7:25–26	40, 133, 146	5:1–13	134, 139	13:3–6	89	
		5:1	92	13:3	205	
7:25	201	5:3–4	93	13:4–5	172	
7:26	79	5:4–5	93, 180	13:15–22	152	
9–10	152	5:6	181	13:15–16	31, 91, 207	
9:1–15	216	5:7–13	139			
9:1–8	32	5:7	94	13:16	99	
9:1–2	138	5:8	181	13:17–18	100	
9:2	80	5:9–10	181	13:19–21	139	
9:5–15	101	5:9	94, 135, 180, 182	13:19	140	
9:7–9	167			13:21	139	
		5:10	94	13:23–25	136	

Nehemiah (cont.)

13:25	170
13:26	166
13:28	50, 67, 172

Psalms

46:7–9	71
110:1–2	15

Isaiah

1:9	71
1:24	71
4:2	76
7:3	102
10:21	102
11:1	76
20:1	136
41:27	158
42:6	106
44:28	213
45:1–3	49
45:1	213
52:1–2	158
52:7–10	158
60:1–22	183
60:3	183
60:21	157
66:1–5	152
66:12	101
66:16	213

Jeremiah

11:3–4	165
13:1–27	214
22:24	70, 71
23:3	106
23:4	106
23:5	76
24:9–10	101
25:8–11	167
25:11–12	169
25:11	160
25:20	136
25:21	136
29:3	101, 170
29:5	101, 170
29:10	169
29:14	167
29:16–17	167
29:28	170
31:4	166
31:31–34	166
32:6–25	87
32:8–15	160
32:14–15	87
32:16–44	160
32:31–38	192
33:15	76, 194
39:10	61
40:6	61
52:16	61, 86

Ezekiel

7:3	169
10	83
10:1–22	166
11	215
11:1–20	214
11:16	215
11:22–24	215
17:22–24	76
20:33–36	88
20:41–42	169
30:14	213
33:23–25	87
33:29	87
38:22	213

Daniel

7:10	213

Joel

2:1–17	223

Haggai

1:1–2	67
1:1	75
1:2–4	146
1:12	72, 75
1:14	72, 75
2	70
2:1–9	68
2:2	72, 75
2:4	72
2:6–8	71
2:17	168
2:19	65
2:20–23	68, 70, 76
2:21–23	68, 70, 72
2:21	75
2:23	69

Zechariah

1–8	56, 57, 175, 176
1:1–5	177
1:6–8	57
1:12	160
2:4	58
2:5	59, 205, 213
2:6–7	177
2:8 HB	58
2:10–11	57
2:11–13	59
2:11–12	215
2:12	58, 154
3	61, 70, 72
3:2	60
3:7	60
3:8	72
3:9	61
4:3	209
4:6–10	76
4:6–7	175
4:7	76
4:8–14	65
4:9	76
5:6–7	173
5:10–11	173
6	76
6:9–15	61, 68, 77
6:9–14	59, 70
6:10	178
6:11–14	175
6:11	61, 72, 76, 176
6:12–13	176
6:12	72, 76, 77
7:9–14	144

Index of References

8:3	70	MIDRASH		Pliny	
8:7–8	178	*Genesis Rabbah*		*Historia naturalis*	
8:11–12	106	8:9	231	18.11	93
8:14–15	62				
8:20–22	77	*Seder 'Olam Rabbah*		Seneca	
9:6	136	3	231	*Epistles*	
10:9–12	200			89	93
13:2	193	JEWISH AUTHORS			
		Shir ha-Shirim Rabbah		INSCRIPTIONS AND	
Malachi		2:18	226	PAPYRI	
1:8	126			Elephantine Papyrus	
3:13–21	152	Maimonides		Cowley 30	51
4:1	223	*Mishneh Torah*			
		2:9	189	QURAN	
Matthew		8:2	154, 155	2.9	231
5:30	232			2.218	188
22:21	42	*Mishneh Torah,*		4.97–98	188
		Hilkhot Mamrim		4.100	188
John		3.1	231	6.59	224
12:28–31	155			7.54	222
15:19–20	46	*Mishneh Torah,*		7.3180	227
17:14–16	46	*Hilkhot Teshuvah*		8.20	188
		3.7	231	8.72	188
Hebrews				8.74	188
9:3–7	80	CLASSICAL AUTHORS		8.75	188
		Aquinas		9.20	188
Revelation		*Summa Theologica*		16.1	222
2:17	233	91.2	225	16.106–107	46
2:26	227			16.110	188
		Aristotle		25.45–49	155
BABYLONIAN TALMUD		*Politics*		63.4	231
Ketubbot		1.1252a	92		
100b	221			HADITH	
		Josephus		*Bukhari*	
Sanhedrin		*Antiquities*		9 93:481	112
90b	231	11.297–301	51		
				Muslim	
		Contra Apion		20:4541	46
		1.187–89	99		

INDEX OF AUTHORS

Ackroyd, P. R. 40
Abrahamian, E. 51, 123
Abu-Sahlieh, S. A. A. 188
Ahlström, G. W. 32, 33, 45, 50, 61, 70, 72, 76, 90, 100, 142, 147, 168, 171, 175, 217
Ahmed, A. S. 227
Ainsa, F. 180
Ake, C. 17, 113, 114, 118, 120, 122, 127
Albright, W. F. 20
Alexander, J. C. 34, 169
Alt, A. 65, 105
Amjad, M. 123
Armstrong, D. 35
Árnason, J. P. 24, 27, 28
Assmann, J. 5, 6, 21, 39, 79, 186
Avigad, N. 99, 143

Balcer, J. M. 57, 95, 141
Barag, D. P. 51, 98, 157
Barkin, J. S. 117, 129
Barstad, H. M. 47, 63, 64, 204
Bascom, W. R. 182
Baskauskas, L. 35
Bausani, A. 207
Becking, B. 63, 91
Bedford, P. R. 47, 57, 65, 102
Bellah, R. 8, 21, 23–26, 152
Berger, P. L. 1, 15, 39, 56, 158, 199, 205
Berquist, J. L. 9, 13, 47, 69, 142, 158, 203
Berry, J. 194–96
Betlyon, J. W. 141, 157
Bhavnani, K.-K. 196, 202
Blenkinsopp, J. 44, 65, 70, 141, 145, 147, 152, 204, 206, 211, 216
Boer, R. 88
Borowitz, E. B. 188, 226
Bourdieu, P. 13, 29, 43, 44, 49, 52, 53, 85, 110, 117, 118, 121, 161, 184, 191, 192, 198
Briant, P. 95, 141, 184, 210
Bright, J. 59, 68, 131, 160, 170
Brown, J. A. C. 224, 231, 232
Burns, G. 123

Capps, L. 88, 165
Carr, E. H. 129

Carrier, N. 129
Carroll, R. P. 45, 47, 63, 68, 69, 86, 160, 161, 204
Carter, C. E. 31, 45, 57, 63, 90, 141
Cataldo, J. W. 18, 44, 51, 63, 77, 80, 86, 88, 91, 98, 99, 124, 143, 176, 178
Cerulo, K. A. 189, 191, 202
Childs, B. S. 210
Cladis, M. S. 164
Clines, D. J. A. 200
Coats, G. W. 149
Coggins, R. J. 56, 59, 69, 71, 175
Cook, S. L. 57–59, 69–72, 76, 126, 175, 176
Cosman, C. 164
Cross, F. M. 65, 68, 90, 176, 178
Crouch, D. 174, 175

Dandamaev, M. A. 64, 95–98, 143, 148
Dauenhauer, B. P. 194, 208
Davies, P. R. 20, 47, 63, 88, 115, 116, 130, 186, 209
Davis, R. 195, 196
De Bremond, A. 95, 96
de Haardt, M. 228
De Long-Bas, N. J. 42, 97, 188, 227, 233
de Vaux, R. 107, 181
Deleuze, G. 16, 35, 37, 41, 43–45, 52, 55, 56, 66, 70, 73, 84, 85, 109, 115, 116, 126, 153, 158, 159, 171, 180, 181, 190, 197, 203, 229
Dever, W. G. 107
Dion, P.-E. 59, 126, 143
Donald, M. 26
Donnelly, S. J. M. 145
Douglas, M. 80, 83, 100, 199, 213
Dozeman, T. B. 48, 130, 157, 177
Driver, F. 36
Durkheim, E. 29, 34, 164
Dyck, J. E. 59, 107, 178

Earle, T. K. 61
Easterly, W. 96
Edelman, D. 69, 70, 73, 90, 91, 103, 148, 172, 207, 211
Eisenstadt, S. N. 22–25, 27, 28

Index of Authors

Eliade, M. 14, 189
Elkana, Y. 26
Elvin, M. 24
Eph'al, I. 33, 46, 176, 208
Erikson, K. 188
Eskenazi, T. C. 53, 100, 131, 176, 210, 211
Esposito, J. L. 42, 97, 188, 227, 233

Ferguson, J. 180
Finkelstein, I. 211
Fishman, G. 195, 196
Flood, G. D. 10, 11
Ford, T. 187, 188, 193
Foucault, M. 35, 36, 42, 43, 52, 54, 61, 62, 64, 69, 78, 80, 92, 135, 138–40, 158, 203
Freedman, D. N. 88
Fried, L. S. 50, 59, 60, 65, 66, 73, 74, 90, 91, 95, 128, 143, 146, 147, 168, 171, 175, 184
Friedland, R. 195, 198
Friedman, R. E. 150

Galambush, J. 48, 87, 173, 177, 204
Garbini, G. 68, 72, 104, 133, 156, 179, 202, 208
Gibbs, R. 62, 163
Girard, R. 191
Glaserfield, E. von 130
Gnuse, R. K. 11, 17, 20, 22
Gottwald, N. K. 69, 92, 105, 108, 159, 168
Grabbe, L. L. 64, 145, 146
Green, W. S. 51, 199
Gropp, D. M. 33
Guattari, F. 16, 35, 37, 41, 43–45, 52, 55, 56, 66, 70, 73, 84, 85, 109, 115, 116, 126, 153, 158, 159, 171, 180, 181, 190, 197, 203, 229

Habel, N. C. 149, 162, 171, 173
Hall, D. J. 121, 125, 192
Hall, R. B. 39, 40
Hanson, P. 107
Harris, M. 49
Hart, H. L. A. 113–15, 118–21, 134
Hartman, D. 110, 229–32
Harvey, B. A. 127
Hocart, A. M. 20
Hoglund, K. G. 33, 34, 55, 66, 83, 107, 128, 139, 143, 200, 210, 216
Hornblower, S. 95
Howard, J. A. 166
Hurtado, L. W. 18

Jackson, B. S. 137
Jaffee, M. S. 12, 18, 186
James, E. O. 19
Janzen, D. 146
Japhet, S. 70, 74, 75, 130, 208, 214
Jaspers, K. 21, 26
Joannès, F. 91
Jospe, R. 221

Karen, R. 7
Karp, D. J. 31, 129, 131–33
Kenzle, S. C. 101, 102, 106, 212
Kessler, J. 32, 33, 68–72
Khaldun, I. 42, 94
Khomeini, R. 124, 125
King, R. 10
Kislev, I. 177
Kollock, P. 43
Krisciunas, R. G. 35
Küng, H. 112, 187, 188
Lawson, E. T. 197

LeFebvre, M. 116
Lefebvre, H. 133–35, 137–40, 142–45, 154
Leith, M. J. W. 32, 33, 141, 152, 209, 215
Lemaire, A. 33, 91, 147, 206, 211
Lemche, N. P. 165
Lipshits, O. 90, 106
Liverani, M. 30, 31, 60, 65, 85, 89, 102, 103, 149, 151, 166, 176, 195, 201, 207, 216
Luhmann, N. 129
Lukonin, V. G. 64, 95, 143, 148

Macnicol, N. 11
Mannheim, K. 29
Margalith, O. 68
Marx, K. 43, 47, 52, 86–88, 108, 173
Matar, A. 21
McEvenue, S. 65
McKenzie, J. L. 101
Mendenhall, G. 15, 105, 117, 145
Merry, S. E. 139, 140
Mesch, G. 195, 196
Meshorer, Y. 157
Meyers, C. L. 59, 61, 72, 73, 141, 143, 178
Meyers, E. M. 59, 61, 72, 73, 141, 143, 178
Mohler, R. A. 222
Momigliano, A. 21
Moore, M. 210
More, T. 159, 170, 173, 182
Morgenstern, J. 69

Mouffe, C. 193, 194
Murphy, P. 198
Myers, J. 200

Nasr, S. H. 193, 234
Nelson, R. D. 155
Neusner, J. 128, 196
Nicholson, E. 126
Nietzsche, F. W. 93, 223, 227
Nikiprowetzky, V. 20
Niogosian, S. A. 24
Noth, M. 149
Novak, D. 226, 235

O'Connor, M. P. 94, 103, 206
Obama, B. 115
Ochs, E. 88, 165
Oded, B. 47, 63, 69, 164, 204
Oppenheim, A. L. 144, 145, 213
Otto, R. 19

Pakkala, J. 20
Parker, G. 174, 175
Pearce, L. 91
Peri, C. 20
Phoenix, A. 196, 202
Pierre, L. 197
Pinsky, R. 80
Plöger, O. 107
Porten, B. 101, 168

Radin, P. 19
Rappaport, U. 99, 143, 157
Rasch, W. 129
Ravasi, G. 216
Reay, D. 85
Riches, D. 183, 204
Robinson, H. W. 182
Rudolph, W. 200
Rustomji, N. 234

Safi, L. M. 223, 232
Said, E. 23, 58
Schaeffer, F. A. 224
Schaper, J. 65, 91
Schiffrin, D. 88
Schimmelfennig, F. 82, 84, 203
Schmid, C. 154
Schwartz, B. I. 22
Silberman, N. A. 211
Smith, D. L. 32, 45, 66, 131, 185

Smith, M. 70, 195
Smith, M. 33, 48, 67, 69, 90, 100, 145, 162, 201, 204, 218, 220
Smith, M. S. 7
Smith, R. S. 16
Soggin, J. A. 57, 69, 73, 143
Soja, E. 154
Sonn, T. 128, 196
Steinberg, N. 134
Stolper, M. W. 65, 91
Summers, D. 153, 156, 157, 211
Swaine, L. A. 124
Sweeney, M. A. 97

Tajfel, H. 187, 190, 196, 198
Teubner, G. 117
Thompson, T. L. 20
Tigay, J. H. 220
Tillich, P. 120
Tonander, G. 187, 188, 193
Torrey, C. C. 175, 178
Tozer, A. W. 113
Trible, P. 100
Tucker, K. H. 88
Turjeman, H. 195, 196
Turner, J. C. 187, 190, 196

Ussishkin, D. 211

Valliere, P. 124
Van Seters, J. 20, 104
Van de Mieroop, M. 97, 106
VanderKam, J. C. 50, 59, 65, 67, 69, 72–74, 76, 90, 99, 100, 137, 171, 172, 175, 177
Verhay, A. 124
Volf, M. 89, 187, 228

Weber, M. 39, 44, 50, 63, 69, 79, 198
Webster, D. 106, 191
Weinberg, J. 57, 59, 65, 69, 73, 74, 90, 106, 107, 147
Wellhausen, J. 102, 107
Westbrook, R. 134, 137
Williams, J. 186
Williamson, H. G. M. 200, 216
Wilson, R. R. 59, 114, 117
Wittrock, B. 24, 27, 28

Zayani, M. 36
Zertal, A. 65
Zorn, J. 211

www.ingramcontent.com/pod-product-compliance
Lightning Source LLC
Chambersburg PA
CBHW070024010526
44117CB00011B/1700